MANGA EDITION

NARUTO

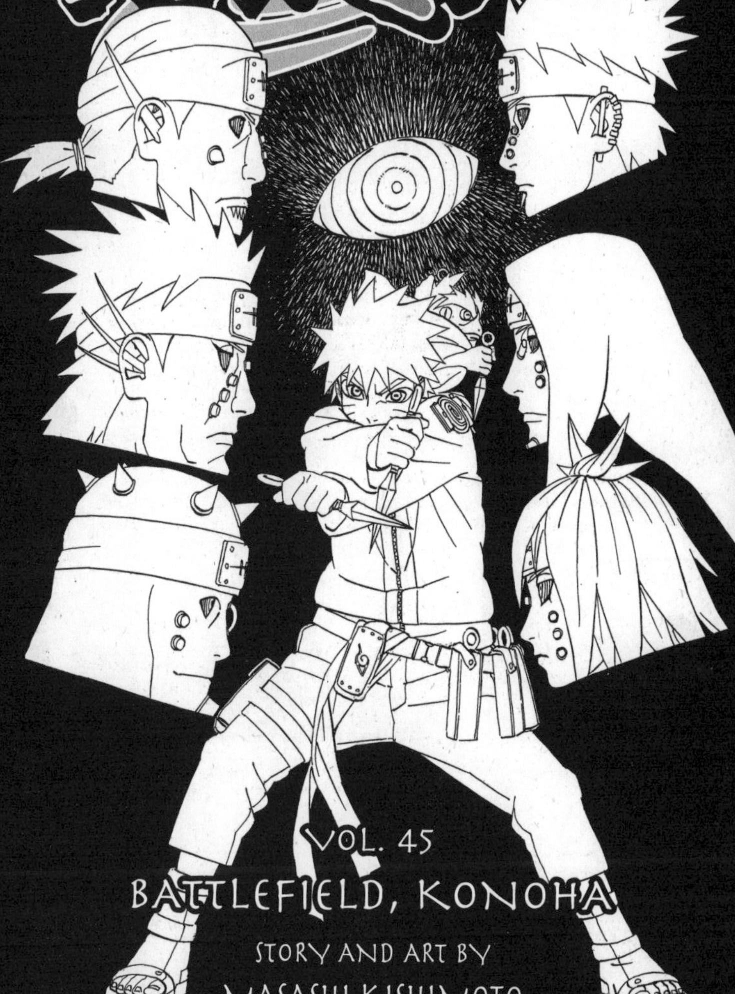

VOL. 45

BATTLEFIELD, KONOHA

STORY AND ART BY
MASASHI KISHIMOTO

CHARACTERS

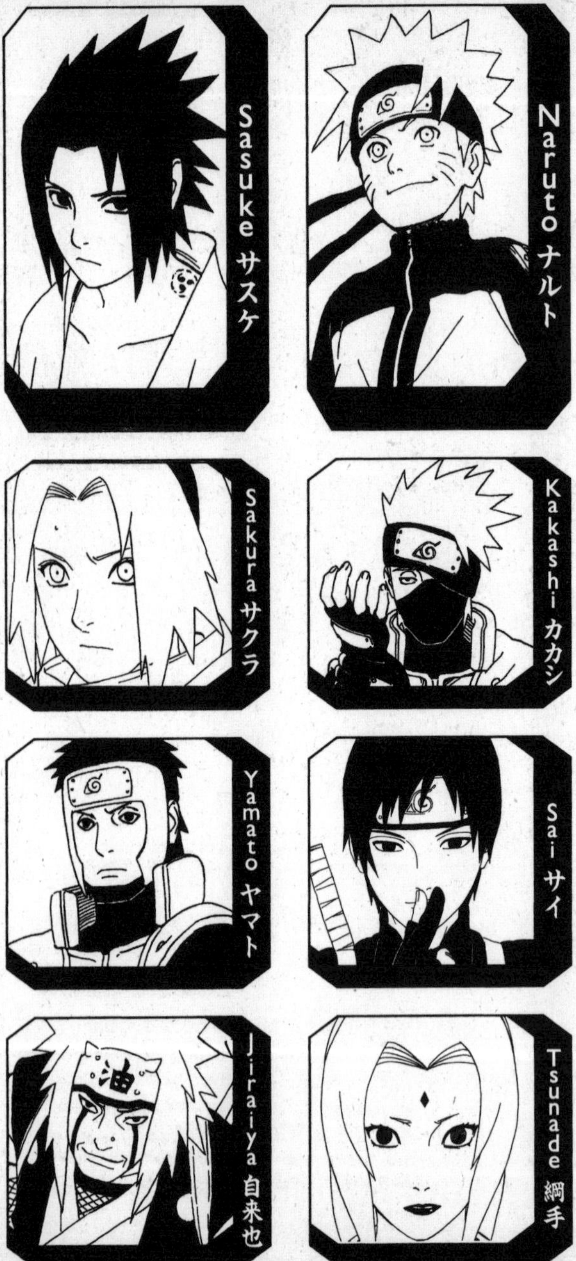
Naruto ナルト
Sasuke サスケ
Kakashi カカシ
Sakura サクラ
Sai サイ
Yamato ヤマト
Tsunade 綱手
Jiraiya 自来也
油

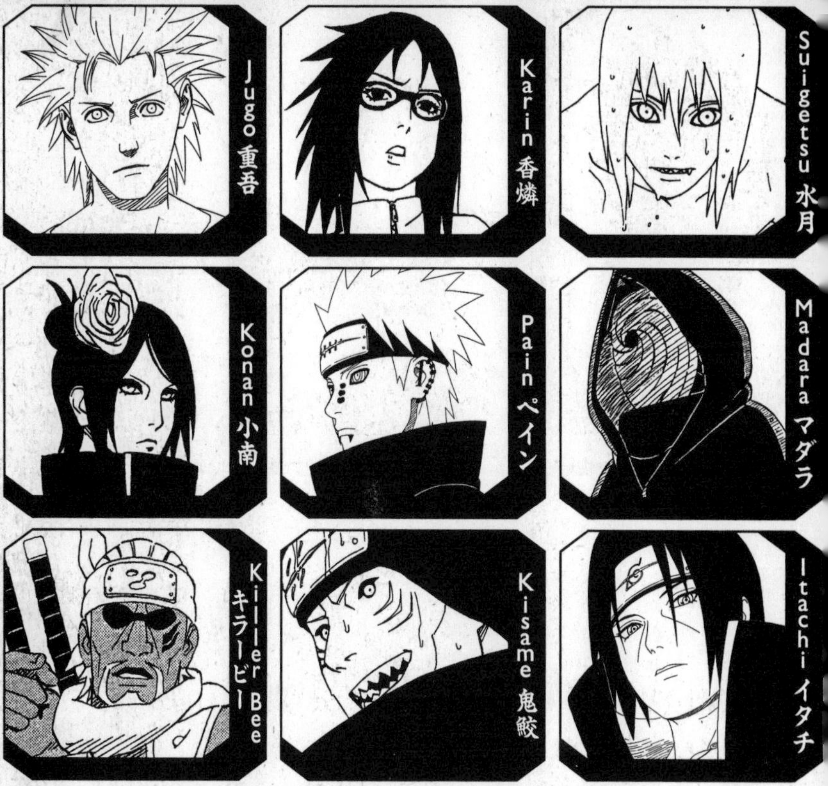
Suigetsu 水月
Karin 香燐
Jugo 重吾
Madara マダラ
Pain ペイン
Konan 小南
Itachi イタチ
Kisame 鬼鮫
Killer Bee キラービー

THE STORY SO FAR...

Naruto, the biggest troublemaker at the Ninja Academy in Konohagakure, finally becomes a ninja along with his classmates Sasuke and Sakura. They grow and mature through countless trials and battles. However, Sasuke, unable to give up his quest for vengeance, leaves Konohagakure to seek Orochimaru and his power...

Two years pass. Naruto and his comrades grow up and head out once more. As their fierce battles against the Tailed Beast-targeting Akatsuki rage on, Sasuke rebels against Orochimaru and eventually absorbs him completely! Sasuke then gathers new companions and chases after his brother Itachi.

But the Uchiha brother confrontation has an unexpected result. Sasuke learns a secret about Itachi that causes him to swear vengeance...on Konoha! To start his quest, he allies with the enemies of the Leaf Ninja, the Akatsuki, and sets out to capture the Eight-Tailed Beast!

NARUTO

VOL. 45
BATTLEFIELD, KONOHA

CONTENTS

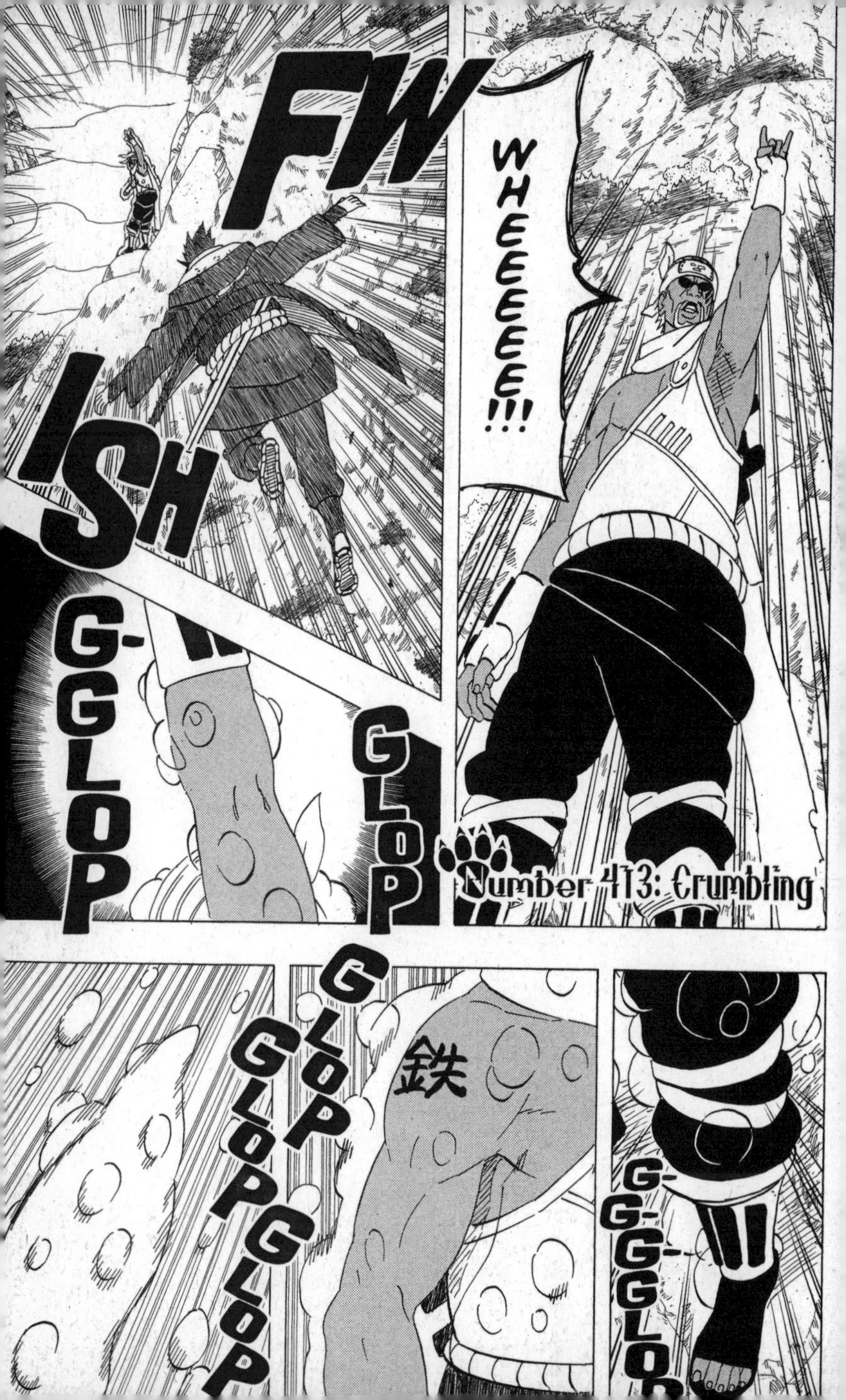
WHEEEEEE!!!
Number 413: Crumbling
FWISH
GLOP
G-GGLOP
G-G-GGGLO
GLOP
GLOPGLOP

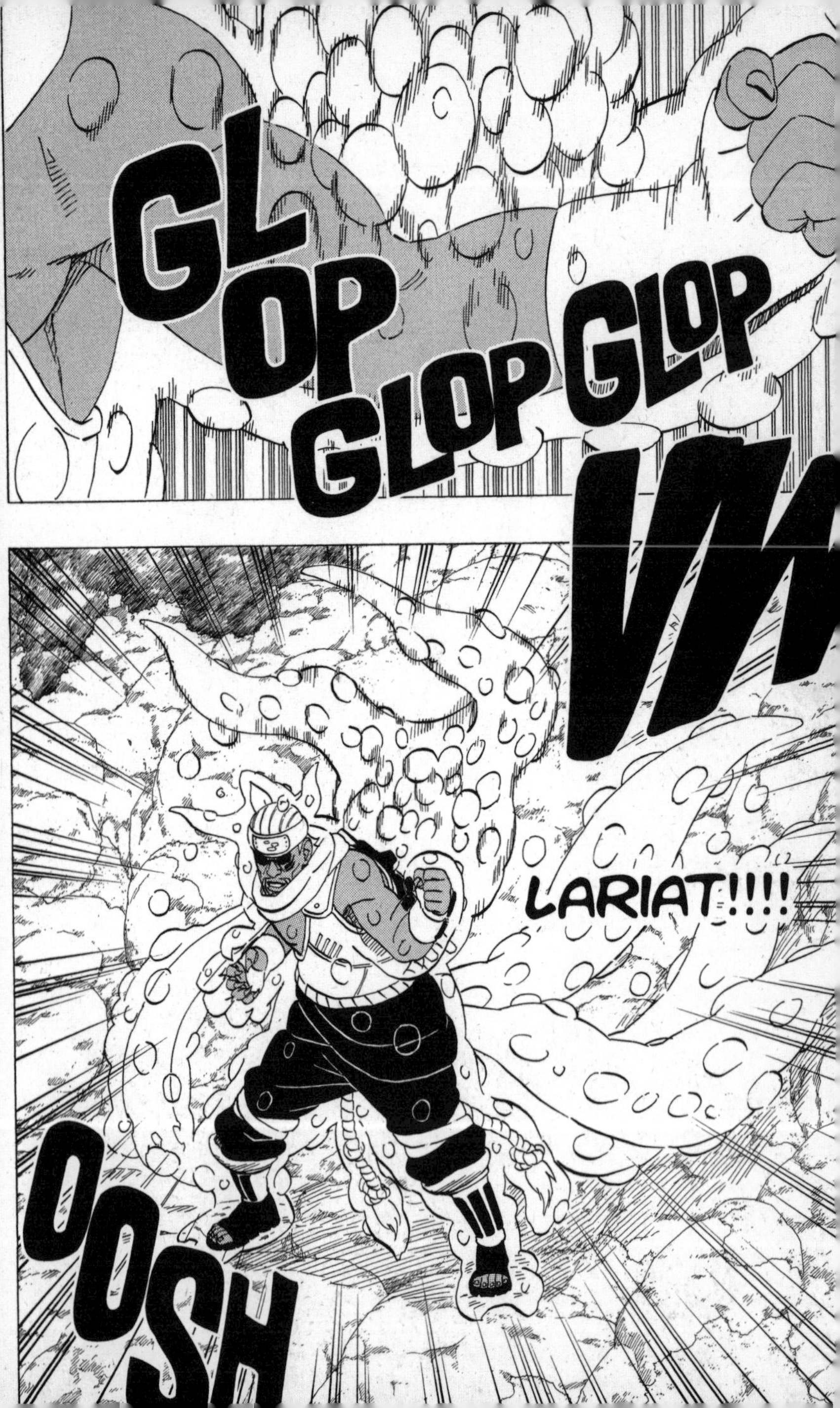
GLOP GLOP GLOP GLOP
VVOOSH
LARIAT!!!!

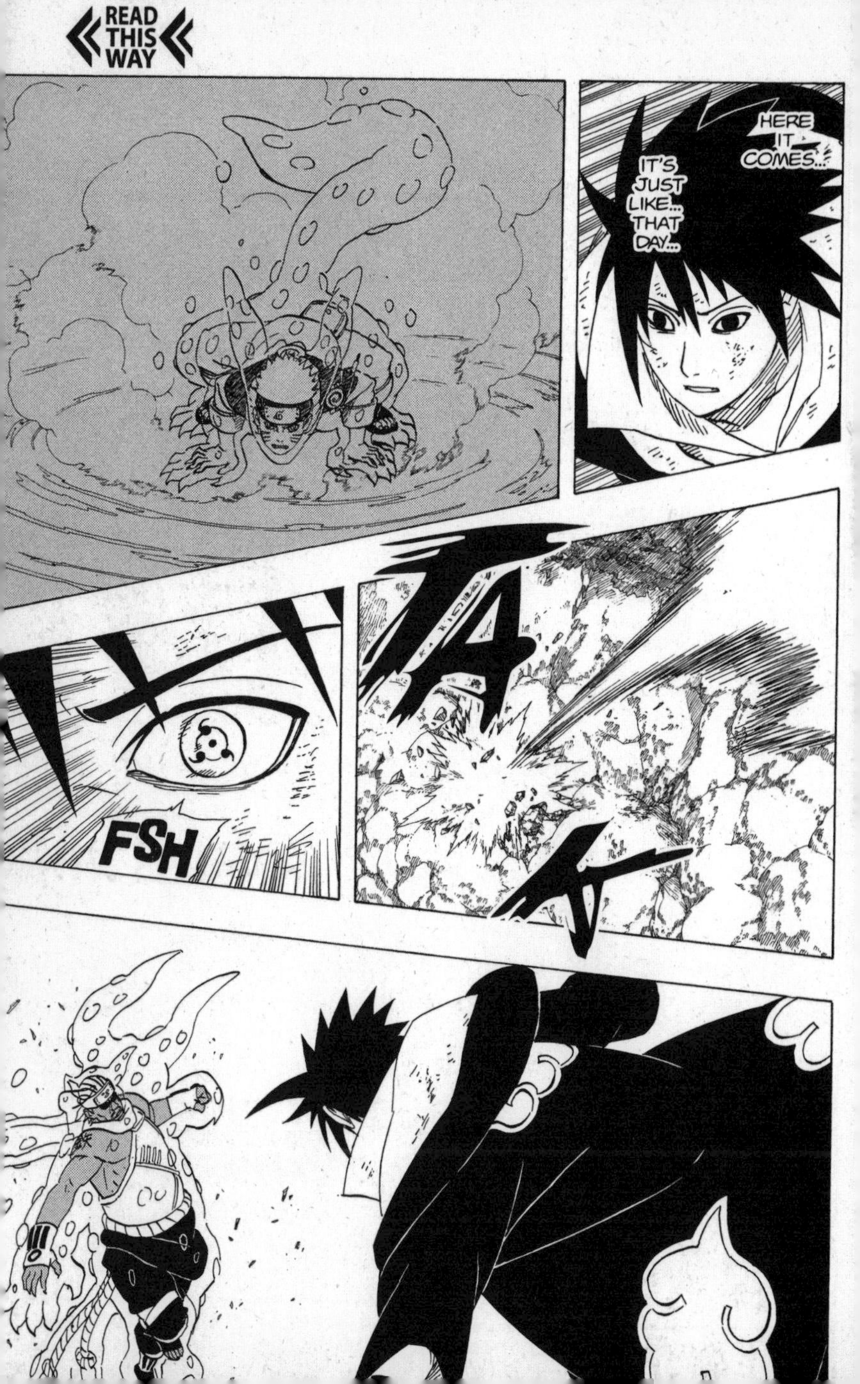
READ THIS WAY
HERE IT COMES...
IT'S JUST LIKE... THAT DAY...
FSH

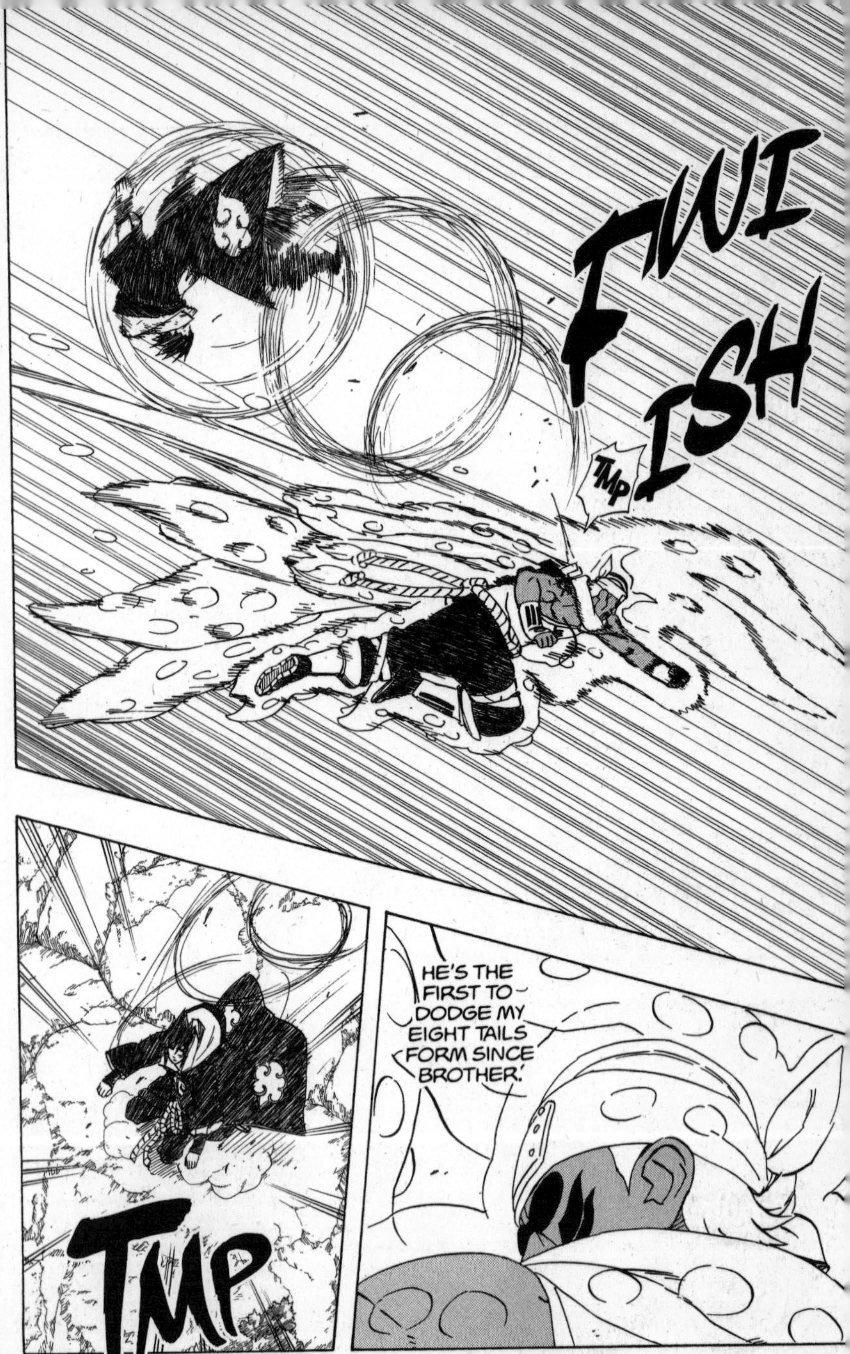
FWIISH
TMP
HE'S THE FIRST TO DODGE MY EIGHT TAILS FORM SINCE BROTHER.
TMP

READ THIS WAY

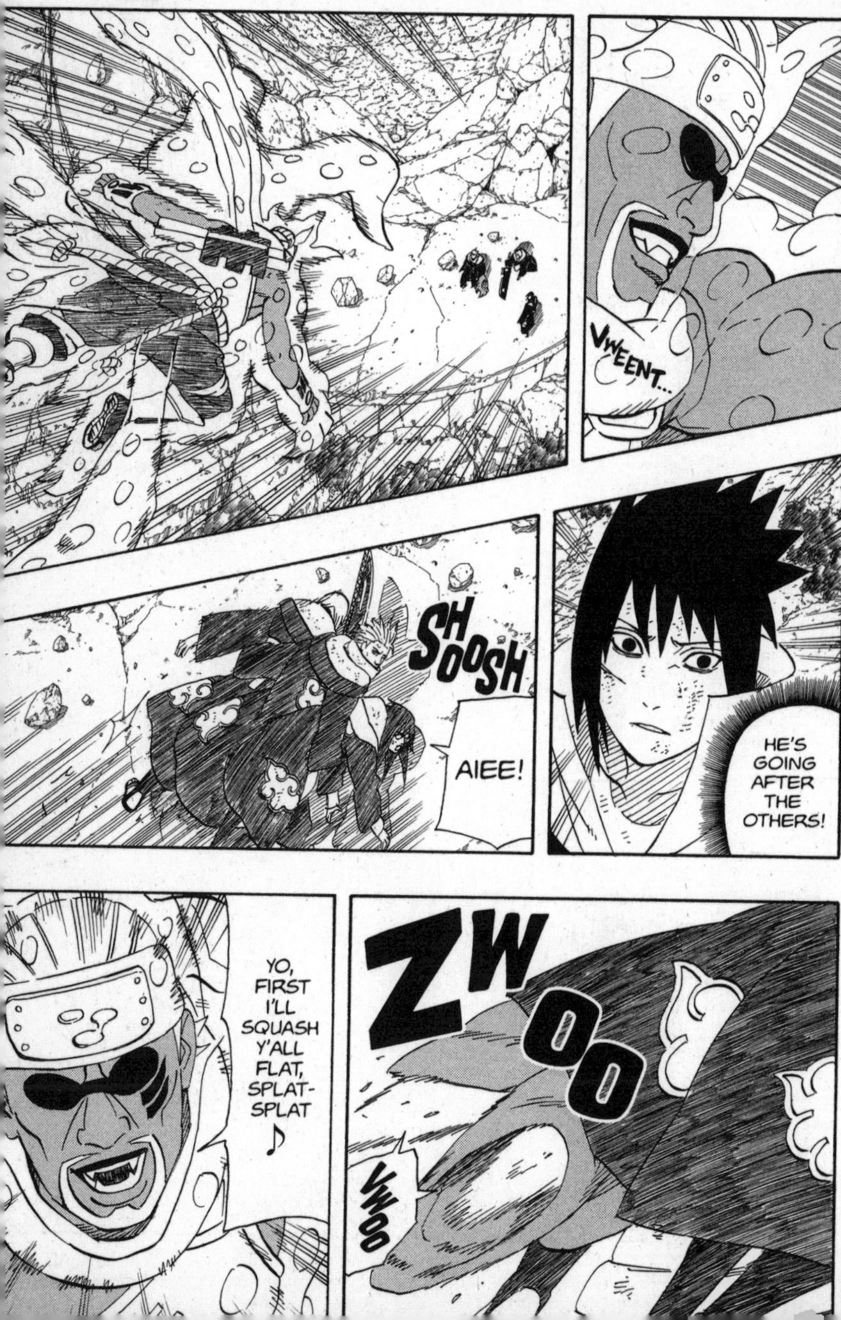
VWEENT...
HE'S GOING AFTER THE OTHERS!
SHOOSH
AIEE!
ZWOO
VWOO
YO, FIRST I'LL SQUASH Y'ALL FLAT, SPLAT-SPLAT ♪

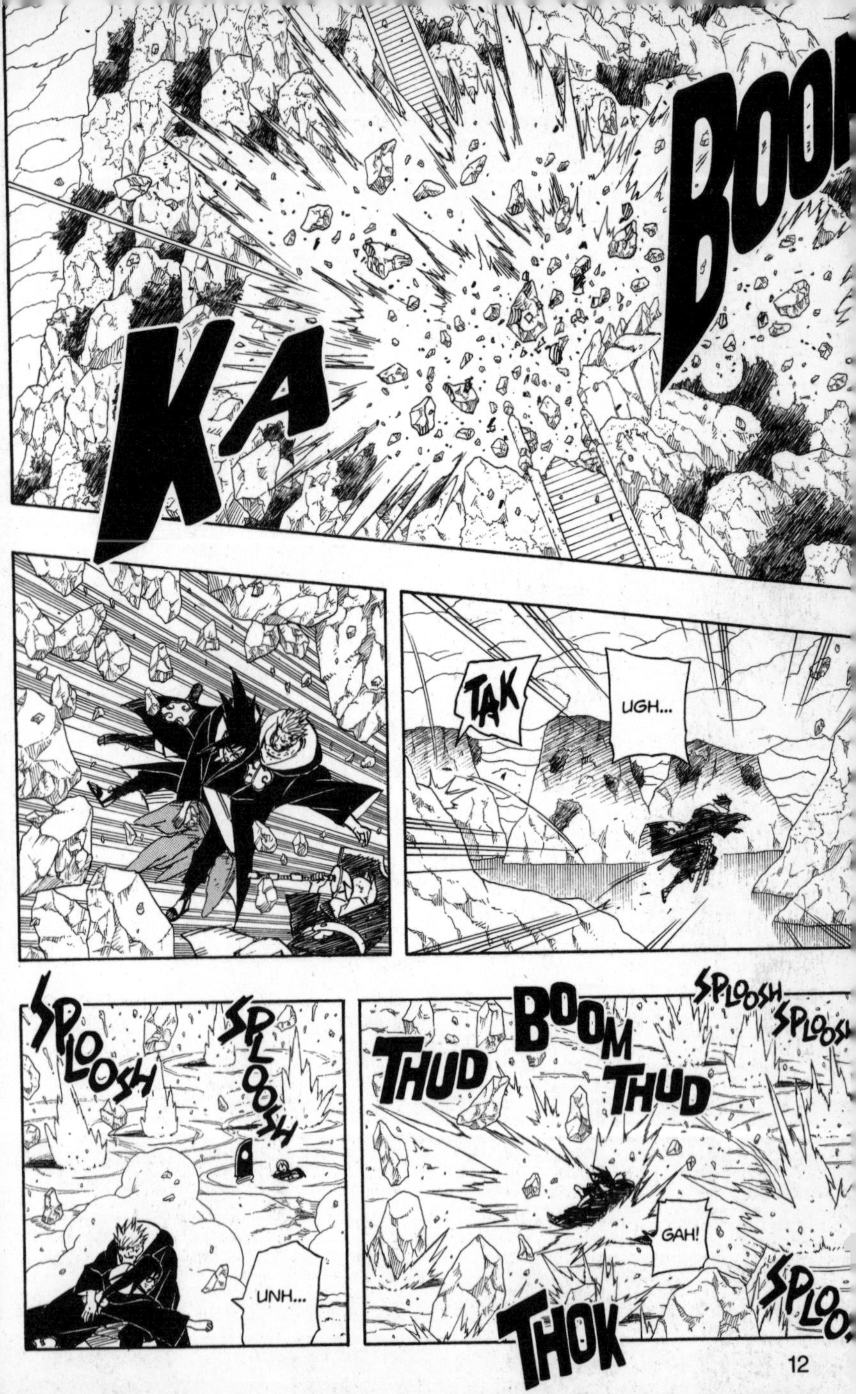
KA
BOO
TAK
UGH...
SPLOOSH
SPLOOS
BOOM
THUD
THUD
GAH!
SPLOO
THOK
SPLOOSH
SPLOOSH
UNH...

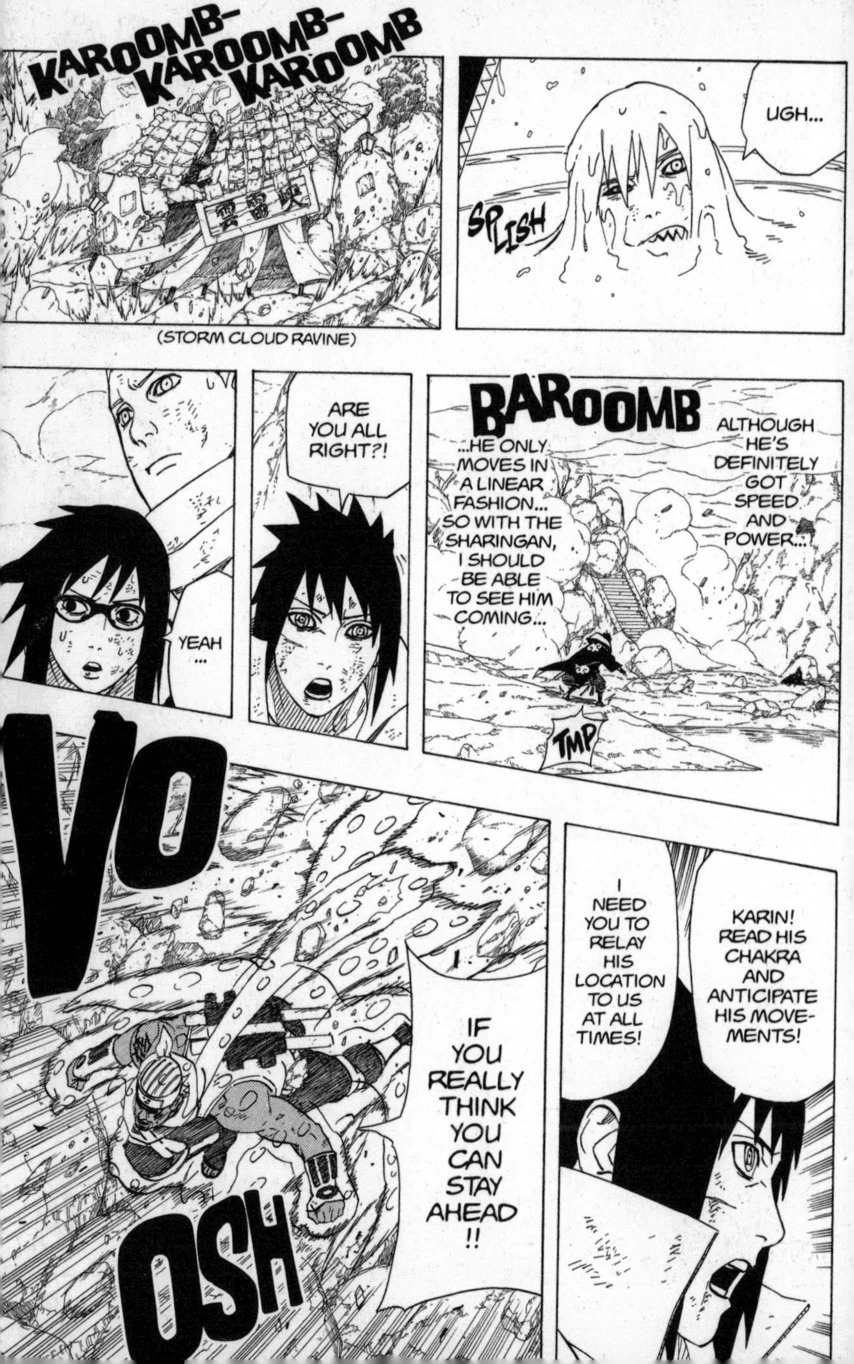
UGH...
SPLISH
KAROOMB-KAROOMB-KAROOMB
雲雷峡
(STORM CLOUD RAVINE)
BAROOMB
ALTHOUGH HE'S DEFINITELY GOT SPEED AND POWER...
...HE ONLY MOVES IN A LINEAR FASHION... SO WITH THE SHARINGAN, I SHOULD BE ABLE TO SEE HIM COMING...
TMP
ARE YOU ALL RIGHT?!
YEAH ...
KARIN! READ HIS CHAKRA AND ANTICIPATE HIS MOVEMENTS!
I NEED YOU TO RELAY HIS LOCATION TO US AT ALL TIMES!
VOOSH
IF YOU REALLY THINK YOU CAN STAY AHEAD!!

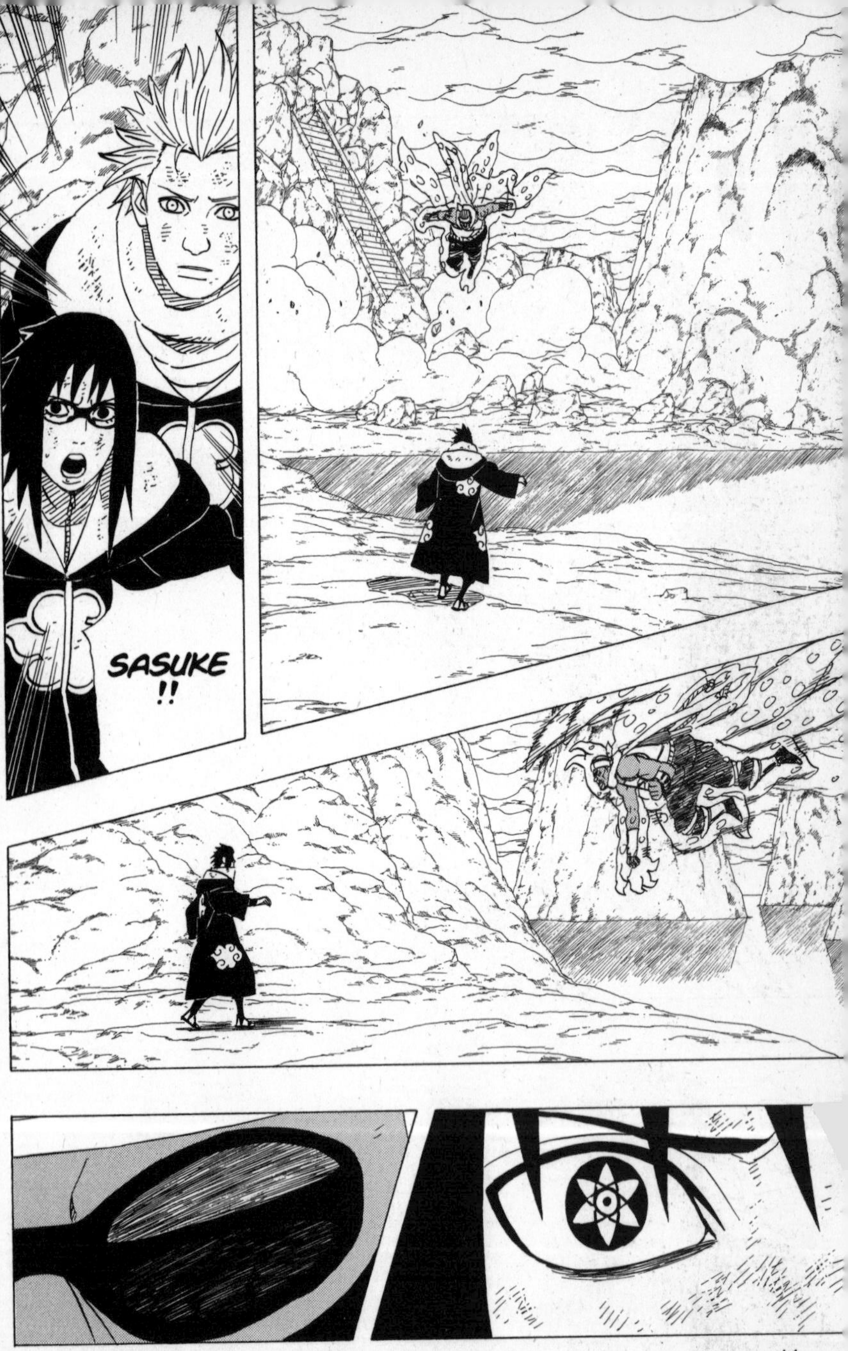
SASUKE
!!

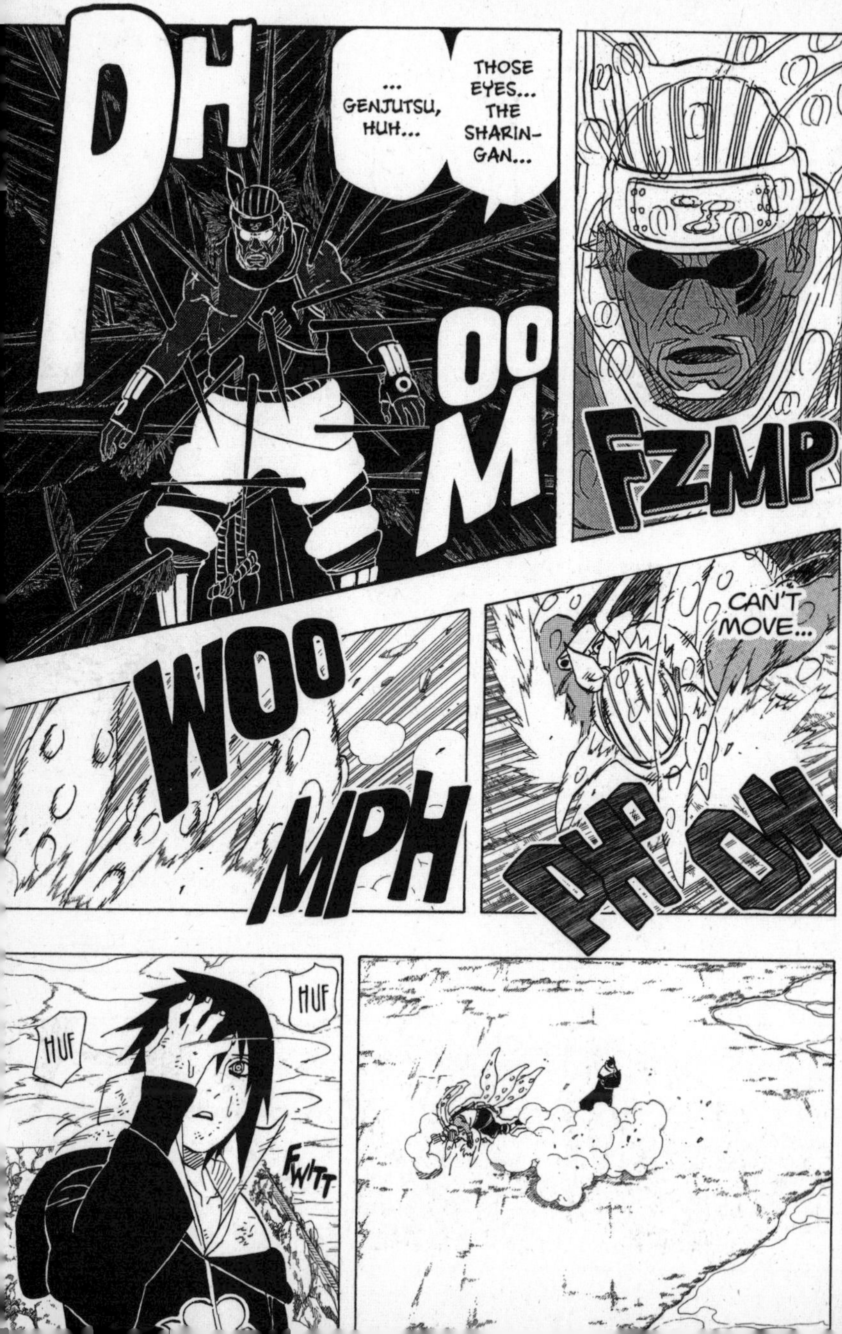

FZMP
THOSE EYES... THE SHARIN-GAN...
... GENJUTSU, HUH...
PHOOM
CAN'T MOVE...
WOOMPH
HUF
HUF
FWITT

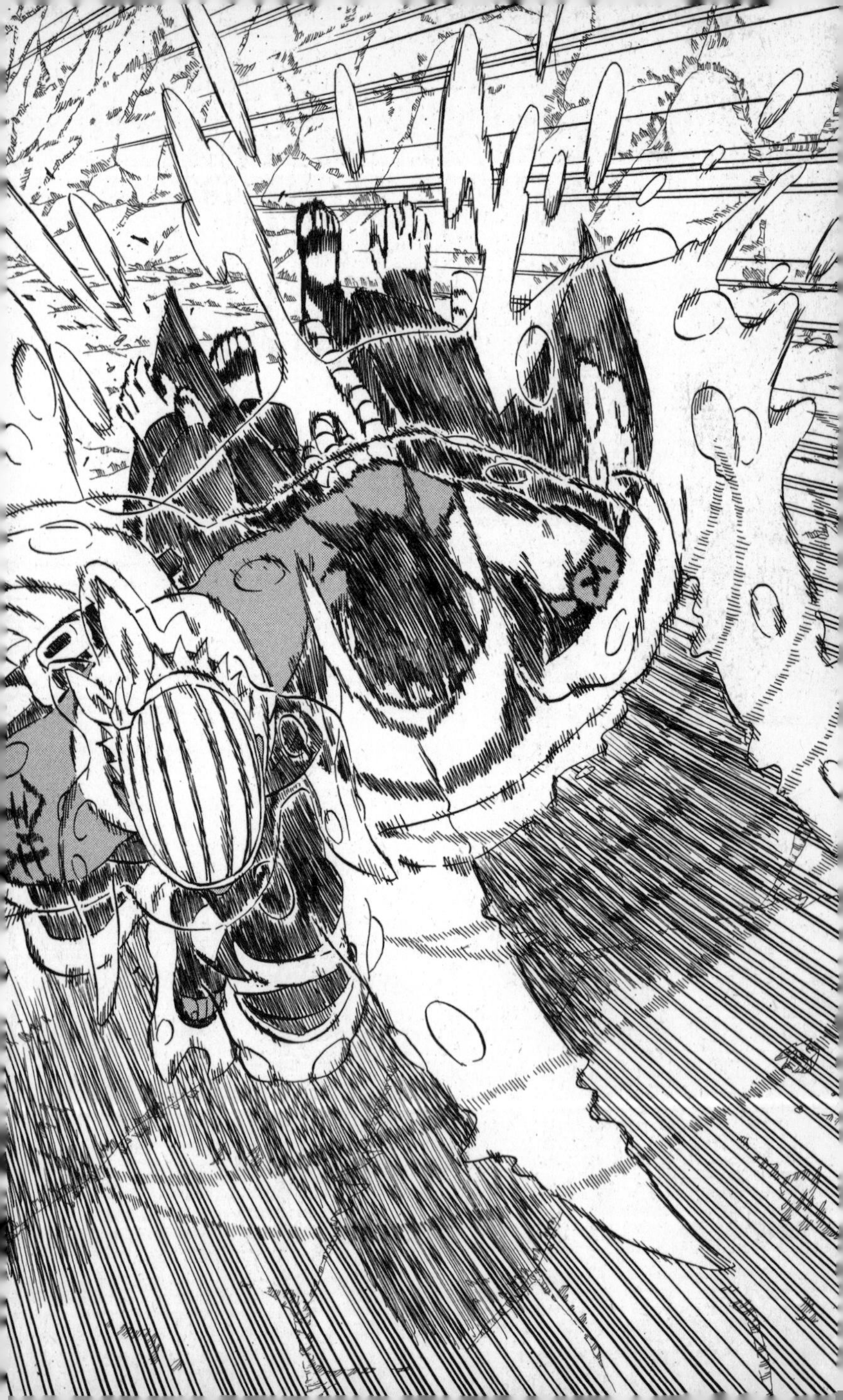

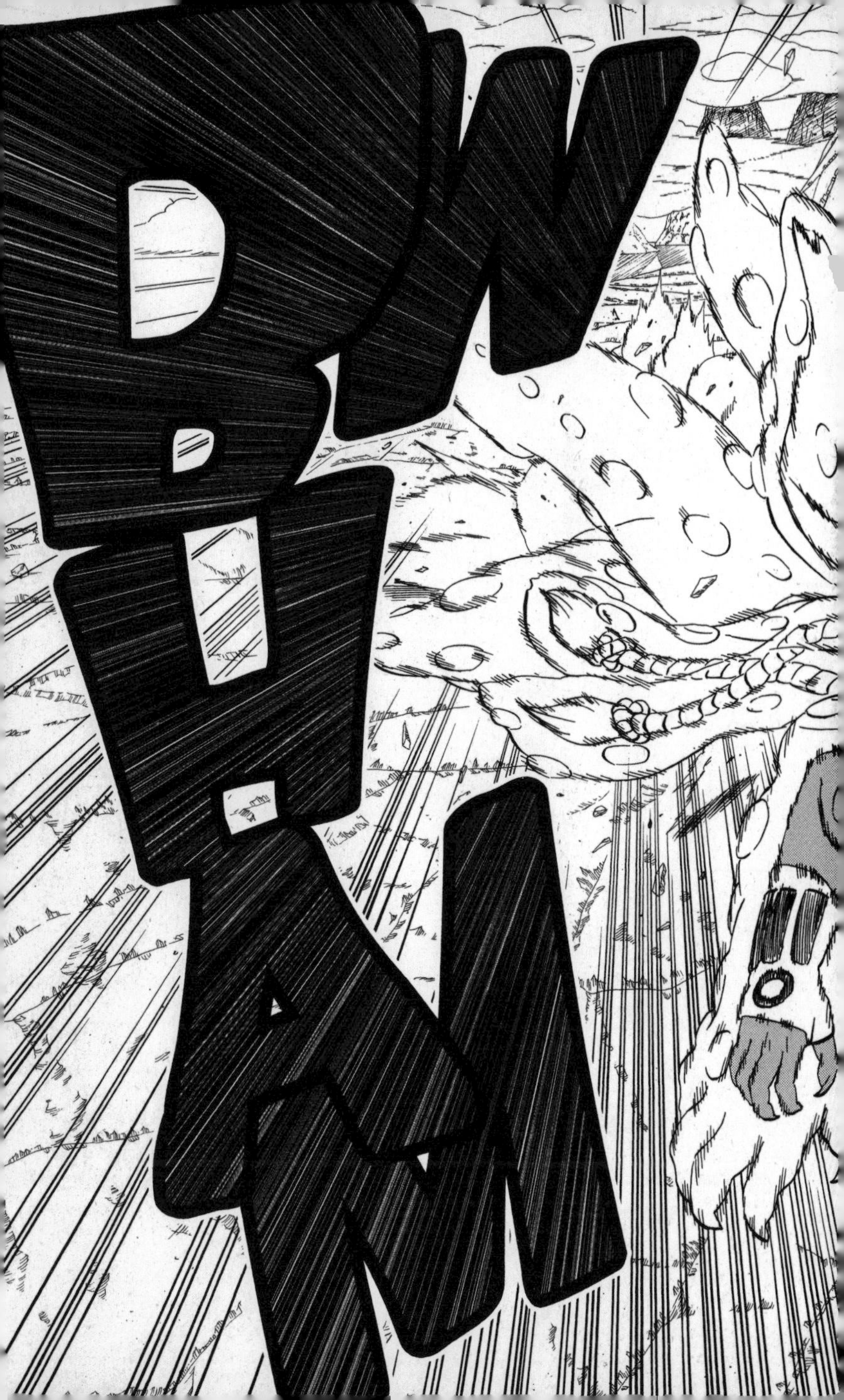

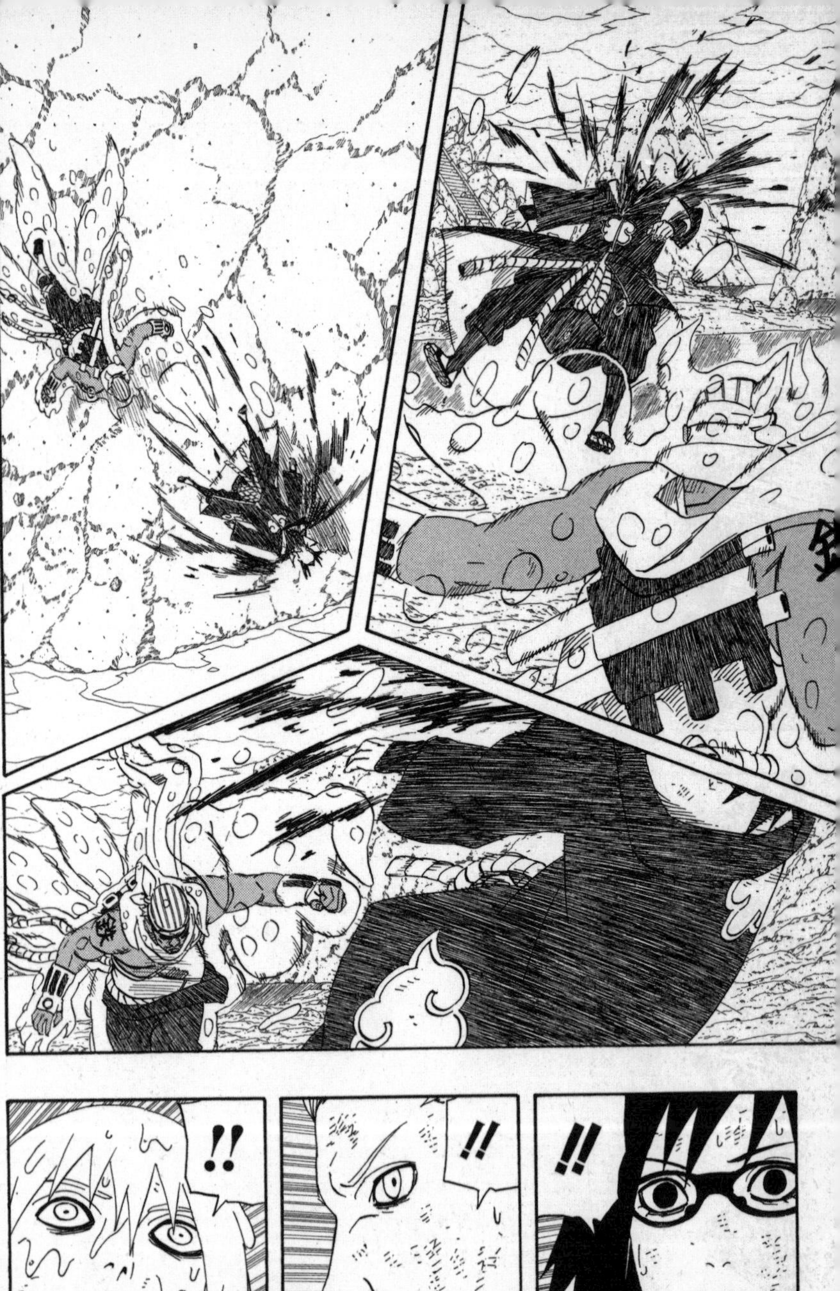
!!
!!
!!

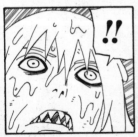

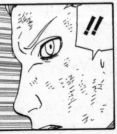

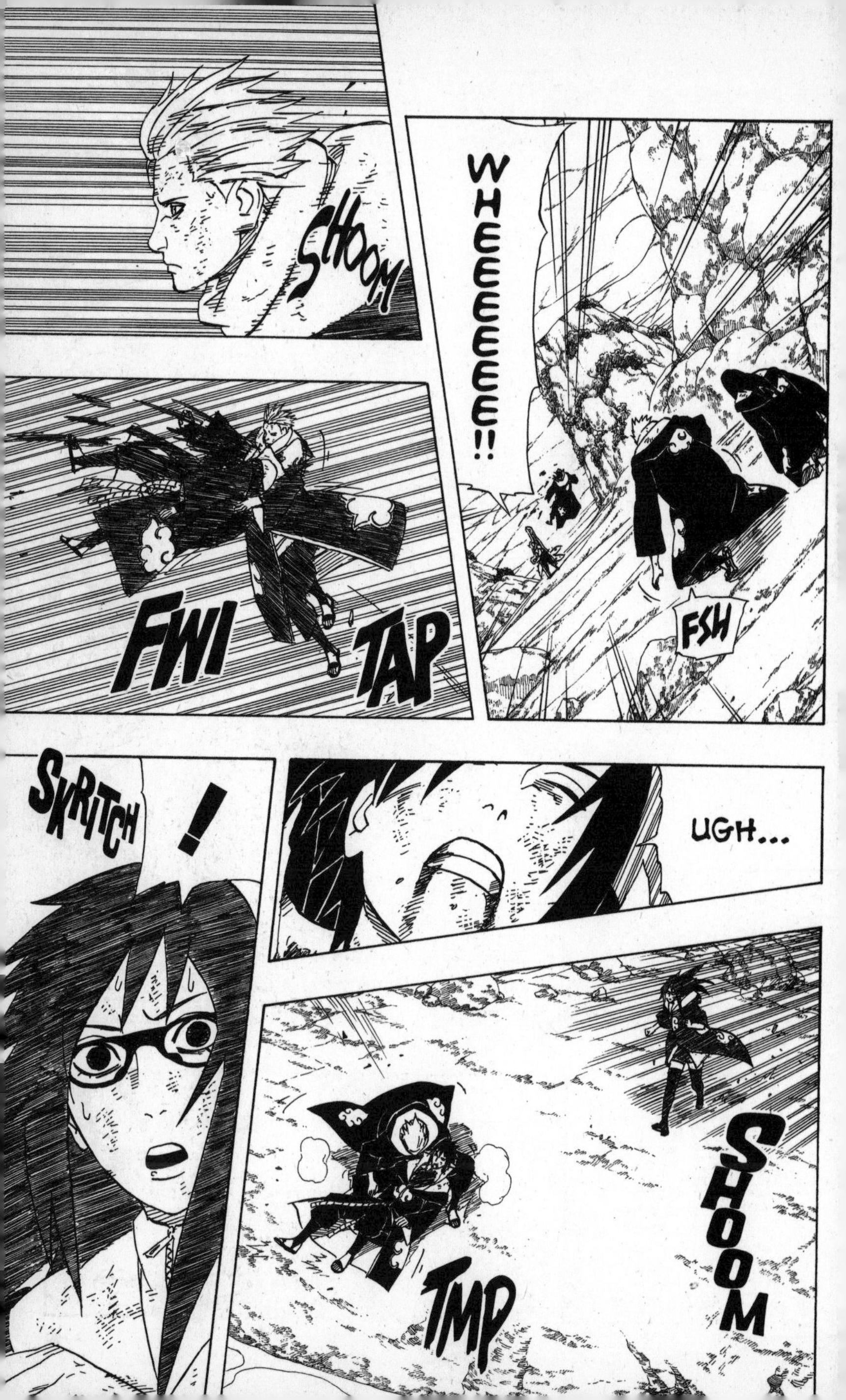
WHEEEEEEEE!!
FSH
SHOOM
FWI
TAP
UGH...
SHOOM
TMP
SKRITCH
!

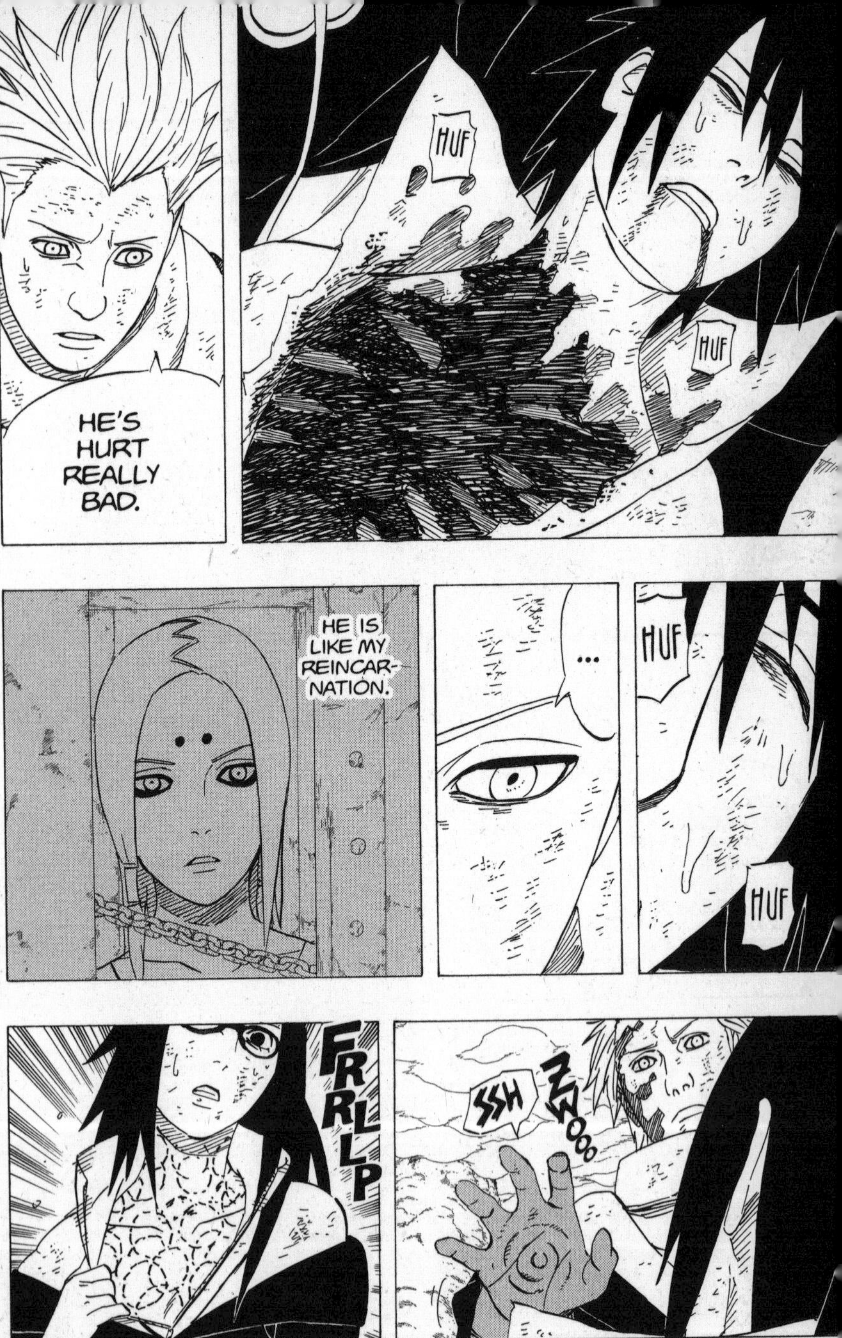
HUF
HUF
HE'S HURT REALLY BAD.
HUF
HUF
...
HE IS LIKE MY REINCAR-NATION.
SSH
ZWOOO
FRRLLP

READ THIS WAY

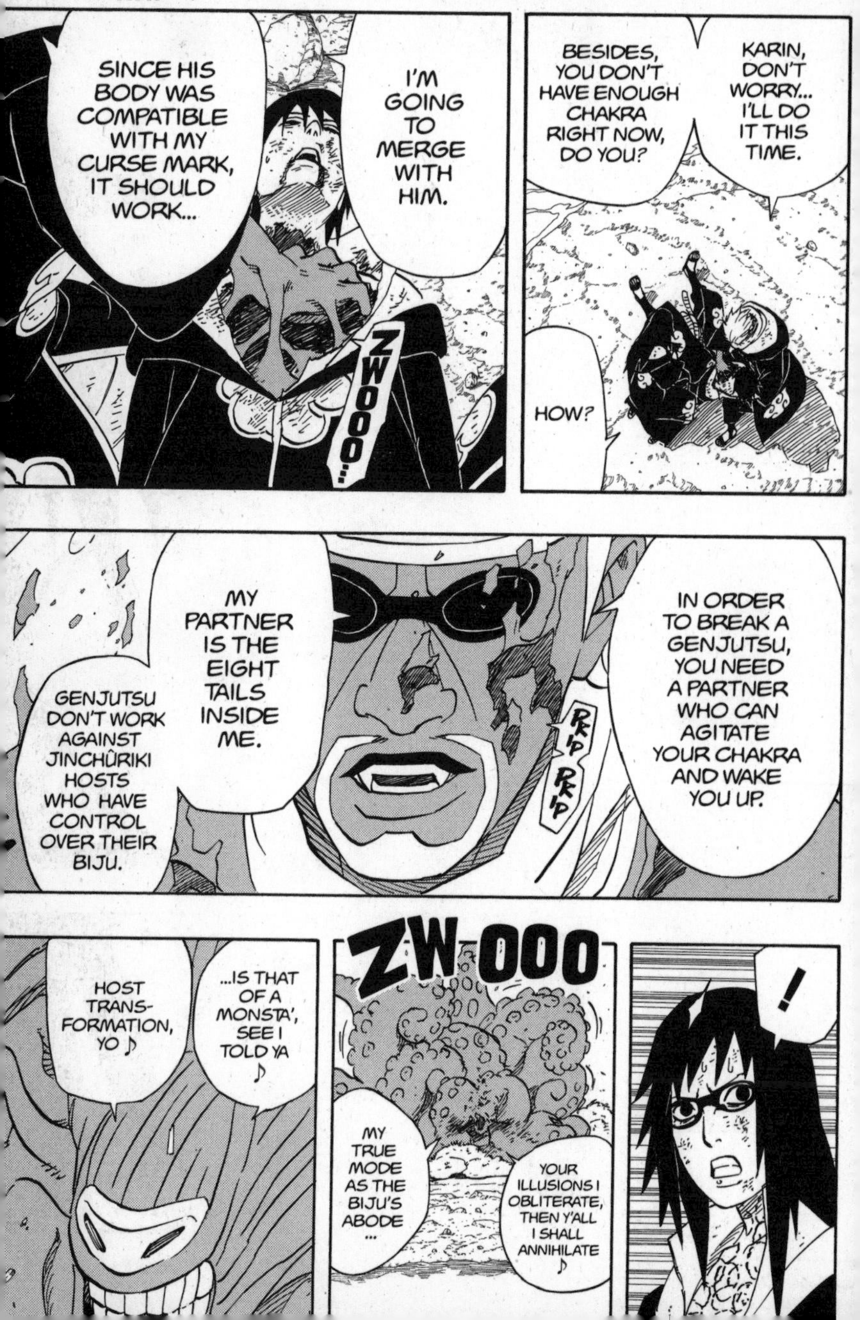

KARIN, DON'T WORRY... I'LL DO IT THIS TIME.
BESIDES, YOU DON'T HAVE ENOUGH CHAKRA RIGHT NOW, DO YOU?
HOW?
I'M GOING TO MERGE WITH HIM.
ZWOOOO...
SINCE HIS BODY WAS COMPATIBLE WITH MY CURSE MARK, IT SHOULD WORK...
IN ORDER TO BREAK A GENJUTSU, YOU NEED A PARTNER WHO CAN AGITATE YOUR CHAKRA AND WAKE YOU UP.
PKIP PKIP
MY PARTNER IS THE EIGHT TAILS INSIDE ME.
GENJUTSU DON'T WORK AGAINST JINCHÛRIKI HOSTS WHO HAVE CONTROL OVER THEIR BIJU.
!
ZW OOO
YOUR ILLUSIONS I OBLITERATE, THEN Y'ALL I SHALL ANNIHILATE ♪
MY TRUE MODE AS THE BIJU'S ABODE ...
...IS THAT OF A MONSTA', SEE I TOLD YA ♪
HOST TRANS-FORMATION, YO ♪

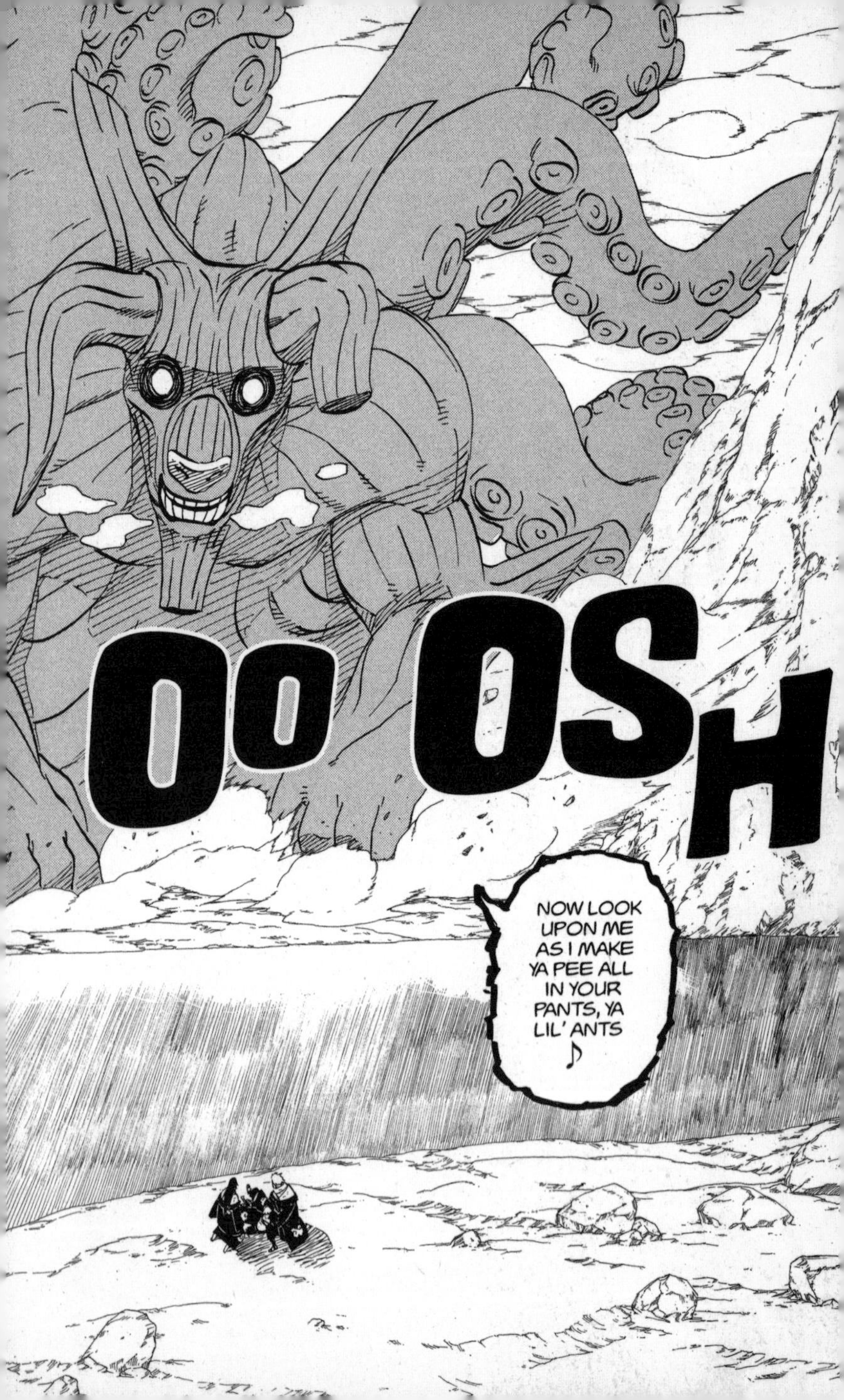
OOOOSH
NOW LOOK UPON ME AS I MAKE YA PEE ALL IN YOUR PANTS, YA LIL' ANTS ♪

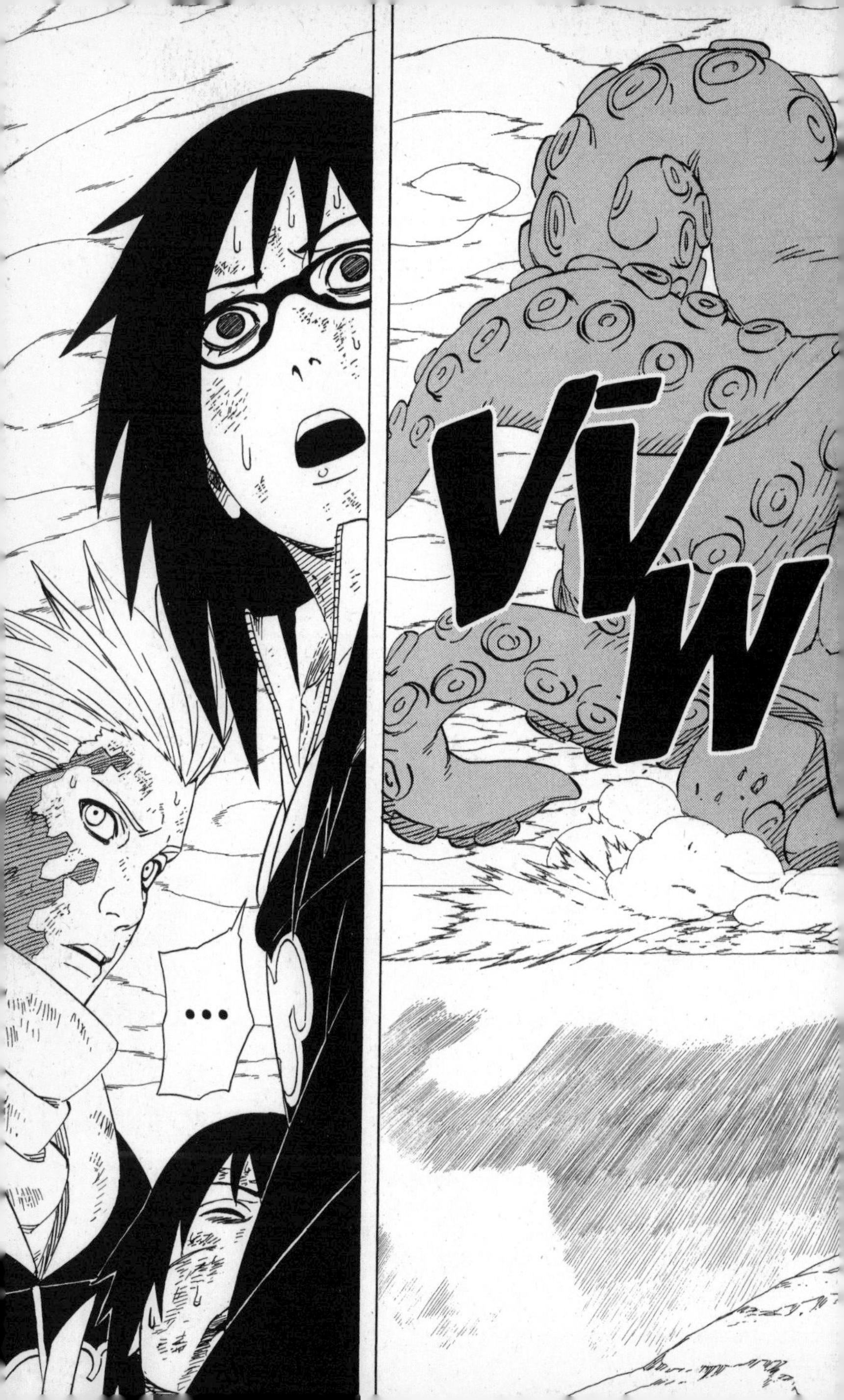
VVVW
...

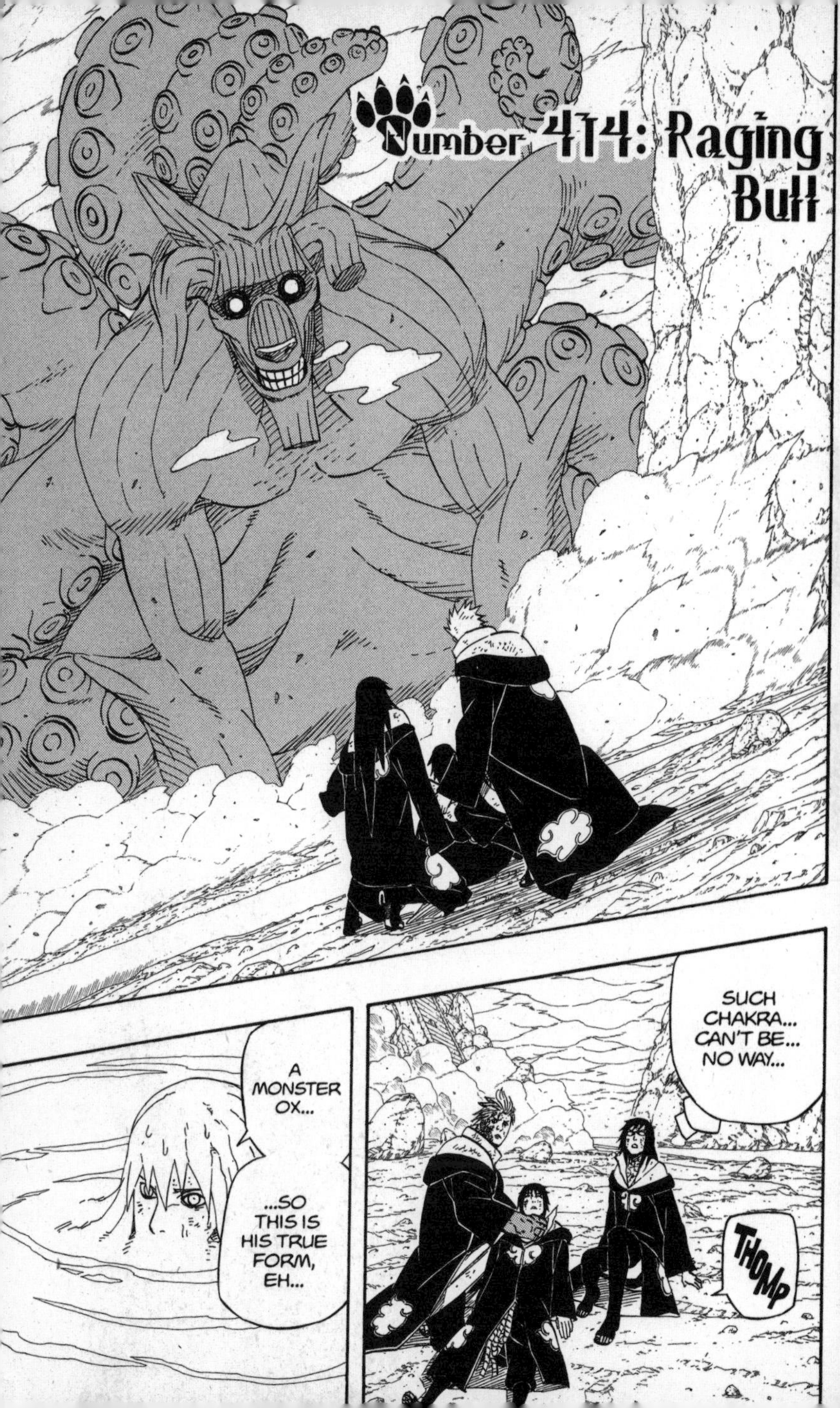
Number 414: Raging Bull
SUCH CHAKRA... CAN'T BE... NO WAY...
THOMP
A MONSTER OX...
...SO THIS IS HIS TRUE FORM, EH...

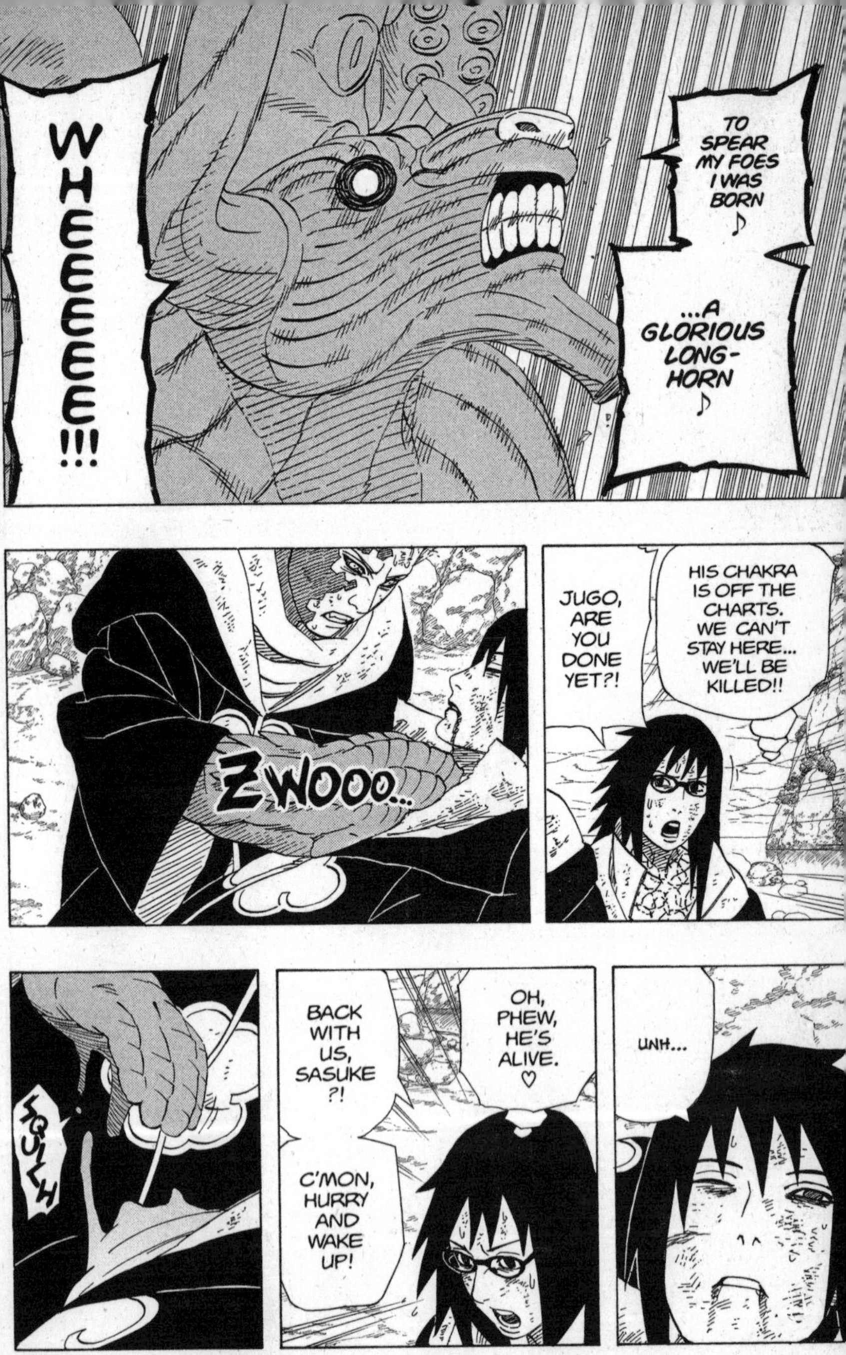
TO SPEAR MY FOES I WAS BORN ♪
...A GLORIOUS LONG-HORN ♪
WHEEEEEEE!!!
HIS CHAKRA IS OFF THE CHARTS. WE CAN'T STAY HERE... WE'LL BE KILLED!!
JUGO, ARE YOU DONE YET?!
ZWOOO...
UNH...
OH, PHEW, HE'S ALIVE. ♡
BACK WITH US, SASUKE?!
C'MON, HURRY AND WAKE UP!
SQULH

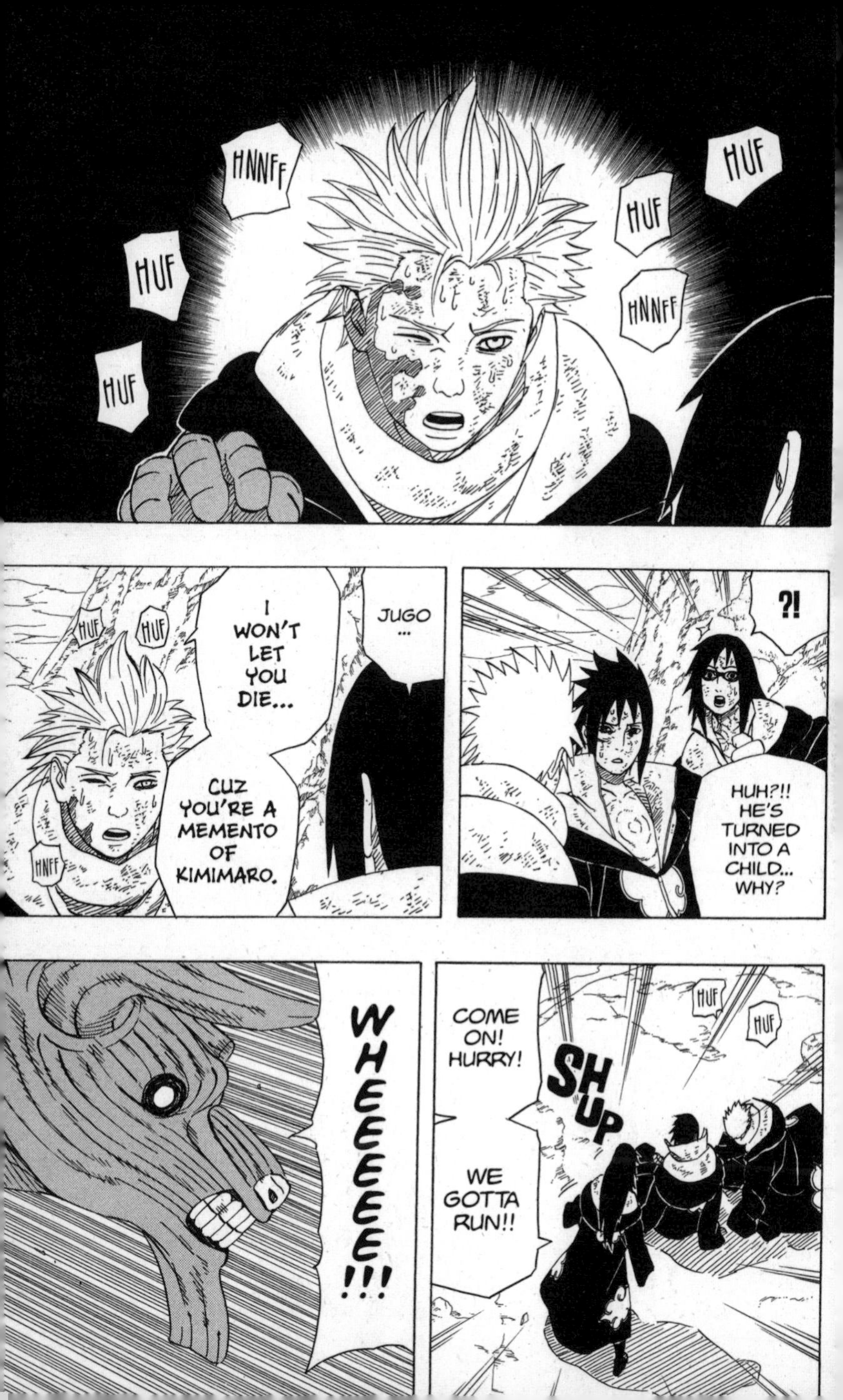
HUF
HUF
HNNFF
HNNFF
HUF
HUF
?!
HUH?!! HE'S TURNED INTO A CHILD... WHY?
JUGO...
HUF
HUF
I WON'T LET YOU DIE...
CUZ YOU'RE A MEMENTO OF KIMIMARO.
HNFF
HUF
HUF
COME ON! HURRY!
SHUP
WE GOTTA RUN!!
WHEEEEEE!!!

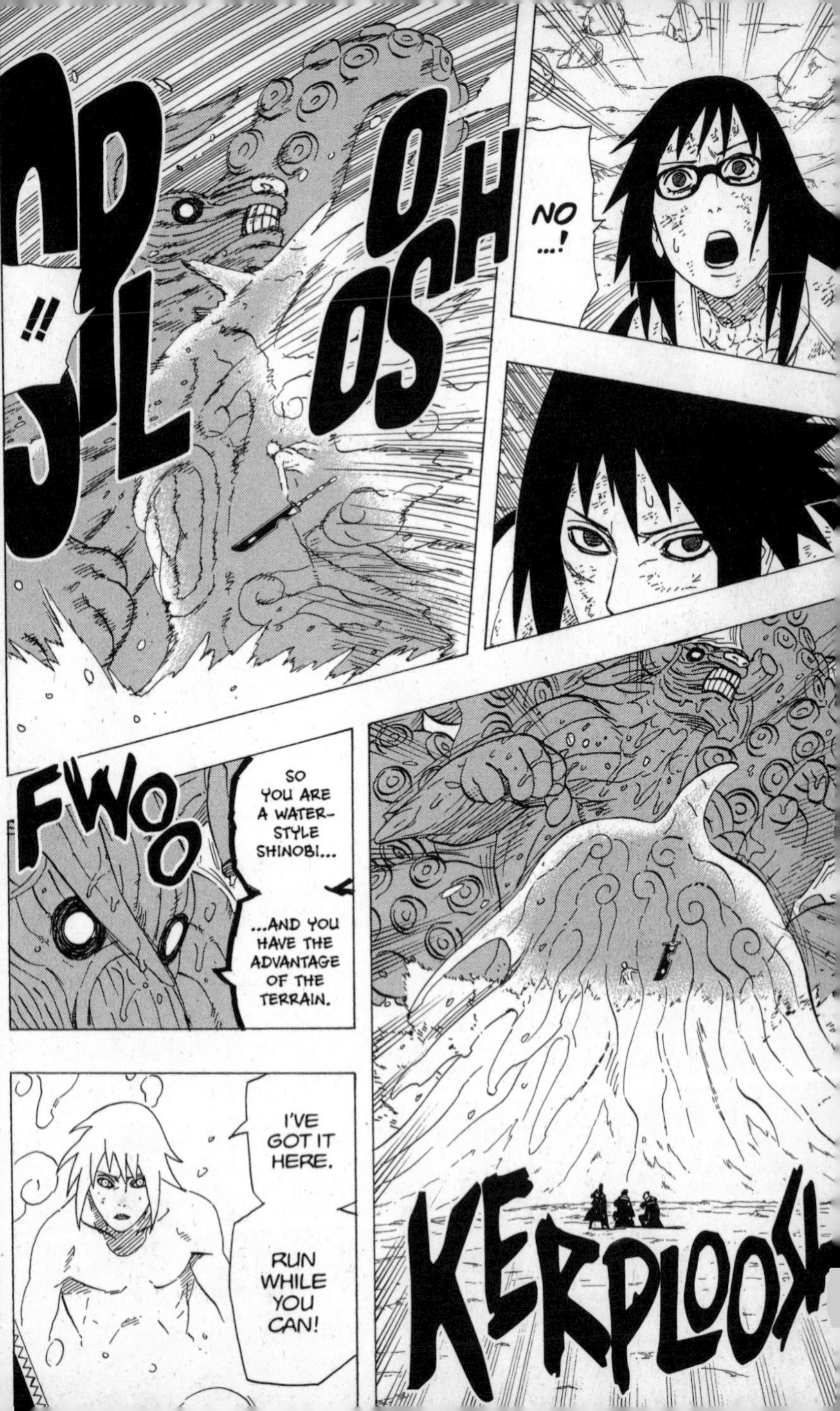
NO ...!
SPLOOSH
!!
KERPLOOSH
FWOO
SO YOU ARE A WATER-STYLE SHINOBI...
...AND YOU HAVE THE ADVANTAGE OF THE TERRAIN.
I'VE GOT IT HERE.
RUN WHILE YOU CAN!

READ THIS WAY

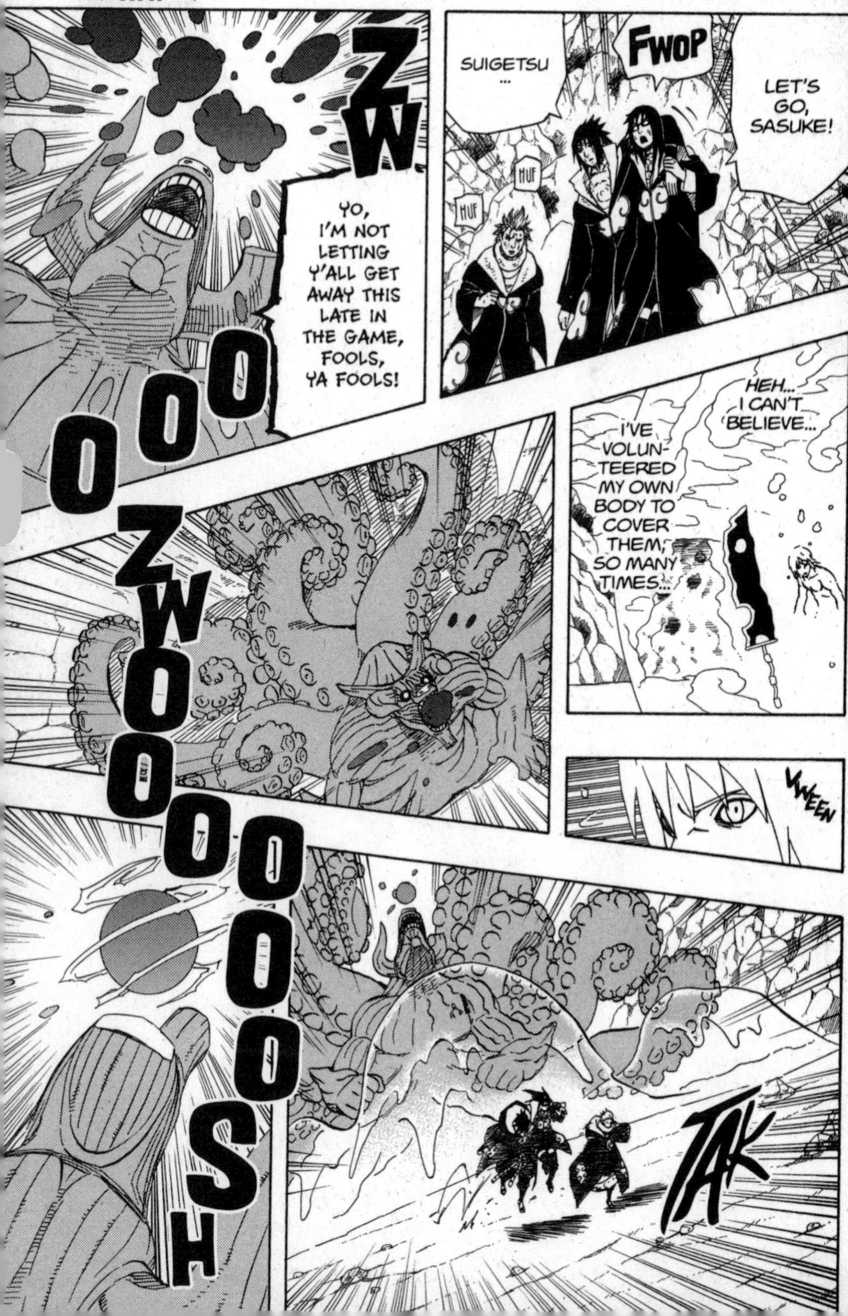
LET'S GO, SASUKE!
FWOP
SUIGETSU ...
HUF
HUF
ZW
YO, I'M NOT LETTING Y'ALL GET AWAY THIS LATE IN THE GAME, FOOLS, YA FOOLS!
OOOO
HEH... I CAN'T BELIEVE...
I'VE VOLUNTEERED MY OWN BODY TO COVER THEM; SO MANY TIMES...
VWEEN
ZWOOOOOOOSH
TAK

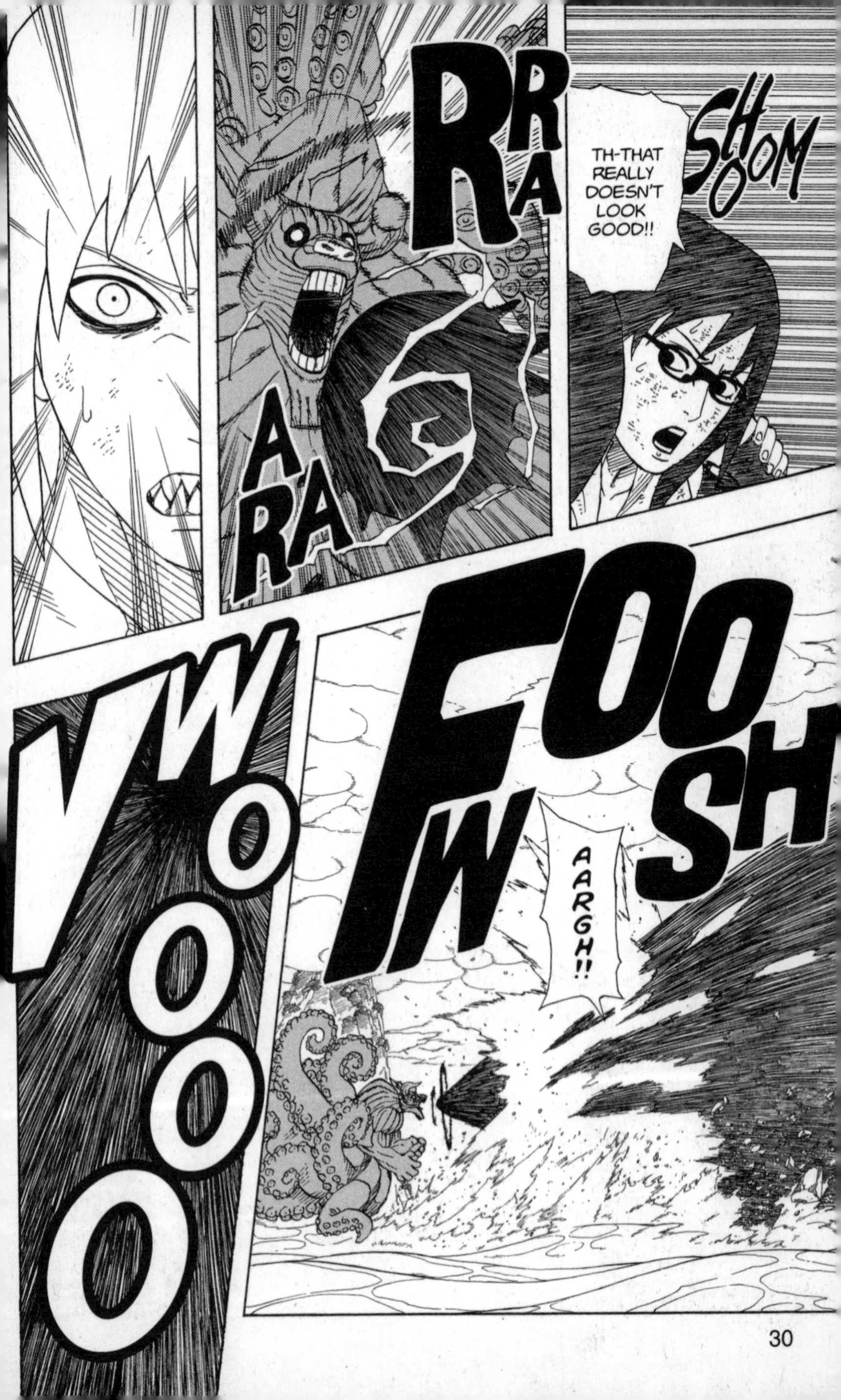
SHOOM
TH-THAT REALLY DOESN'T LOOK GOOD!!
RRA
ARA
FOOWSH
AARGH!!
VWOOOOO

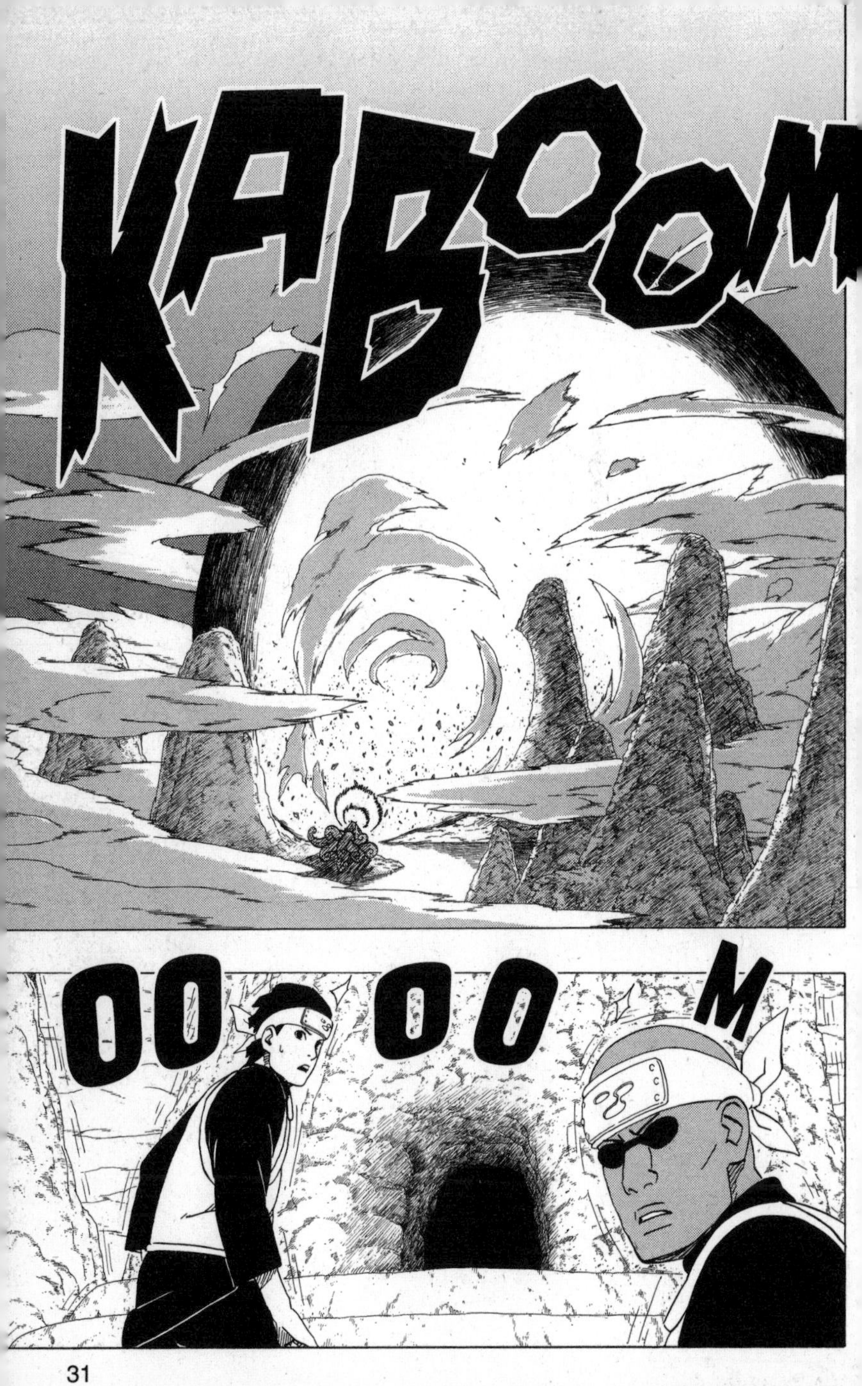
KABOOM
OOOOOM

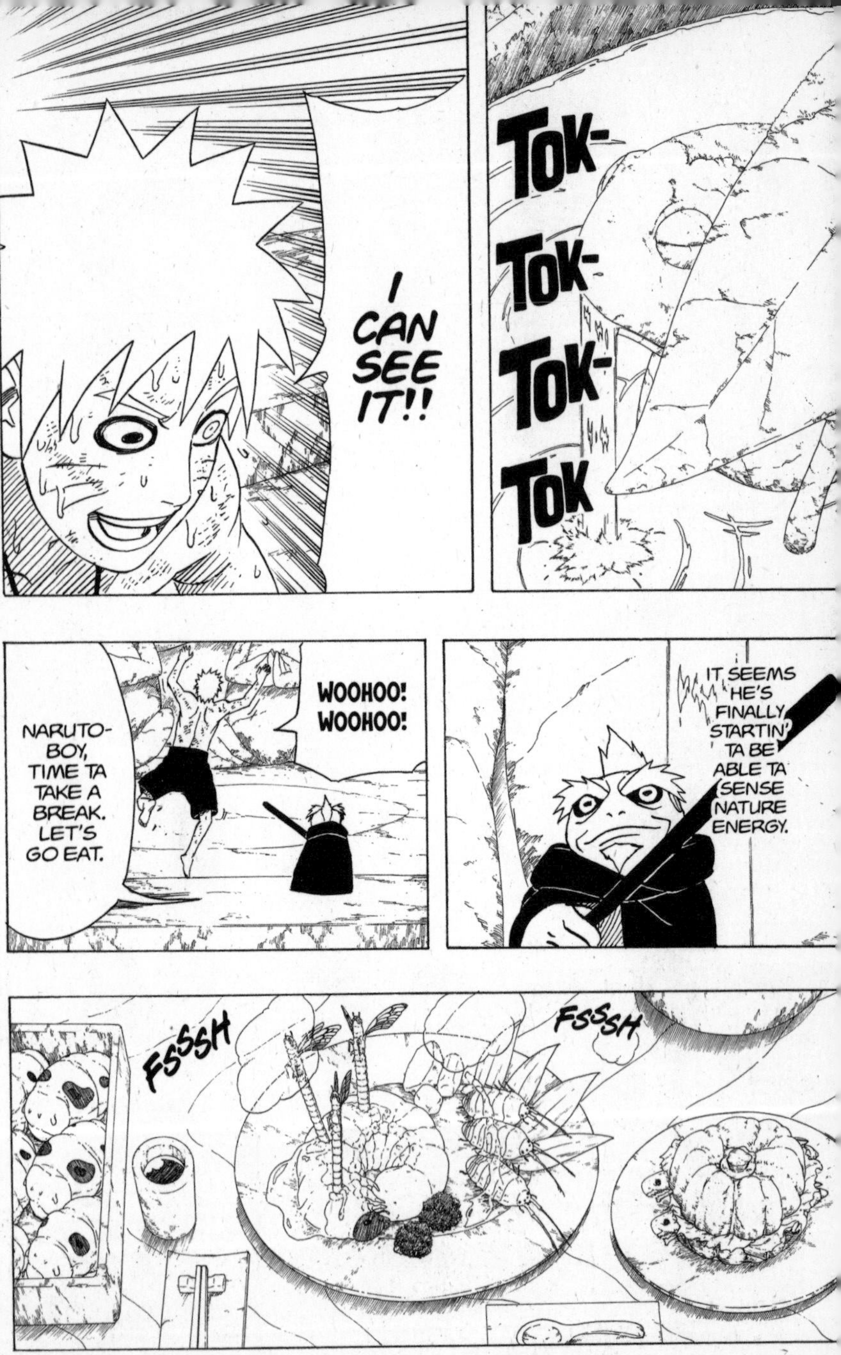
TOK-
TOK-
TOK-
TOK
I CAN SEE IT!!
IT SEEMS HE'S FINALLY STARTIN' TA BE ABLE TA SENSE NATURE ENERGY.
WOOHOO! WOOHOO!
NARUTO-BOY, TIME TA TAKE A BREAK. LET'S GO EAT.
FSSSH
FSSSH

READ THIS WAY

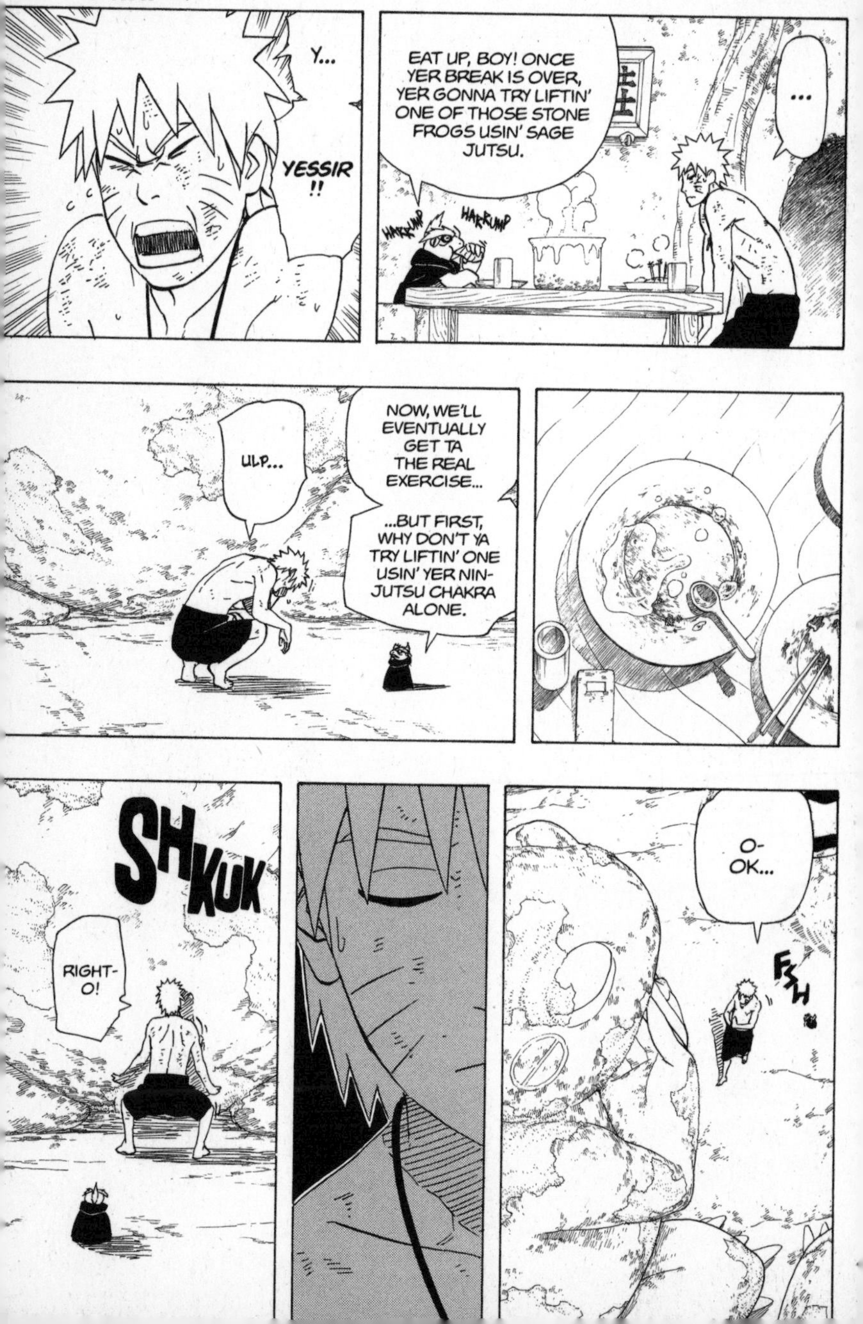
...
EAT UP, BOY! ONCE YER BREAK IS OVER, YER GONNA TRY LIFTIN' ONE OF THOSE STONE FROGS USIN' SAGE JUTSU.
HARRUMP
HARRUMP
Y...
YESSIR!!
NOW, WE'LL EVENTUALLY GET TA THE REAL EXERCISE...
...BUT FIRST, WHY DON'T YA TRY LIFTIN' ONE USIN' YER NINJUTSU CHAKRA ALONE.
ULP...
O-OK...
SHKUK
RIGHT-O!

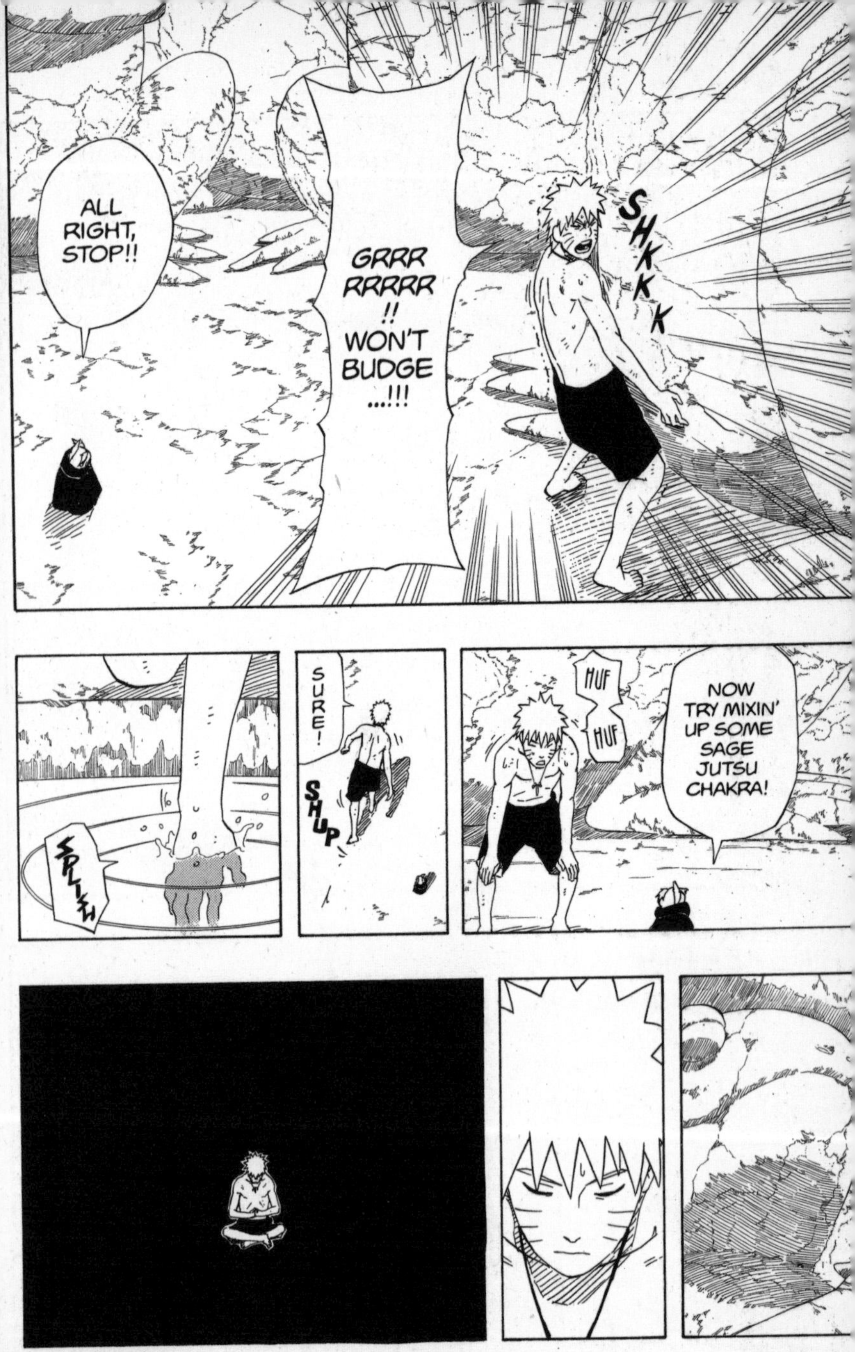
SHKKK
GRRR RRRRR!! WON'T BUDGE...!!!
ALL RIGHT, STOP!!
NOW TRY MIXIN' UP SOME SAGE JUTSU CHAKRA!
HUF
HUF
SURE!
SHUP
SPLISH

READ THIS WAY

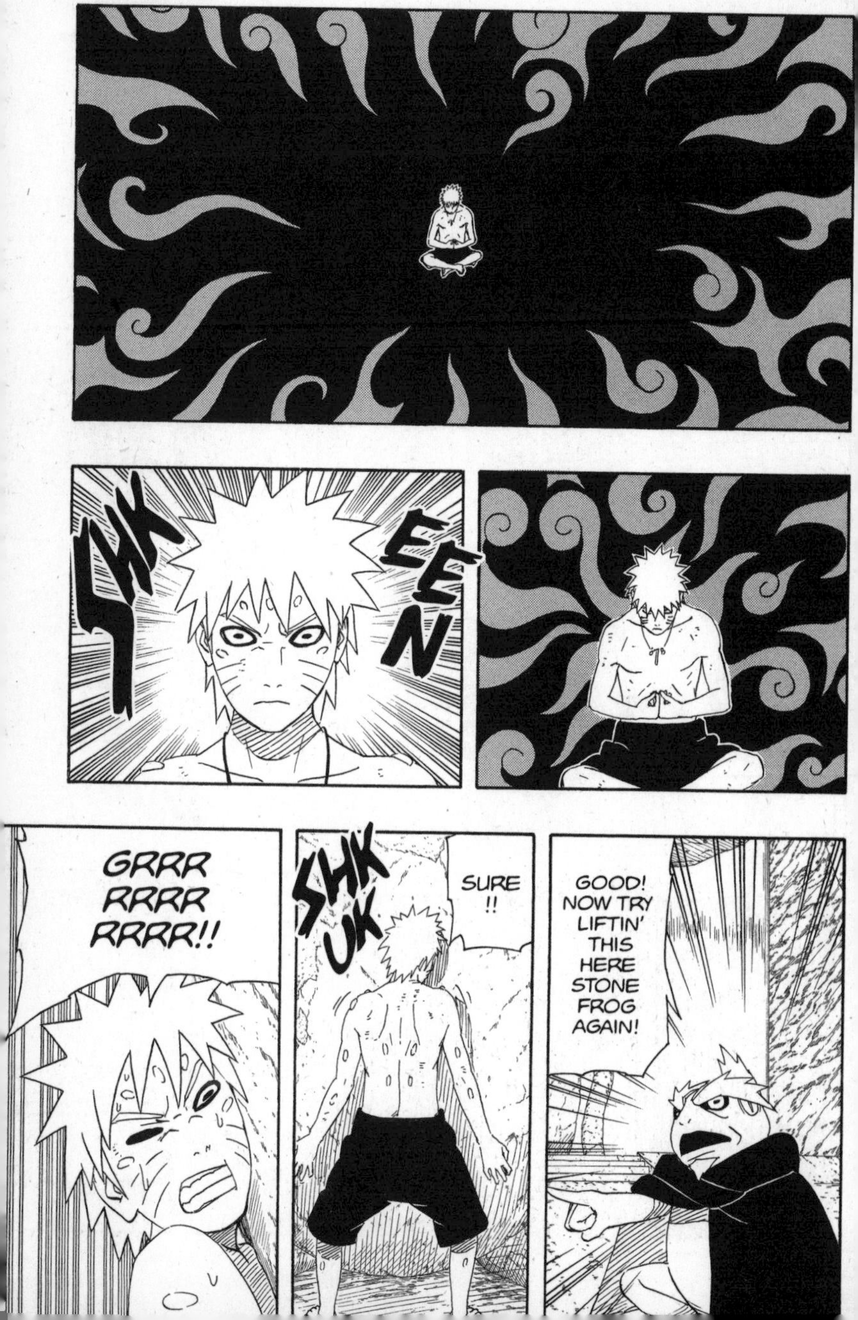
SHKEEN
GOOD! NOW TRY LIFTIN' THIS HERE STONE FROG AGAIN!
SURE !!
SHKUK
GRRRR RRRR RRRR!!

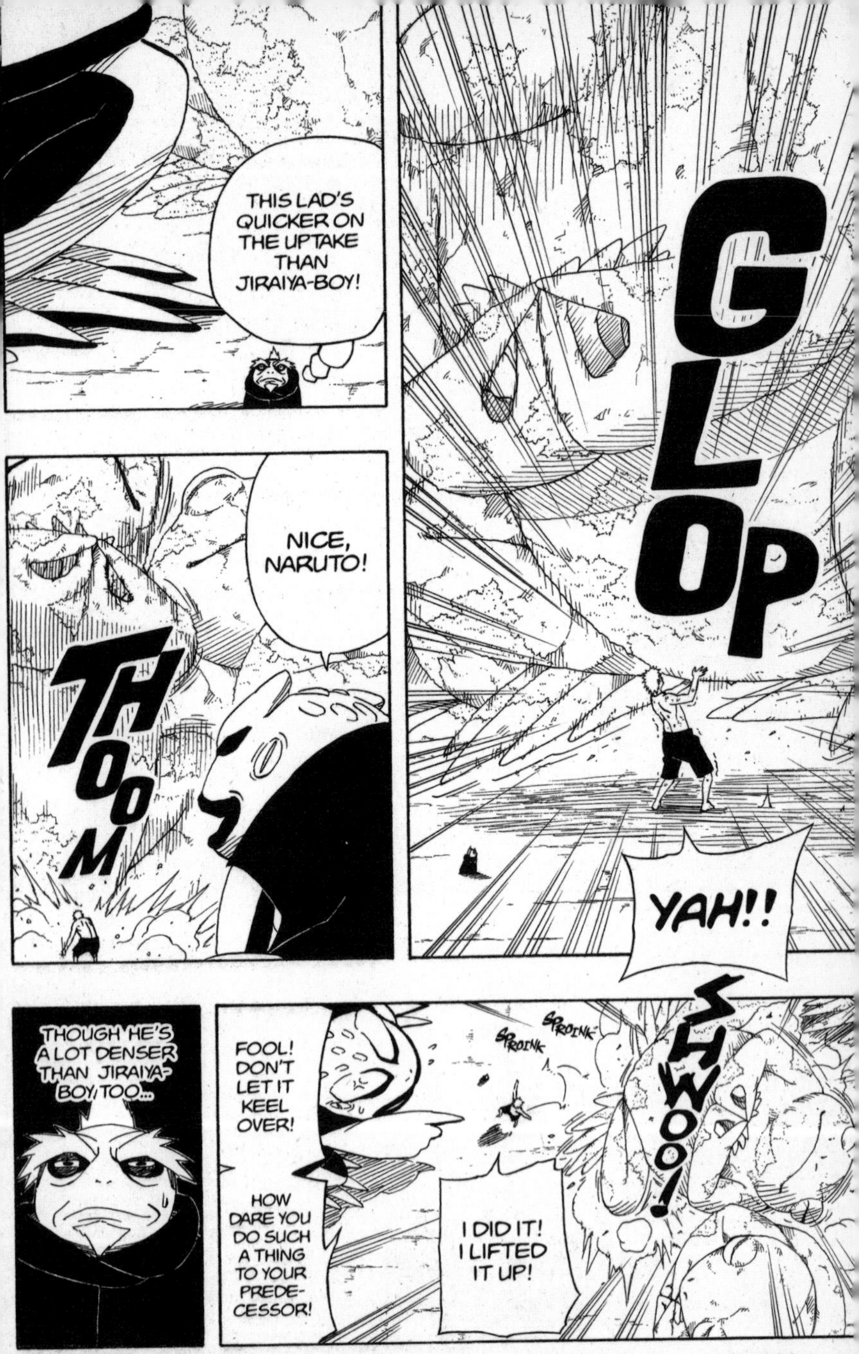
GLOP
YAH!!
THIS LAD'S QUICKER ON THE UPTAKE THAN JIRAIYA-BOY!
NICE, NARUTO!
THOOM
SHWOOO!
SPROINK
SPROINK
I DID IT! I LIFTED IT UP!
FOOL! DON'T LET IT KEEL OVER!
HOW DARE YOU DO SUCH A THING TO YOUR PREDE-CESSOR!
THOUGH HE'S A LOT DENSER THAN JIRAIYA-BOY, TOO...

READ THIS WAY

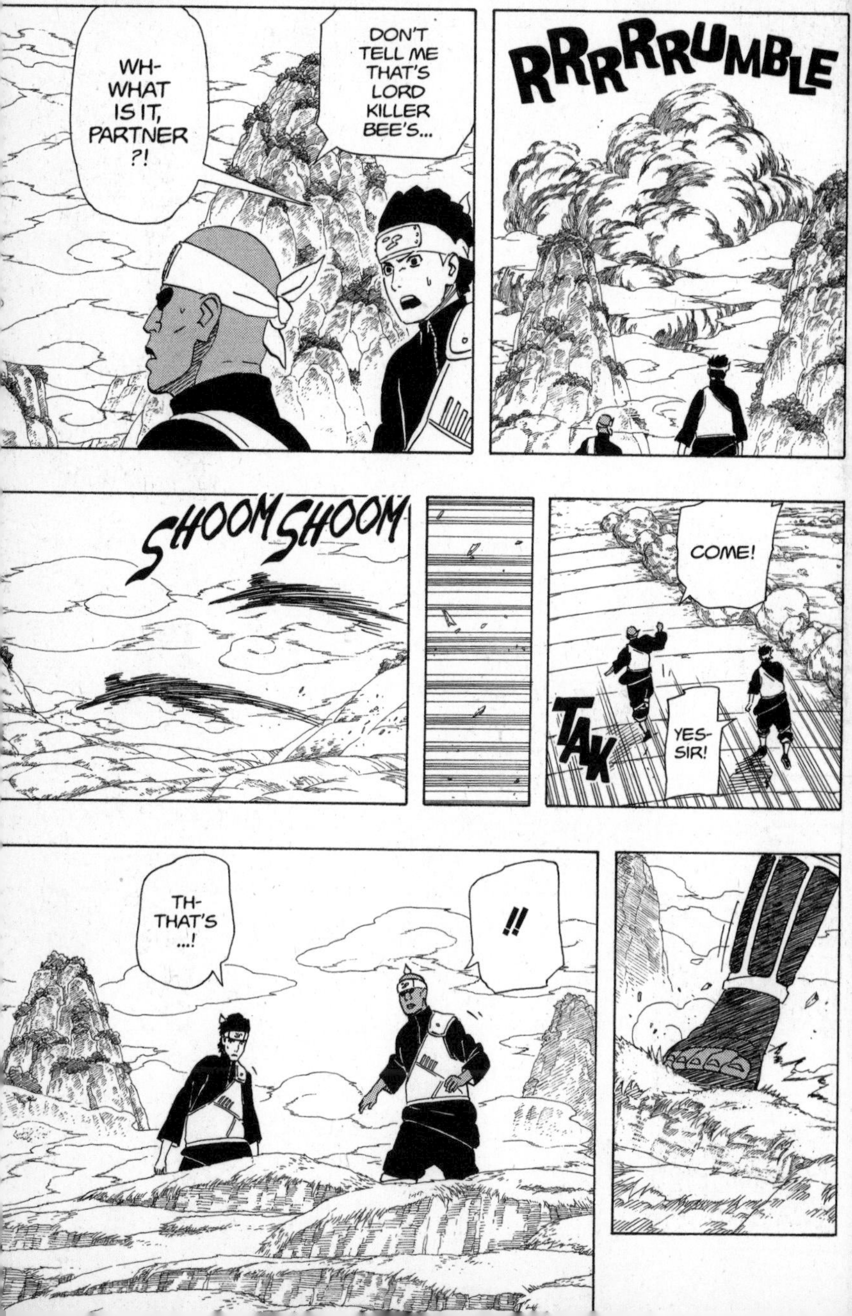
RRRRRUMBLE
DON'T TELL ME THAT'S LORD KILLER BEE'S...
WH-WHAT IS IT, PARTNER?!
COME!
TAK
YES-SIR!
SHOOM SHOOM
!!
TH-THAT'S...!

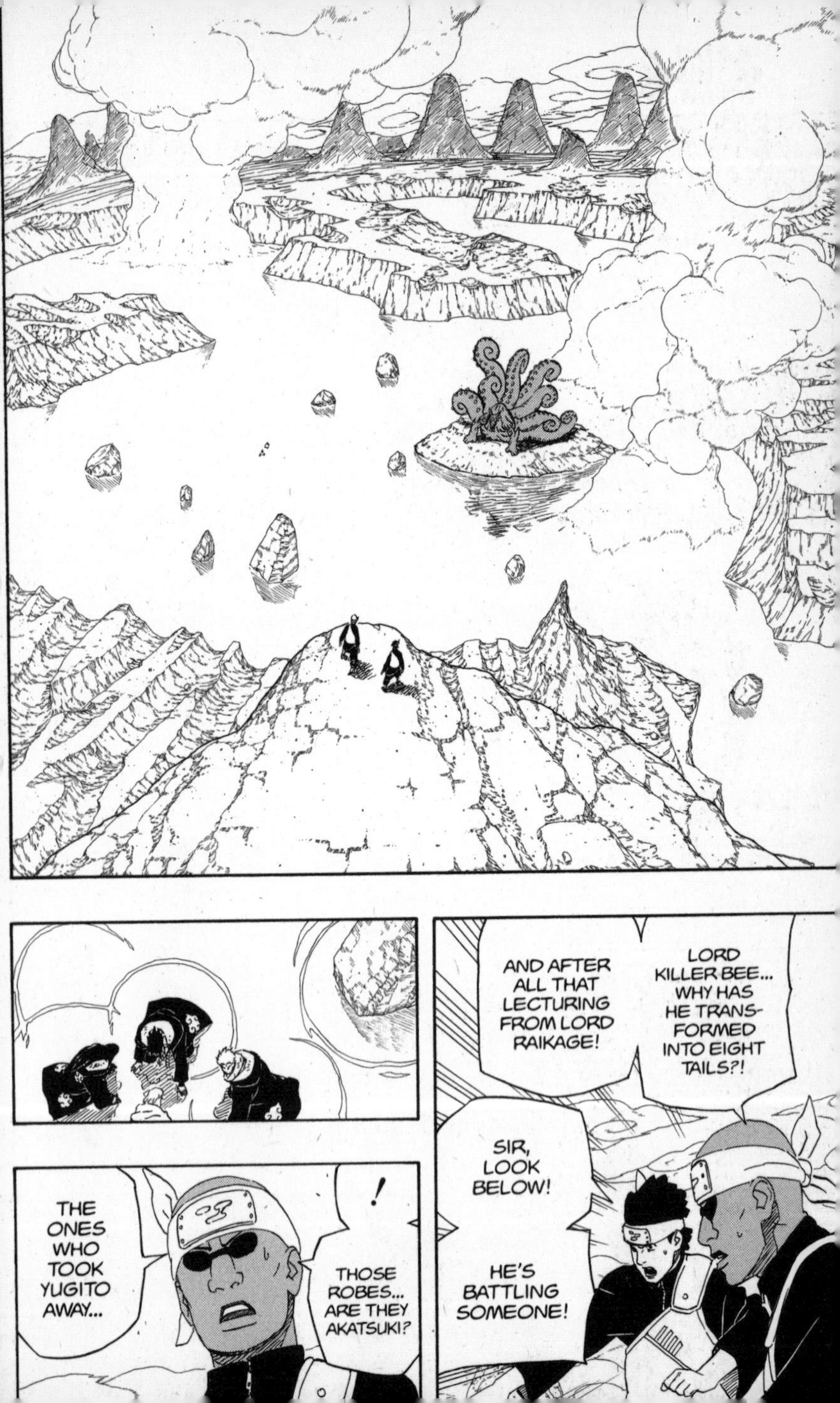
LORD KILLER BEE... WHY HAS HE TRANS-FORMED INTO EIGHT TAILS?!
AND AFTER ALL THAT LECTURING FROM LORD RAIKAGE!
SIR, LOOK BELOW!
HE'S BATTLING SOMEONE!
!
THOSE ROBES... ARE THEY AKATSUKI?
THE ONES WHO TOOK YUGITO AWAY...

READ THIS WAY

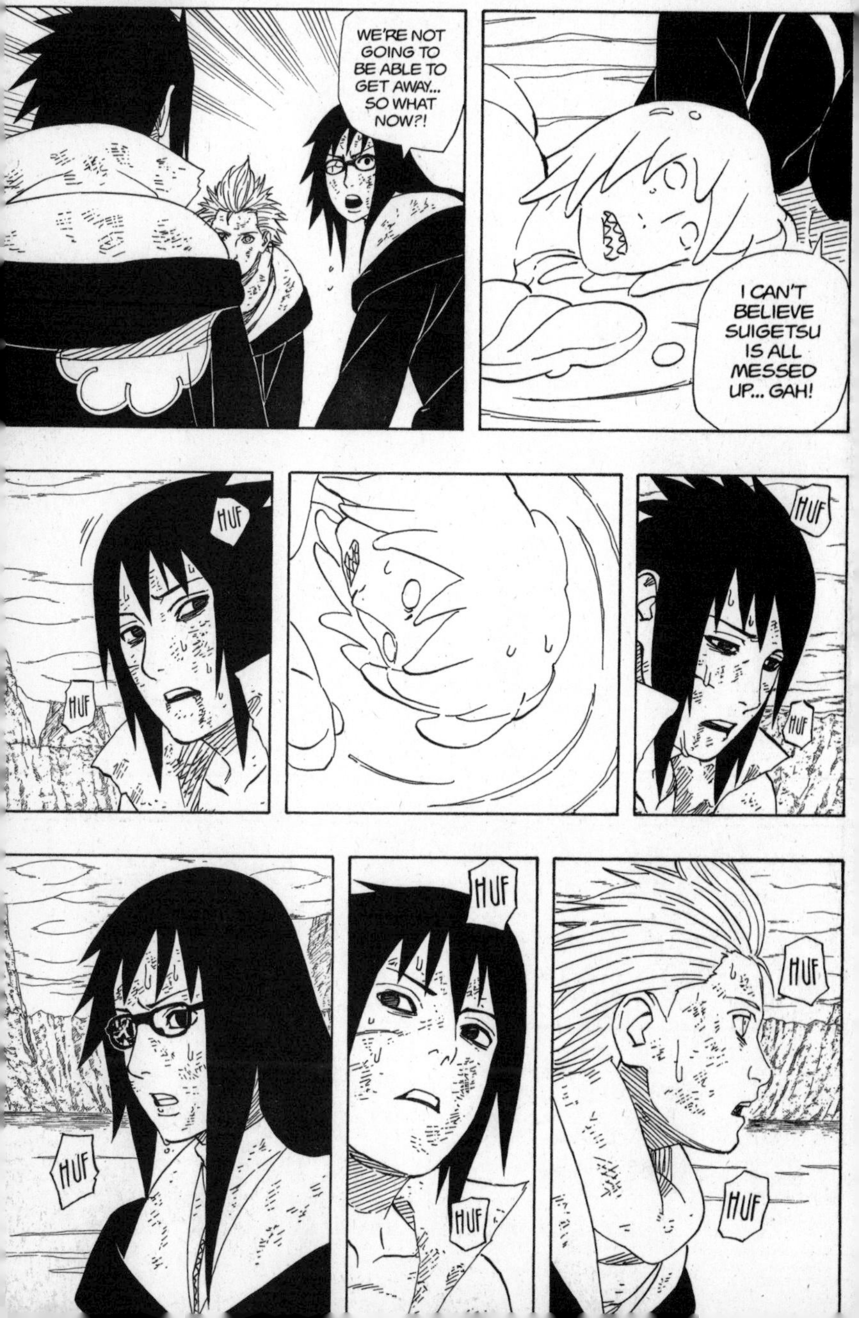
I CAN'T BELIEVE SUIGETSU IS ALL MESSED UP... GAH!
WE'RE NOT GOING TO BE ABLE TO GET AWAY... SO WHAT NOW?!
HUF
HUF
HUF
HUF
HUF
HUF
HUF
HUF
HUF

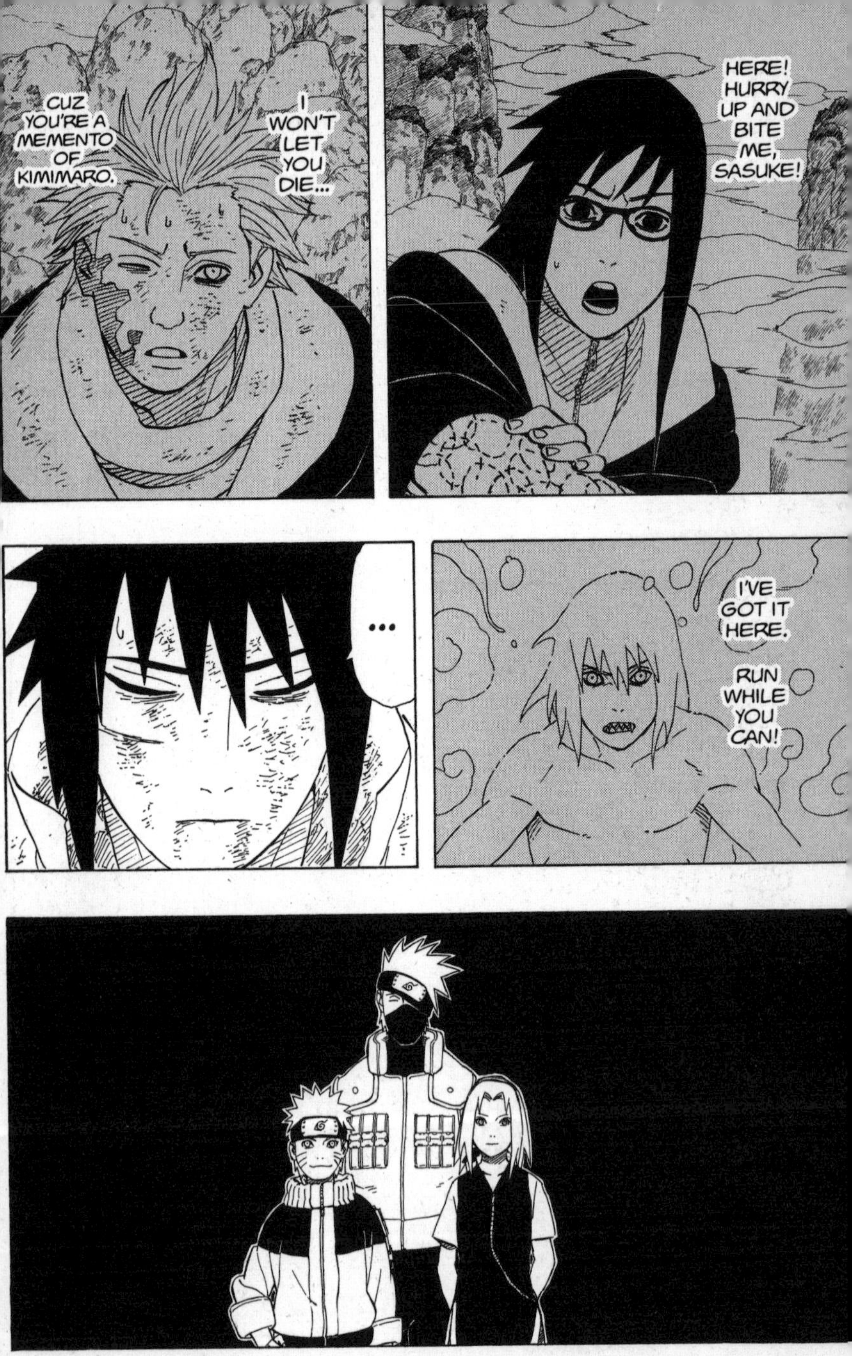
HERE! HURRY UP AND BITE ME, SASUKE!
I WON'T LET YOU DIE...
CUZ YOU'RE A MEMENTO OF KIMIMARO.
I'VE GOT IT HERE.
RUN WHILE YOU CAN!
...

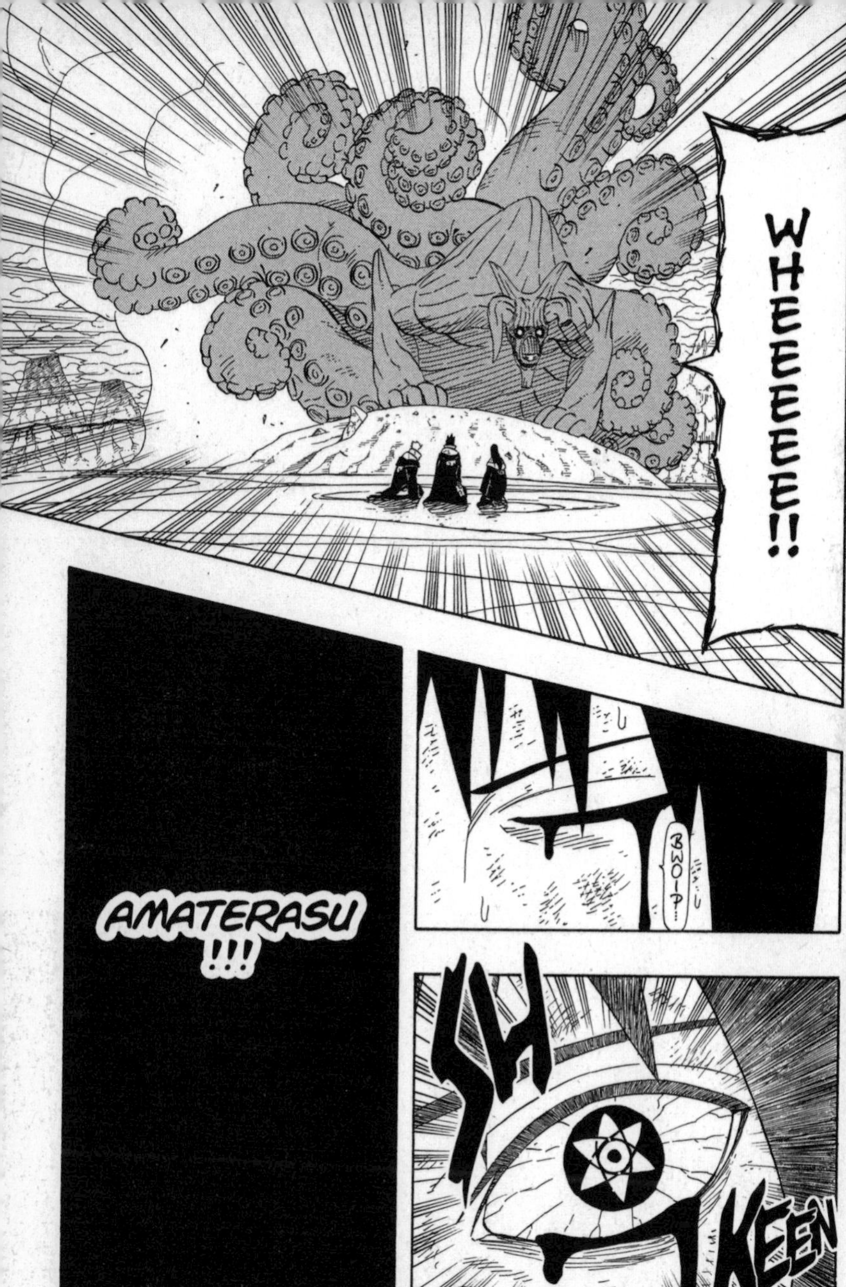
WHEEEEEEE!!
BWOIP...
SHKEEN
AMATERASU!!!

NARUTO

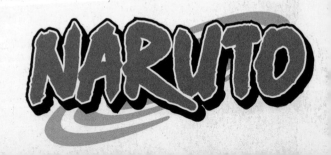

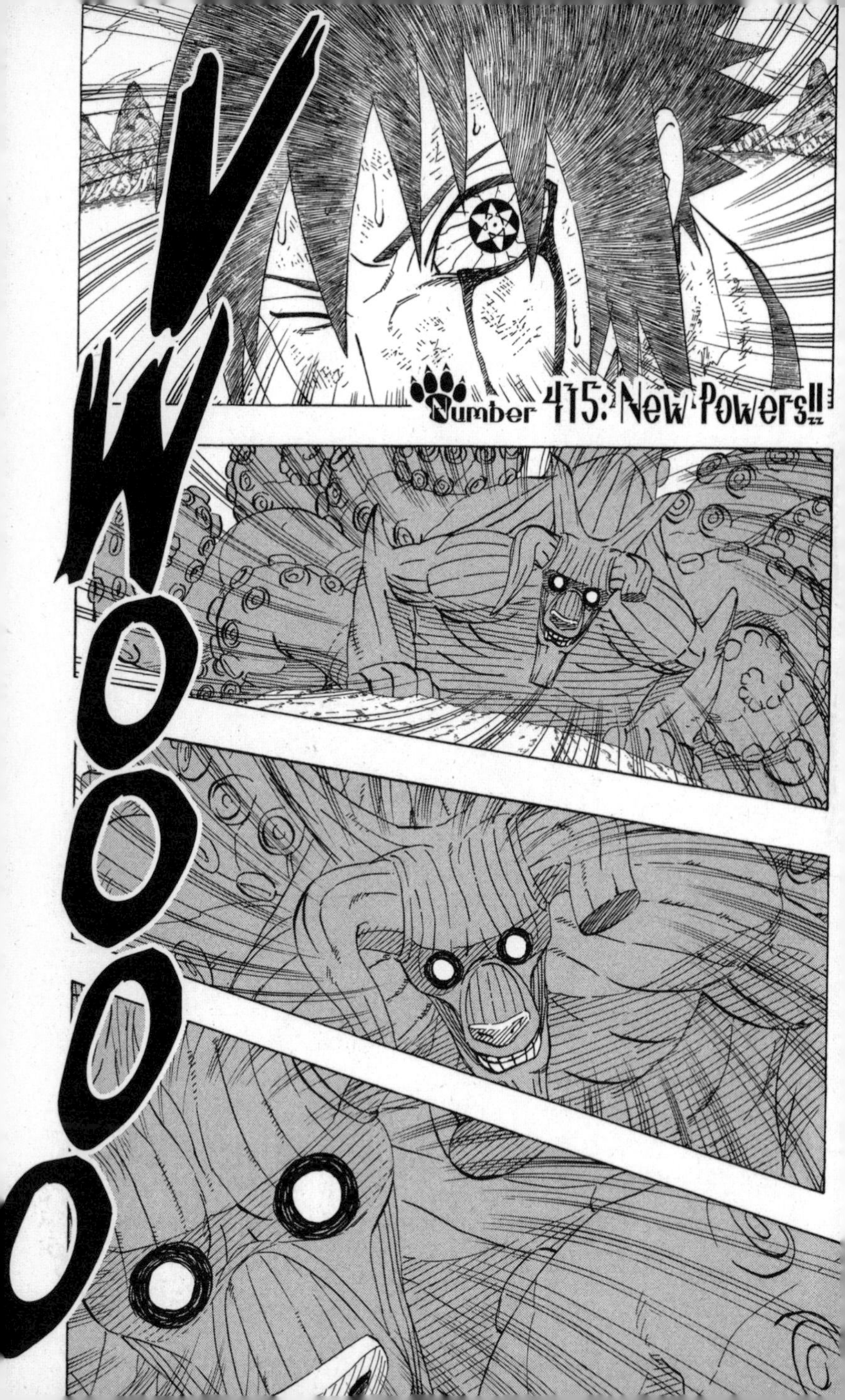
Number 415: New Powers!!
KWOOOOOO

Number 415: New Powers!!

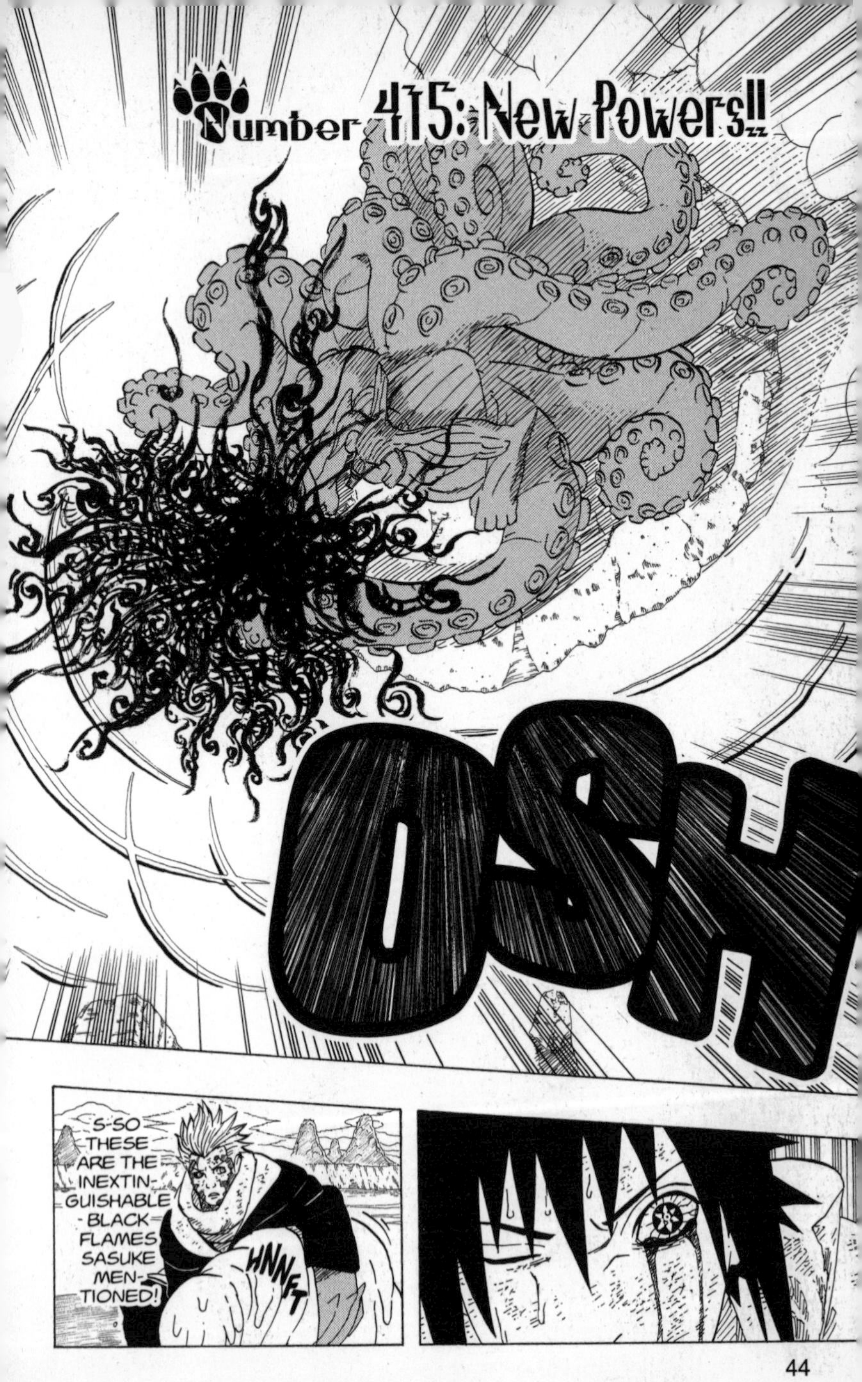

OSH
S-SO THESE ARE THE INEXTIN-GUISHABLE BLACK FLAMES SASUKE MEN-TIONED!
HNNFT

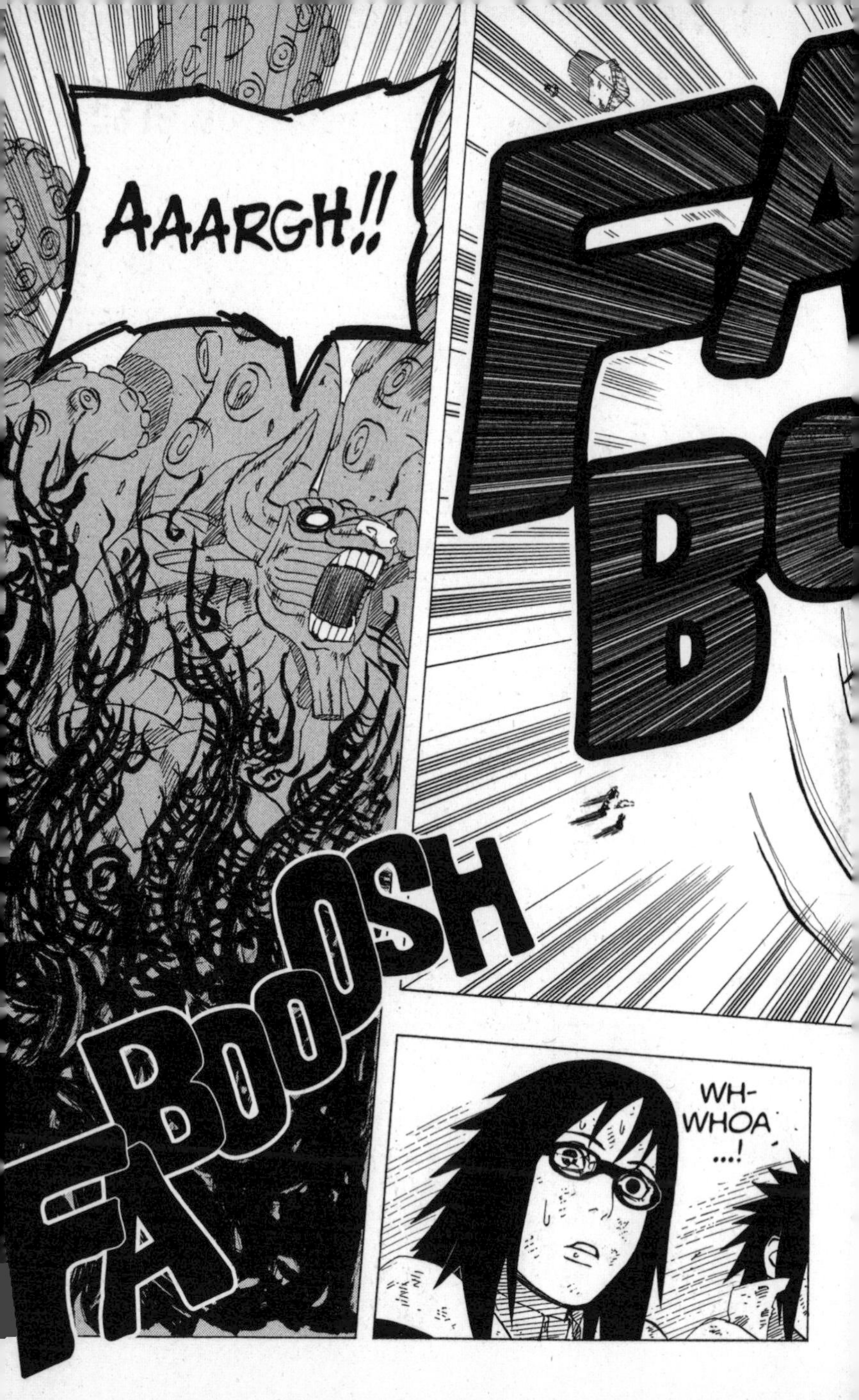
AAARGH!!
FABOOOSH
WH-WHOA ...!

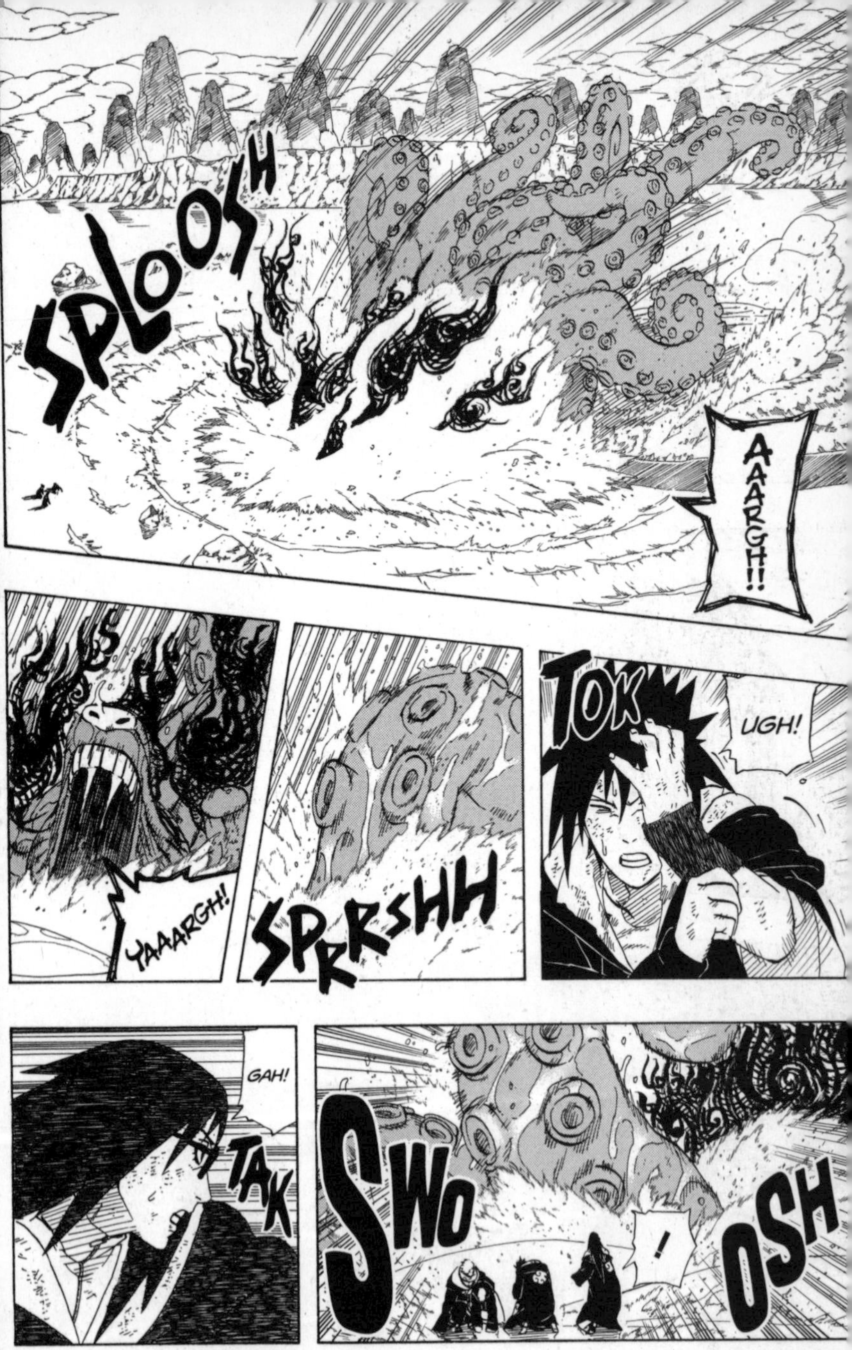
AAARGH!!
SPLOOSH
UGH!
TOK
SPRRSHH
YAAARGH!
SWO
!
OSH
GAH!
TAK

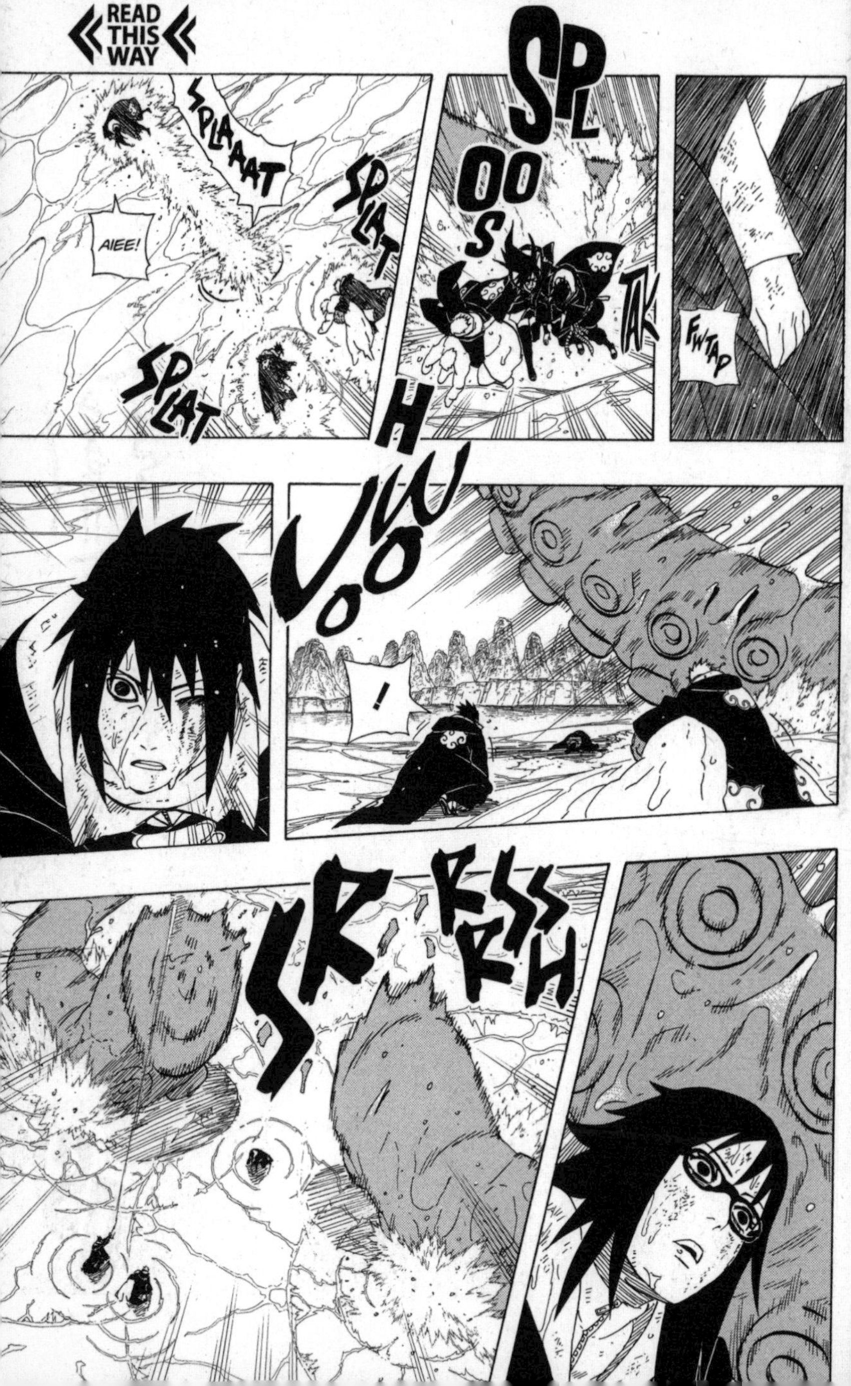

READ THIS WAY
FWTAP
SPLOOOSH
TAK
SPLAT
SPLAAAAT
AIEE!
SPLAT
WOOOO
!
SKRISSH

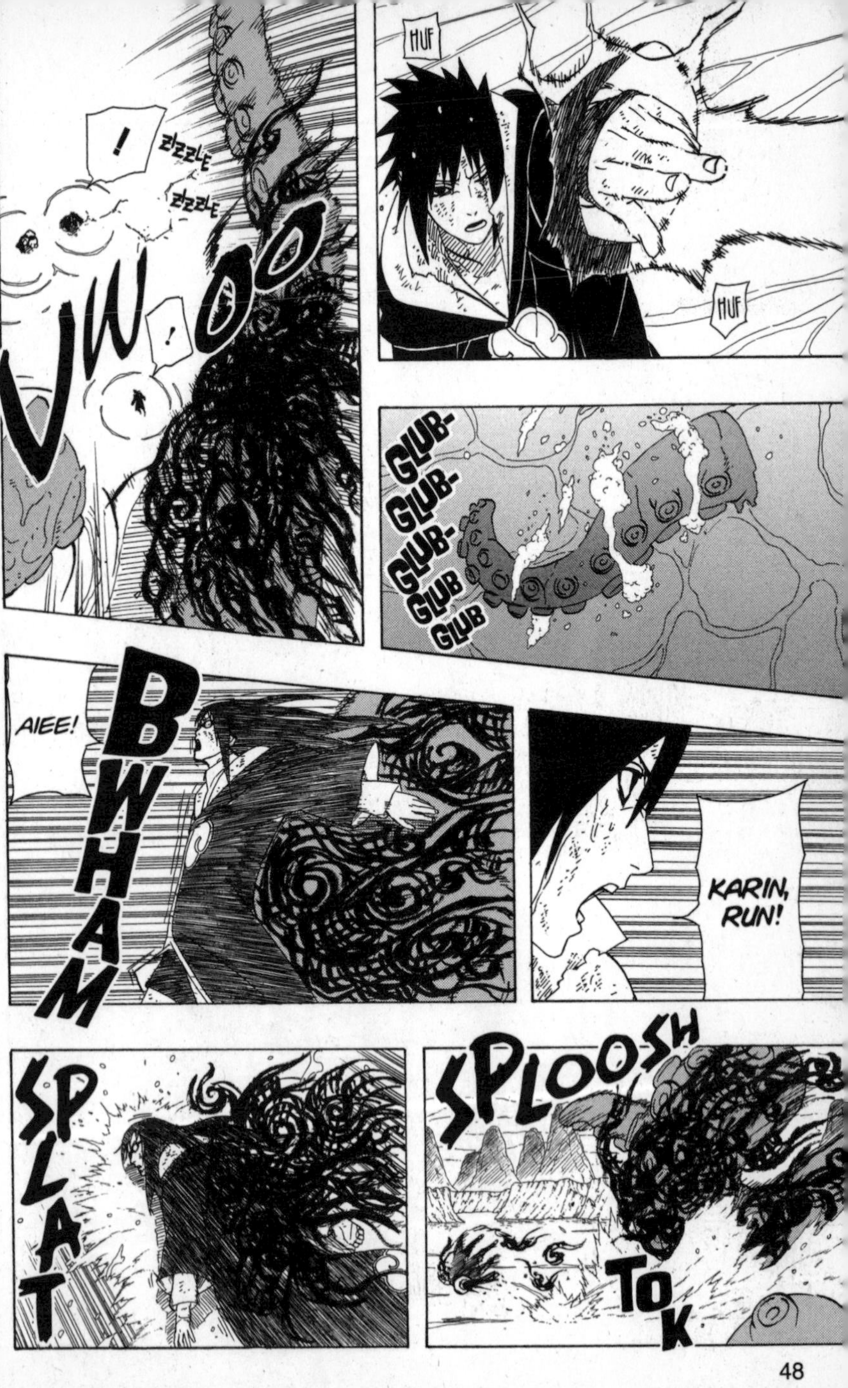
HUF
HUF
GLUB-
GLUB-
GLUB-
GLUB
GLUB
!
ZIZZLE
ZIZZLE
VWOOO
!
KARIN, RUN!
AIEE!
BWHAM
SPLOOSH
TOK
SPLAT

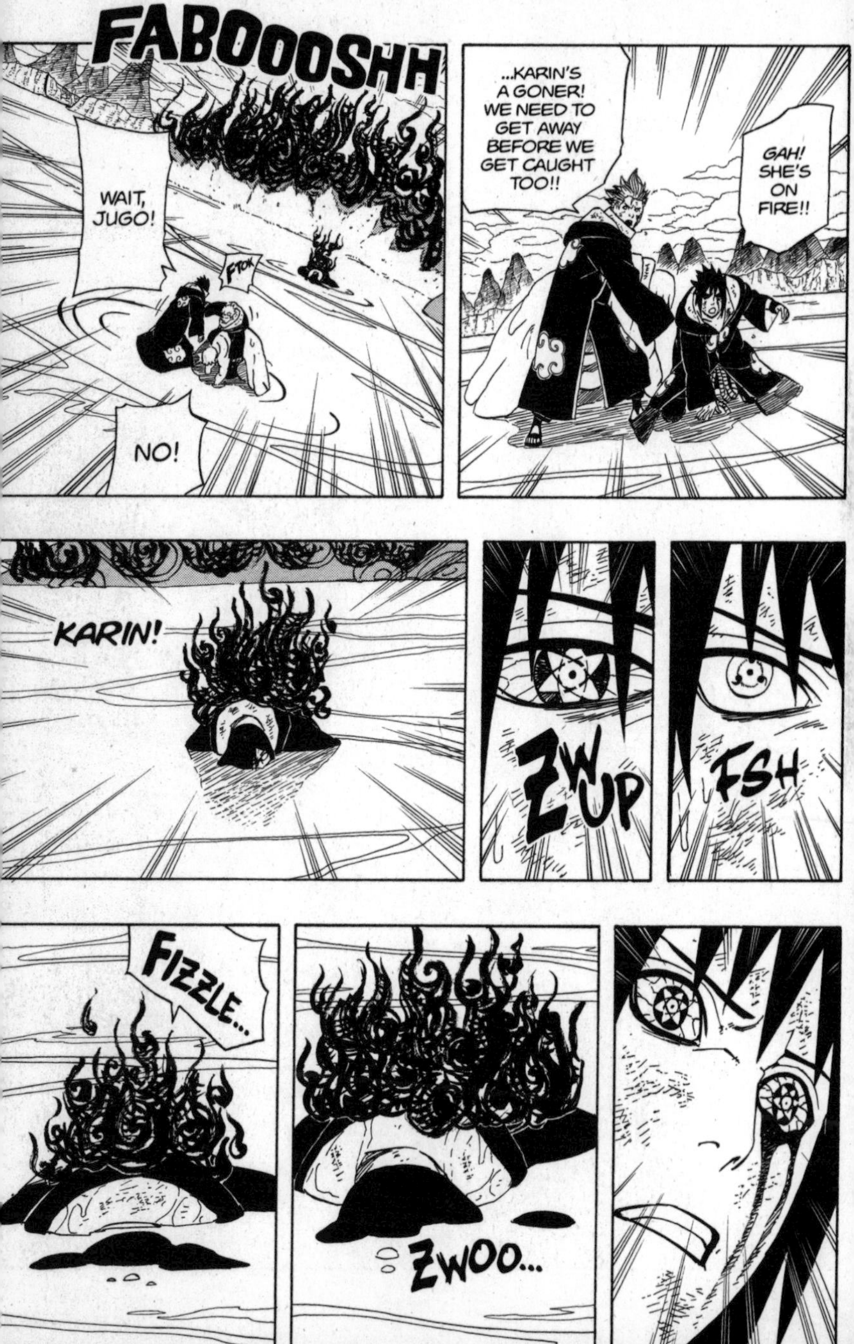
GAH! SHE'S ON FIRE!!
...KARIN'S A GONER! WE NEED TO GET AWAY BEFORE WE GET CAUGHT TOO!!
FABOOOSHH
WAIT, JUGO!
FTOK
NO!
FSH
ZWUP
KARIN!
ZWOO...
FIZZLE...

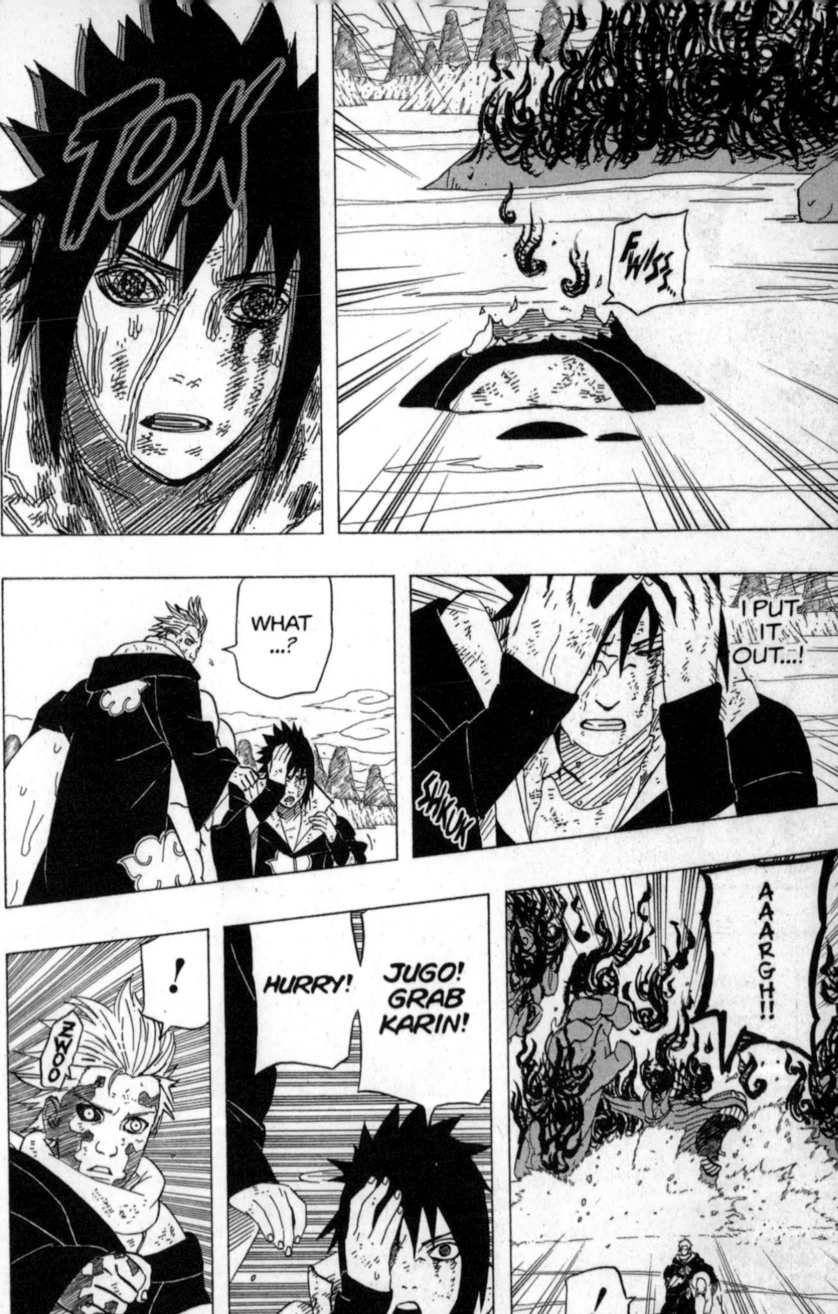
FWISS...
I PUT IT OUT...!
SHKUK
WHAT ...?
AAARGH!!
!
JUGO! GRAB KARIN!
HURRY!
!
ZWOO

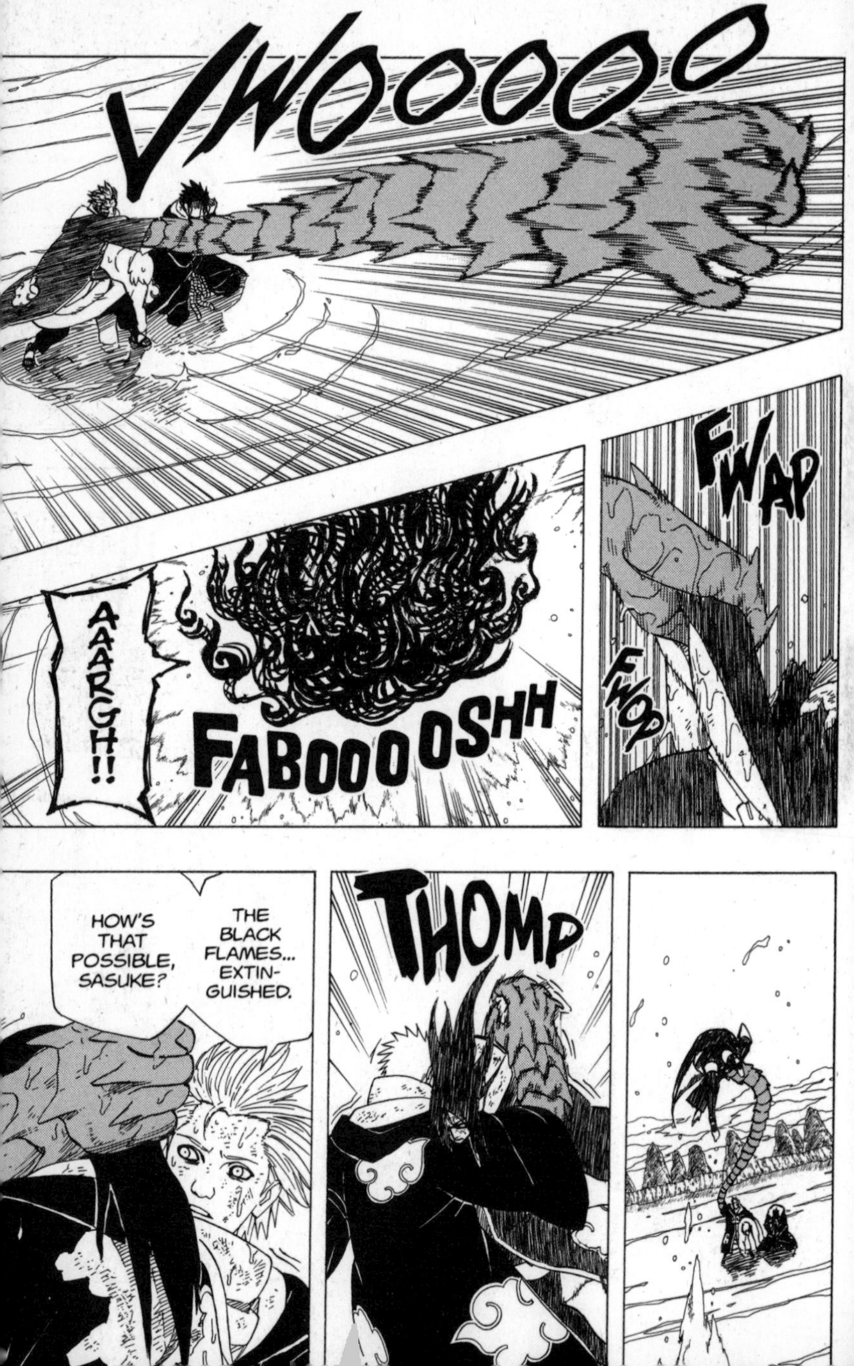
VWOOOOO
FWAP
FWOP
FABOOOOSHH
AAARGH!!
THOMP
THE BLACK FLAMES... EXTINGUISHED.
HOW'S THAT POSSIBLE, SASUKE?

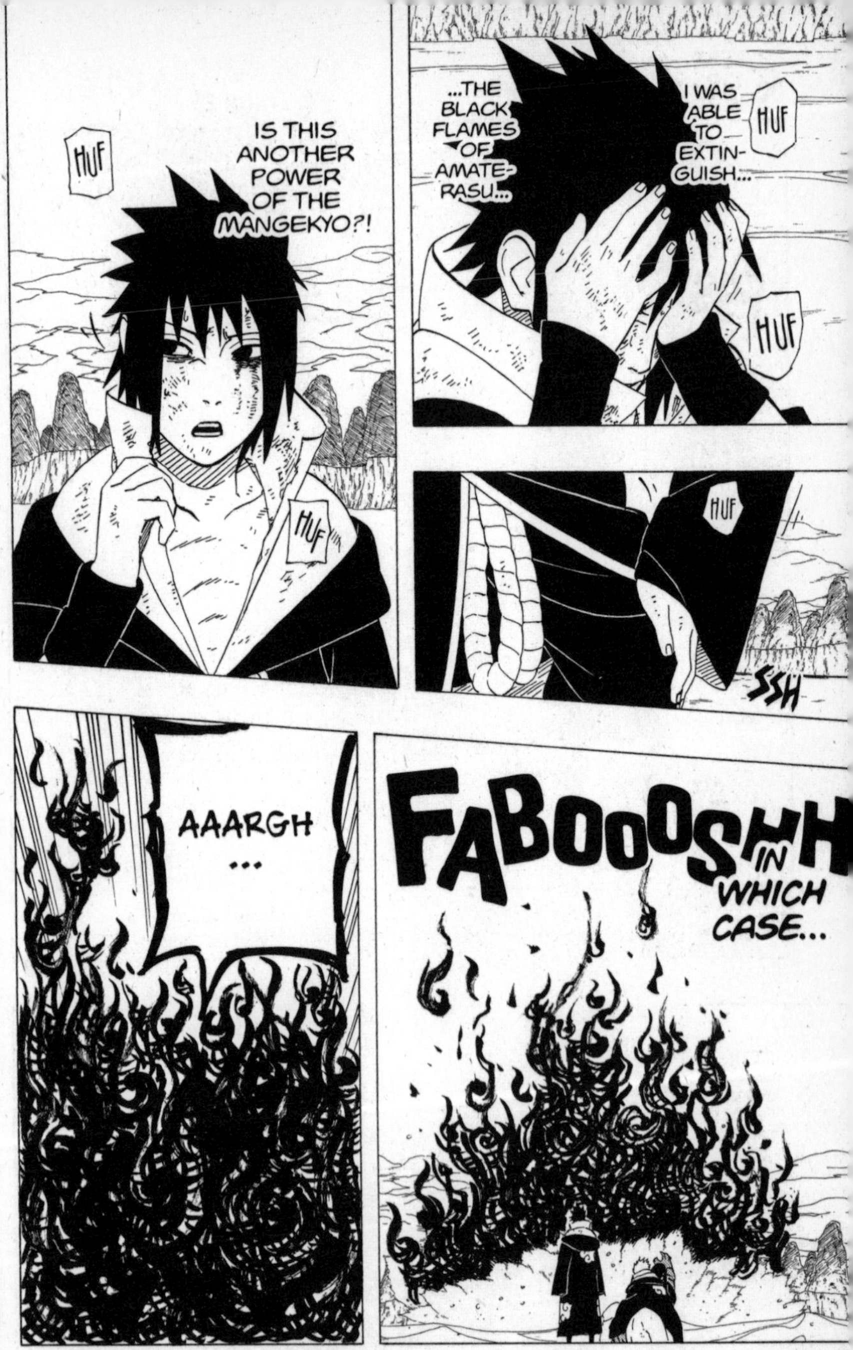
HUF
I WAS ABLE TO EXTIN-GUISH...
...THE BLACK FLAMES OF AMATE-RASU...
HUF
HUF
SSH
HUF
IS THIS ANOTHER POWER OF THE MANGEKYO?!
HUF
FABOOOSHH
IN WHICH CASE...
AAARGH ...

READ THIS WAY

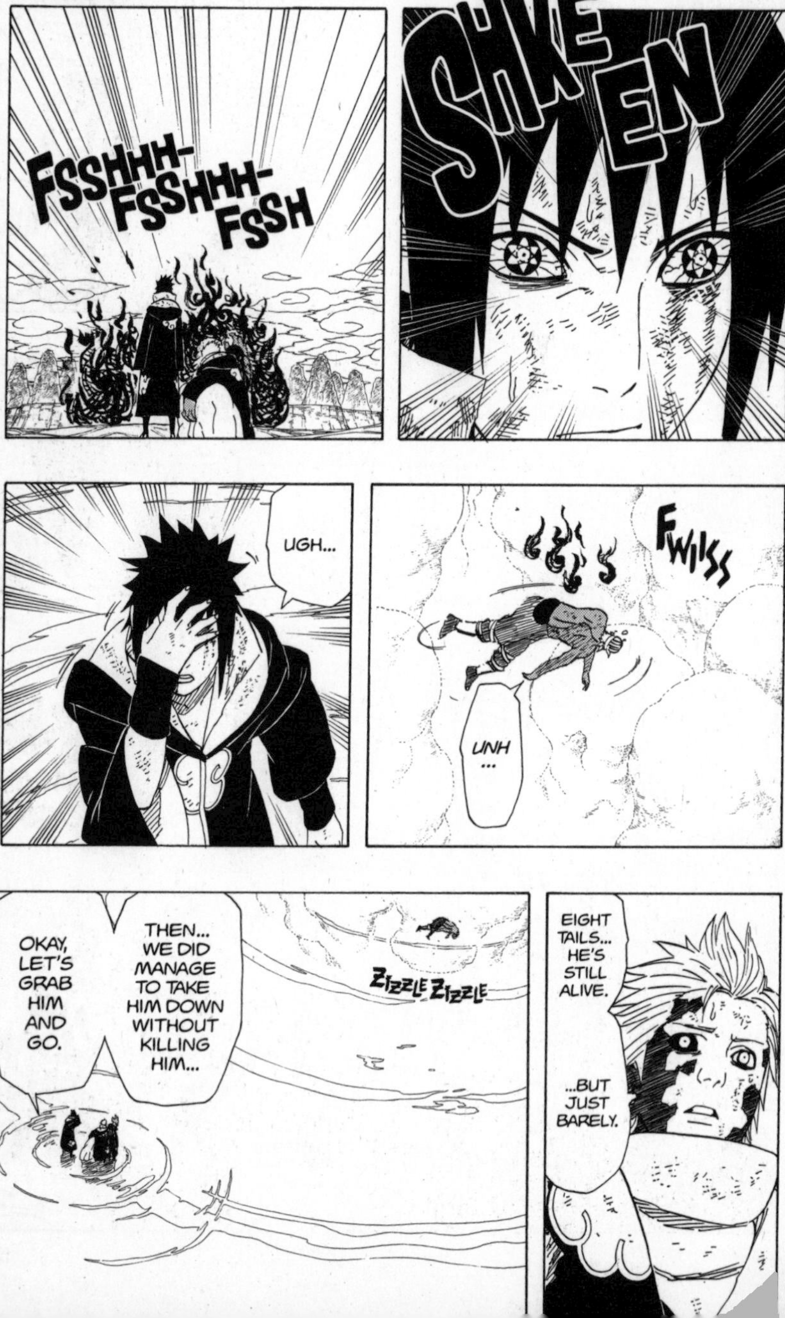
SHKEEN
FSSHHH-FSSHHH-FSSH
FWISS
UNH...
UGH...
EIGHT TAILS... HE'S STILL ALIVE.
...BUT JUST BARELY.
THEN... WE DID MANAGE TO TAKE HIM DOWN WITHOUT KILLING HIM...
OKAY, LET'S GRAB HIM AND GO.
ZIZZLE ZIZZLE

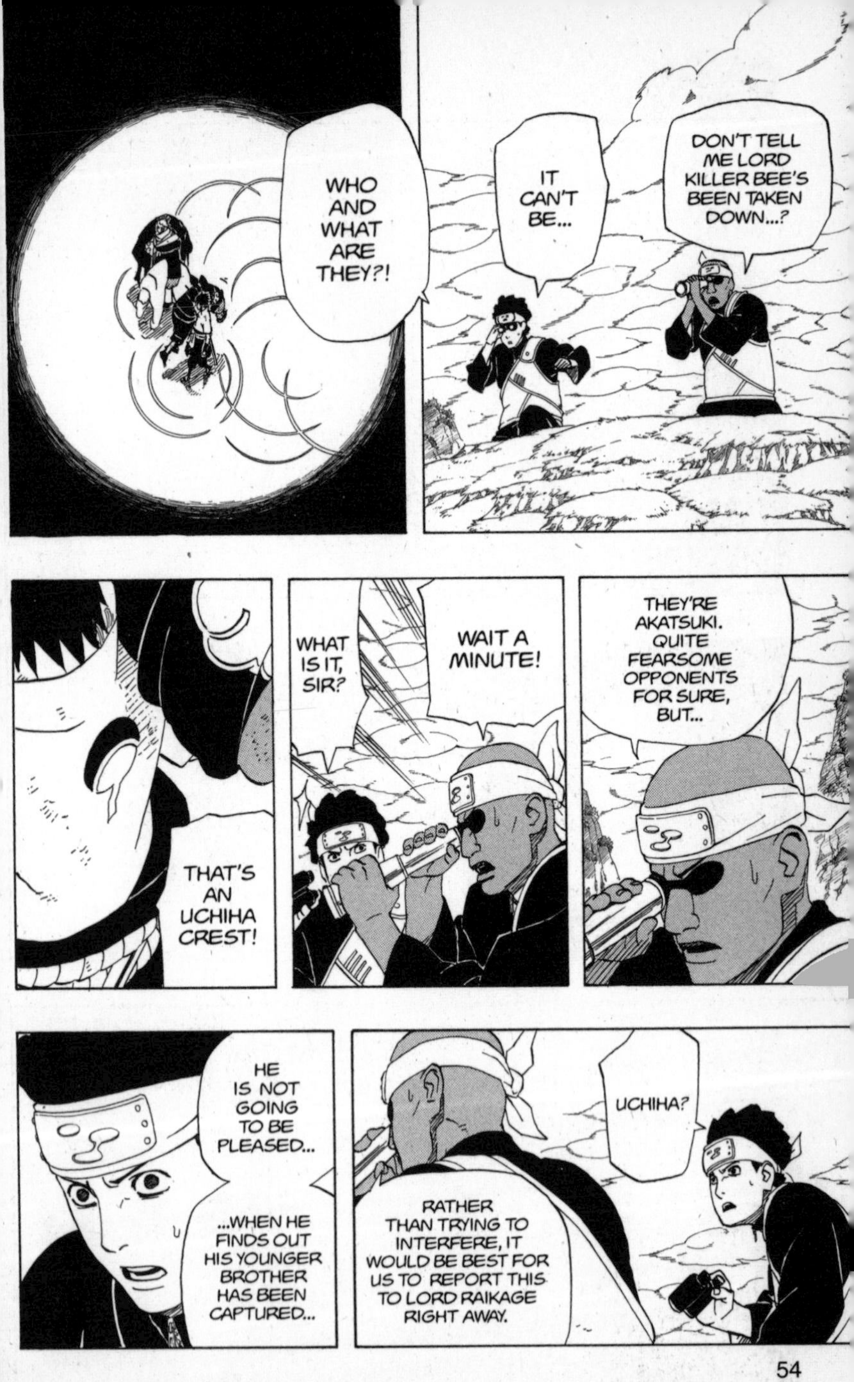
DON'T TELL ME LORD KILLER BEE'S BEEN TAKEN DOWN...?
IT CAN'T BE...
WHO AND WHAT ARE THEY?!
THEY'RE AKATSUKI. QUITE FEARSOME OPPONENTS FOR SURE, BUT...
WAIT A MINUTE!
WHAT IS IT, SIR?
THAT'S AN UCHIHA CREST!
UCHIHA?
RATHER THAN TRYING TO INTERFERE, IT WOULD BE BEST FOR US TO REPORT THIS TO LORD RAIKAGE RIGHT AWAY.
HE IS NOT GOING TO BE PLEASED...
...WHEN HE FINDS OUT HIS YOUNGER BROTHER HAS BEEN CAPTURED...

READ THIS WAY

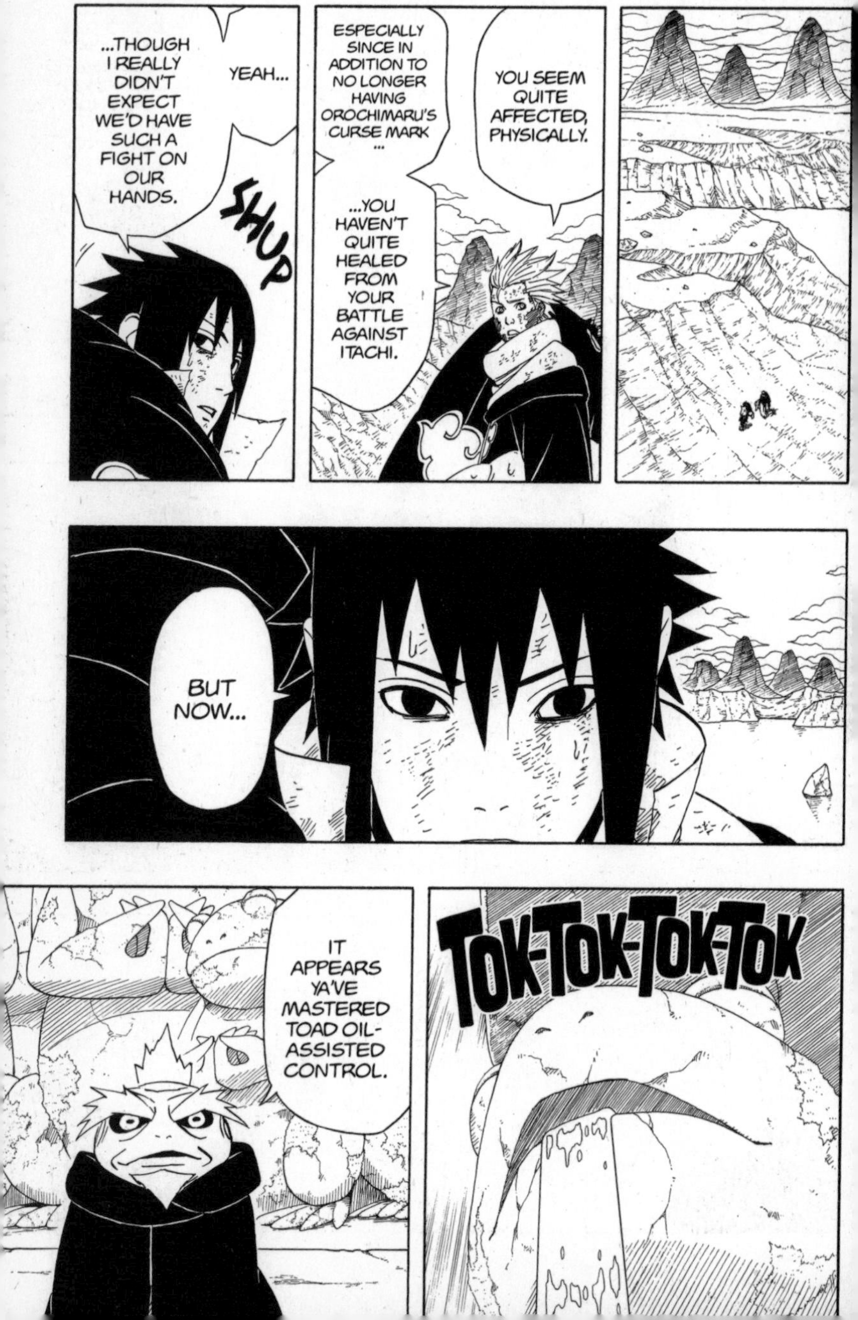

YOU SEEM QUITE AFFECTED, PHYSICALLY.
ESPECIALLY SINCE IN ADDITION TO NO LONGER HAVING OROCHIMARU'S CURSE MARK...
...YOU HAVEN'T QUITE HEALED FROM YOUR BATTLE AGAINST ITACHI.
YEAH...
...THOUGH I REALLY DIDN'T EXPECT WE'D HAVE SUCH A FIGHT ON OUR HANDS.
SHUP
BUT NOW...
TOK-TOK-TOK-TOK
IT APPEARS YA'VE MASTERED TOAD OIL-ASSISTED CONTROL.

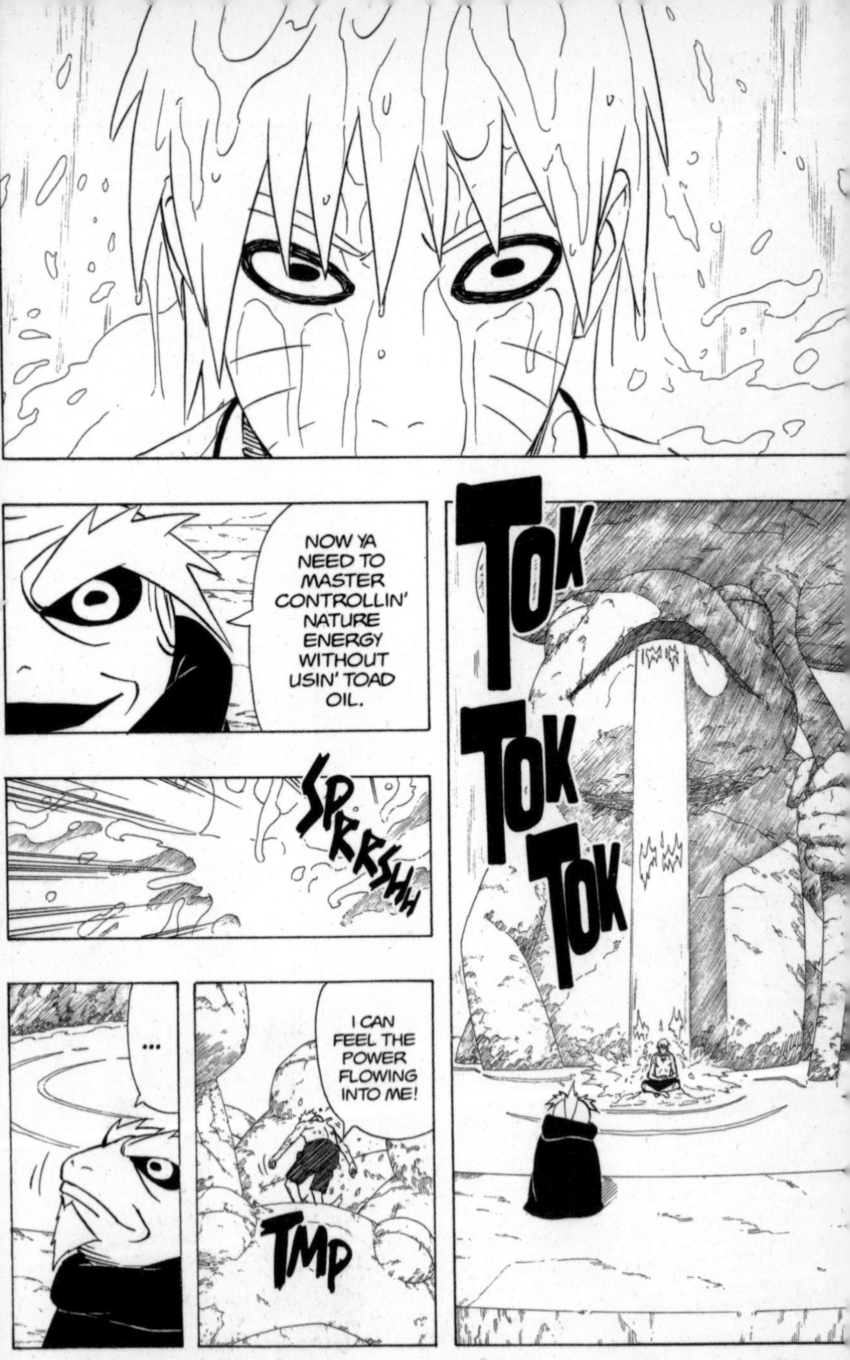
TOK
TOK
TOK
NOW YA NEED TO MASTER CONTROLLIN' NATURE ENERGY WITHOUT USIN' TOAD OIL.
SPRRSHHH
I CAN FEEL THE POWER FLOWING INTO ME!
TMP
...

READ THIS WAY

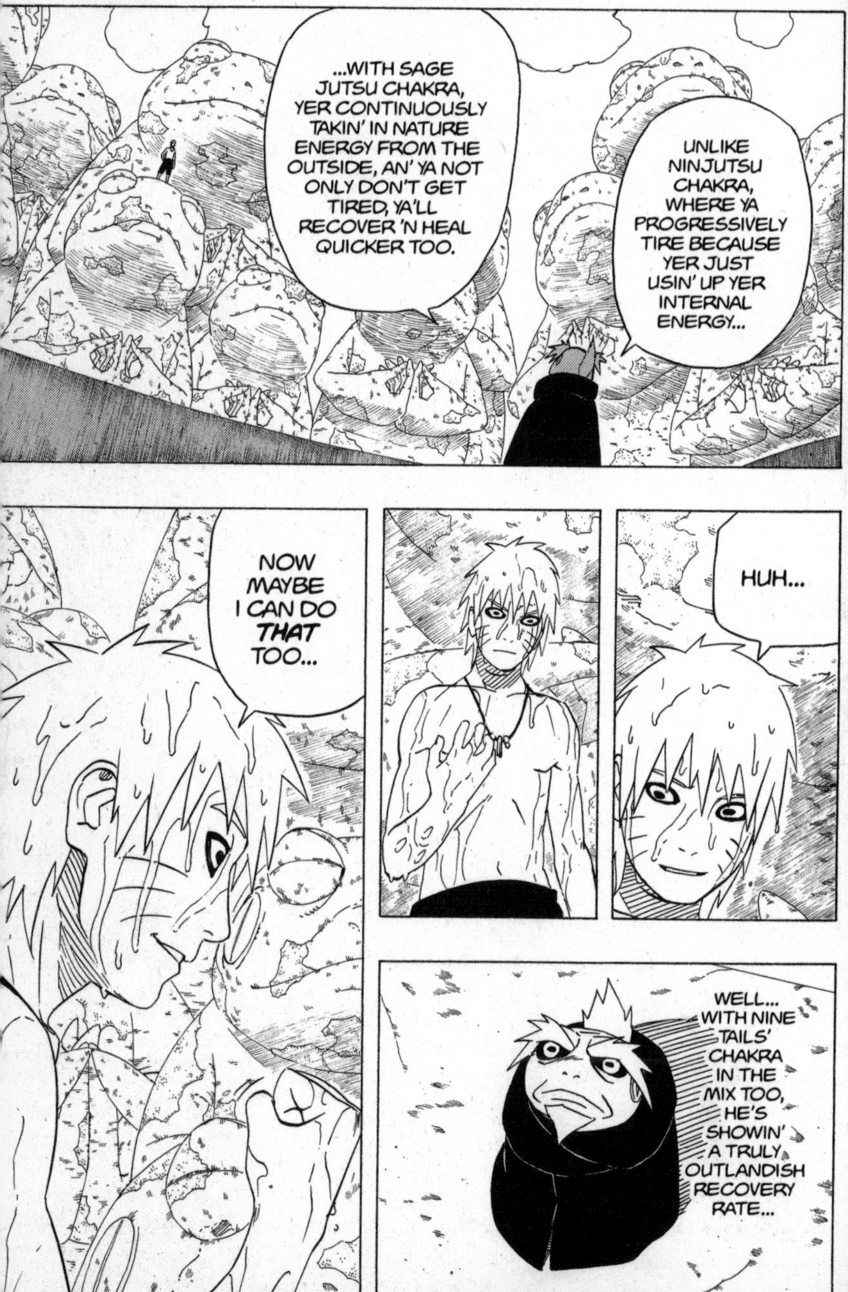

UNLIKE NINJUTSU CHAKRA, WHERE YA PROGRESSIVELY TIRE BECAUSE YER JUST USIN' UP YER INTERNAL ENERGY...
...WITH SAGE JUTSU CHAKRA, YER CONTINUOUSLY TAKIN' IN NATURE ENERGY FROM THE OUTSIDE, AN' YA NOT ONLY DON'T GET TIRED, YA'LL RECOVER 'N HEAL QUICKER TOO.
HUH...
WELL... WITH NINE TAILS' CHAKRA IN THE MIX TOO, HE'S SHOWIN' A TRULY OUTLANDISH RECOVERY RATE...
NOW MAYBE I CAN DO *THAT* TOO...

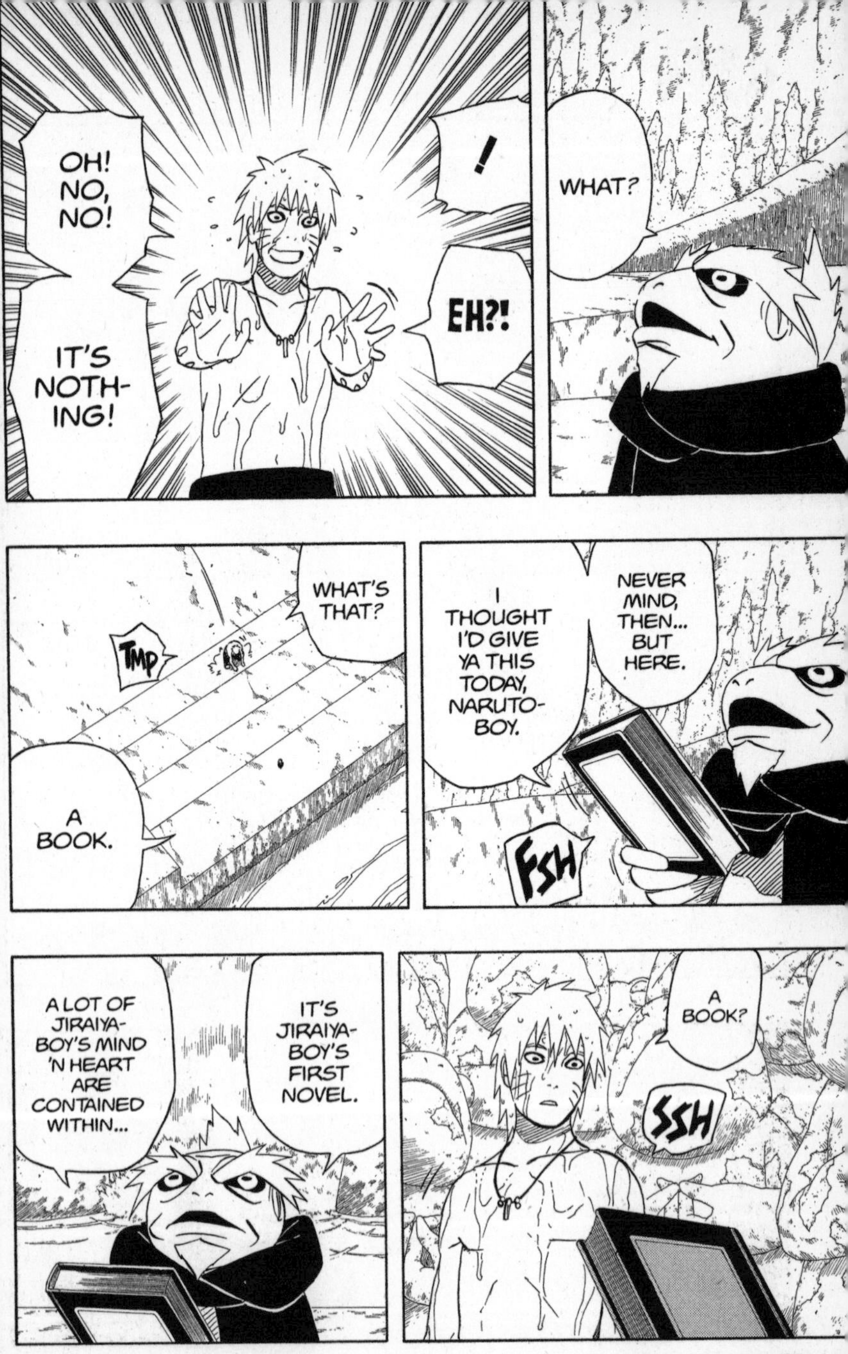
WHAT?
!
EH?!
OH! NO, NO!
IT'S NOTHING!
NEVER MIND, THEN... BUT HERE.
I THOUGHT I'D GIVE YA THIS TODAY, NARUTO-BOY.
FSH
WHAT'S THAT?
TMP
A BOOK.
A BOOK?
SSH
IT'S JIRAIYA-BOY'S FIRST NOVEL.
A LOT OF JIRAIYA-BOY'S MIND 'N HEART ARE CONTAINED WITHIN...

READ THIS WAY

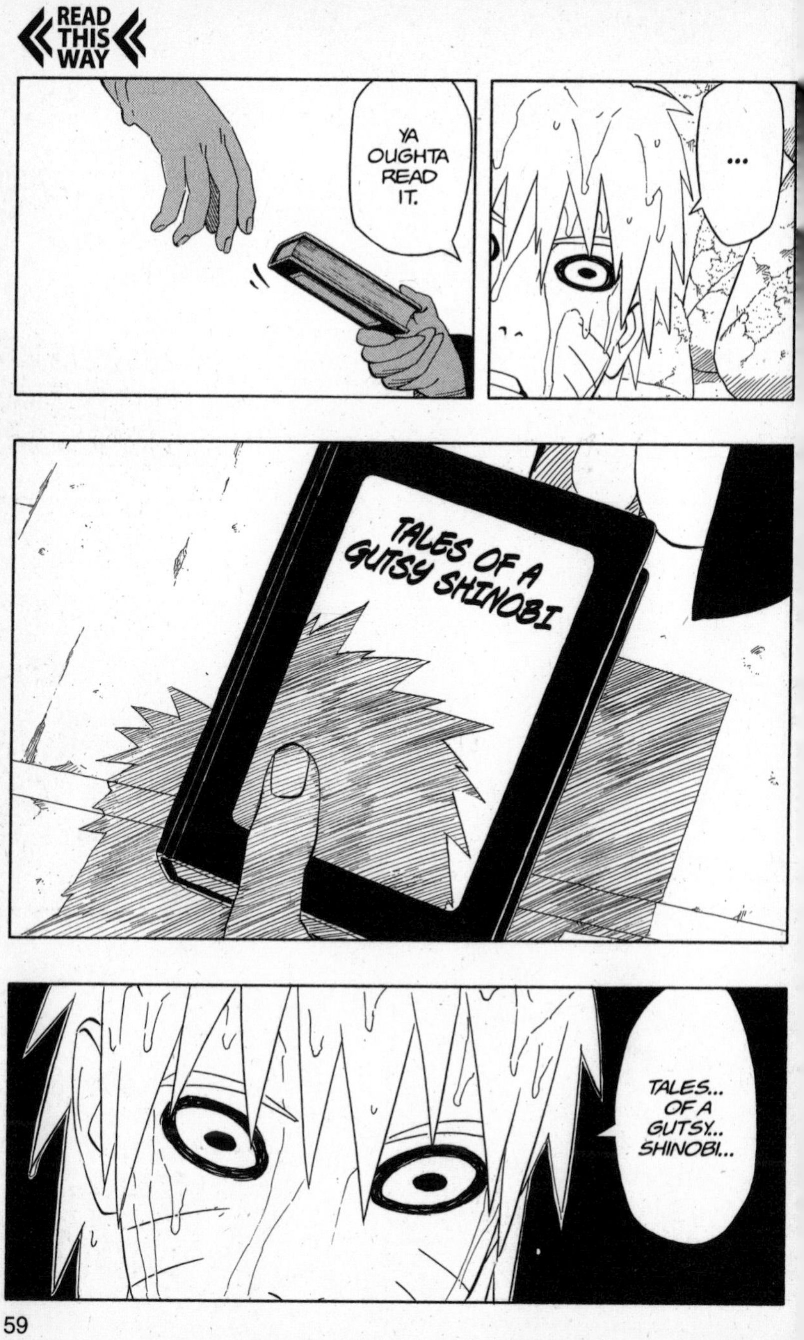
...
YA OUGHTA READ IT.
TALES OF A GUTSY SHINOBI
TALES... OF A GUTSY... SHINOBI...

NARUTO

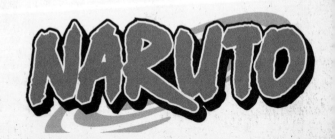

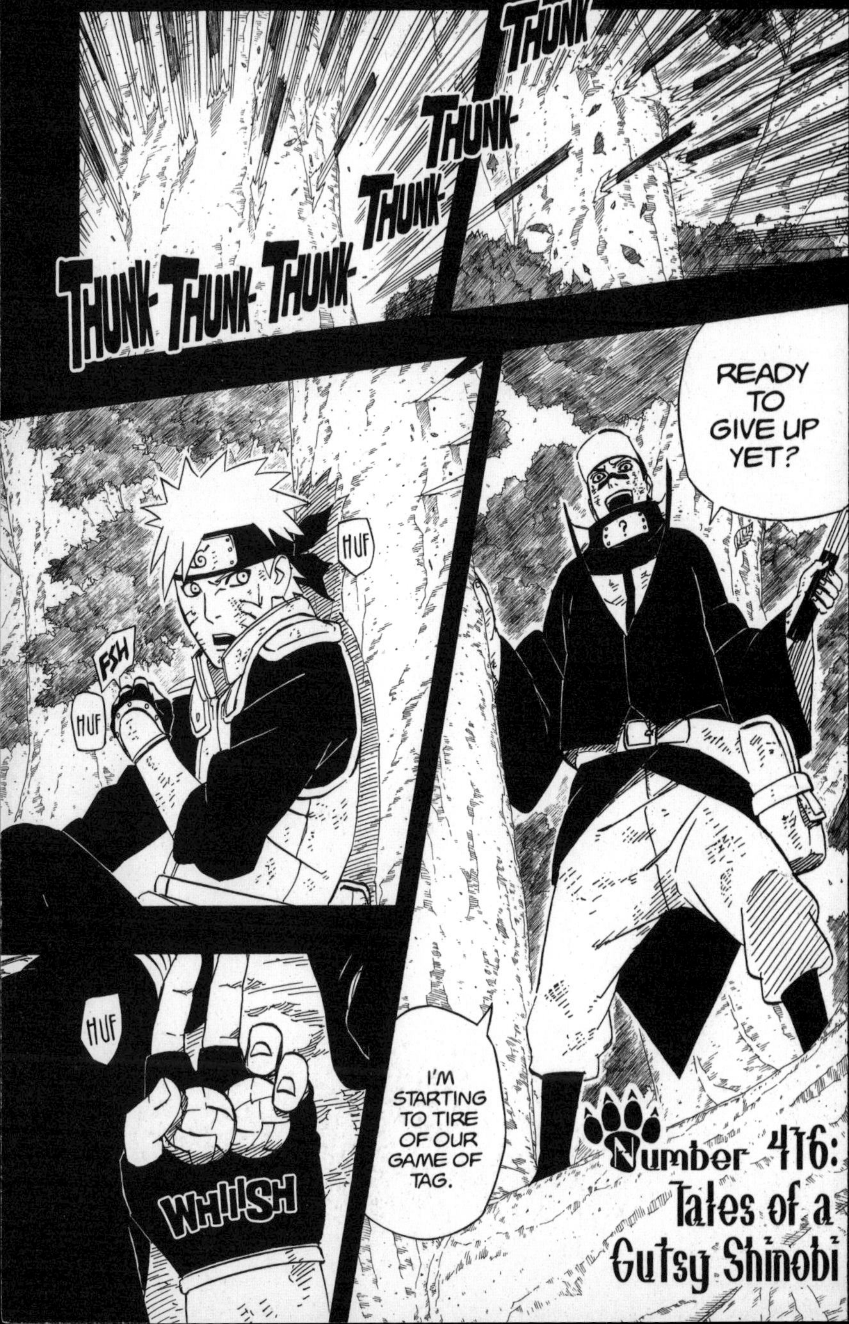
THUNK
THUNK
THUNK
THUNK-THUNK-THUNK
READY TO GIVE UP YET?
HUF
FSH
HUF
Number 416: Tales of a Gutsy Shinobi
I'M STARTING TO TIRE OF OUR GAME OF TAG.
HUF
WHIISH

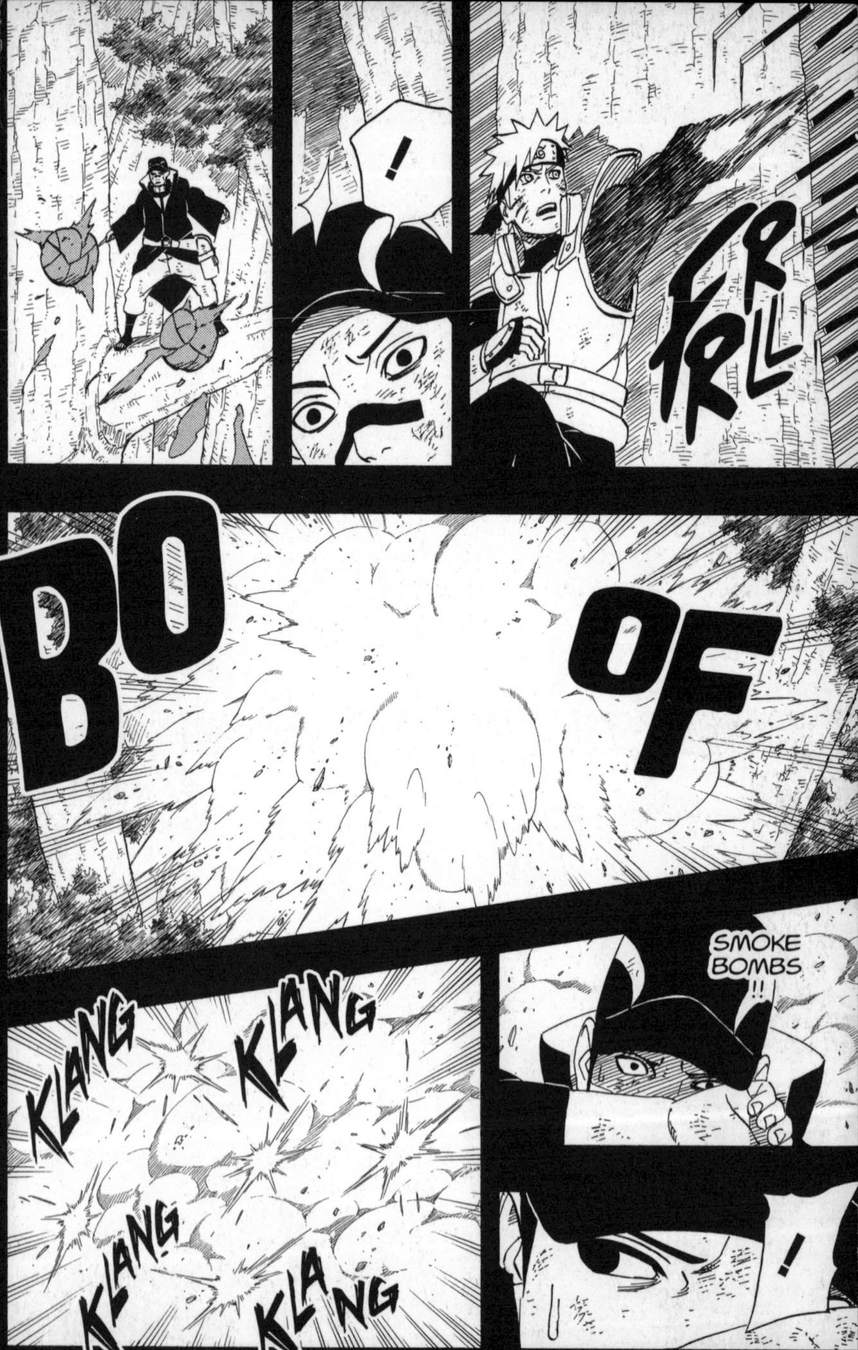

FRRLL
!
BOOF
SMOKE BOMBS!!
KLANG KLANG KLANG KLANG
!

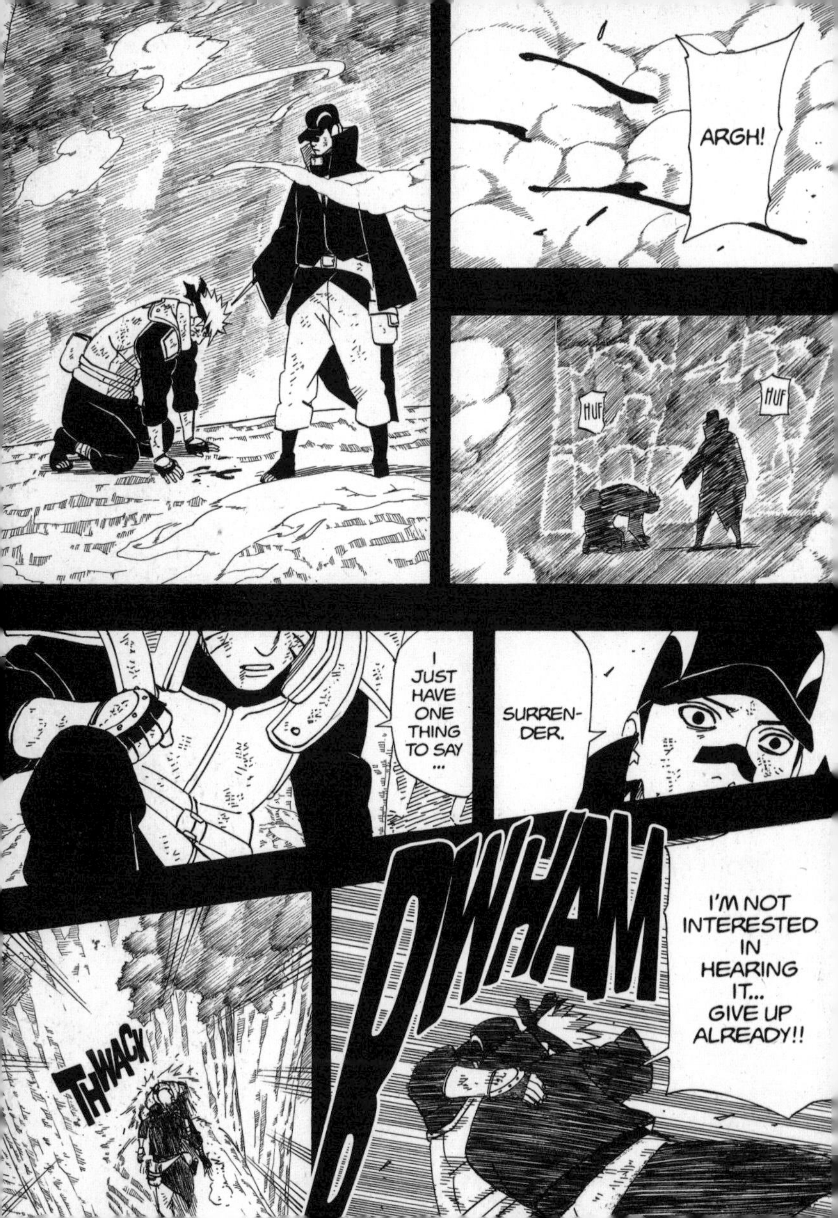
ARGH!
HUF
HUF
SURREN-DER.
I JUST HAVE ONE THING TO SAY ...
DWHAM
I'M NOT INTERESTED IN HEARING IT... GIVE UP ALREADY!!
THWACK

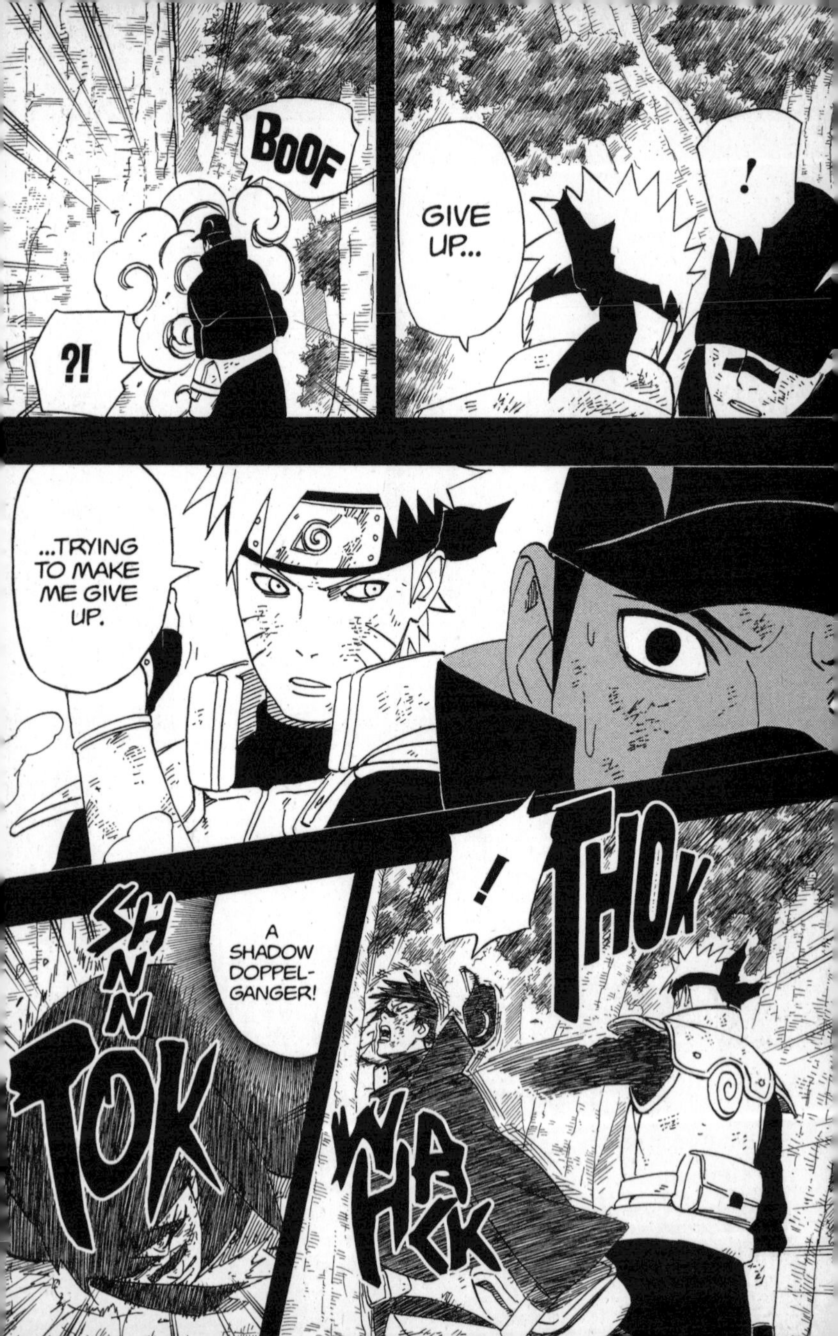
!
GIVE UP...
BOOF
?!
...TRYING TO MAKE ME GIVE UP.
THOK
!
WHACK
SHNNN
TOK
A SHADOW DOPPEL-GANGER!

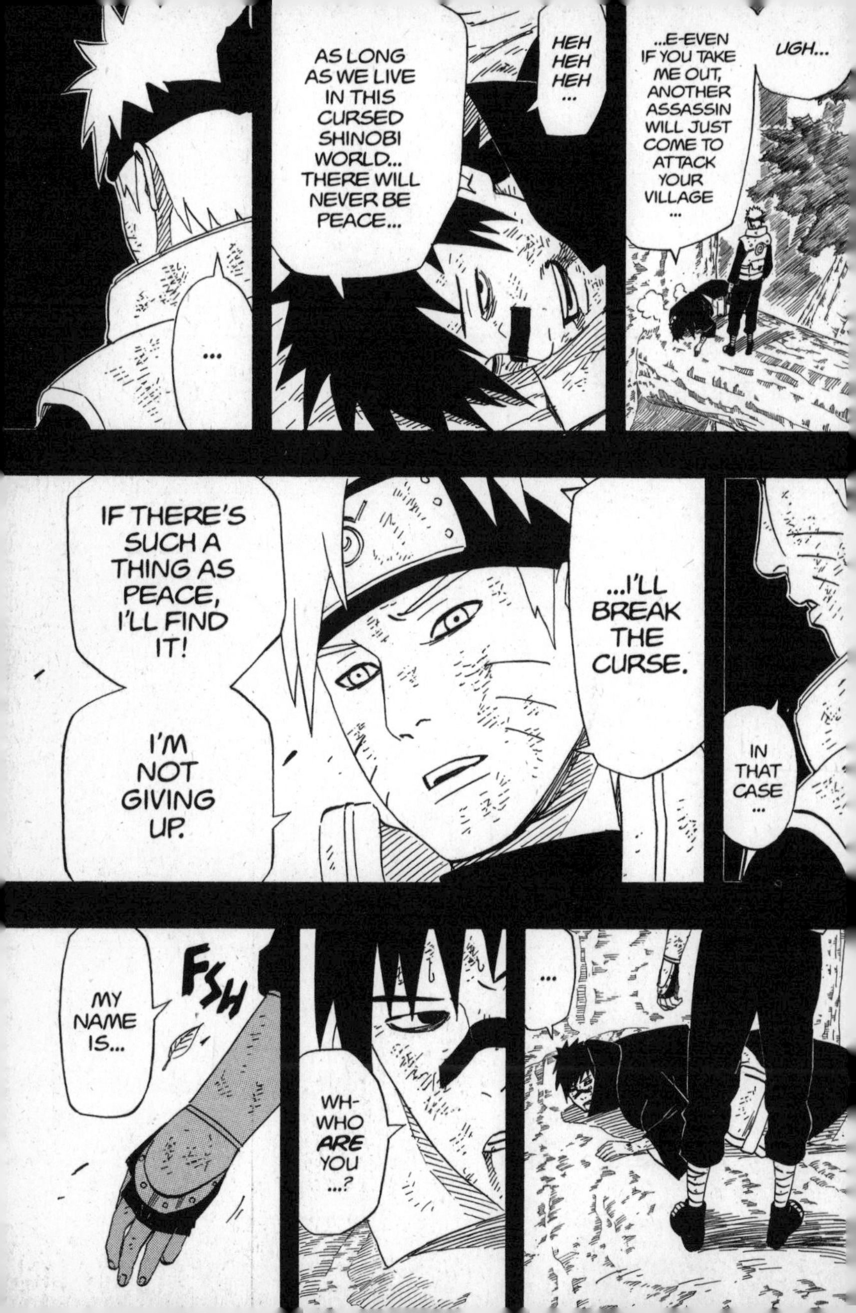
UGH...
...E-EVEN IF YOU TAKE ME OUT, ANOTHER ASSASSIN WILL JUST COME TO ATTACK YOUR VILLAGE ...
HEH HEH HEH ...
AS LONG AS WE LIVE IN THIS CURSED SHINOBI WORLD... THERE WILL NEVER BE PEACE...
...
IN THAT CASE ...
...I'LL BREAK THE CURSE.
IF THERE'S SUCH A THING AS PEACE, I'LL FIND IT!
I'M NOT GIVING UP.
...
WH- WHO ARE YOU ...?
FSH
MY NAME IS...

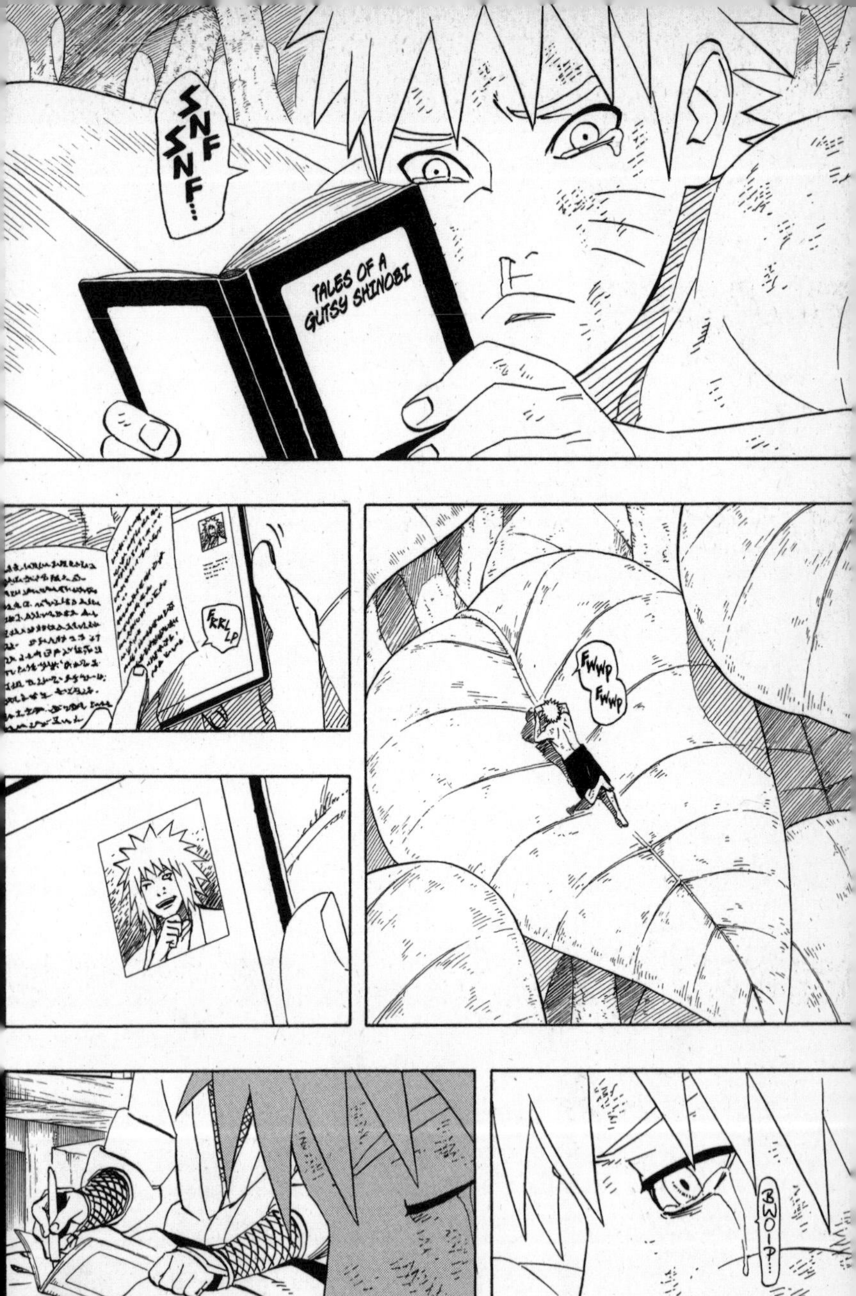
SNF SNF...
TALES OF A GUTSY SHINOBI
FRRLLP
FWWP FWWP
BWO-P...

READ THIS WAY

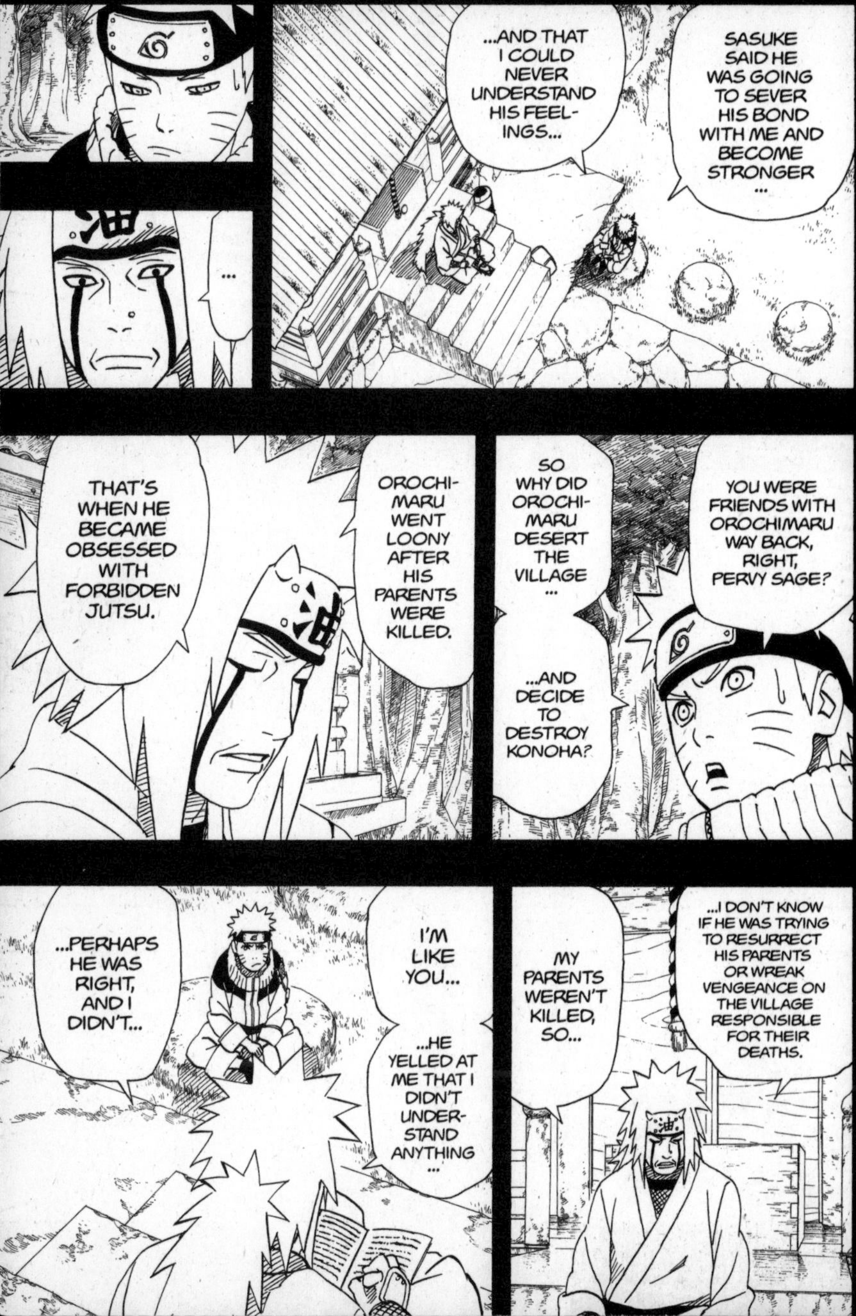
SASUKE SAID HE WAS GOING TO SEVER HIS BOND WITH ME AND BECOME STRONGER ...
...AND THAT I COULD NEVER UNDERSTAND HIS FEEL-INGS...
...
YOU WERE FRIENDS WITH OROCHIMARU WAY BACK, RIGHT, PERVY SAGE?
SO WHY DID OROCHI-MARU DESERT THE VILLAGE ...
...AND DECIDE TO DESTROY KONOHA?
OROCHI-MARU WENT LOONY AFTER HIS PARENTS WERE KILLED.
THAT'S WHEN HE BECAME OBSESSED WITH FORBIDDEN JUTSU.
...I DON'T KNOW IF HE WAS TRYING TO RESURRECT HIS PARENTS OR WREAK VENGEANCE ON THE VILLAGE RESPONSIBLE FOR THEIR DEATHS.
MY PARENTS WEREN'T KILLED, SO...
I'M LIKE YOU...
...HE YELLED AT ME THAT I DIDN'T UNDER-STAND ANYTHING ...
...PERHAPS HE WAS RIGHT, AND I DIDN'T...

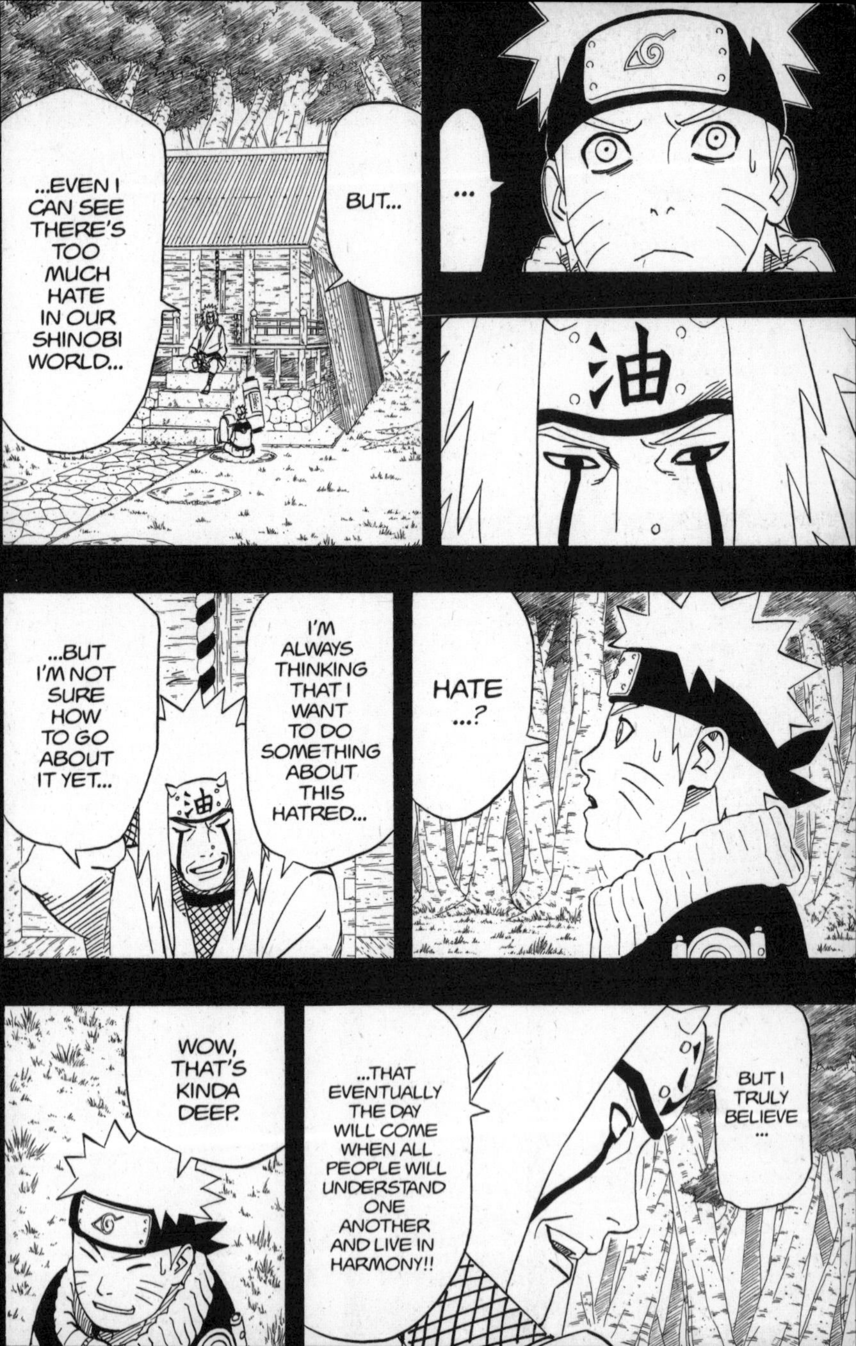
...
BUT...
...EVEN I CAN SEE THERE'S TOO MUCH HATE IN OUR SHINOBI WORLD...
HATE ...?
I'M ALWAYS THINKING THAT I WANT TO DO SOMETHING ABOUT THIS HATRED...
...BUT I'M NOT SURE HOW TO GO ABOUT IT YET...
BUT I TRULY BELIEVE ...
...THAT EVENTUALLY THE DAY WILL COME WHEN ALL PEOPLE WILL UNDERSTAND ONE ANOTHER AND LIVE IN HARMONY!!
WOW, THAT'S KINDA DEEP.

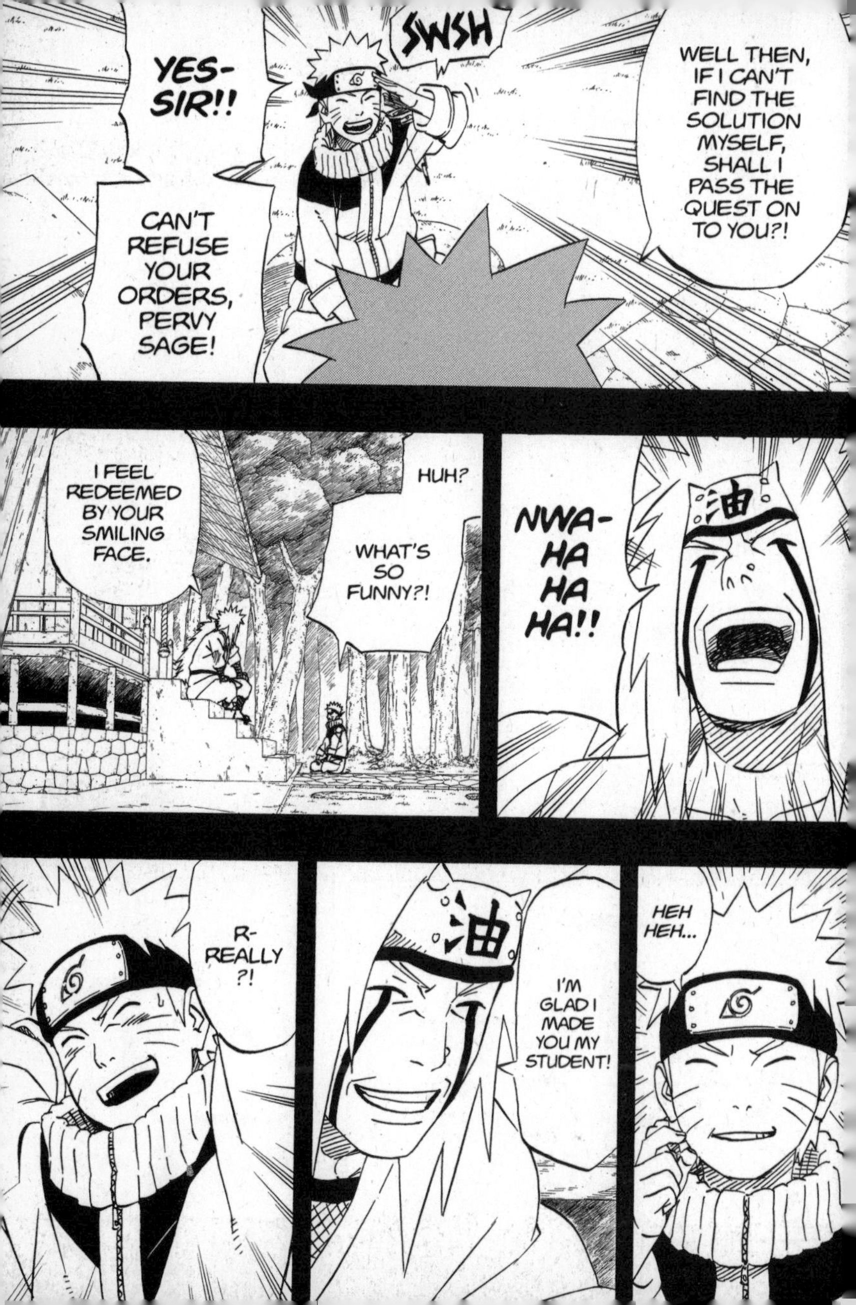
WELL THEN, IF I CAN'T FIND THE SOLUTION MYSELF, SHALL I PASS THE QUEST ON TO YOU?!
SWSH
YES-SIR!!
CAN'T REFUSE YOUR ORDERS, PERVY SAGE!
NWA-HA HA HA!!
HUH?
WHAT'S SO FUNNY?!
I FEEL REDEEMED BY YOUR SMILING FACE.
HEH HEH...
I'M GLAD I MADE YOU MY STUDENT!
R-REALLY?!

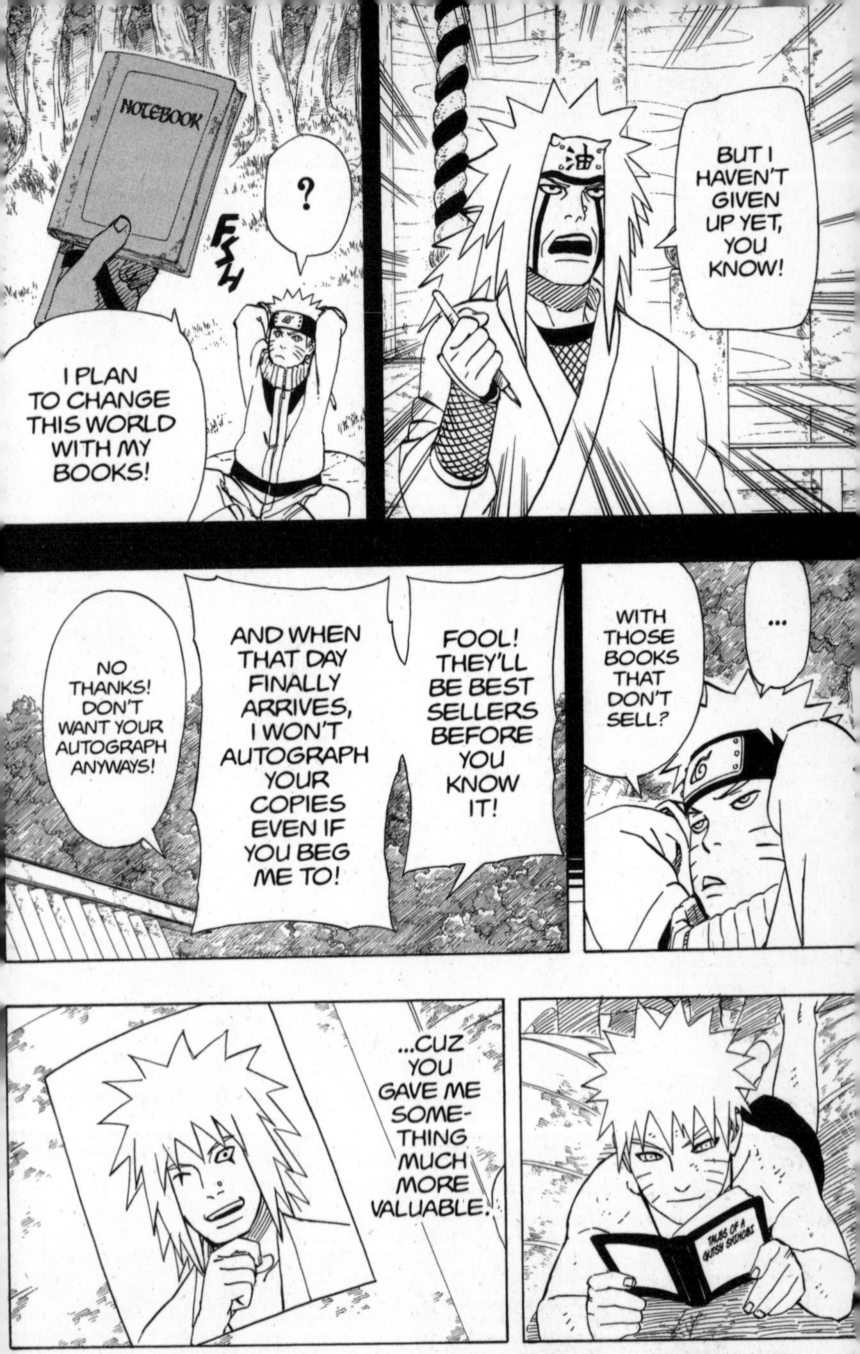
BUT I HAVEN'T GIVEN UP YET, YOU KNOW!
?
NOTEBOOK
FSH
I PLAN TO CHANGE THIS WORLD WITH MY BOOKS!
...
WITH THOSE BOOKS THAT DON'T SELL?
FOOL! THEY'LL BE BEST SELLERS BEFORE YOU KNOW IT!
AND WHEN THAT DAY FINALLY ARRIVES, I WON'T AUTOGRAPH YOUR COPIES EVEN IF YOU BEG ME TO!
NO THANKS! DON'T WANT YOUR AUTOGRAPH ANYWAYS!
TALES OF A GUTSY SHINOBI
...CUZ YOU GAVE ME SOME-THING MUCH MORE VALUABLE.

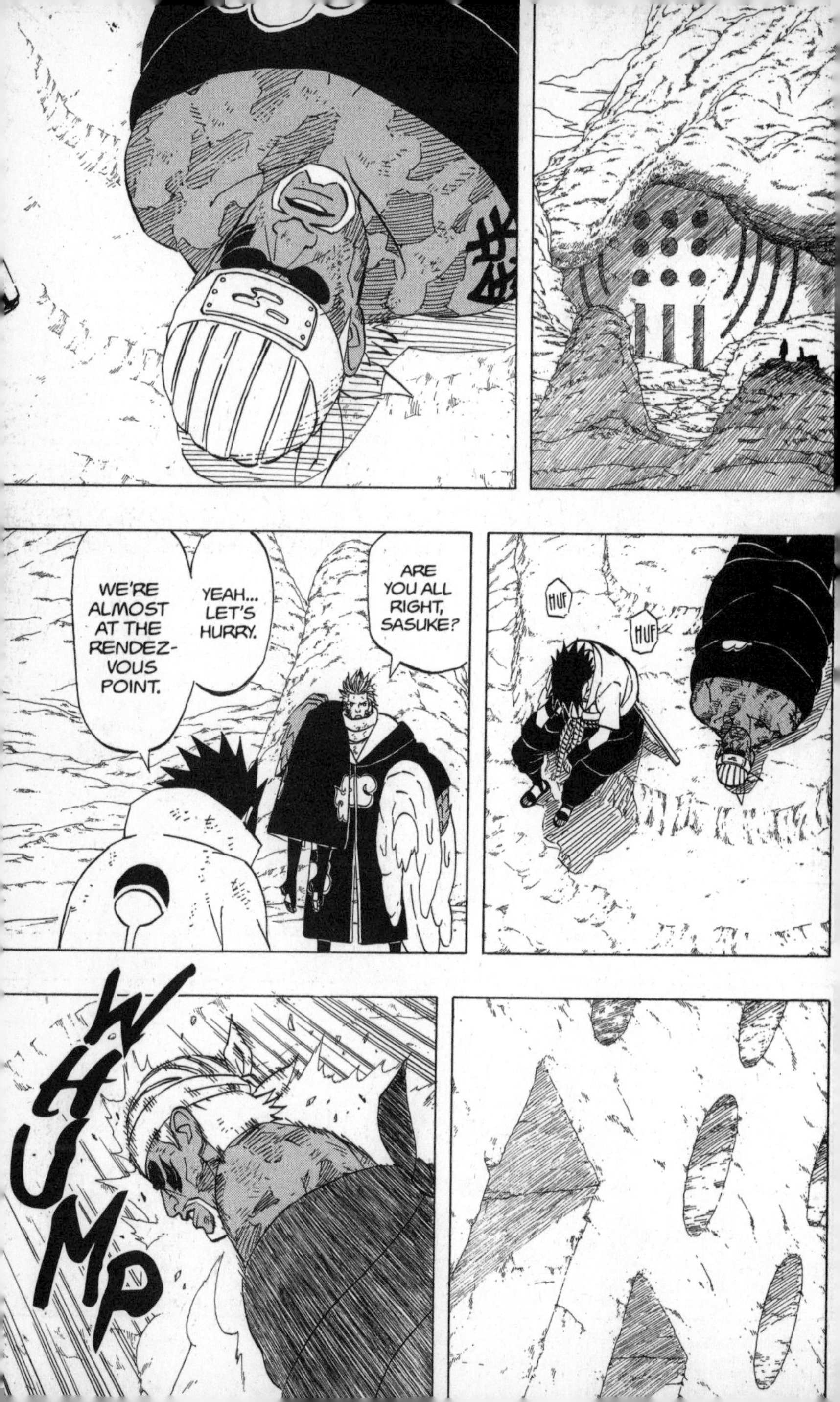
HUF
HUF
ARE YOU ALL RIGHT, SASUKE?
YEAH... LET'S HURRY.
WE'RE ALMOST AT THE RENDEZ-VOUS POINT.
WHUMP

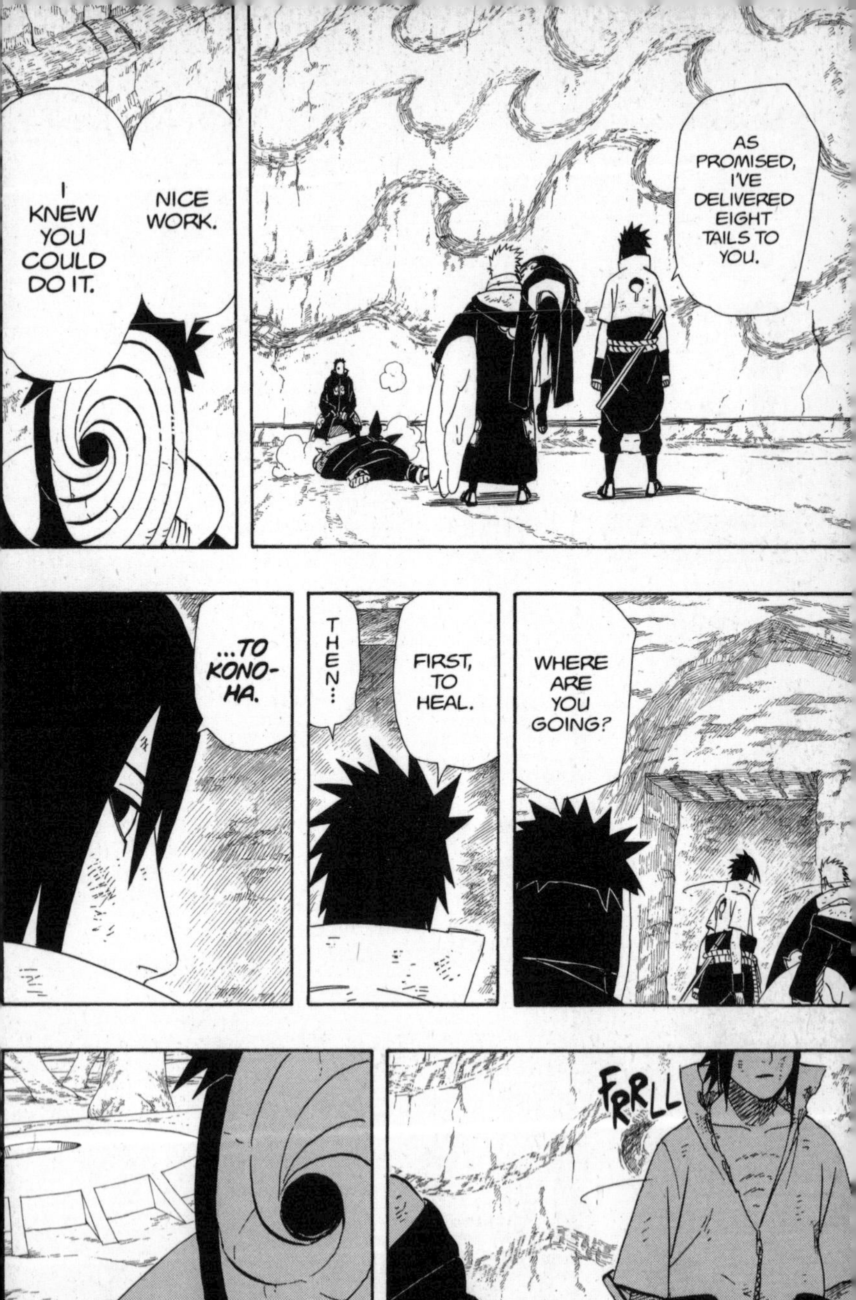
AS PROMISED, I'VE DELIVERED EIGHT TAILS TO YOU.
NICE WORK.
I KNEW YOU COULD DO IT.
WHERE ARE YOU GOING?
FIRST, TO HEAL.
THEN...
...TO KONOHA.
FRRLL

READ THIS WAY

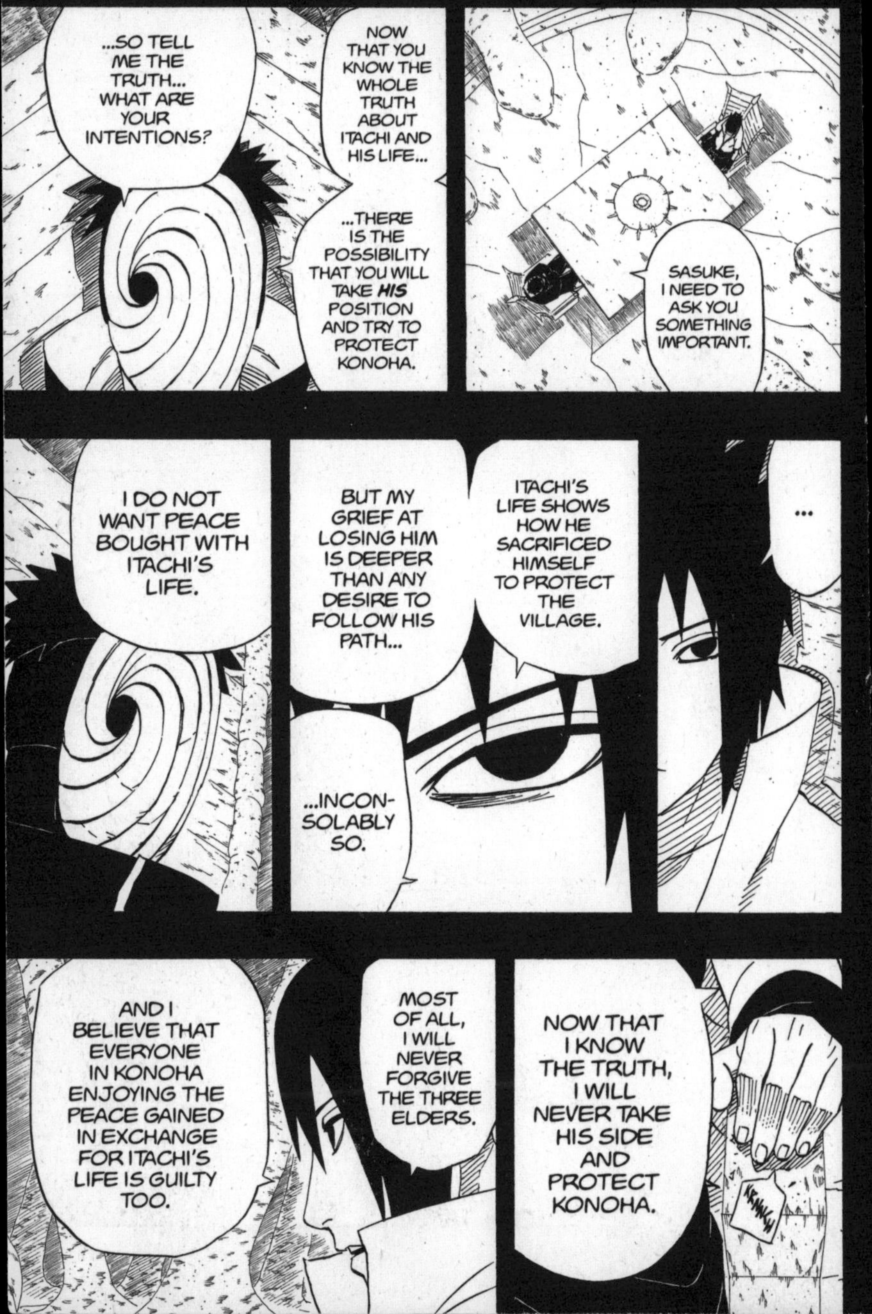

SASUKE, I NEED TO ASK YOU SOMETHING IMPORTANT.
NOW THAT YOU KNOW THE WHOLE TRUTH ABOUT ITACHI AND HIS LIFE...
...THERE IS THE POSSIBILITY THAT YOU WILL TAKE ***HIS*** POSITION AND TRY TO PROTECT KONOHA.
...SO TELL ME THE TRUTH... WHAT ARE YOUR INTENTIONS?
...
ITACHI'S LIFE SHOWS HOW HE SACRIFICED HIMSELF TO PROTECT THE VILLAGE.
BUT MY GRIEF AT LOSING HIM IS DEEPER THAN ANY DESIRE TO FOLLOW HIS PATH...
...INCON-SOLABLY SO.
I DO NOT WANT PEACE BOUGHT WITH ITACHI'S LIFE.
NOW THAT I KNOW THE TRUTH, I WILL NEVER TAKE HIS SIDE AND PROTECT KONOHA.
KRNNCH
MOST OF ALL, I WILL NEVER FORGIVE THE THREE ELDERS.
AND I BELIEVE THAT EVERYONE IN KONOHA ENJOYING THE PEACE GAINED IN EXCHANGE FOR ITACHI'S LIFE IS GUILTY TOO.

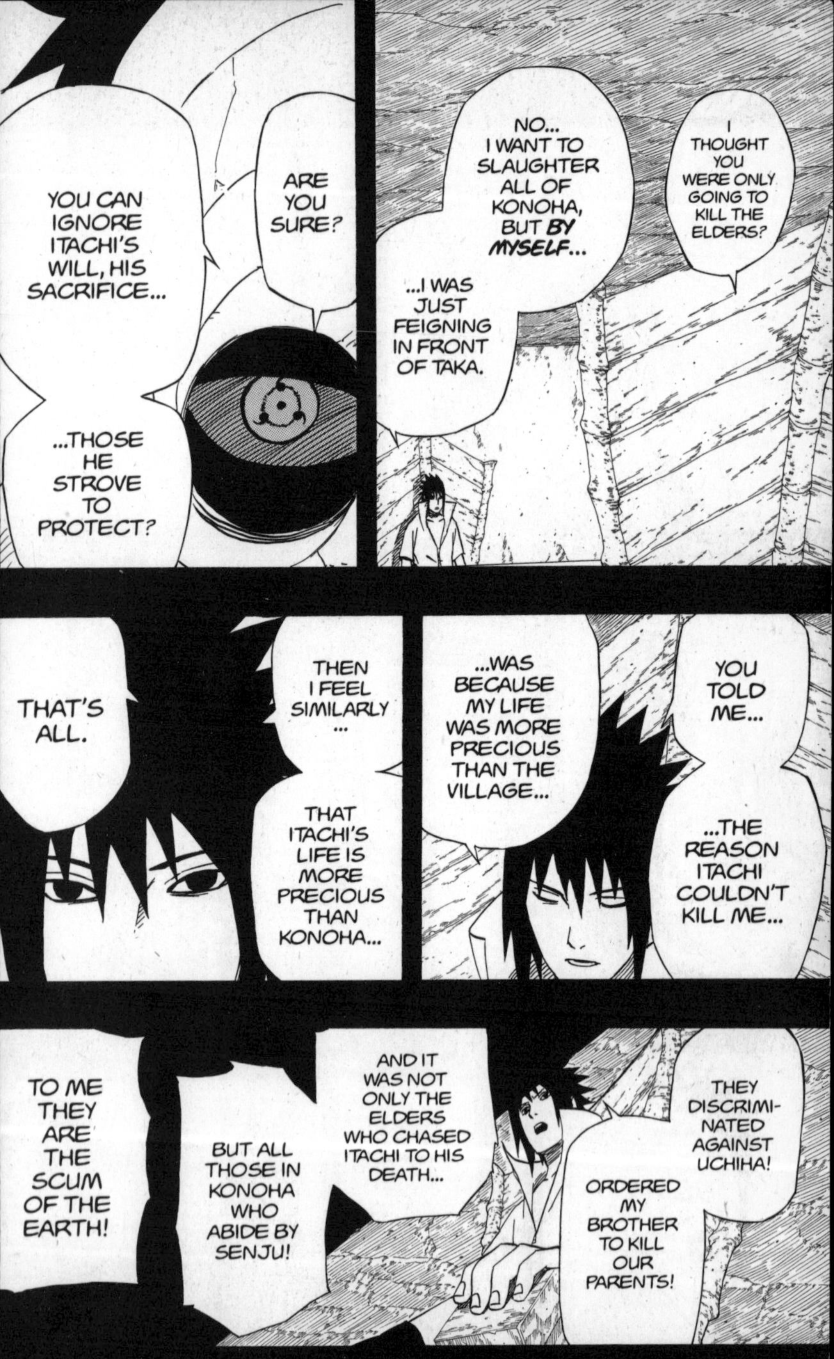
I THOUGHT YOU WERE ONLY GOING TO KILL THE ELDERS?
NO... I WANT TO SLAUGHTER ALL OF KONOHA, BUT ***BY MYSELF***...
...I WAS JUST FEIGNING IN FRONT OF TAKA.
ARE YOU SURE?
YOU CAN IGNORE ITACHI'S WILL, HIS SACRIFICE...
...THOSE HE STROVE TO PROTECT?
YOU TOLD ME...
...THE REASON ITACHI COULDN'T KILL ME...
...WAS BECAUSE MY LIFE WAS MORE PRECIOUS THAN THE VILLAGE...
THEN I FEEL SIMILARLY...
THAT ITACHI'S LIFE IS MORE PRECIOUS THAN KONOHA...
THAT'S ALL.
THEY DISCRIMINATED AGAINST UCHIHA!
ORDERED MY BROTHER TO KILL OUR PARENTS!
AND IT WAS NOT ONLY THE ELDERS WHO CHASED ITACHI TO HIS DEATH...
BUT ALL THOSE IN KONOHA WHO ABIDE BY SENJU!
TO ME THEY ARE THE SCUM OF THE EARTH!

READ THIS WAY

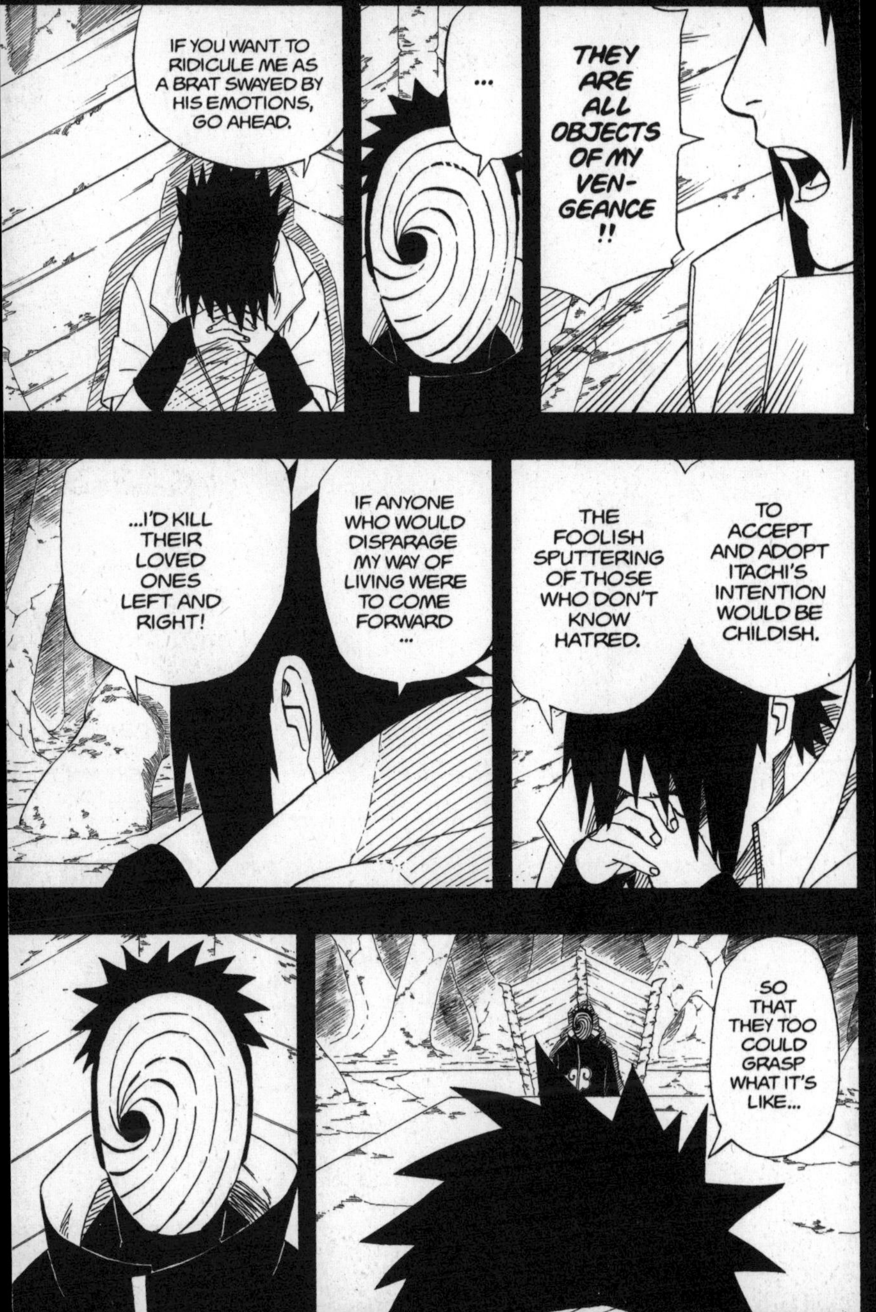
THEY ARE ALL OBJECTS OF MY VENGEANCE!!
...
IF YOU WANT TO RIDICULE ME AS A BRAT SWAYED BY HIS EMOTIONS, GO AHEAD.
TO ACCEPT AND ADOPT ITACHI'S INTENTION WOULD BE CHILDISH.
THE FOOLISH SPUTTERING OF THOSE WHO DON'T KNOW HATRED.
IF ANYONE WHO WOULD DISPARAGE MY WAY OF LIVING WERE TO COME FORWARD...
...I'D KILL THEIR LOVED ONES LEFT AND RIGHT!
SO THAT THEY TOO COULD GRASP WHAT IT'S LIKE...

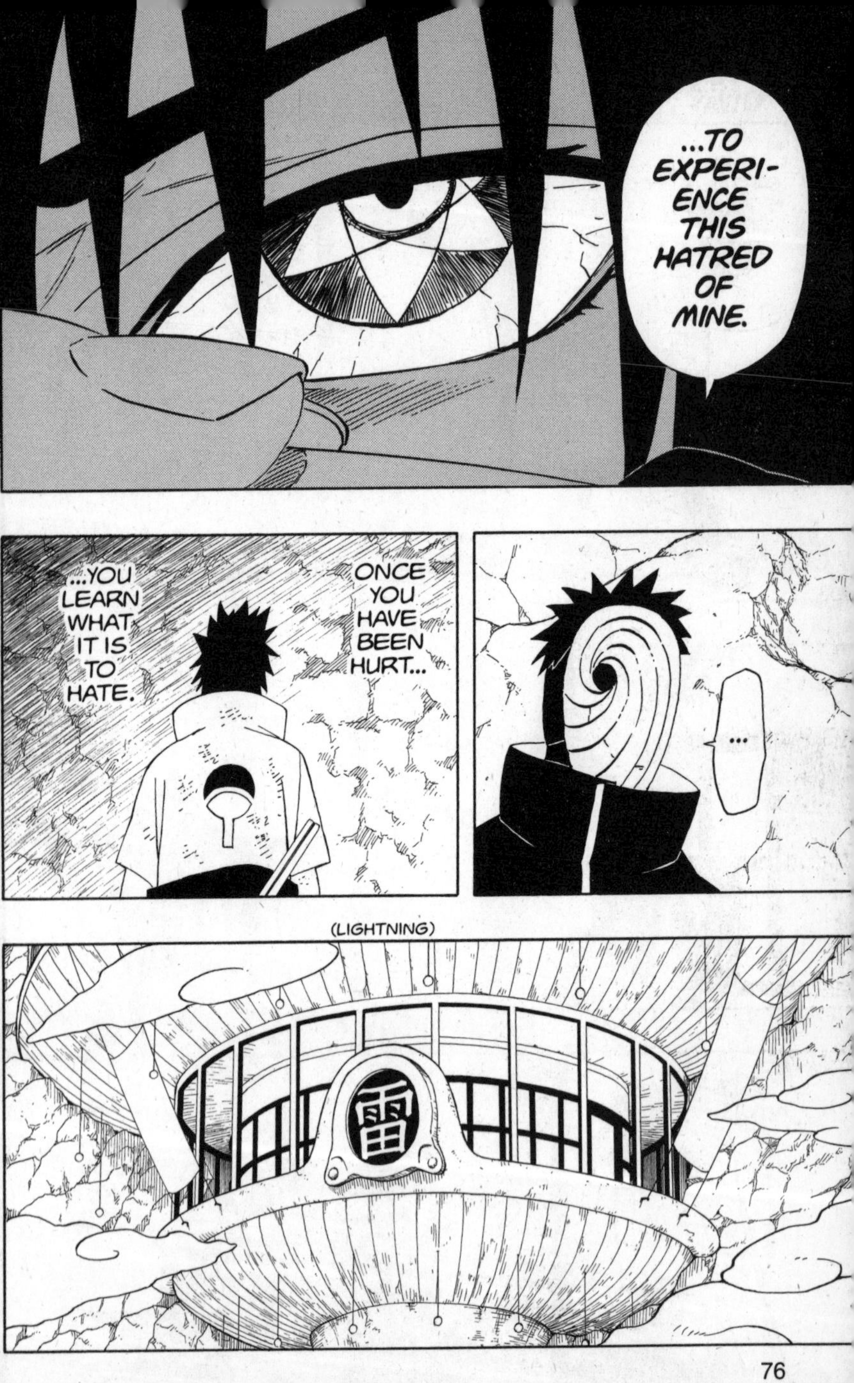
...TO EXPERI-ENCE THIS HATRED OF MINE.
...
ONCE YOU HAVE BEEN HURT...
...YOU LEARN WHAT IT IS TO HATE.
(LIGHTNING)

READ THIS WAY

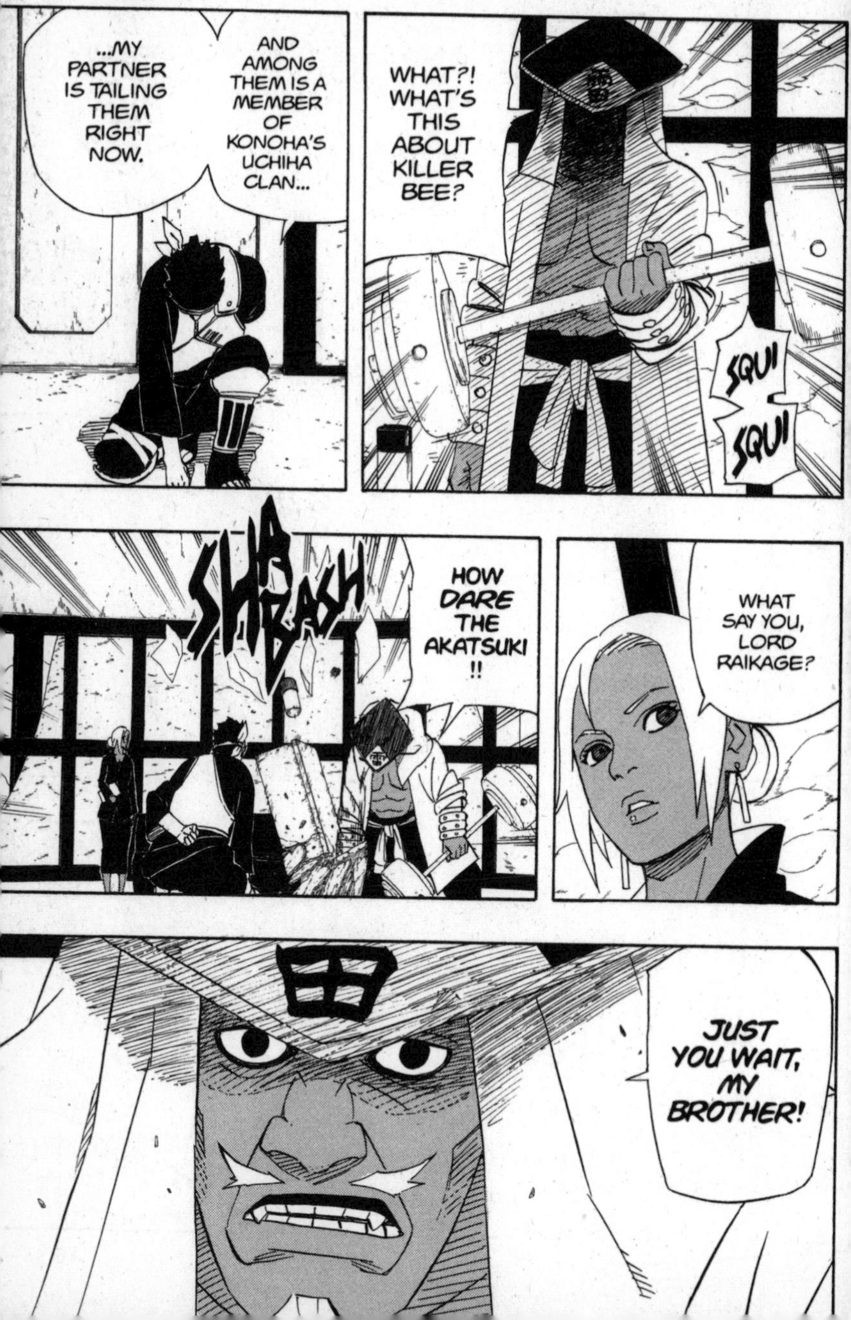
WHAT?! WHAT'S THIS ABOUT KILLER BEE?
SQUI
SQUI
AND AMONG THEM IS A MEMBER OF KONOHA'S UCHIHA CLAN...
...MY PARTNER IS TAILING THEM RIGHT NOW.
WHAT SAY YOU, LORD RAIKAGE?
HOW DARE THE AKATSUKI!!
SHBASH
JUST YOU WAIT, MY BROTHER!

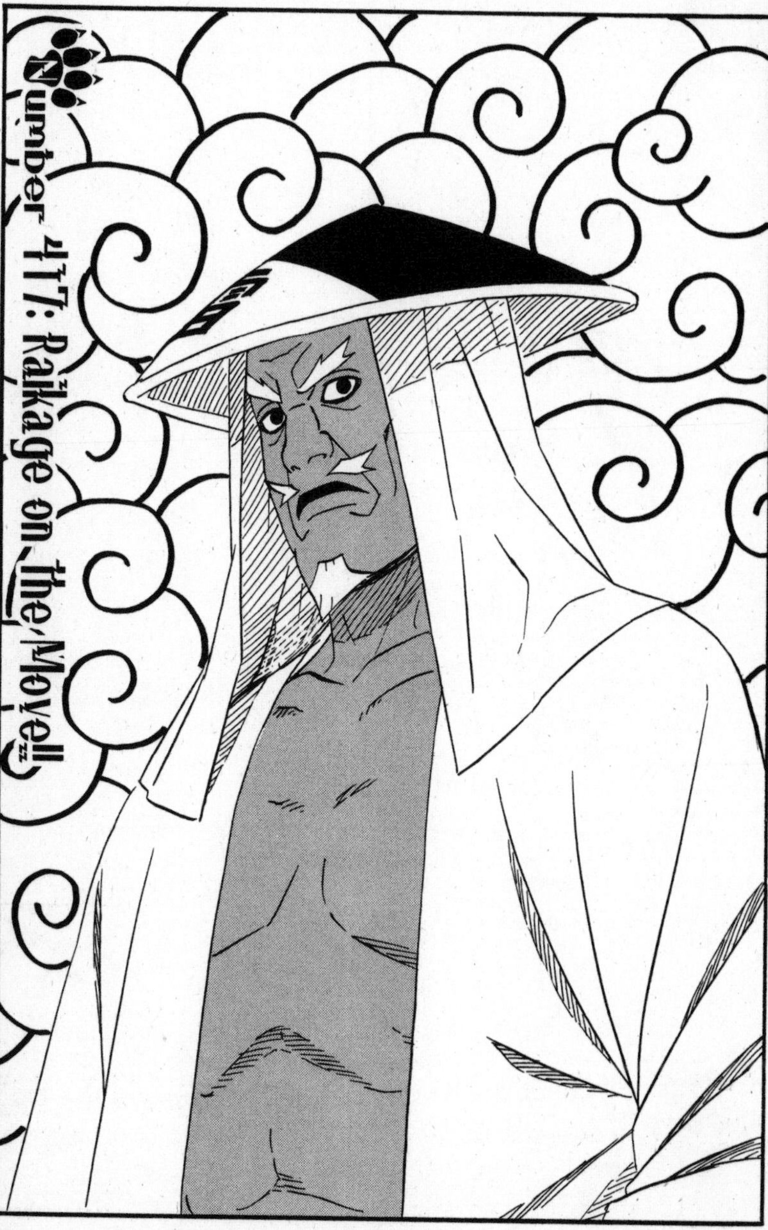
Number 477: Raikage on the Move!!

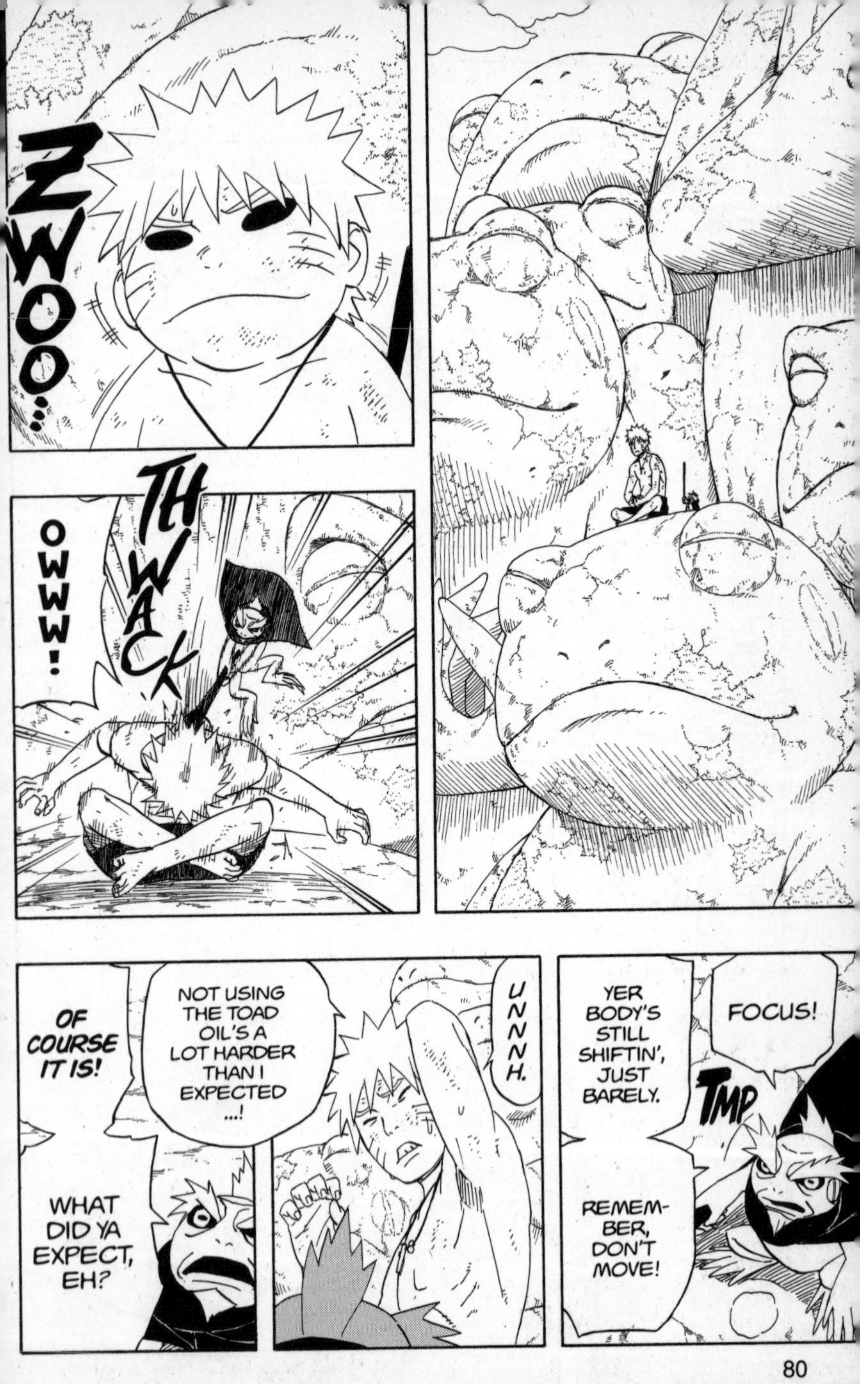
ZWOO...
THWACK
OWWW!
FOCUS!
TMP
YER BODY'S STILL SHIFTIN', JUST BARELY.
REMEMBER, DON'T MOVE!
UNNNH.
NOT USING THE TOAD OIL'S A LOT HARDER THAN I EXPECTED ...!
OF COURSE IT IS!
WHAT DID YA EXPECT, EH?

READ THIS WAY

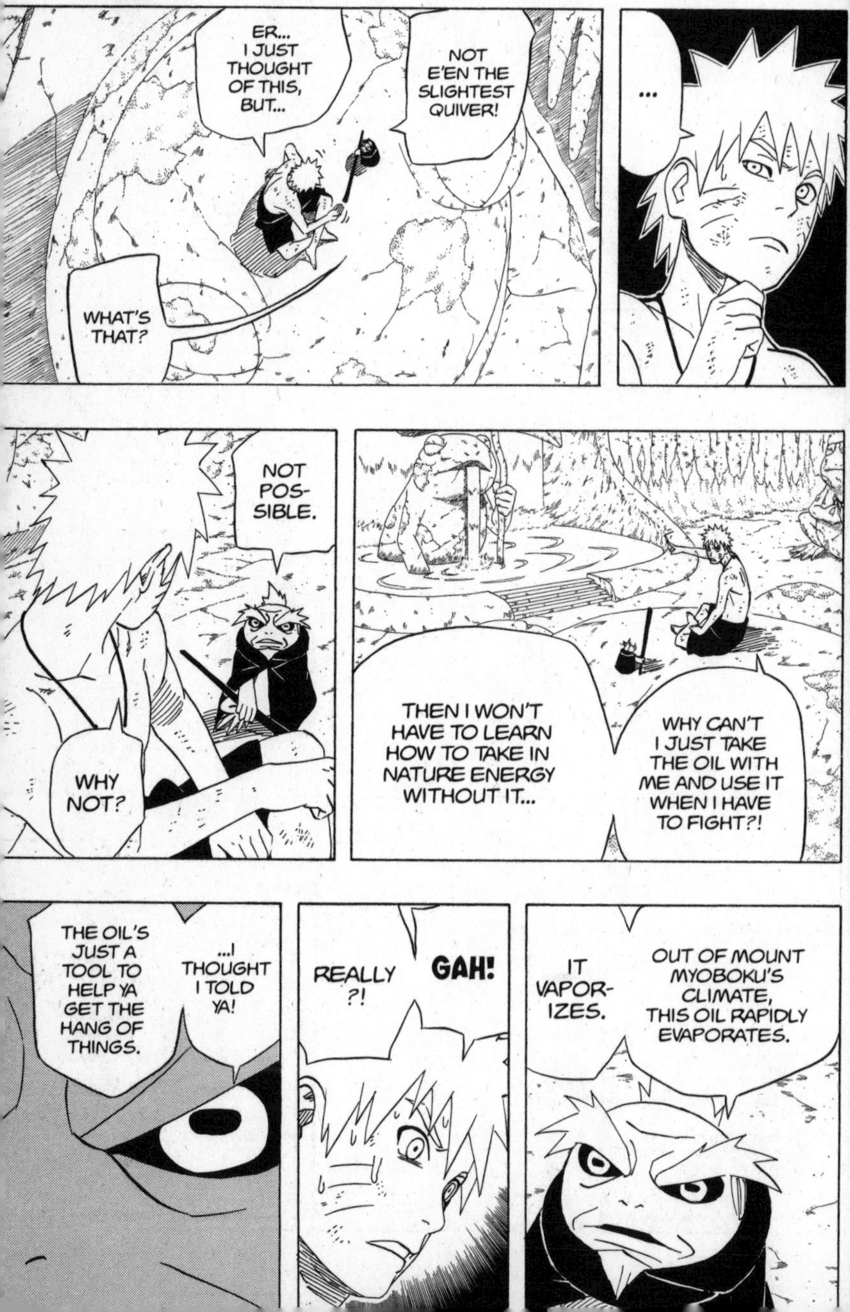
...
NOT E'EN THE SLIGHTEST QUIVER!
ER... I JUST THOUGHT OF THIS, BUT...
WHAT'S THAT?
WHY CAN'T I JUST TAKE THE OIL WITH ME AND USE IT WHEN I HAVE TO FIGHT?!
THEN I WON'T HAVE TO LEARN HOW TO TAKE IN NATURE ENERGY WITHOUT IT...
NOT POS-SIBLE.
WHY NOT?
OUT OF MOUNT MYOBOKU'S CLIMATE, THIS OIL RAPIDLY EVAPORATES.
IT VAPOR-IZES.
GAH!
REALLY ?!
...I THOUGHT I TOLD YA!
THE OIL'S JUST A TOOL TO HELP YA GET THE HANG OF THINGS.

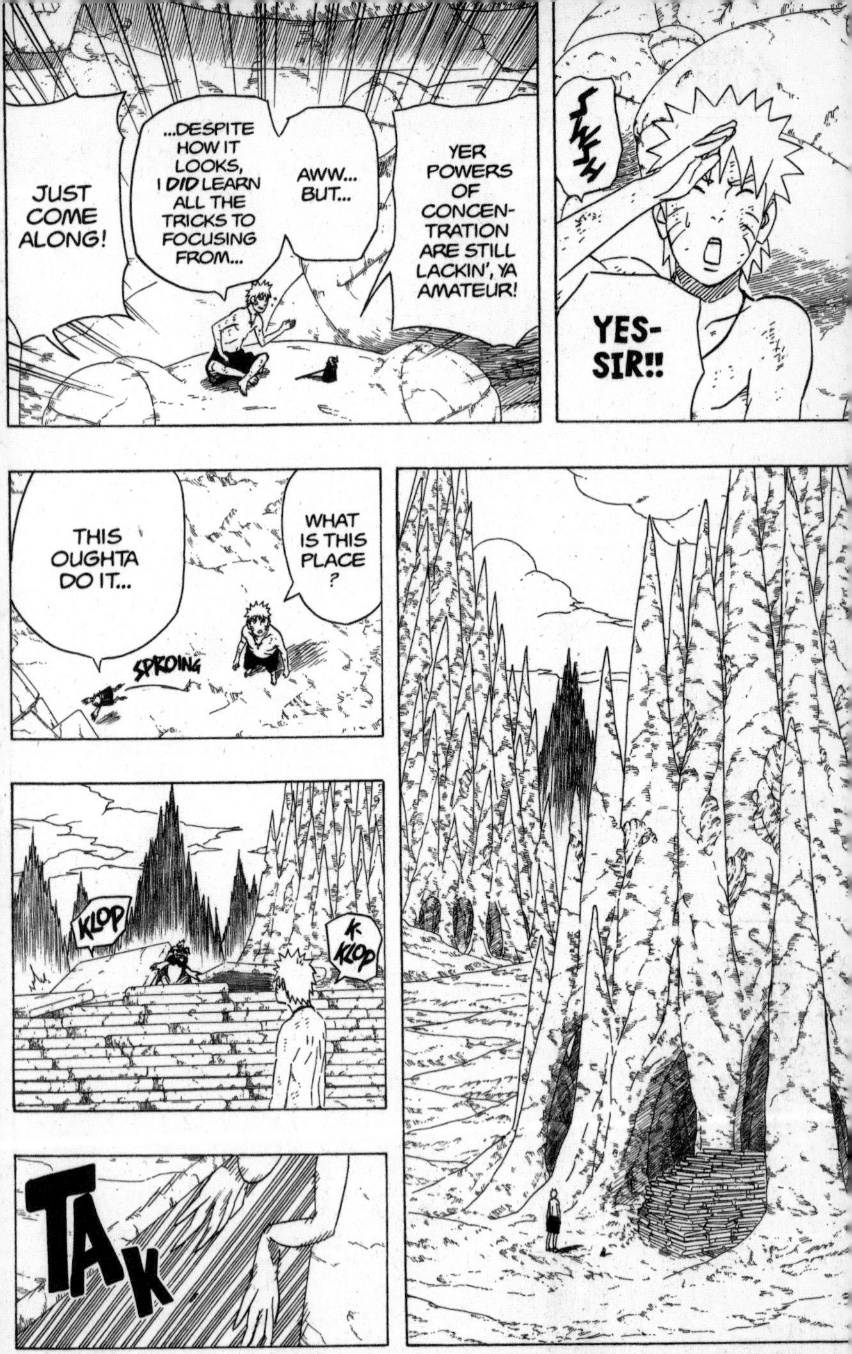
YES-SIR!!
YER POWERS OF CONCENTRATION ARE STILL LACKIN', YA AMATEUR!
AWW... BUT...
...DESPITE HOW IT LOOKS, I DID LEARN ALL THE TRICKS TO FOCUSING FROM...
JUST COME ALONG!
WHAT IS THIS PLACE?
THIS OUGHTA DO IT...
SPROING
K-KLOP
KLOP
TAK

READ THIS WAY

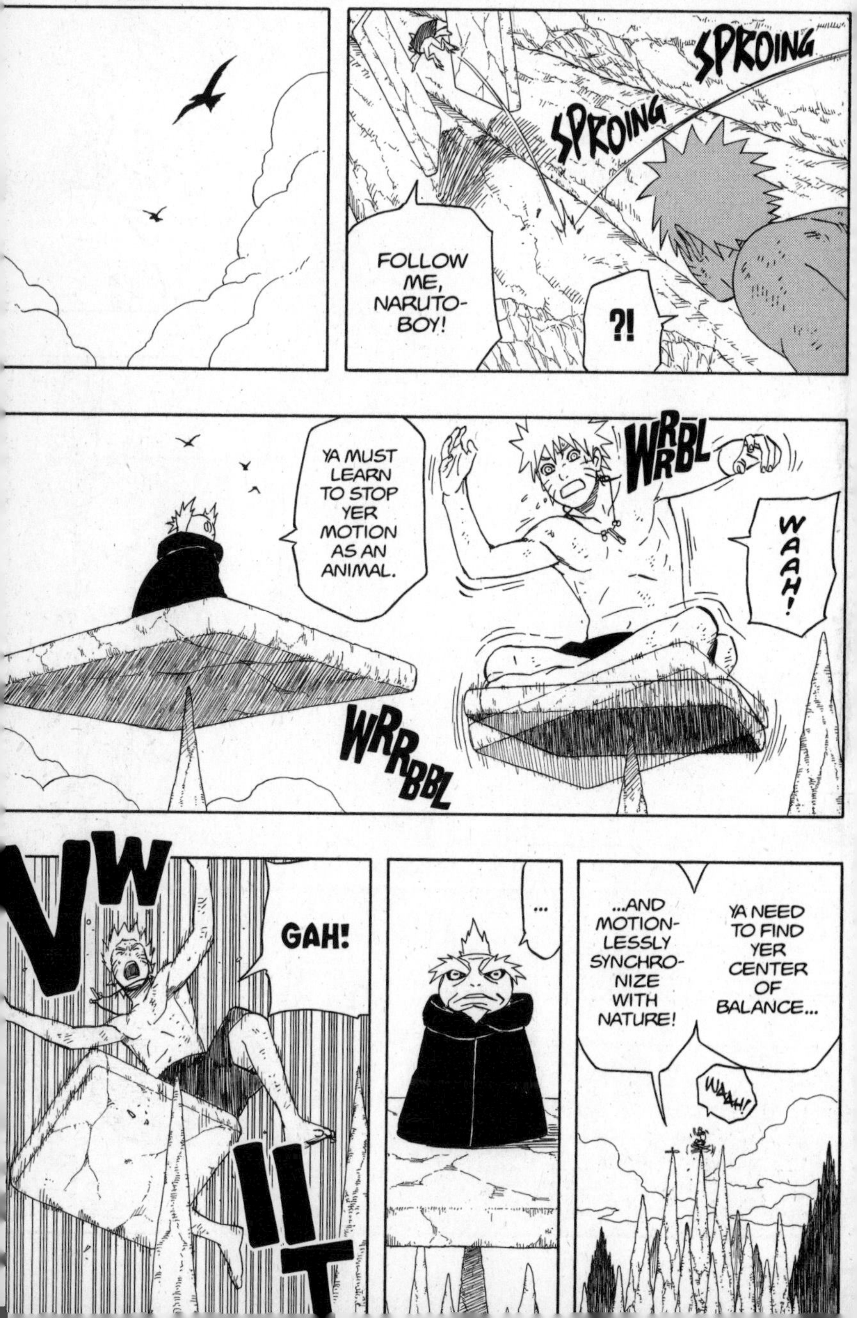

SPROING
SPROING
FOLLOW ME, NARUTO-BOY!
?!
WRRBL
WAAH!
YA MUST LEARN TO STOP YER MOTION AS AN ANIMAL.
WRRBBL
YA NEED TO FIND YER CENTER OF BALANCE...
...AND MOTIONLESSLY SYNCHRONIZE WITH NATURE!
WAAH!
...
GAH!
VWIIT

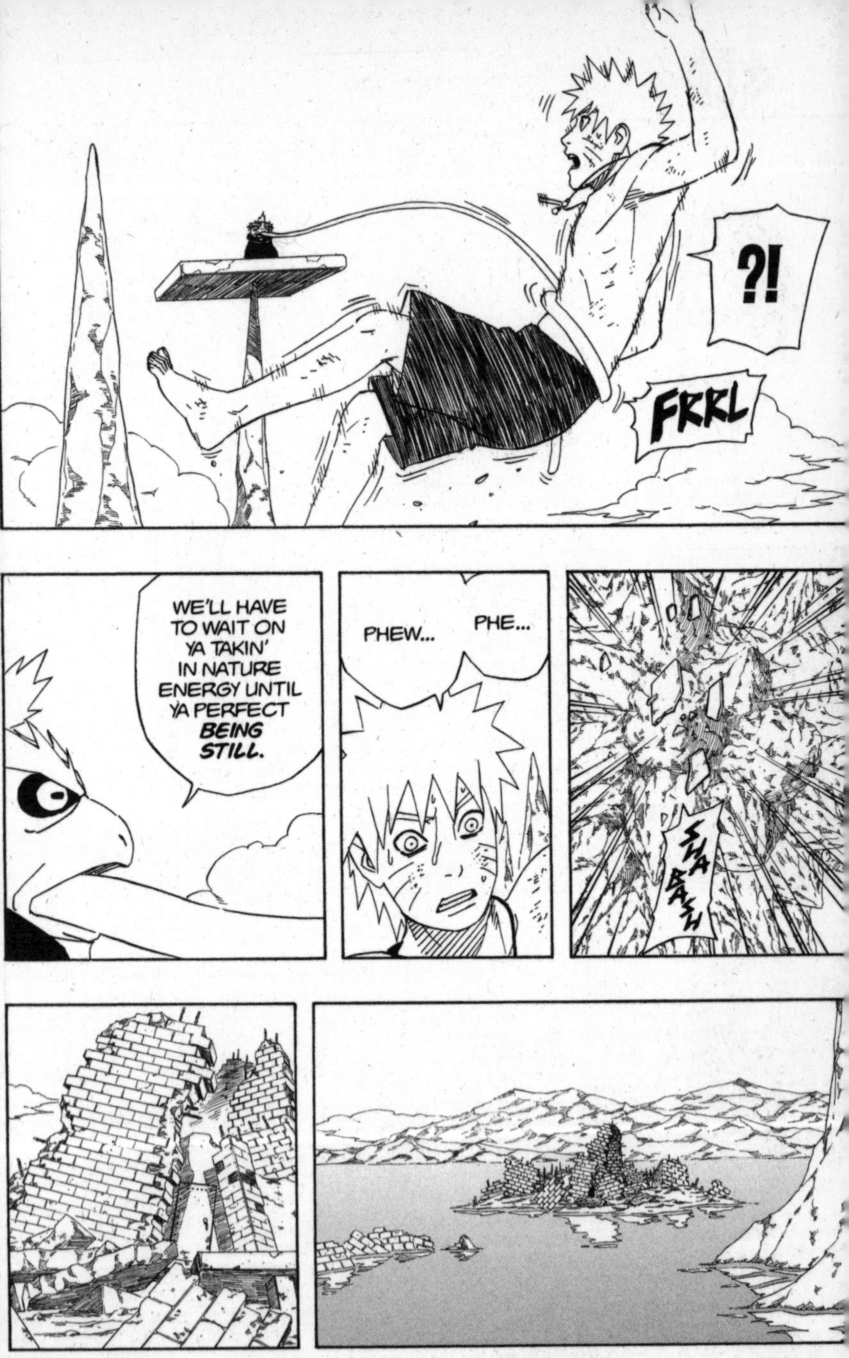
?!
FRRL
SHABASH
PHE...
PHEW...
WE'LL HAVE TO WAIT ON YA TAKIN' IN NATURE ENERGY UNTIL YA PERFECT *BEING STILL*.

READ THIS WAY

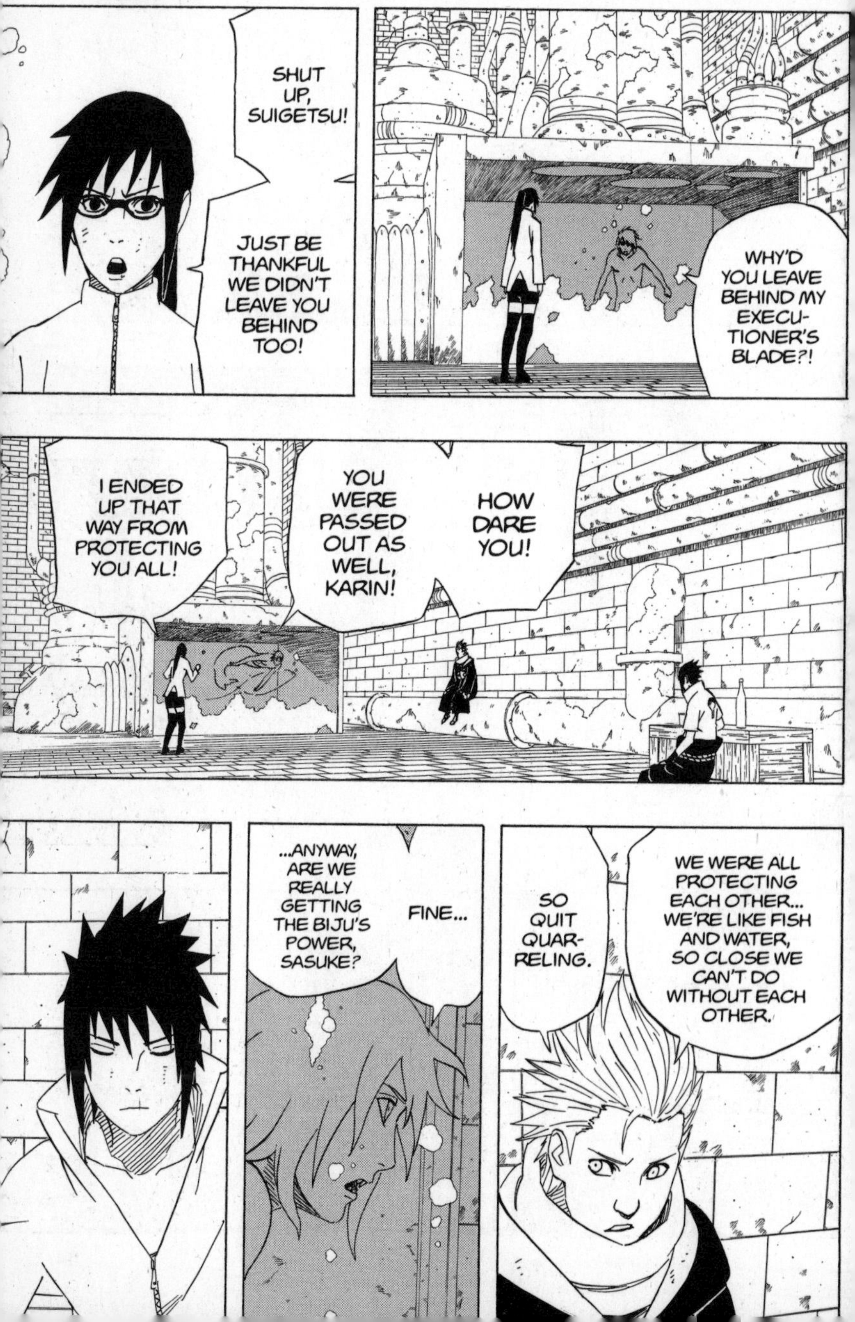
WHY'D YOU LEAVE BEHIND MY EXECUTIONER'S BLADE?!
SHUT UP, SUIGETSU!
JUST BE THANKFUL WE DIDN'T LEAVE YOU BEHIND TOO!
HOW DARE YOU!
YOU WERE PASSED OUT AS WELL, KARIN!
I ENDED UP THAT WAY FROM PROTECTING YOU ALL!
WE WERE ALL PROTECTING EACH OTHER... WE'RE LIKE FISH AND WATER, SO CLOSE WE CAN'T DO WITHOUT EACH OTHER.
SO QUIT QUARRELING.
FINE...
...ANYWAY, ARE WE REALLY GETTING THE BIJU'S POWER, SASUKE?

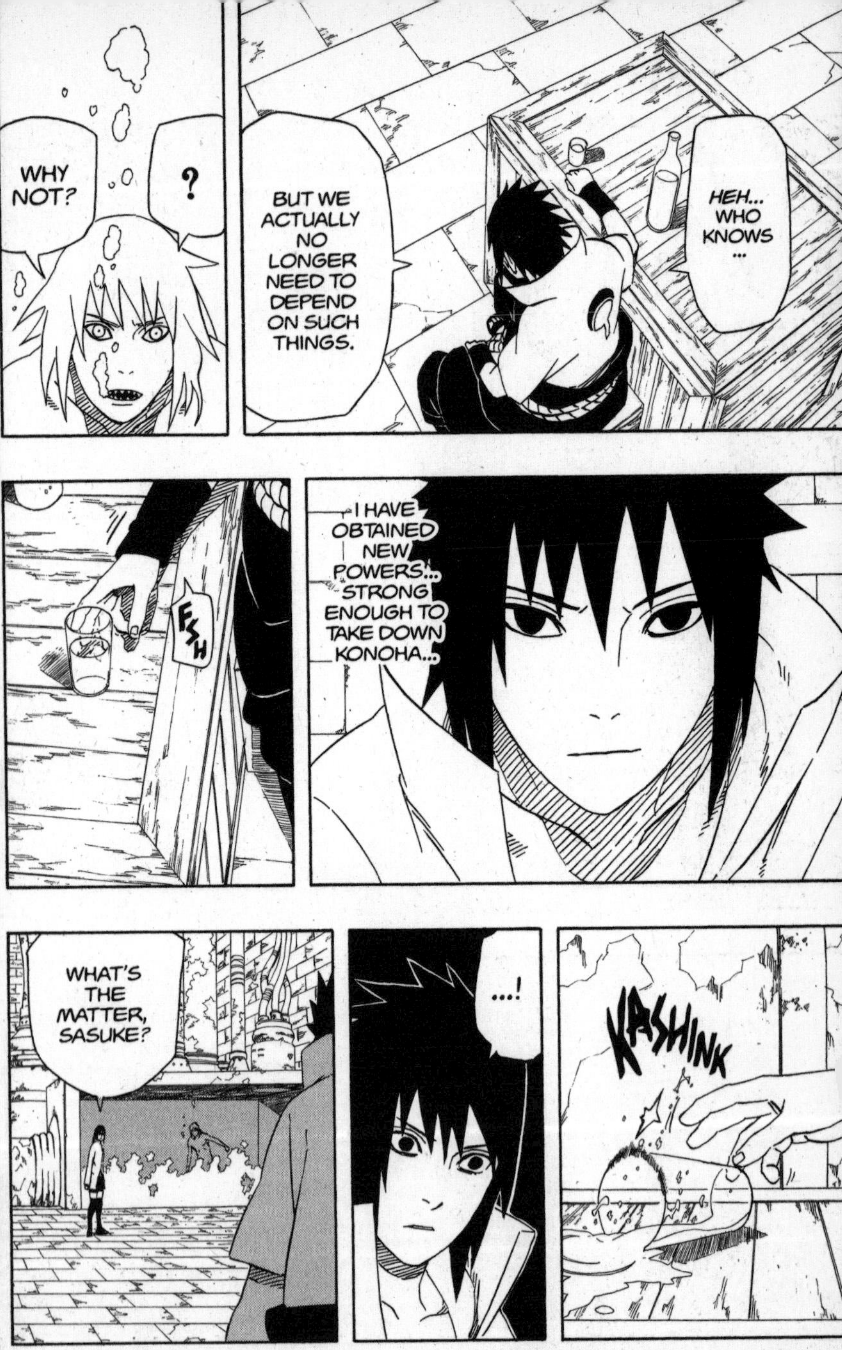
HEH... WHO KNOWS ...
BUT WE ACTUALLY NO LONGER NEED TO DEPEND ON SUCH THINGS.
?
WHY NOT?
I HAVE OBTAINED NEW POWERS... STRONG ENOUGH TO TAKE DOWN KONOHA...
FSH
KASHINK
...!
WHAT'S THE MATTER, SASUKE?

READ THIS WAY

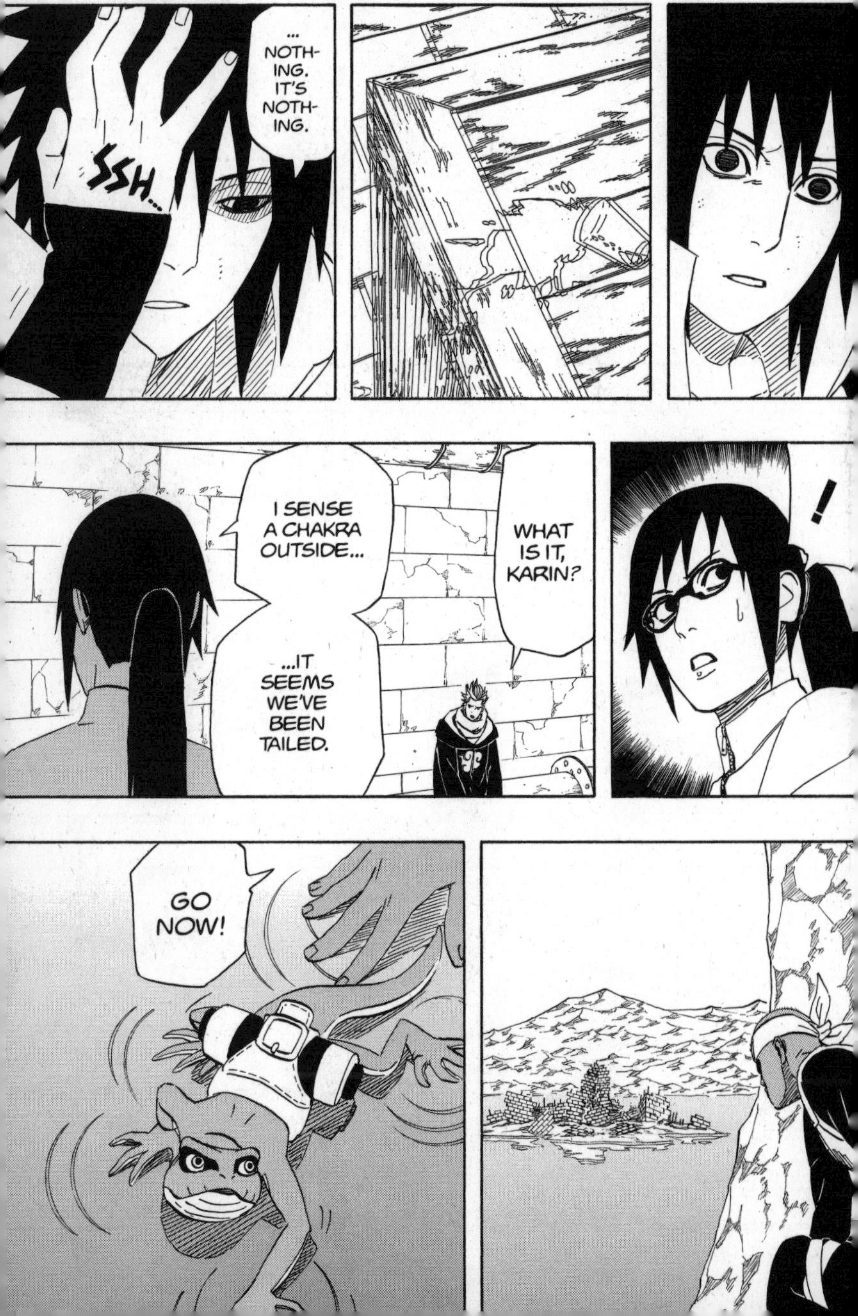
... NOTHING. IT'S NOTHING.
SSH...
!
WHAT IS IT, KARIN?
I SENSE A CHAKRA OUTSIDE...
...IT SEEMS WE'VE BEEN TAILED.
GO NOW!

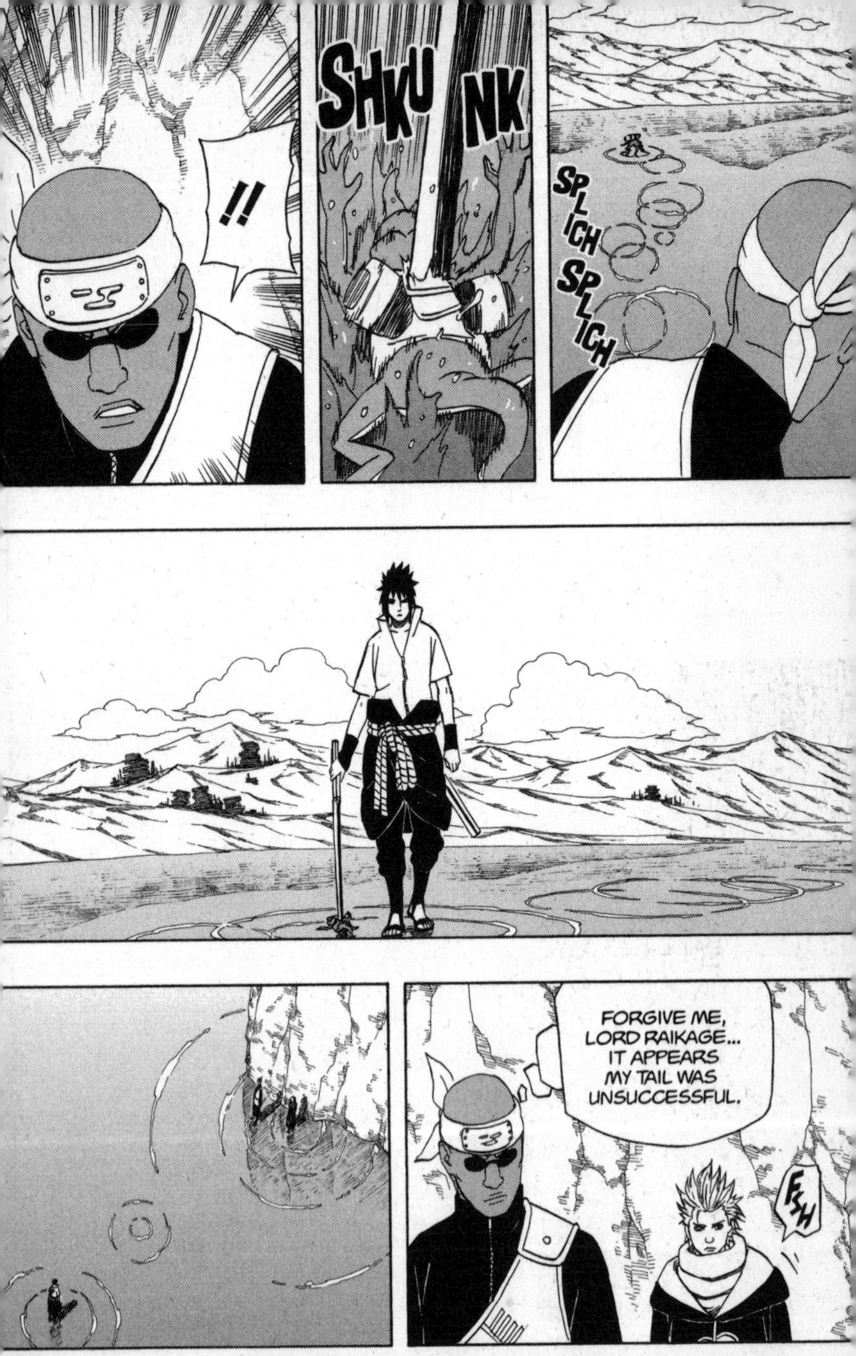
SPLICH
SPLICH
SHKUNK
!!
FORGIVE ME, LORD RAIKAGE... IT APPEARS MY TAIL WAS UNSUCCESSFUL.
FSH

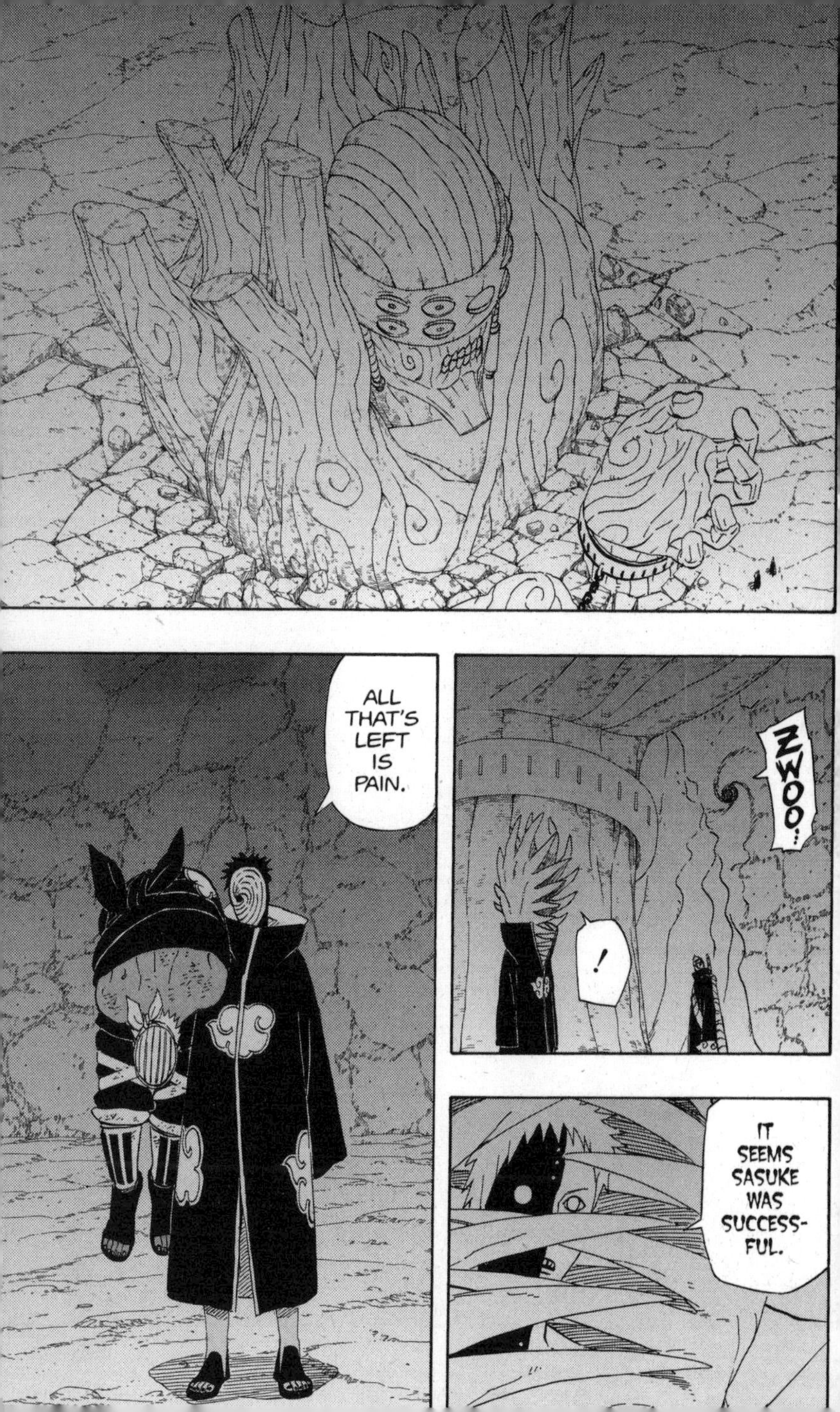
ZWOO...
!
IT SEEMS SASUKE WAS SUCCESSFUL.
ALL THAT'S LEFT IS PAIN.

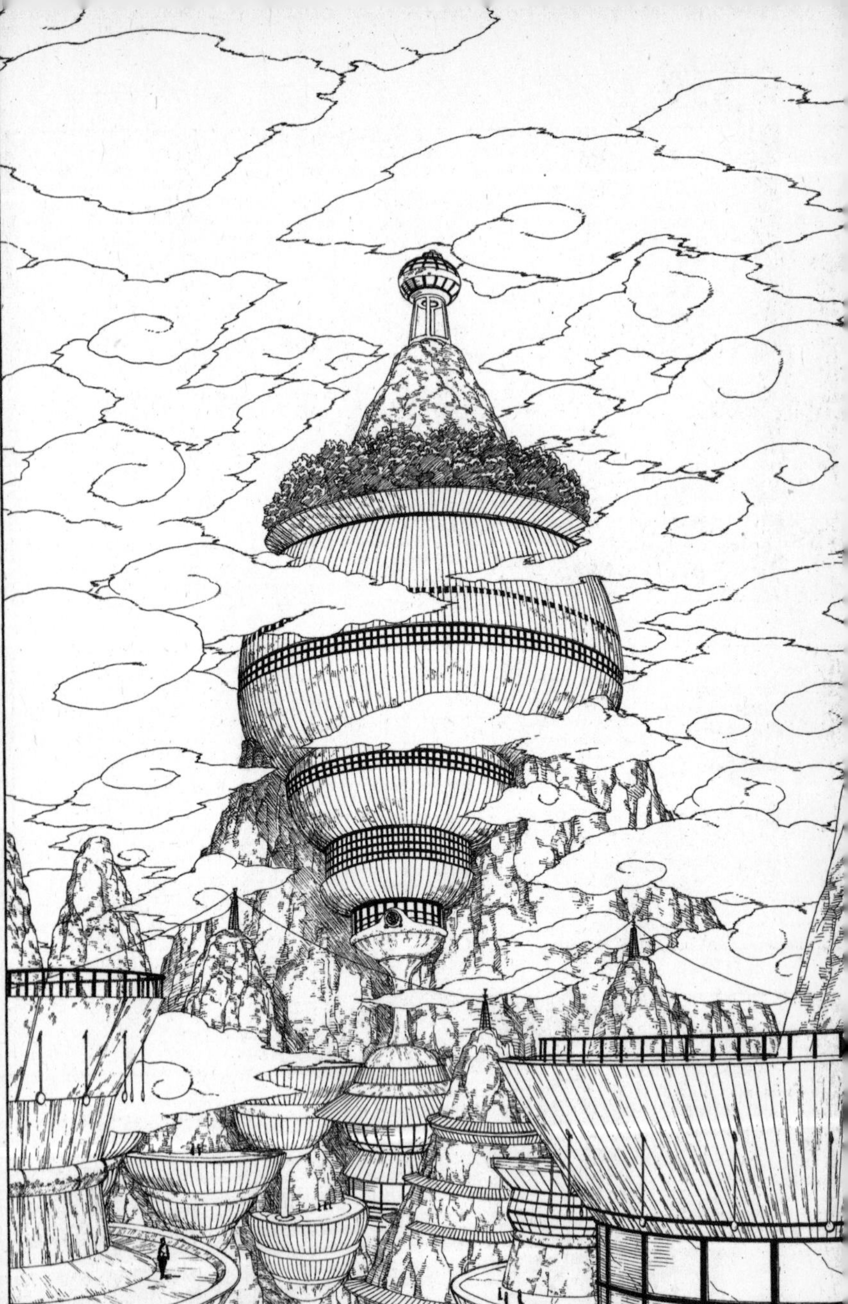

READ THIS WAY

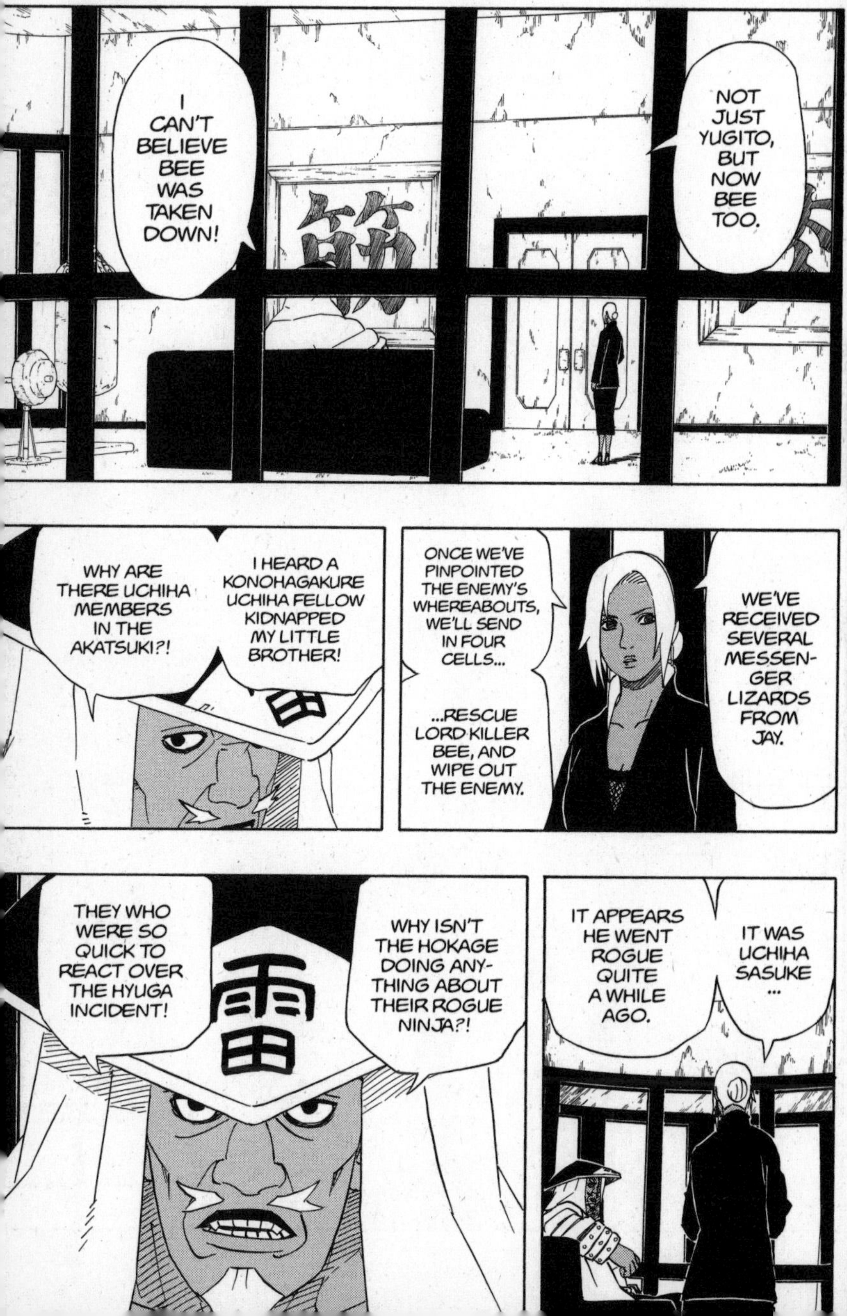
NOT JUST YUGITO, BUT NOW BEE TOO.
I CAN'T BELIEVE BEE WAS TAKEN DOWN!
WE'VE RECEIVED SEVERAL MESSEN-GER LIZARDS FROM JAY.
ONCE WE'VE PINPOINTED THE ENEMY'S WHEREABOUTS, WE'LL SEND IN FOUR CELLS...
...RESCUE LORD KILLER BEE, AND WIPE OUT THE ENEMY.
I HEARD A KONOHAGAKURE UCHIHA FELLOW KIDNAPPED MY LITTLE BROTHER!
WHY ARE THERE UCHIHA MEMBERS IN THE AKATSUKI?!
IT WAS UCHIHA SASUKE ...
IT APPEARS HE WENT ROGUE QUITE A WHILE AGO.
WHY ISN'T THE HOKAGE DOING ANY-THING ABOUT THEIR ROGUE NINJA?!
THEY WHO WERE SO QUICK TO REACT OVER THE HYUGA INCIDENT!

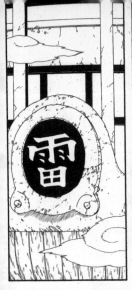

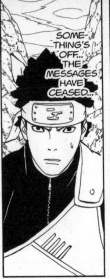

SOME-THING'S OFF... THE MESSAGES HAVE CEASED...
WHAT?!!
IT SEEMS JAY HAS EITHER BEEN KILLED OR CAP-TURED.
NOW WE WILL NO LONGER BE ABLE TO LOCATE THE ENEMY...
FIGURE OUT AS MUCH AS YOU CAN FROM THE INTEL HE'S ALREADY SENT BACK AND START COMBING THE VICINITY!
SEND OUT AN ENTIRE BATTALION IF YOU HAVE TO!

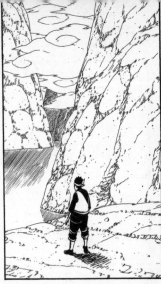

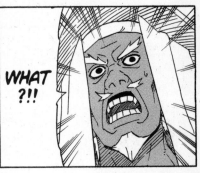

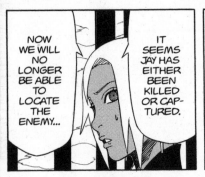

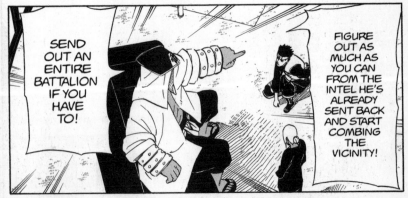

READ THIS WAY

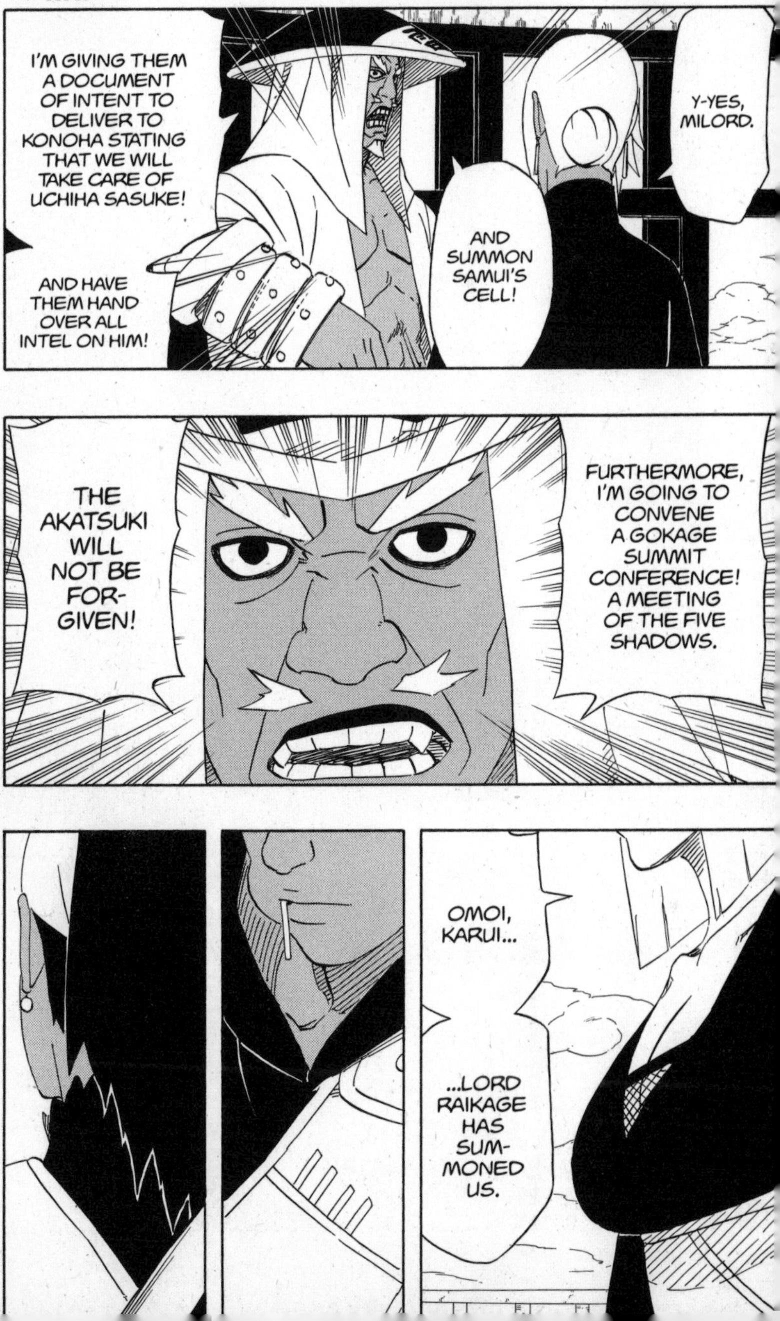
Y-YES, MILORD.
AND SUMMON SAMUI'S CELL!
I'M GIVING THEM A DOCUMENT OF INTENT TO DELIVER TO KONOHA STATING THAT WE WILL TAKE CARE OF UCHIHA SASUKE!
AND HAVE THEM HAND OVER ALL INTEL ON HIM!
FURTHERMORE, I'M GOING TO CONVENE A GOKAGE SUMMIT CONFERENCE! A MEETING OF THE FIVE SHADOWS.
THE AKATSUKI WILL NOT BE FOR-GIVEN!
OMOI, KARUI...
...LORD RAIKAGE HAS SUM-MONED US.

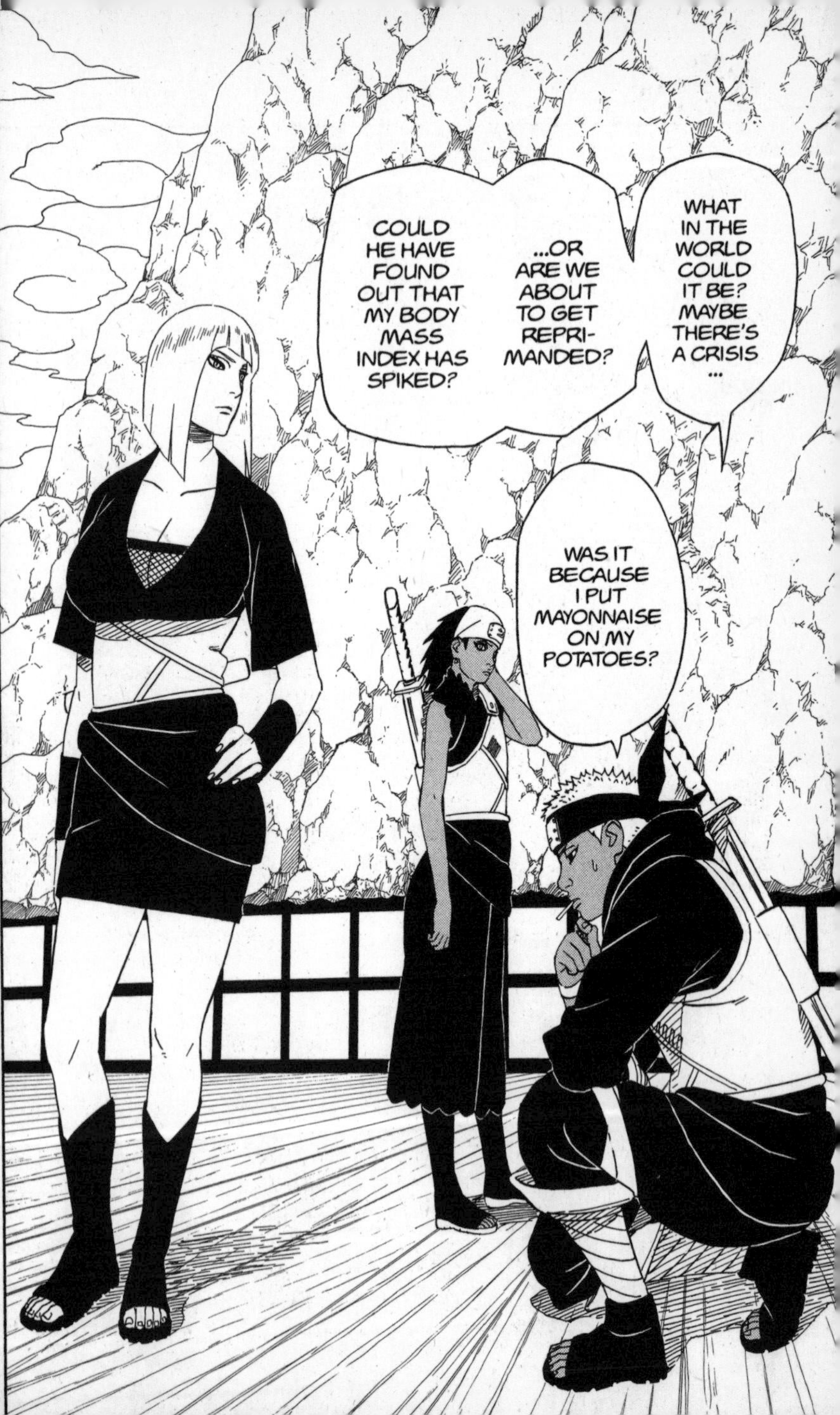
WHAT IN THE WORLD COULD IT BE? MAYBE THERE'S A CRISIS ...
...OR ARE WE ABOUT TO GET REPRI-MANDED?
COULD HE HAVE FOUND OUT THAT MY BODY MASS INDEX HAS SPIKED?
WAS IT BECAUSE I PUT MAYONNAISE ON MY POTATOES?

READ THIS WAY

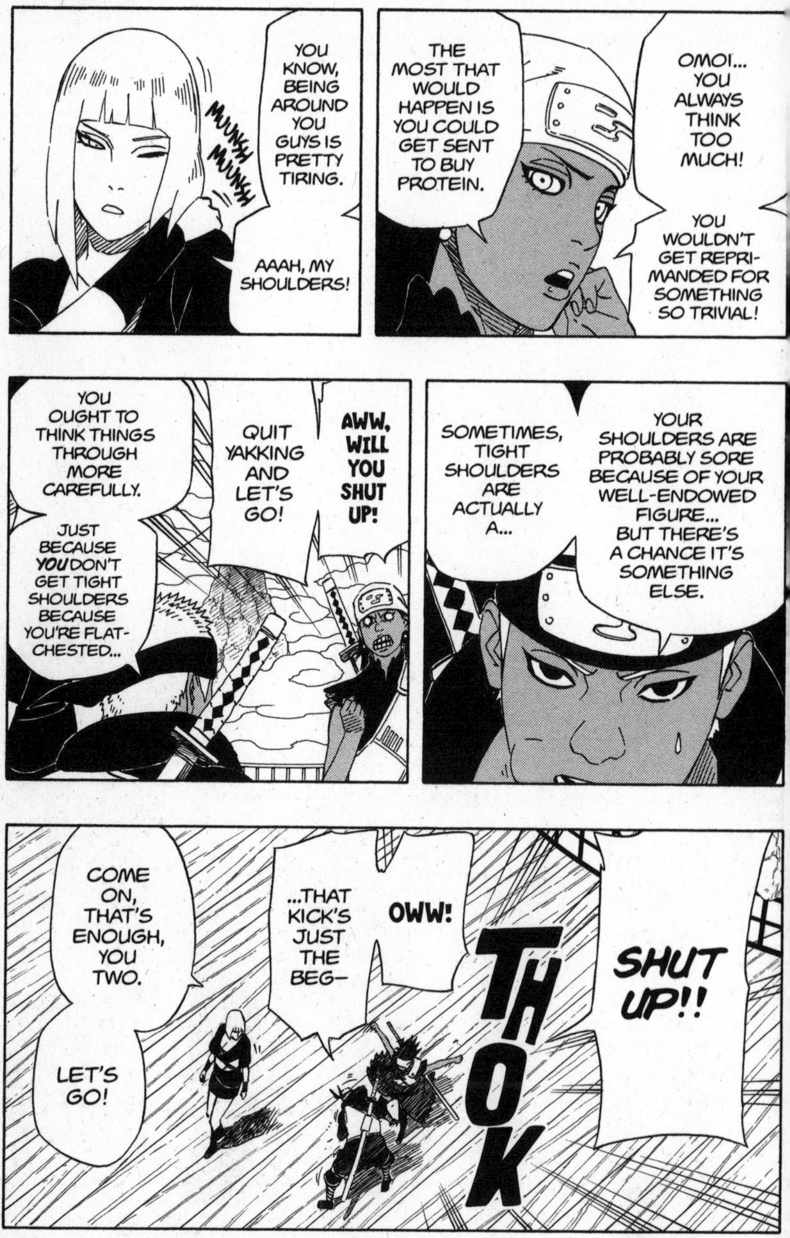
OMOI... YOU ALWAYS THINK TOO MUCH!
YOU WOULDN'T GET REPRIMANDED FOR SOMETHING SO TRIVIAL!
THE MOST THAT WOULD HAPPEN IS YOU COULD GET SENT TO BUY PROTEIN.
YOU KNOW, BEING AROUND YOU GUYS IS PRETTY TIRING.
MUUNH MUUNH
AAAH, MY SHOULDERS!
YOUR SHOULDERS ARE PROBABLY SORE BECAUSE OF YOUR WELL-ENDOWED FIGURE... BUT THERE'S A CHANCE IT'S SOMETHING ELSE.
SOMETIMES, TIGHT SHOULDERS ARE ACTUALLY A...
AWW, WILL YOU SHUT UP!
QUIT YAKKING AND LET'S GO!
YOU OUGHT TO THINK THINGS THROUGH MORE CAREFULLY.
JUST BECAUSE *YOU* DON'T GET TIGHT SHOULDERS BECAUSE YOU'RE FLAT-CHESTED...
SHUT UP!!
THOK
OWW!
...THAT KICK'S JUST THE BEG–
COME ON, THAT'S ENOUGH, YOU TWO.
LET'S GO!

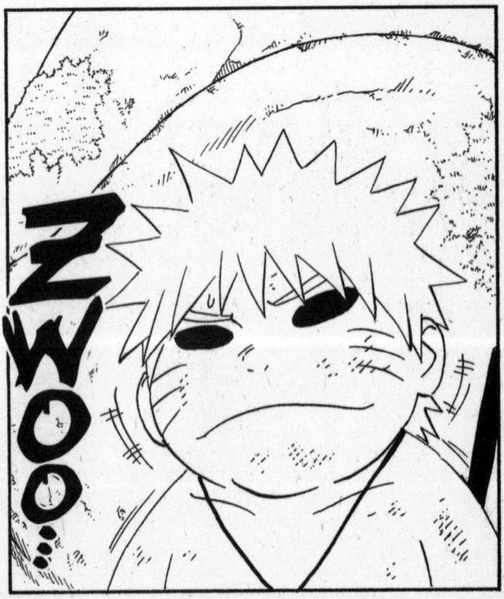
ZWOO...

Number 418: Sage Naruto!!

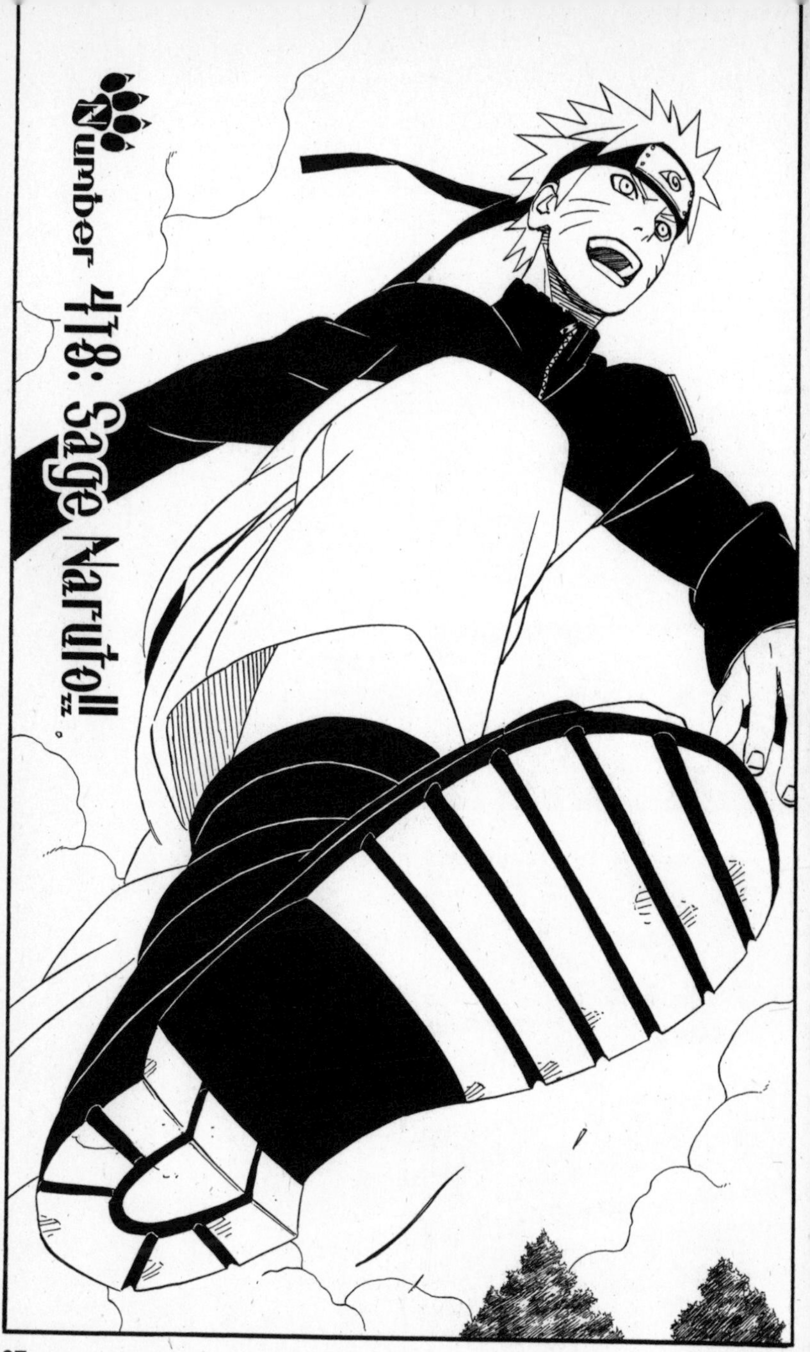

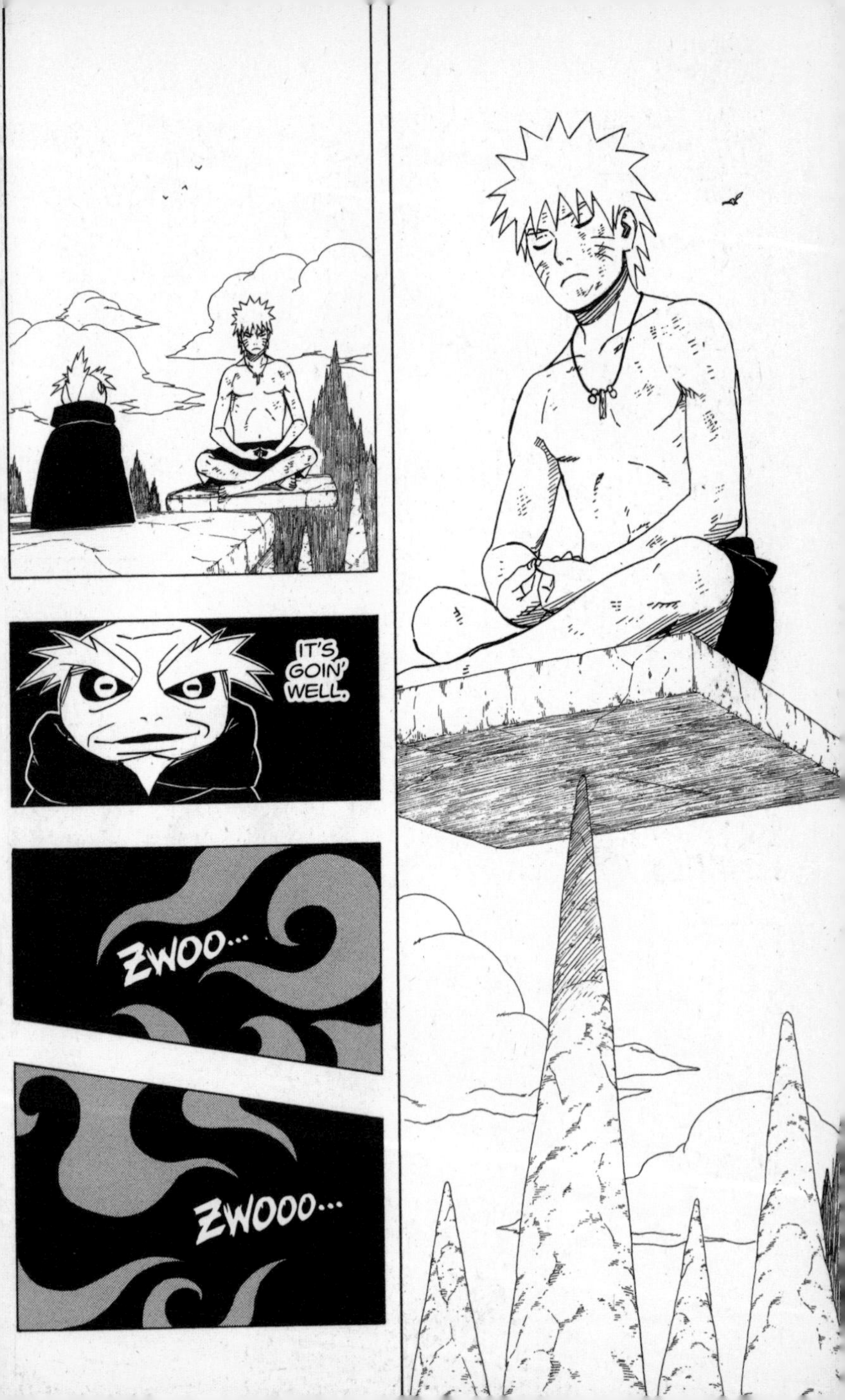
IT'S GOIN' WELL.
ZWOO...
ZWOOO...

READ THIS WAY

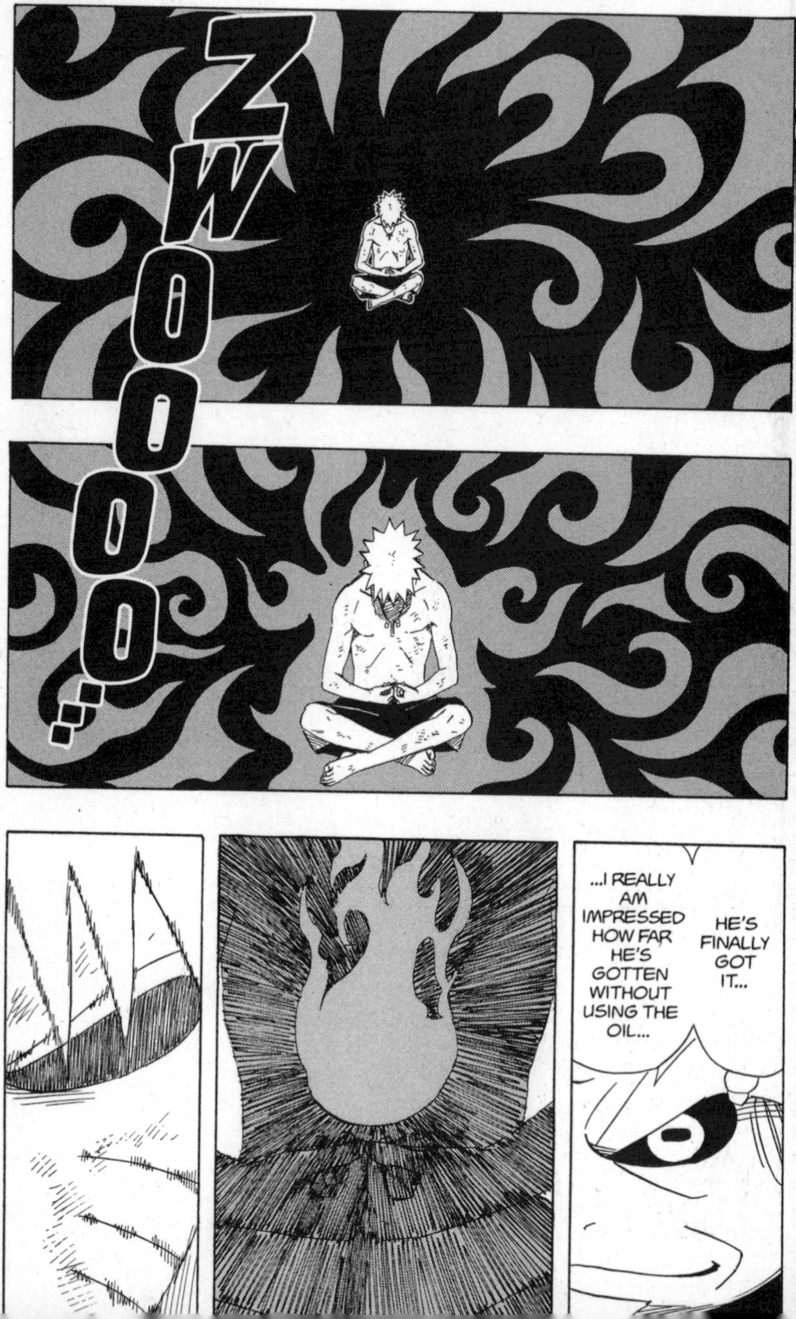
ZWOOOOO...
HE'S FINALLY GOT IT...
...I REALLY AM IMPRESSED HOW FAR HE'S GOTTEN WITHOUT USING THE OIL...

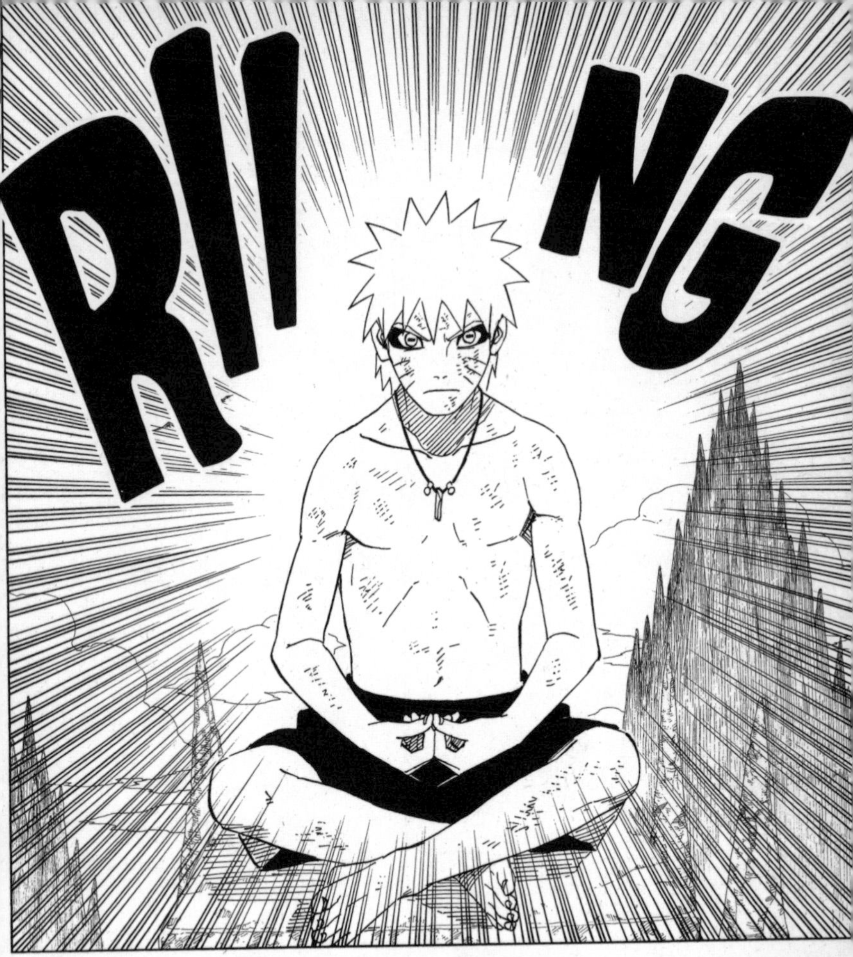
RIING

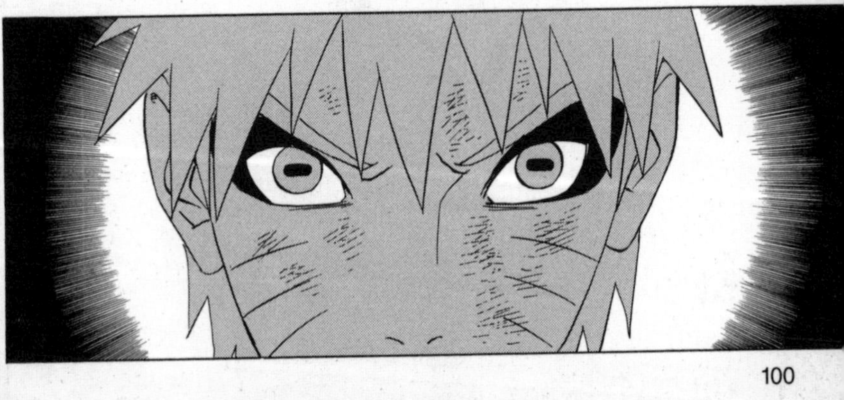

READ THIS WAY

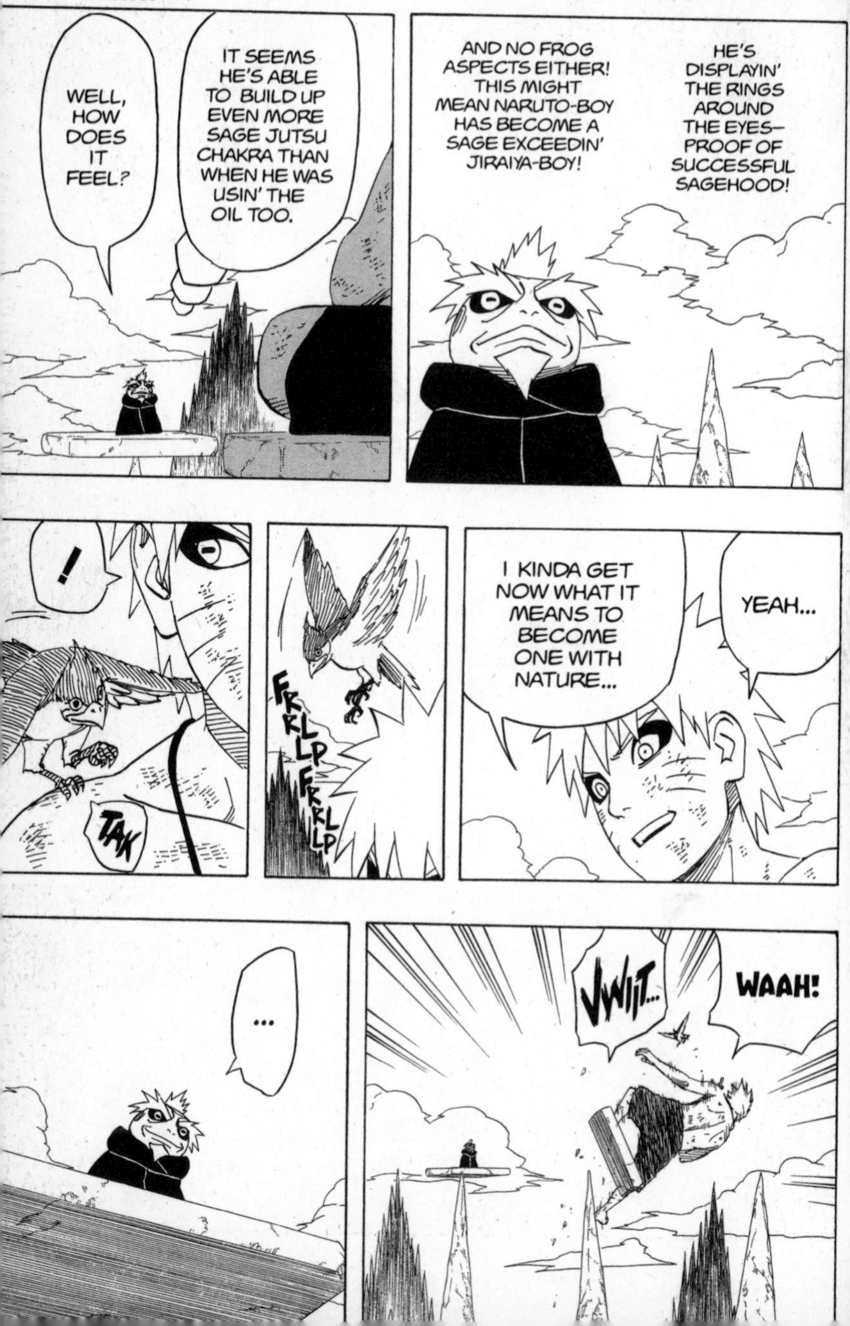
HE'S DISPLAYIN' THE RINGS AROUND THE EYES—PROOF OF SUCCESSFUL SAGEHOOD!
AND NO FROG ASPECTS EITHER! THIS MIGHT MEAN NARUTO-BOY HAS BECOME A SAGE EXCEEDIN' JIRAIYA-BOY!
IT SEEMS HE'S ABLE TO BUILD UP EVEN MORE SAGE JUTSU CHAKRA THAN WHEN HE WAS USIN' THE OIL TOO.
WELL, HOW DOES IT FEEL?
YEAH...
I KINDA GET NOW WHAT IT MEANS TO BECOME ONE WITH NATURE...
FRRLLP
FRRLLP
!
TAK
WAAH!
VWIIT...
...

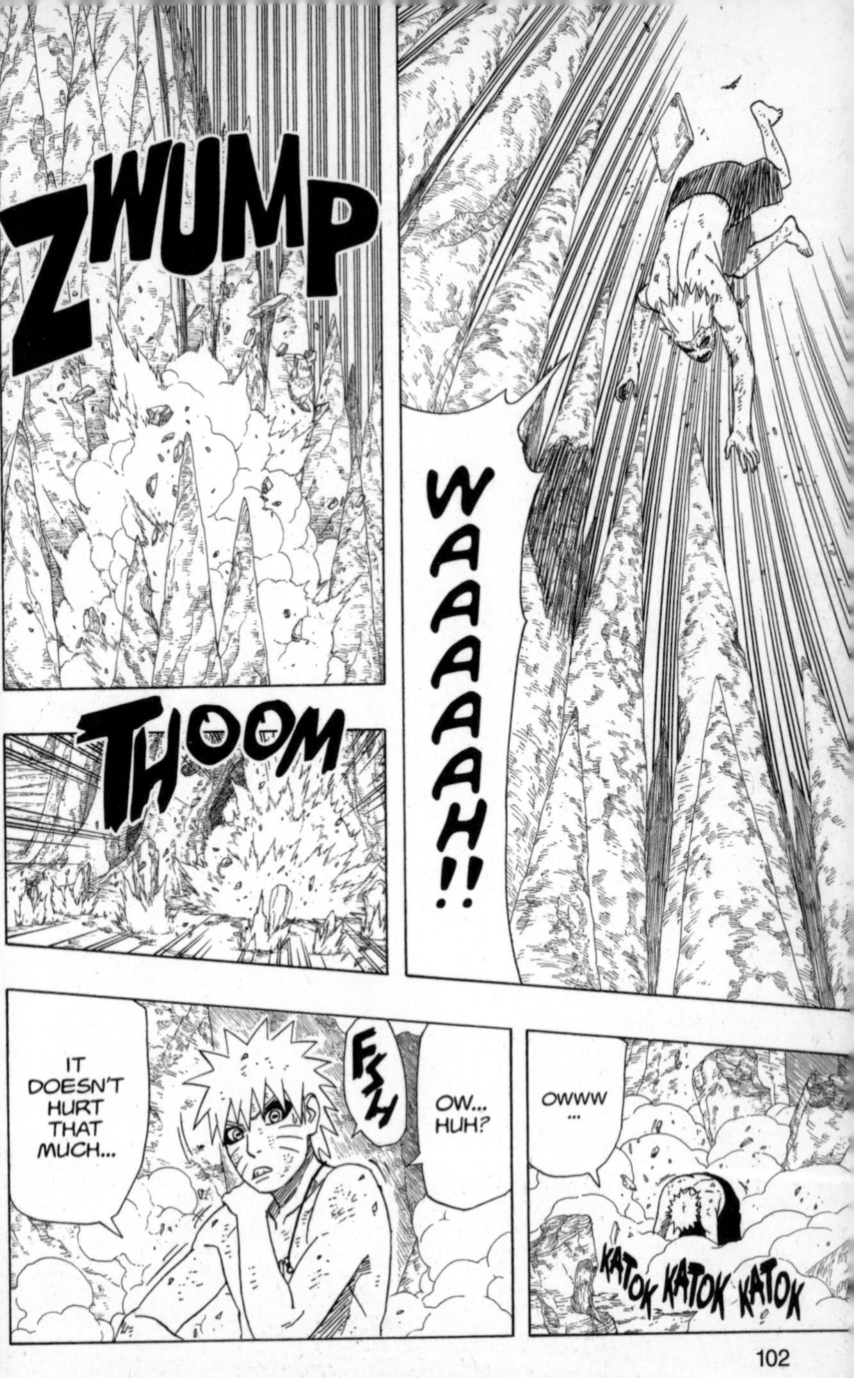
WAAAAAAH!!
ZWUMP
THOOM
OWWW ...
KATOK KATOK KATOK
OW... HUH?
FSH
IT DOESN'T HURT THAT MUCH...

READ THIS WAY

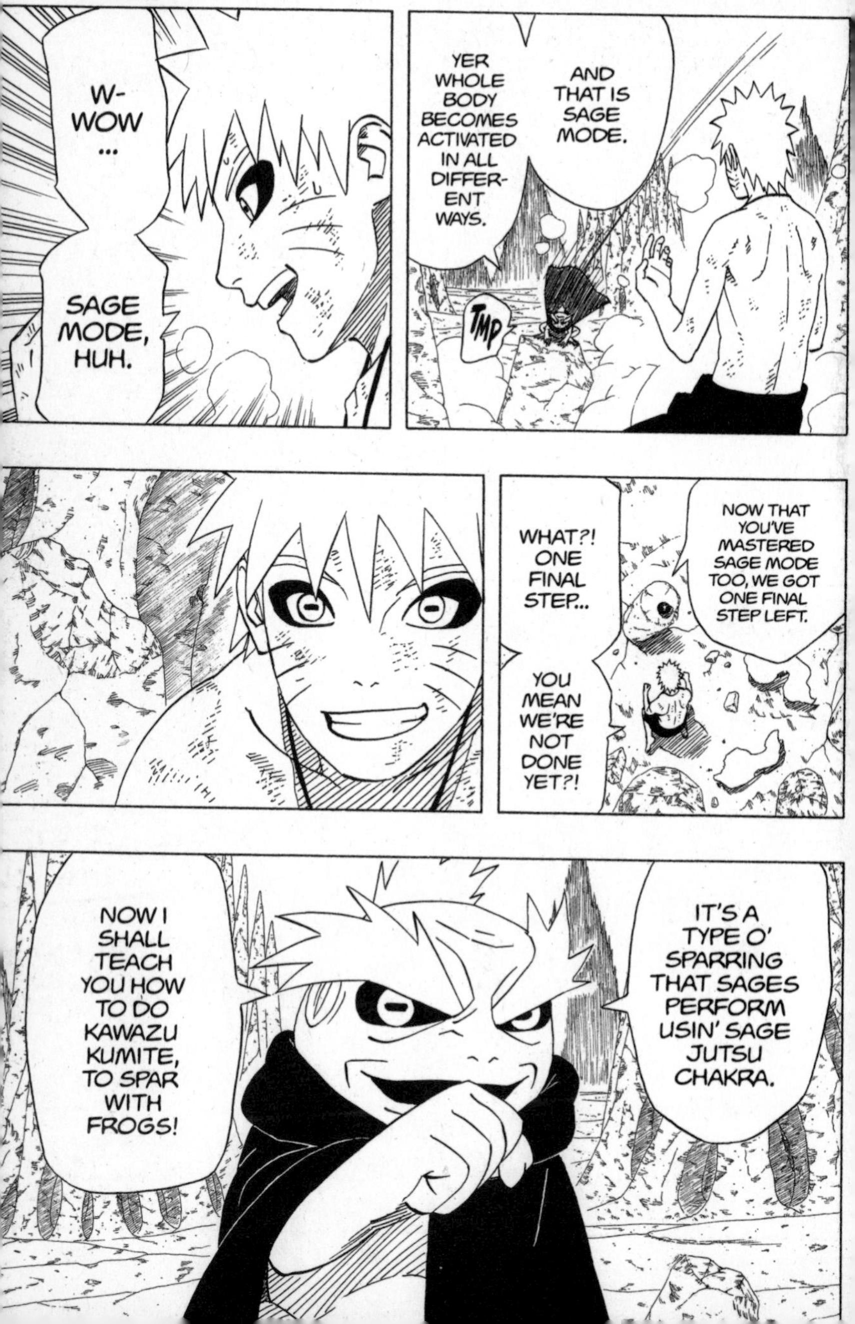

AND THAT IS SAGE MODE.
YER WHOLE BODY BECOMES ACTIVATED IN ALL DIFFER-ENT WAYS.
TMP
W-WOW...
SAGE MODE, HUH.
NOW THAT YOU'VE MASTERED SAGE MODE TOO, WE GOT ONE FINAL STEP LEFT.
WHAT?! ONE FINAL STEP...
YOU MEAN WE'RE NOT DONE YET?!
IT'S A TYPE O' SPARRING THAT SAGES PERFORM USIN' SAGE JUTSU CHAKRA.
NOW I SHALL TEACH YOU HOW TO DO KAWAZU KUMITE, TO SPAR WITH FROGS!

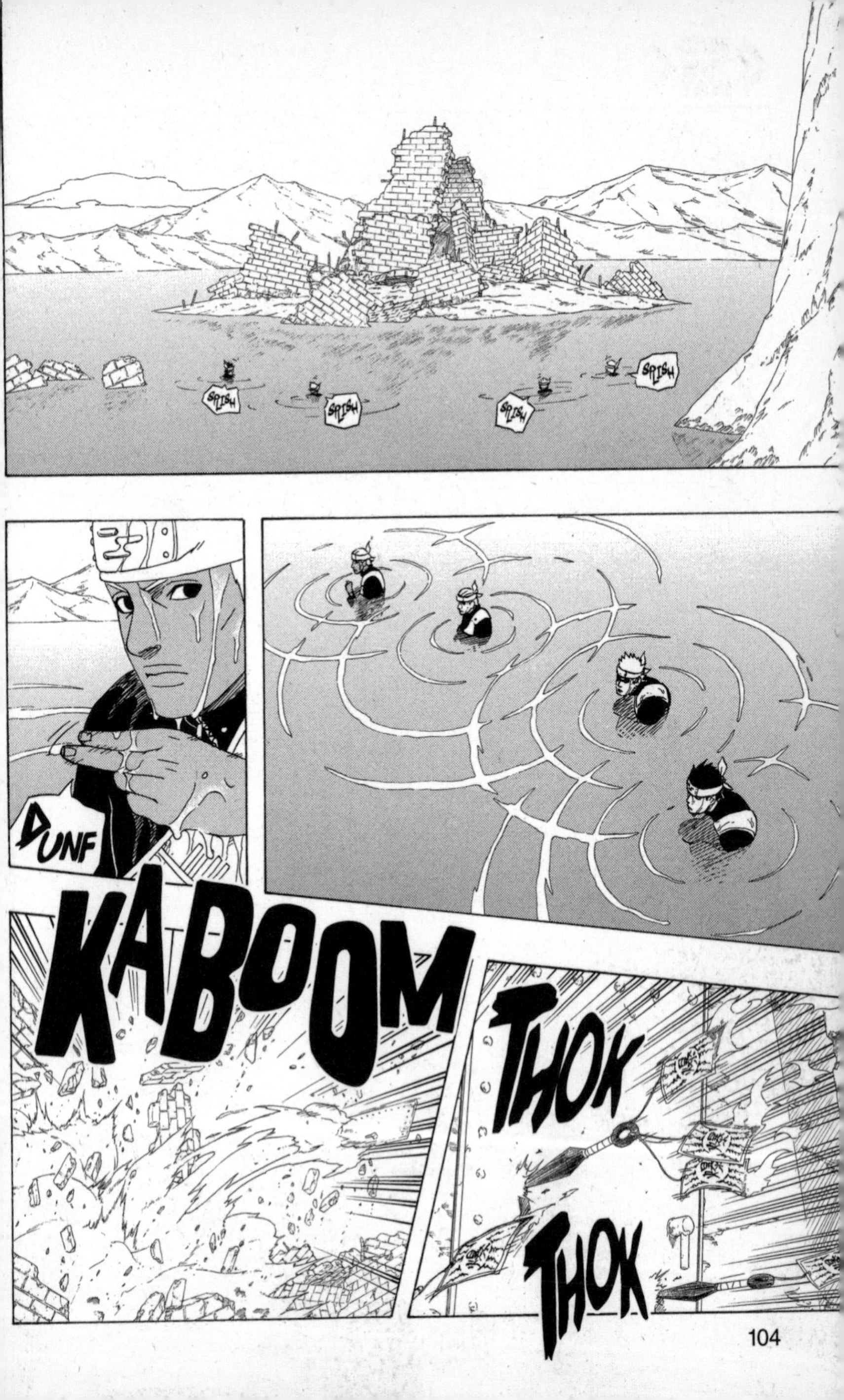
SRISH
SRISH
SRISH
SRISH
DUNF
THOK
THOK
KABOOM

READ THIS WAY

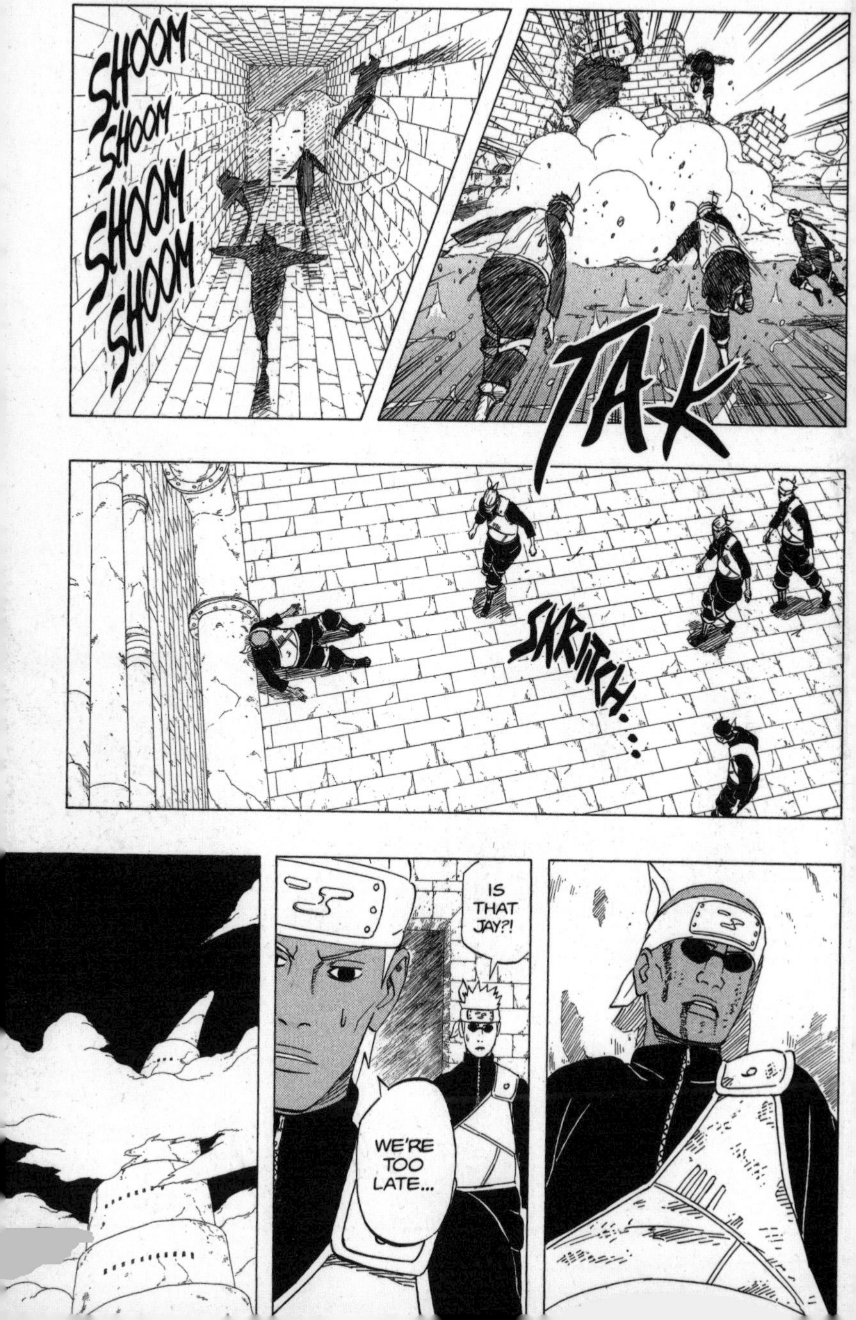
TAK
SHOOM SHOOM SHOOM SHOOM
SKRIITCH...
IS THAT JAY?!
WE'RE TOO LATE...

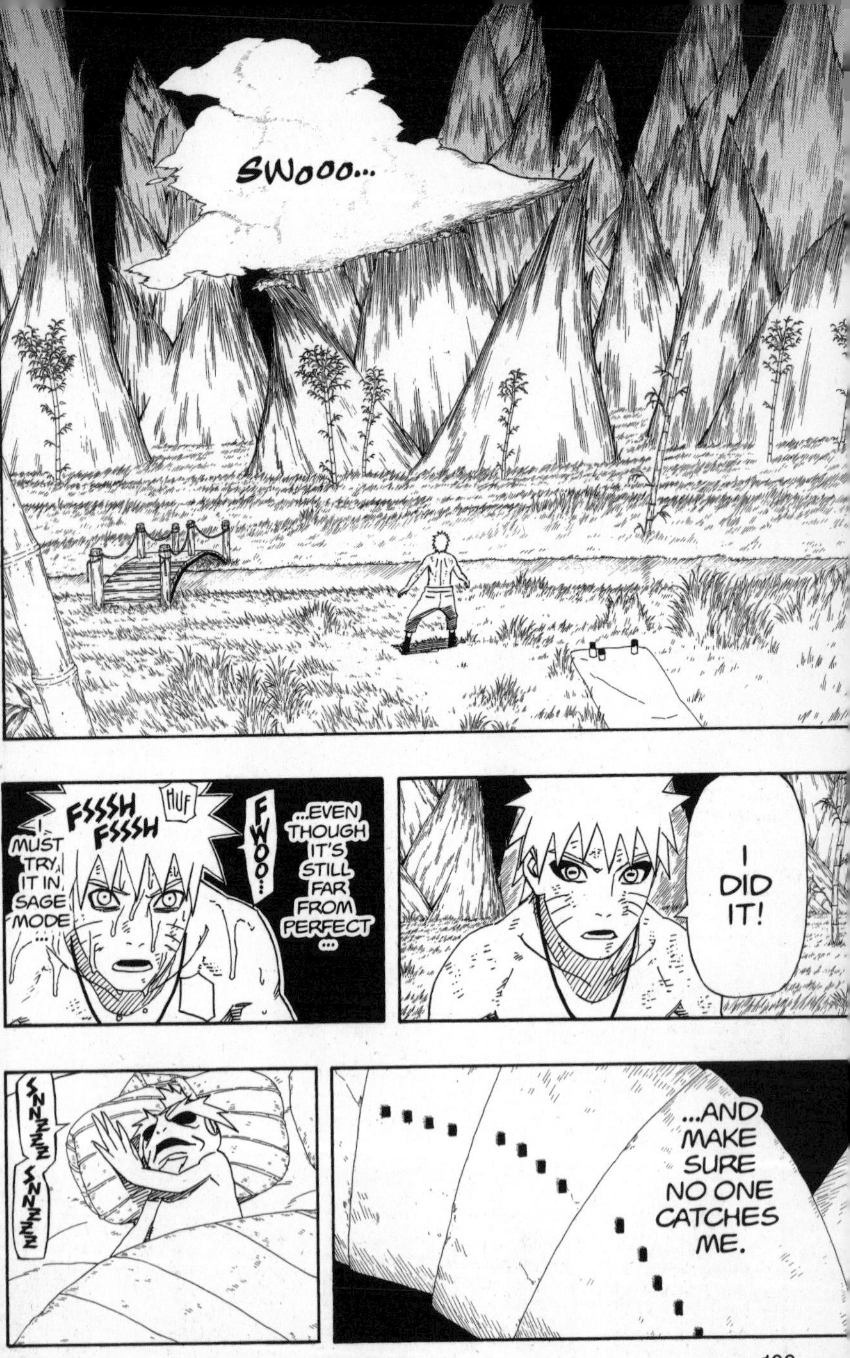
SWOOO...
I DID IT!
...EVEN THOUGH IT'S STILL FAR FROM PERFECT...
FWOO...
HUF
FSSSH FSSSH
I MUST TRY IT IN SAGE MODE...
...AND MAKE SURE NO ONE CATCHES ME.
SNZZZ SNZZZ

READ THIS WAY

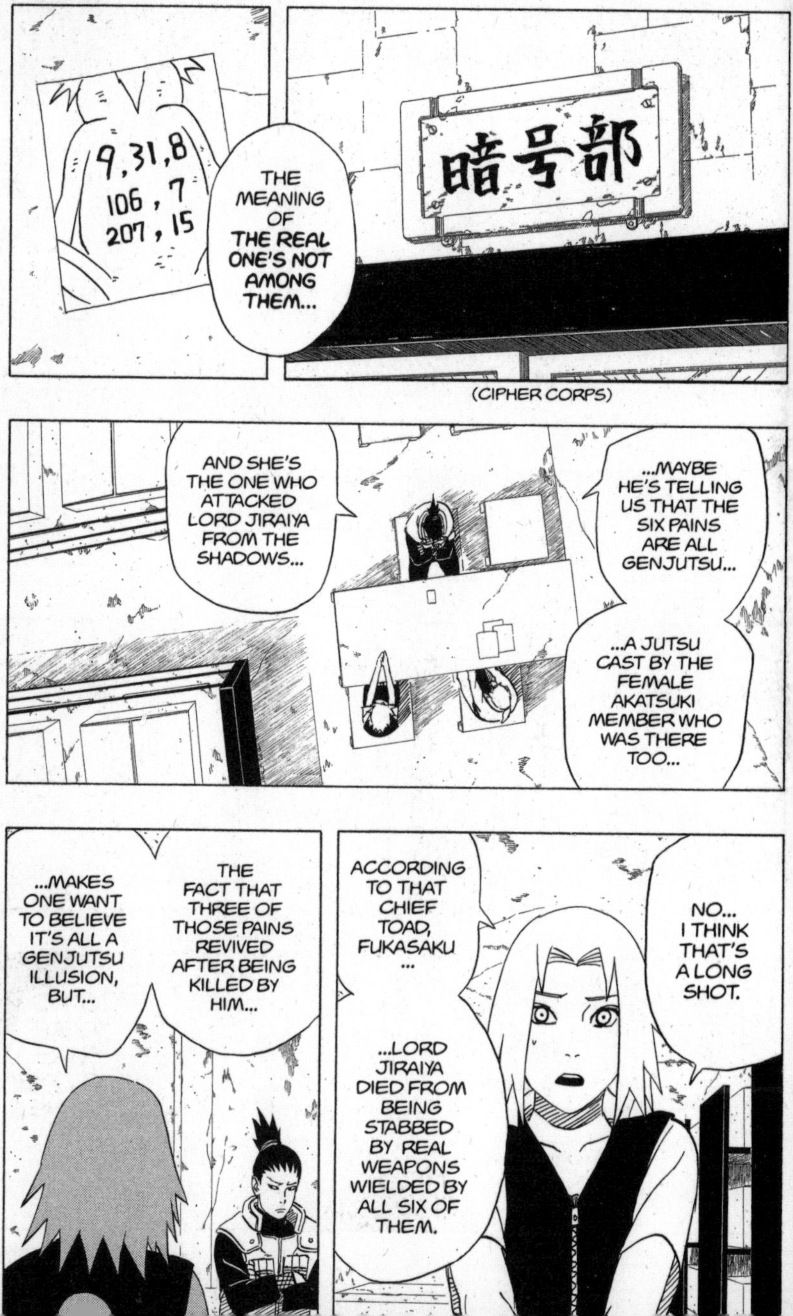

暗号部
(CIPHER CORPS)
9,31,8
106,7
207,15
THE MEANING OF THE REAL ONE'S NOT AMONG THEM...
...MAYBE HE'S TELLING US THAT THE SIX PAINS ARE ALL GENJUTSU...
...A JUTSU CAST BY THE FEMALE AKATSUKI MEMBER WHO WAS THERE TOO...
AND SHE'S THE ONE WHO ATTACKED LORD JIRAIYA FROM THE SHADOWS...
NO... I THINK THAT'S A LONG SHOT.
ACCORDING TO THAT CHIEF TOAD, FUKASAKU...
...LORD JIRAIYA DIED FROM BEING STABBED BY REAL WEAPONS WIELDED BY ALL SIX OF THEM.
THE FACT THAT THREE OF THOSE PAINS REVIVED AFTER BEING KILLED BY HIM...
...MAKES ONE WANT TO BELIEVE IT'S ALL A GENJUTSU ILLUSION, BUT...

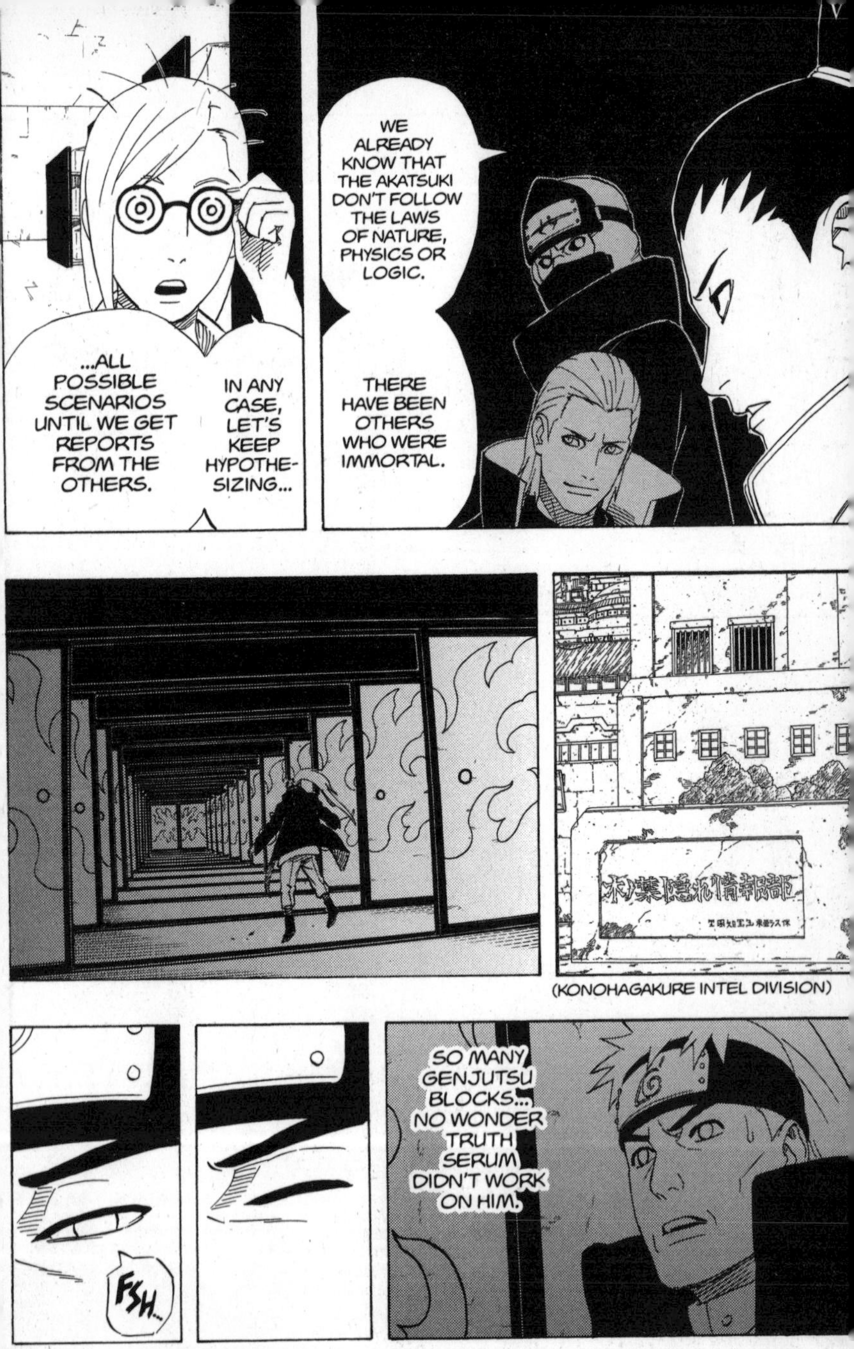

WE ALREADY KNOW THAT THE AKATSUKI DON'T FOLLOW THE LAWS OF NATURE, PHYSICS OR LOGIC.
THERE HAVE BEEN OTHERS WHO WERE IMMORTAL.
IN ANY CASE, LET'S KEEP HYPOTHE-SIZING...
...ALL POSSIBLE SCENARIOS UNTIL WE GET REPORTS FROM THE OTHERS.
(KONOHAGAKURE INTEL DIVISION)
SO MANY GENJUTSU BLOCKS... NO WONDER TRUTH SERUM DIDN'T WORK ON HIM.
FSH...

READ THIS WAY

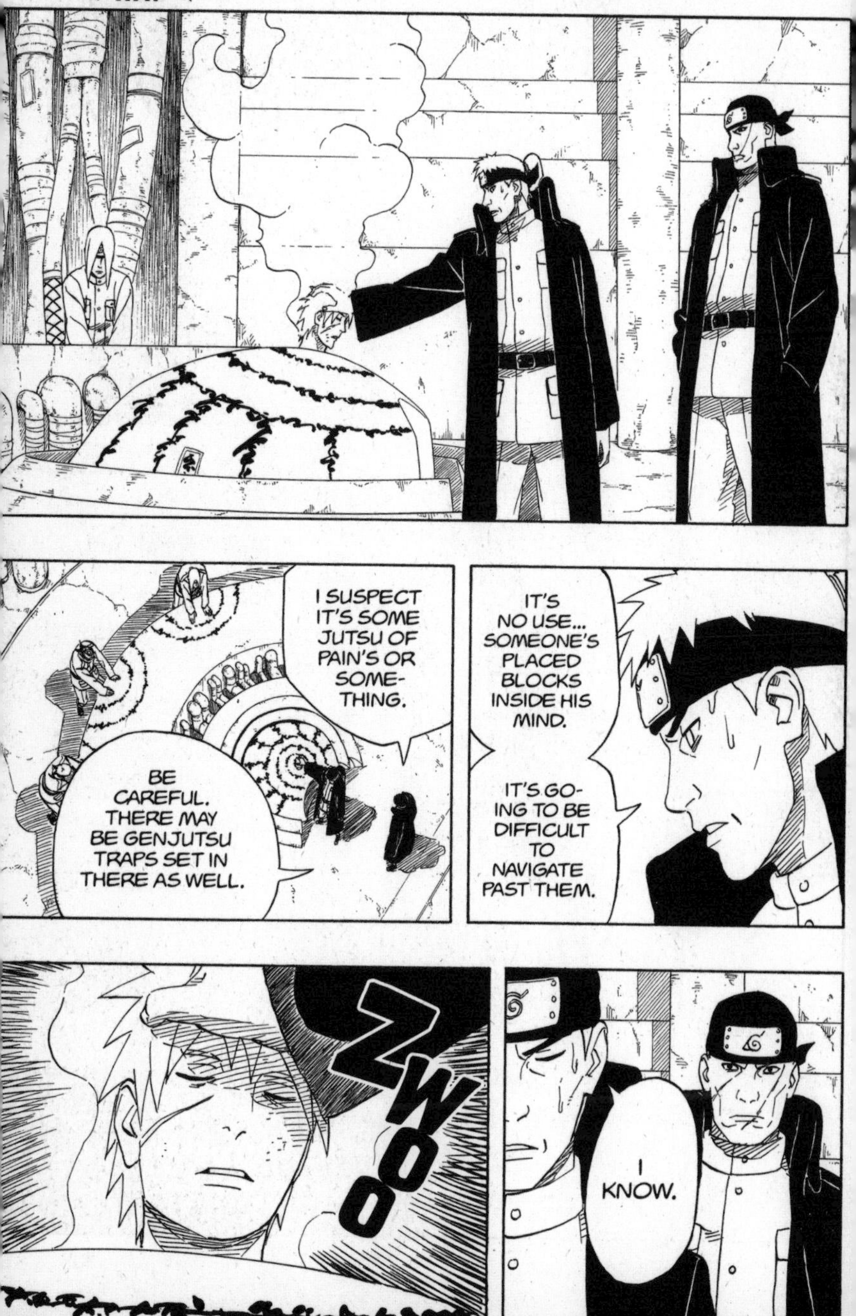
IT'S NO USE... SOMEONE'S PLACED BLOCKS INSIDE HIS MIND.
IT'S GOING TO BE DIFFICULT TO NAVIGATE PAST THEM.
I SUSPECT IT'S SOME JUTSU OF PAIN'S OR SOMETHING.
BE CAREFUL. THERE MAY BE GENJUTSU TRAPS SET IN THERE AS WELL.
I KNOW.
ZWOO

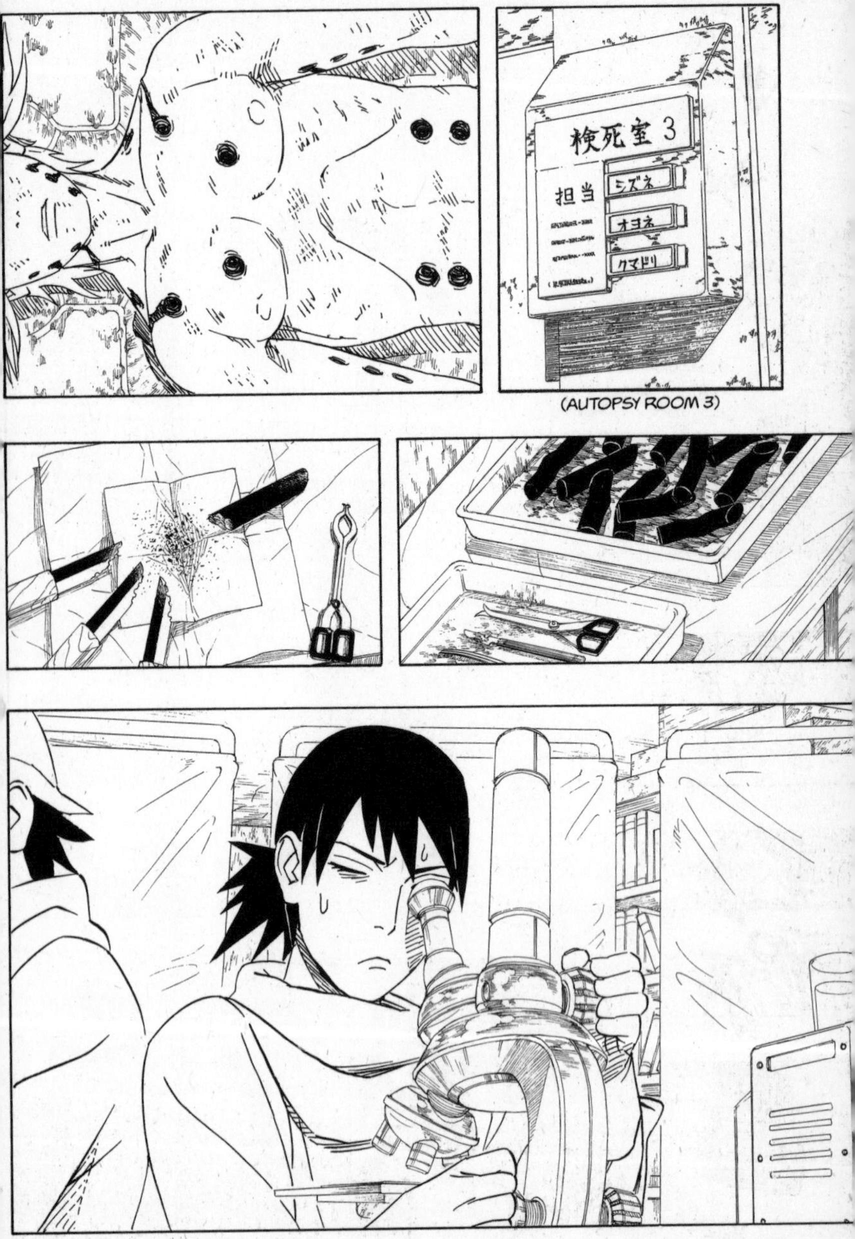
検死室 3
担当
シズネ
オヨネ
クマドリ
(AUTOPSY ROOM 3)

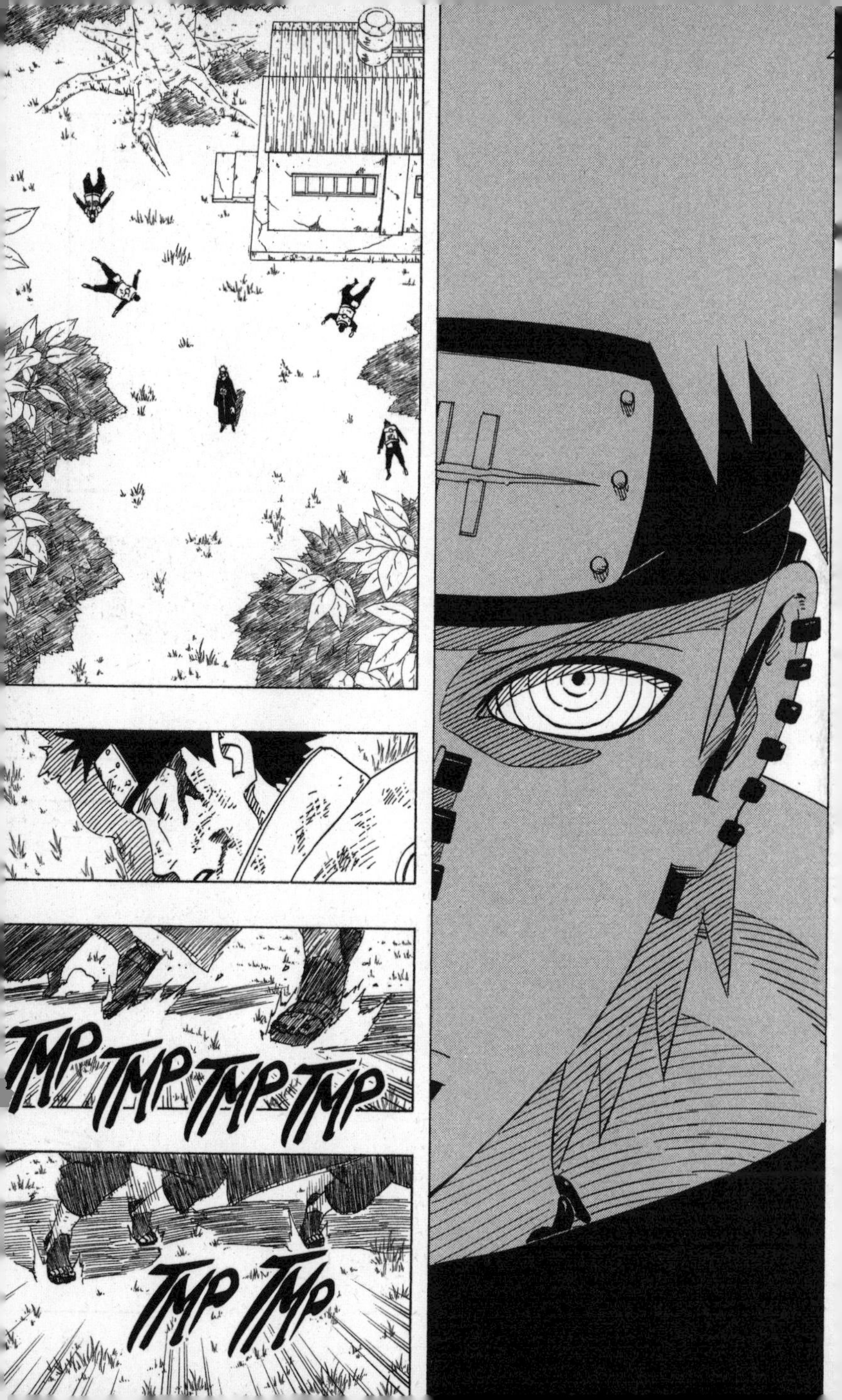
TMP TMP TMP TMP
TMP TMP

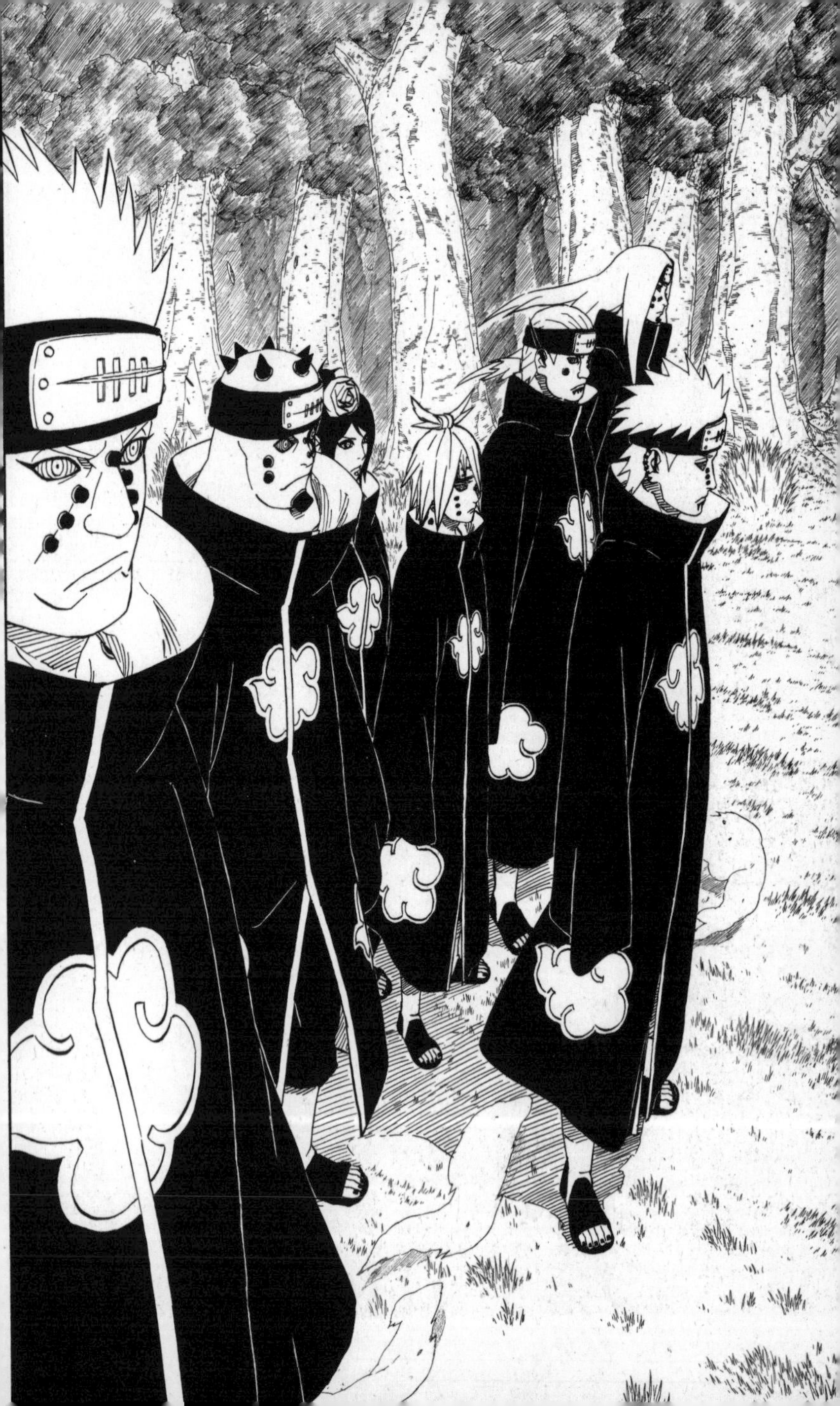

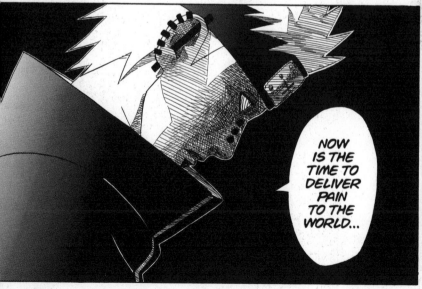

NOW IS THE TIME TO DELIVER PAIN TO THE WORLD...

NARUTO

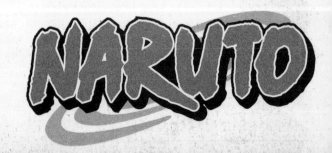

Number 419: Raid!!

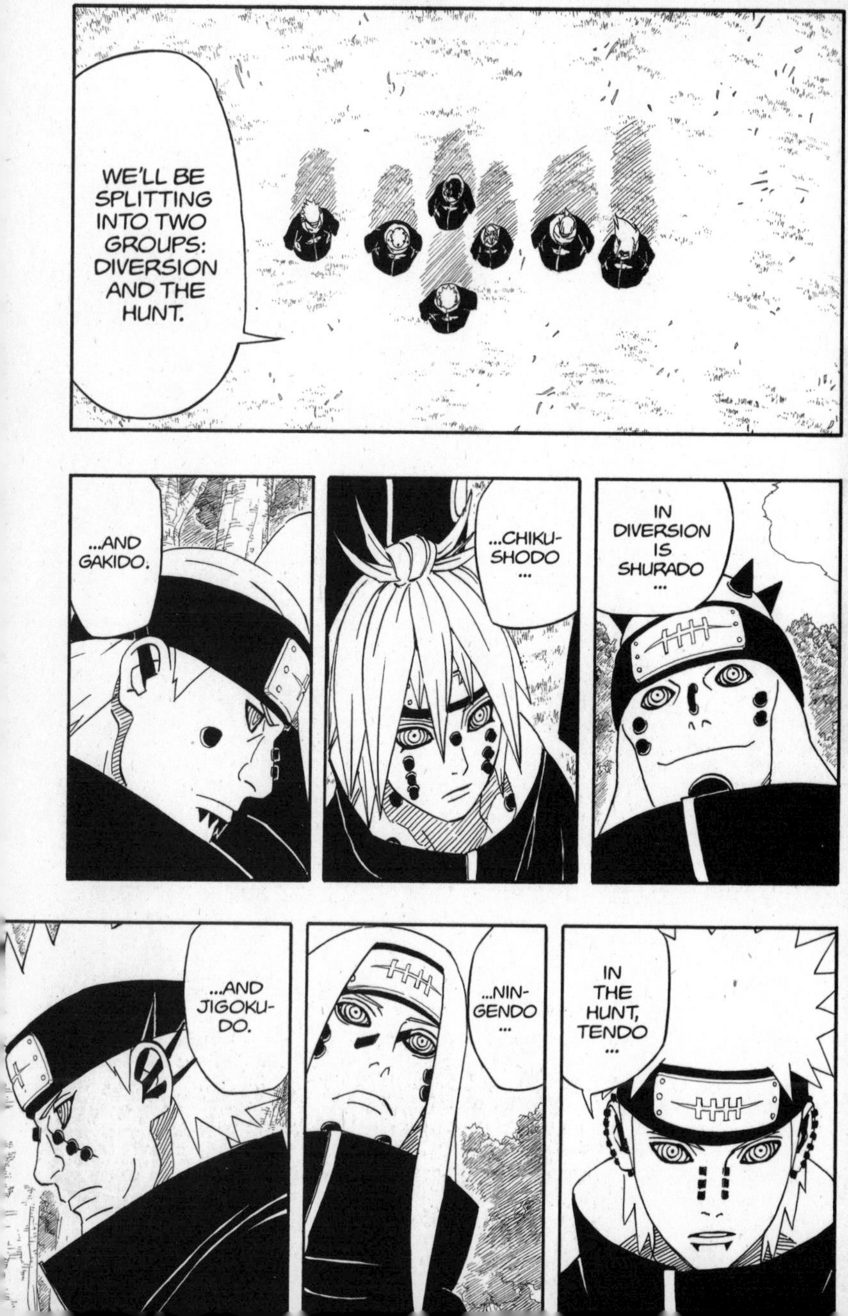
WE'LL BE SPLITTING INTO TWO GROUPS: DIVERSION AND THE HUNT.
IN DIVERSION IS SHURADO ...
...CHIKU-SHODO ...
...AND GAKIDO.
IN THE HUNT, TENDO ...
...NIN-GENDO ...
...AND JIGOKU-DO.

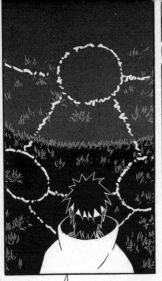

KONAN, YOU'RE WITH THE HUNT.

I KNOW.

KONOHA IS PROTECTED BY A SPHERICAL BARRIER THAT ENCOMPASSES BOTH THE VILLAGE ITSELF AND THE AIR ABOVE IT.

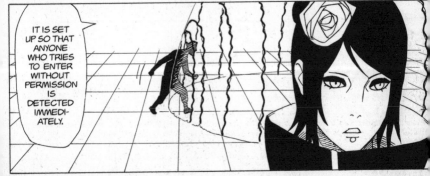

IT IS SET UP SO THAT ANYONE WHO TRIES TO ENTER WITHOUT PERMISSION IS DETECTED IMMEDI-ATELY.

READ THIS WAY

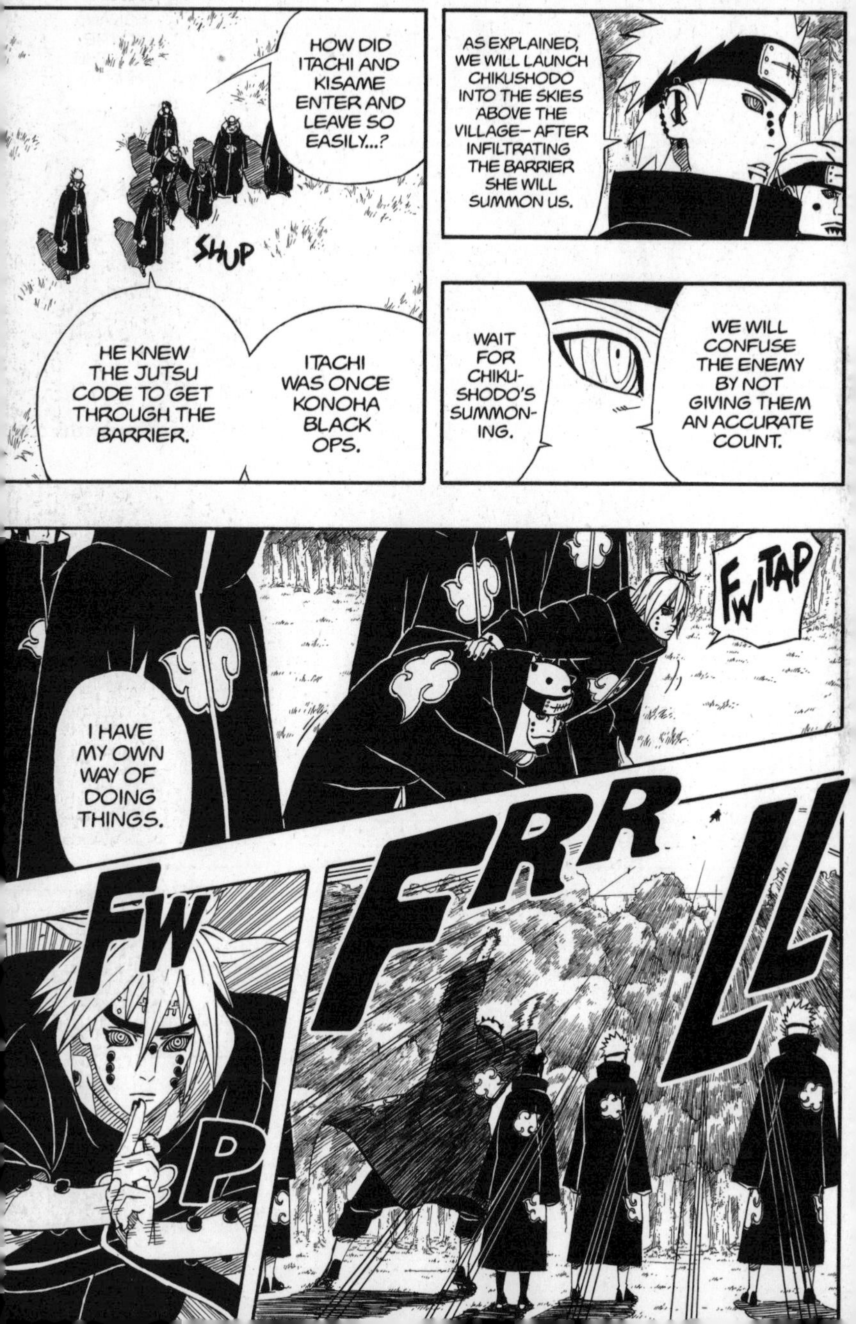

AS EXPLAINED, WE WILL LAUNCH CHIKUSHODO INTO THE SKIES ABOVE THE VILLAGE– AFTER INFILTRATING THE BARRIER SHE WILL SUMMON US.
WE WILL CONFUSE THE ENEMY BY NOT GIVING THEM AN ACCURATE COUNT.
WAIT FOR CHIKU-SHODO'S SUMMON-ING.
HOW DID ITACHI AND KISAME ENTER AND LEAVE SO EASILY...?
SHUP
ITACHI WAS ONCE KONOHA BLACK OPS.
HE KNEW THE JUTSU CODE TO GET THROUGH THE BARRIER.
FWITAP
I HAVE MY OWN WAY OF DOING THINGS.
FW
FRRLL
P

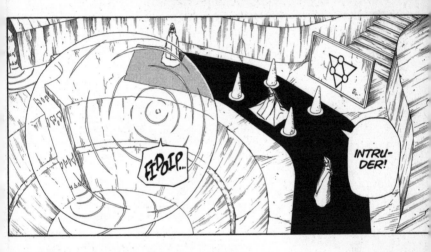

FI-DIP...

INTRU-DER!

FSH

SINGLE TARGET, WEST GATE, SECTOR 1-B.

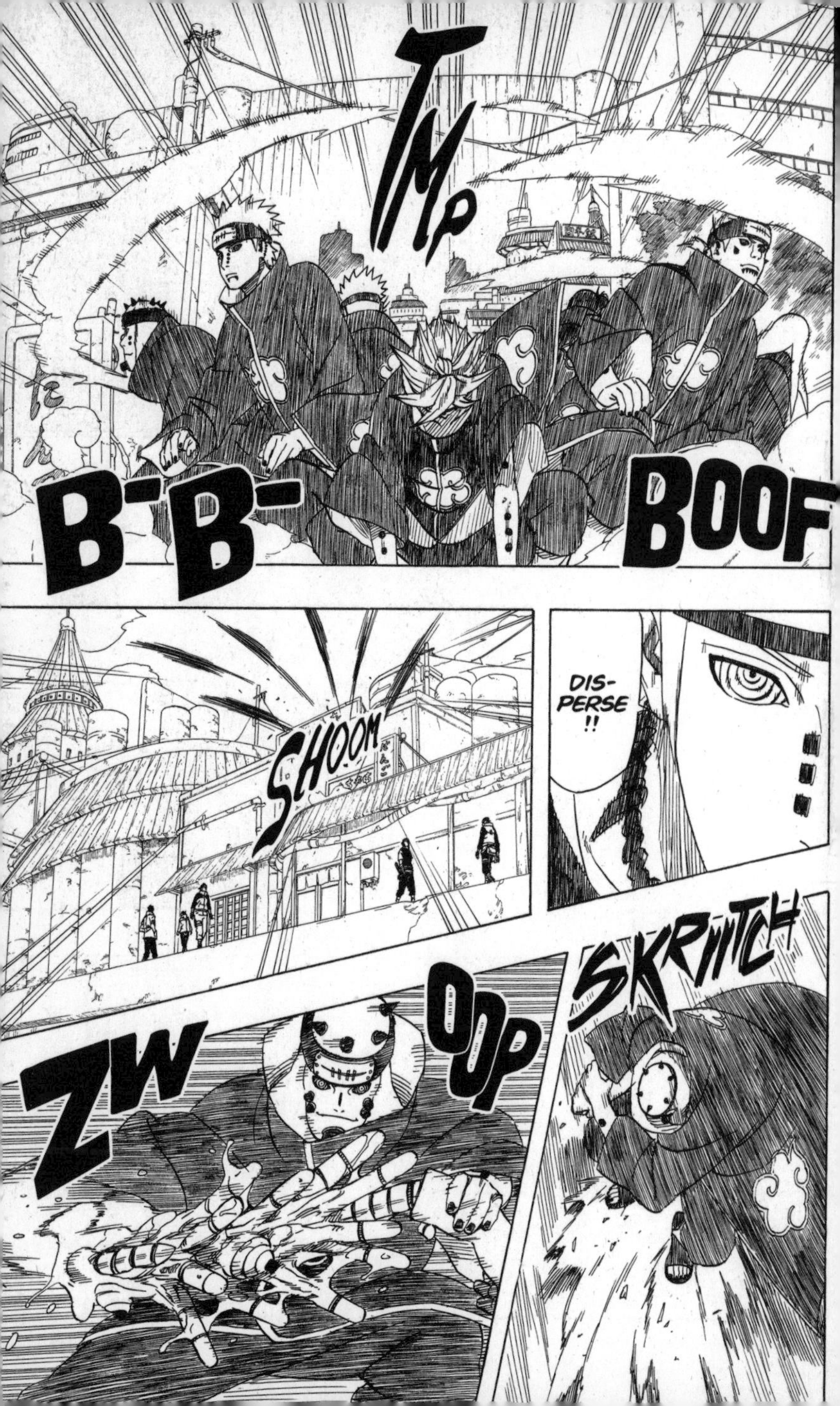
TMP
B-B-BOOF
DIS-PERSE !!
SHOOM
SKRIIITCH
ZWOOP

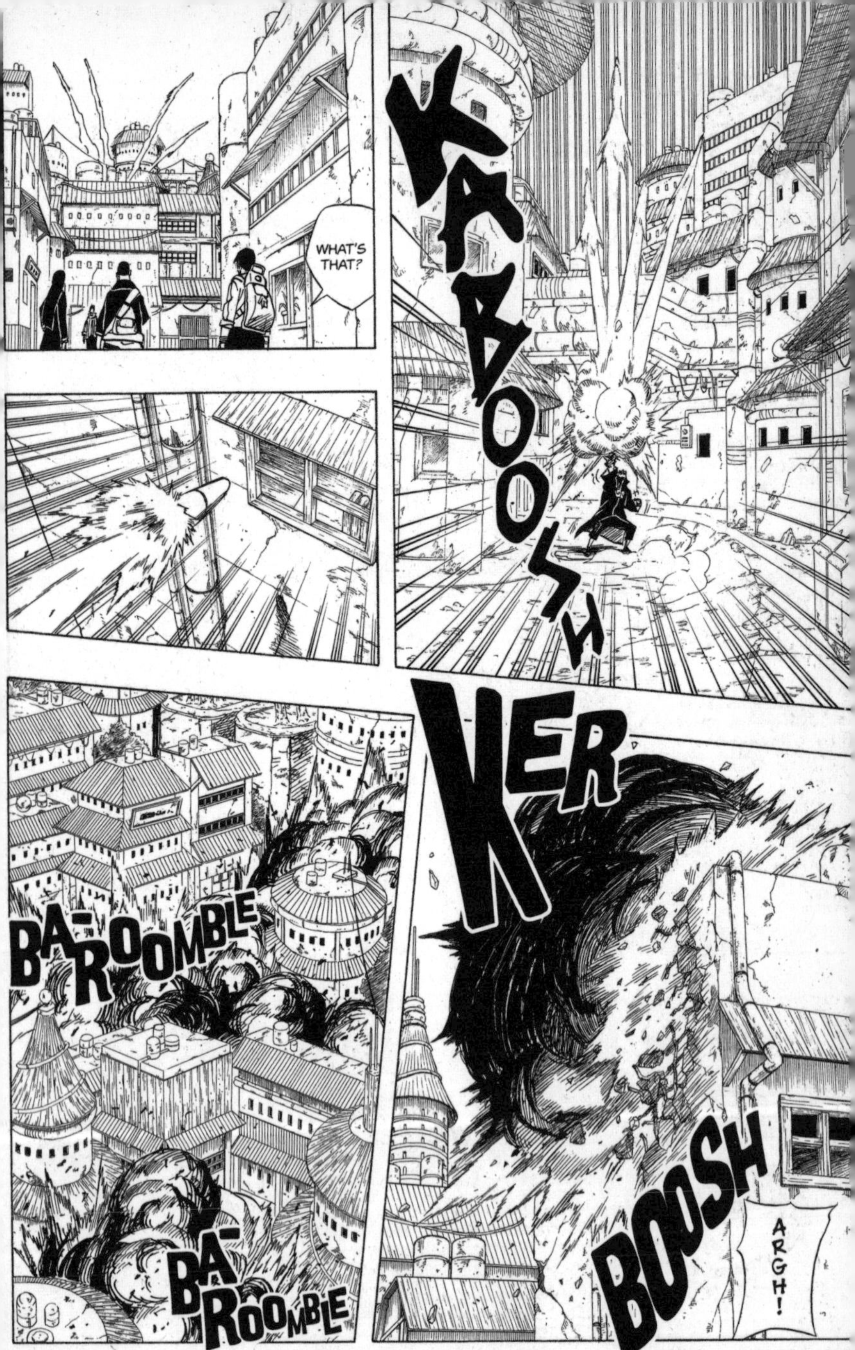
KABOOSH
WHAT'S THAT?
VERK
BOOSH
ARGH!
BA-ROOMBLE
BA-ROOMBLE

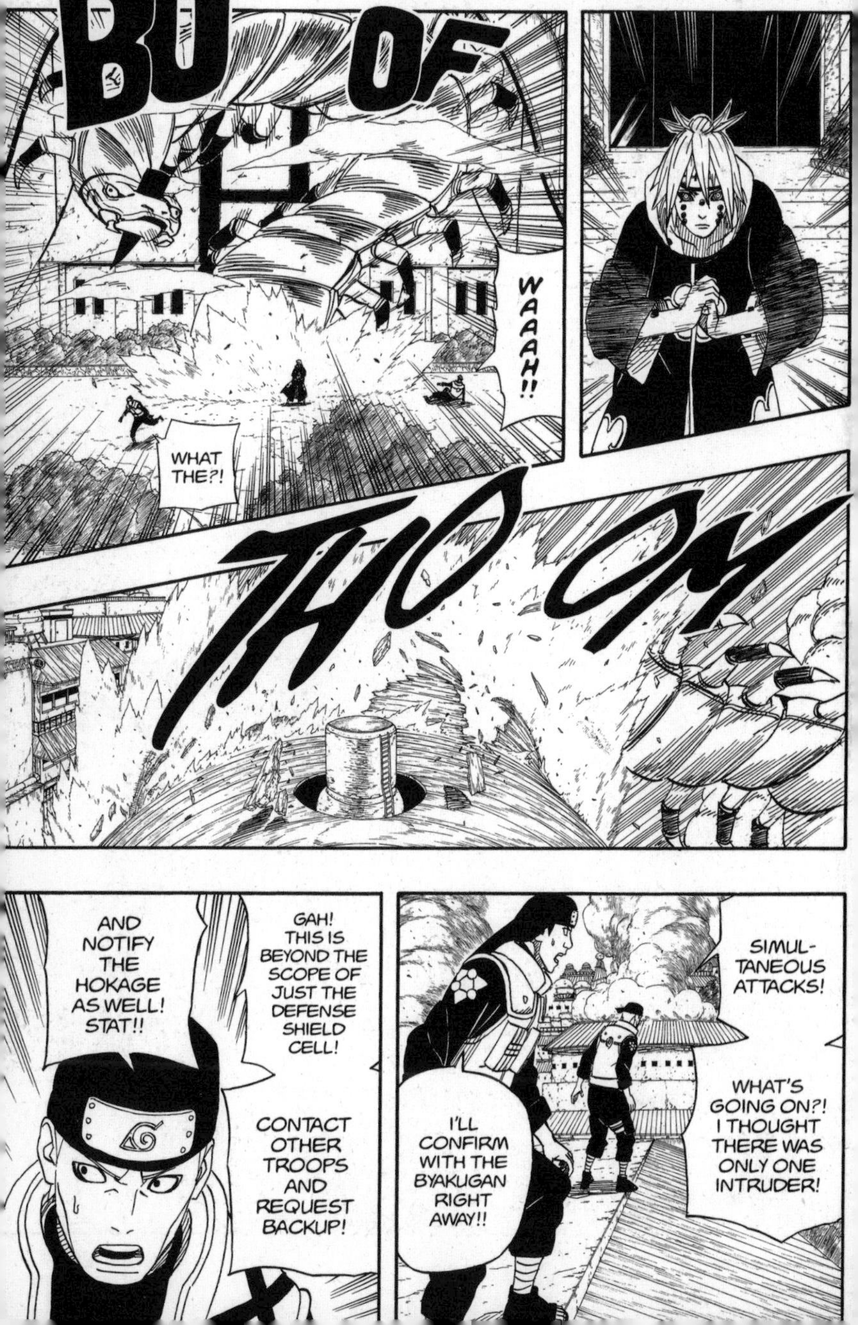
BOOF
WAAAAH!!
WHAT THE?!
THOOM
SIMUL-TANEOUS ATTACKS!
WHAT'S GOING ON?! I THOUGHT THERE WAS ONLY ONE INTRUDER!
I'LL CONFIRM WITH THE BYAKUGAN RIGHT AWAY!!
GAH! THIS IS BEYOND THE SCOPE OF JUST THE DEFENSE SHIELD CELL!
CONTACT OTHER TROOPS AND REQUEST BACKUP!
AND NOTIFY THE HOKAGE AS WELL! STAT!!

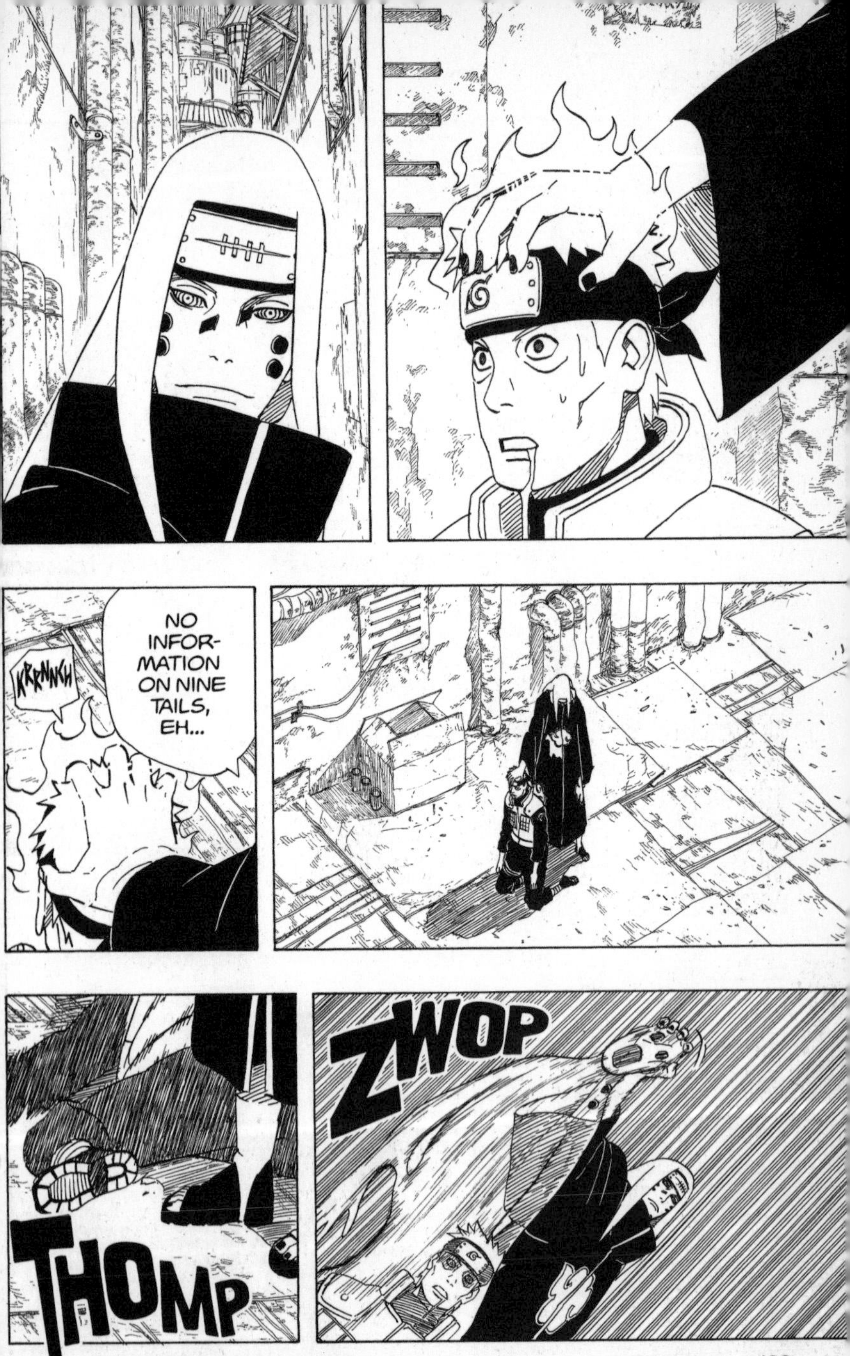
NO INFORMATION ON NINE TAILS, EH...
KRRNNCH
ZWOP
THOMP

READ THIS WAY

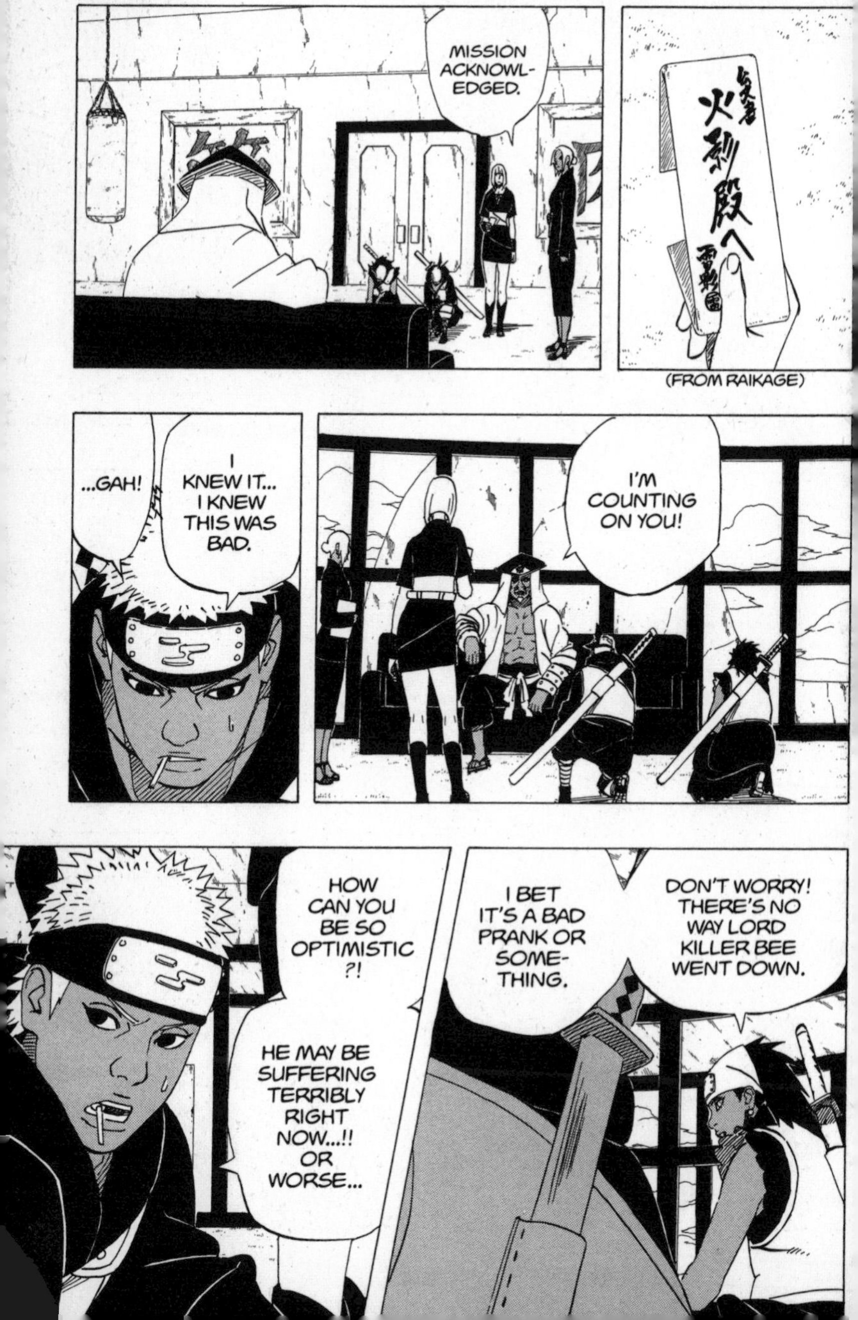

火影殿へ
雷影
(FROM RAIKAGE)
MISSION ACKNOWL-EDGED.
I'M COUNTING ON YOU!
I KNEW IT... I KNEW THIS WAS BAD.
...GAH!
DON'T WORRY! THERE'S NO WAY LORD KILLER BEE WENT DOWN.
I BET IT'S A BAD PRANK OR SOME-THING.
HOW CAN YOU BE SO OPTIMISTIC?!
HE MAY BE SUFFERING TERRIBLY RIGHT NOW...!! OR WORSE...

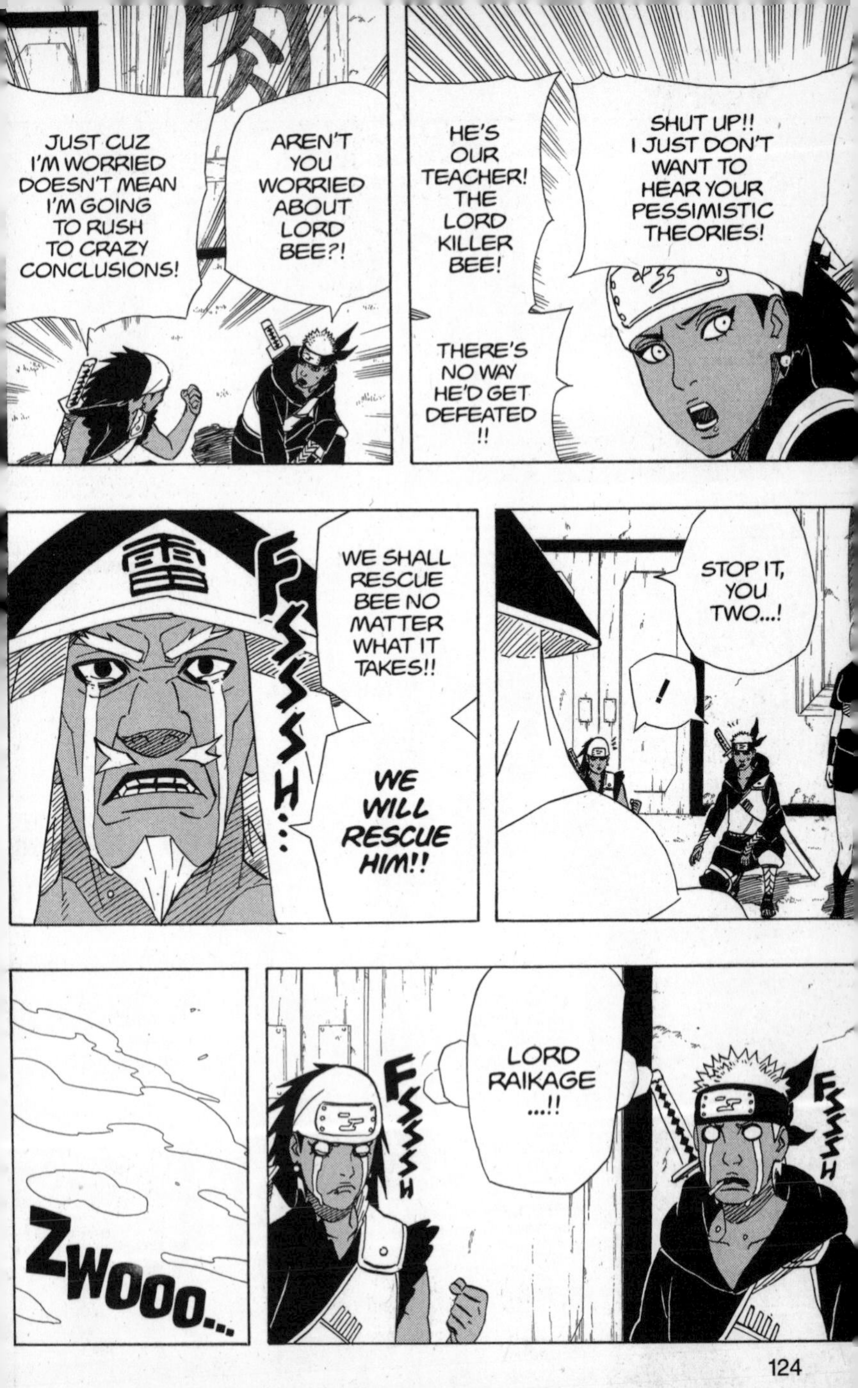

JUST CUZ I'M WORRIED DOESN'T MEAN I'M GOING TO RUSH TO CRAZY CONCLUSIONS!
AREN'T YOU WORRIED ABOUT LORD BEE?!
HE'S OUR TEACHER! THE LORD KILLER BEE!
THERE'S NO WAY HE'D GET DEFEATED !!
SHUT UP!! I JUST DON'T WANT TO HEAR YOUR PESSIMISTIC THEORIES!
FSSSH...
WE SHALL RESCUE BEE NO MATTER WHAT IT TAKES!!
WE WILL RESCUE HIM!!
STOP IT, YOU TWO...!
!
ZWOOO...
FSSSH
LORD RAIKAGE ...!!
FSSSH

READ THIS WAY

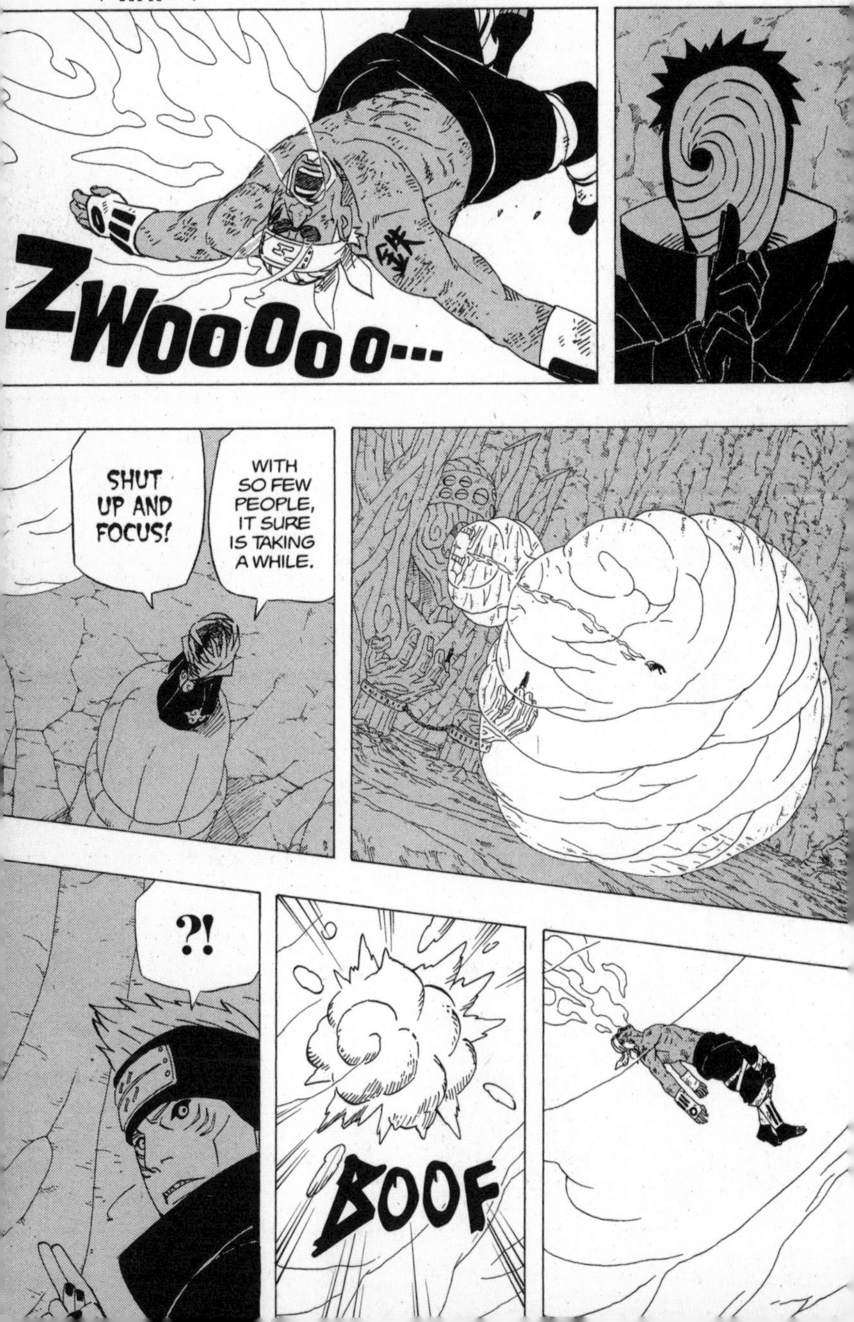
ZWOOOOO...
WITH SO FEW PEOPLE, IT SURE IS TAKING A WHILE.
SHUT UP AND FOCUS!
BOOF
?!

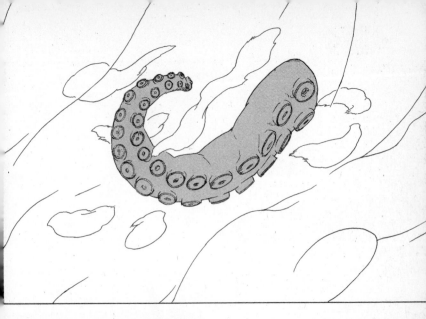

SPLAT

IT APPEARS... SASUKE HAS BLUNDERED ...

SWSH

TK-IK TK-IK

IT'S NOT FUNNY!

A-HA-HA-HA! IT'S AN OCTOPUS LEG!

...

READ THIS WAY

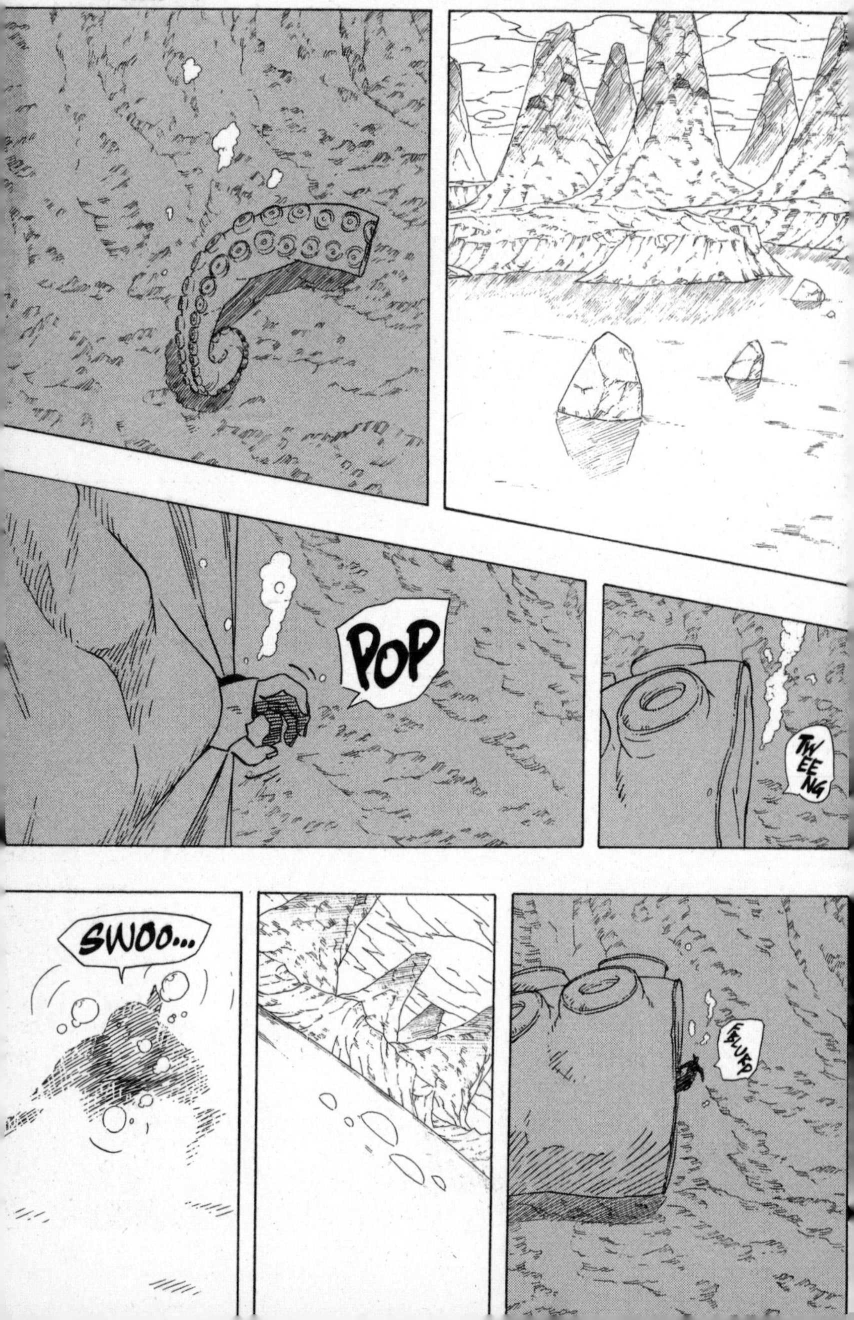
TWEENG
POP
FSLURP
SWOO...

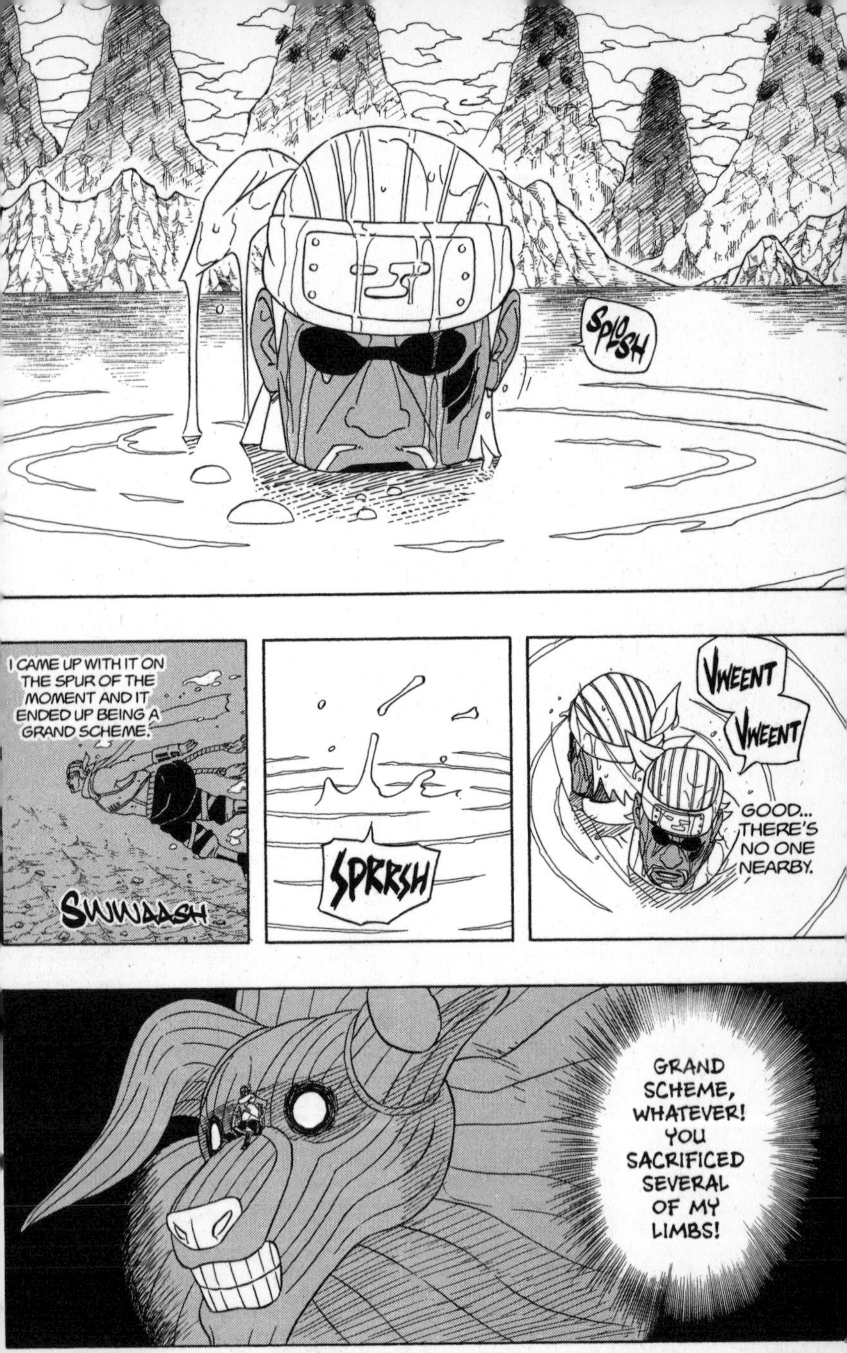
SPLOSH
VWEENT
VWEENT
GOOD... THERE'S NO ONE NEARBY.
SPRRSH
I CAME UP WITH IT ON THE SPUR OF THE MOMENT AND IT ENDED UP BEING A GRAND SCHEME.
SWWAASH
GRAND SCHEME, WHATEVER! YOU SACRIFICED SEVERAL OF MY LIMBS!

READ THIS WAY

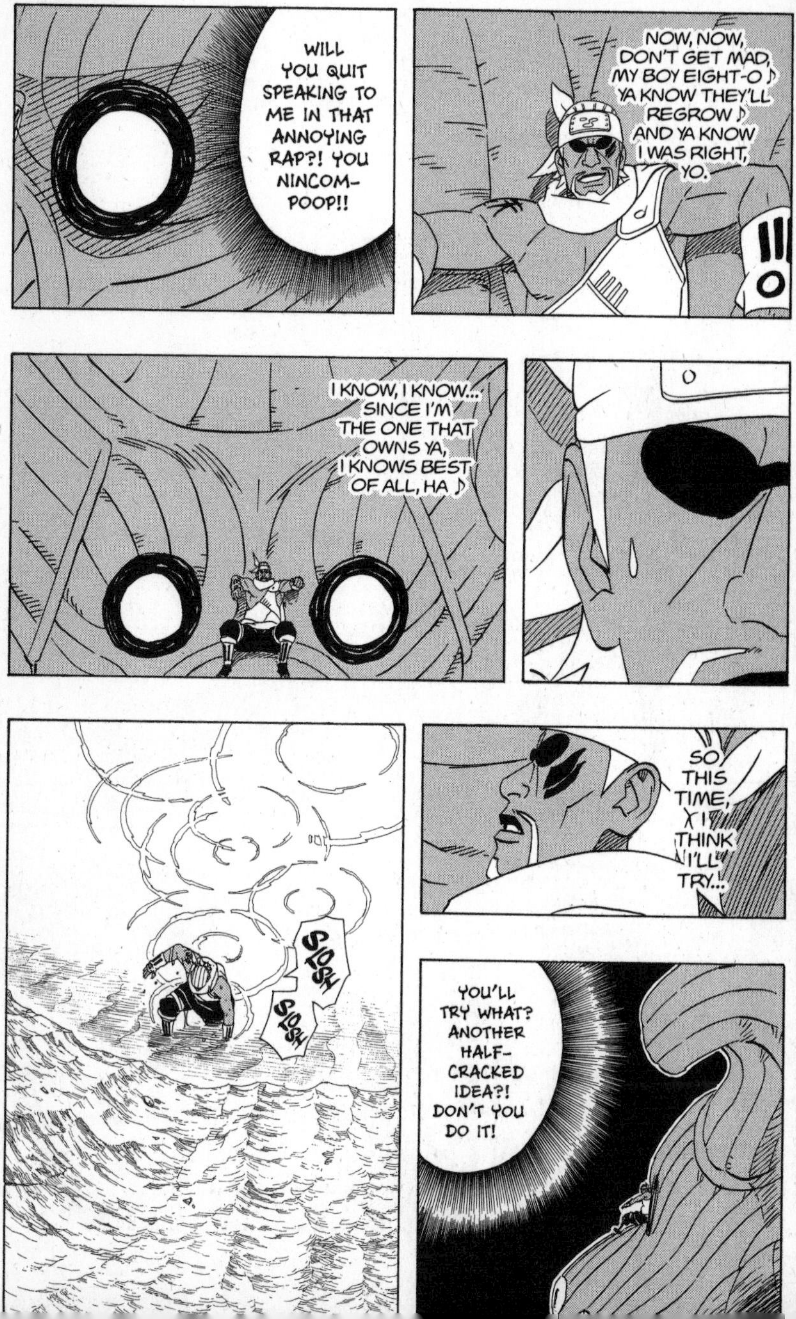

NOW, NOW, DON'T GET MAD, MY BOY EIGHT-O♪ YA KNOW THEY'LL REGROW♪ AND YA KNOW I WAS RIGHT, YO.
WILL YOU QUIT SPEAKING TO ME IN THAT ANNOYING RAP?! YOU NINCOMPOOP!!
I KNOW, I KNOW... SINCE I'M THE ONE THAT OWNS YA, I KNOWS BEST OF ALL, HA♪
SO THIS TIME, I THINK I'LL TRY...
YOU'LL TRY WHAT? ANOTHER HALF-CRACKED IDEA?! DON'T YOU DO IT!
SLOSH
SLOSH

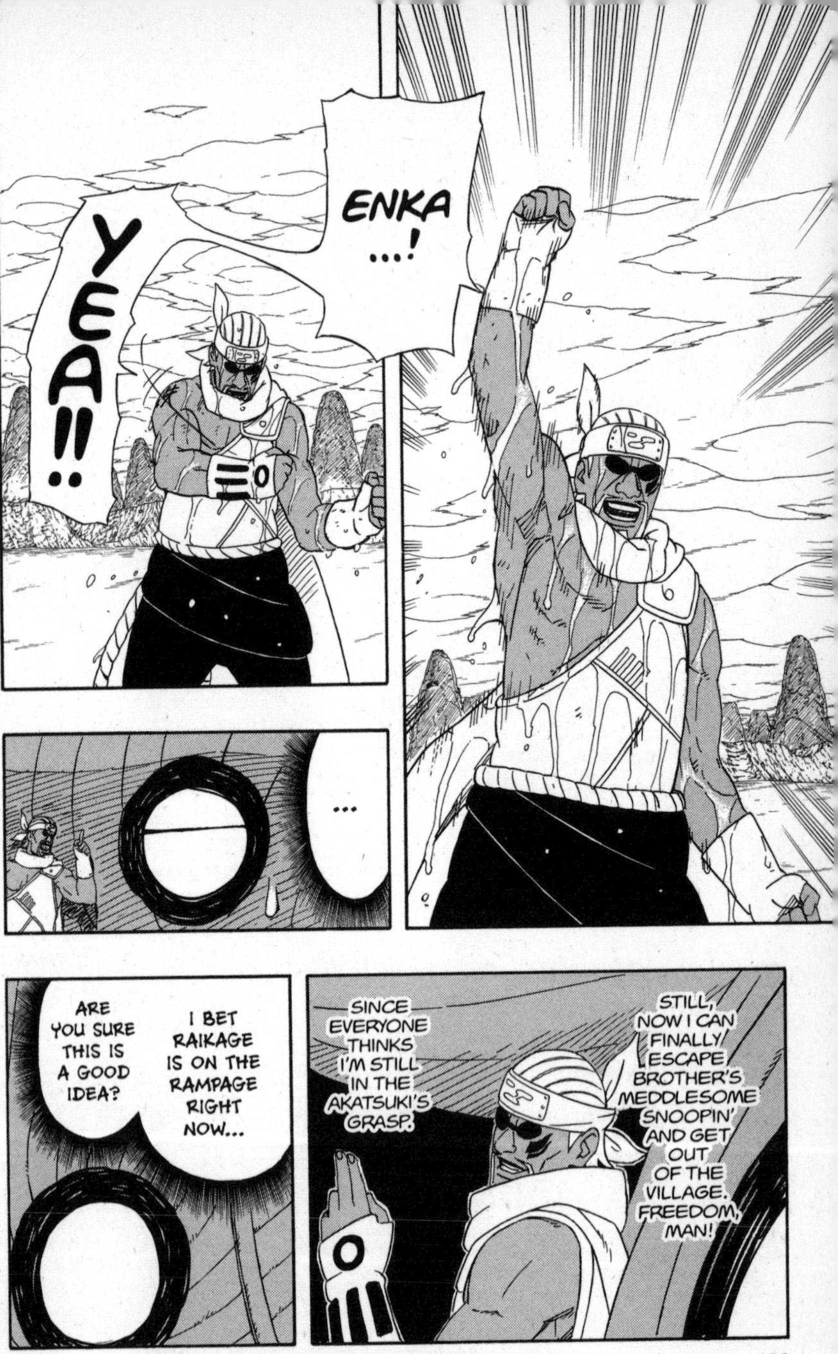
ENKA ...!
YEA!!
...
STILL, NOW I CAN FINALLY ESCAPE BROTHER'S MEDDLESOME SNOOPIN' AND GET OUT OF THE VILLAGE. FREEDOM, MAN!
SINCE EVERYONE THINKS I'M STILL IN THE AKATSUKI'S GRASP.
I BET RAIKAGE IS ON THE RAMPAGE RIGHT NOW...
ARE YOU SURE THIS IS A GOOD IDEA?

READ THIS WAY

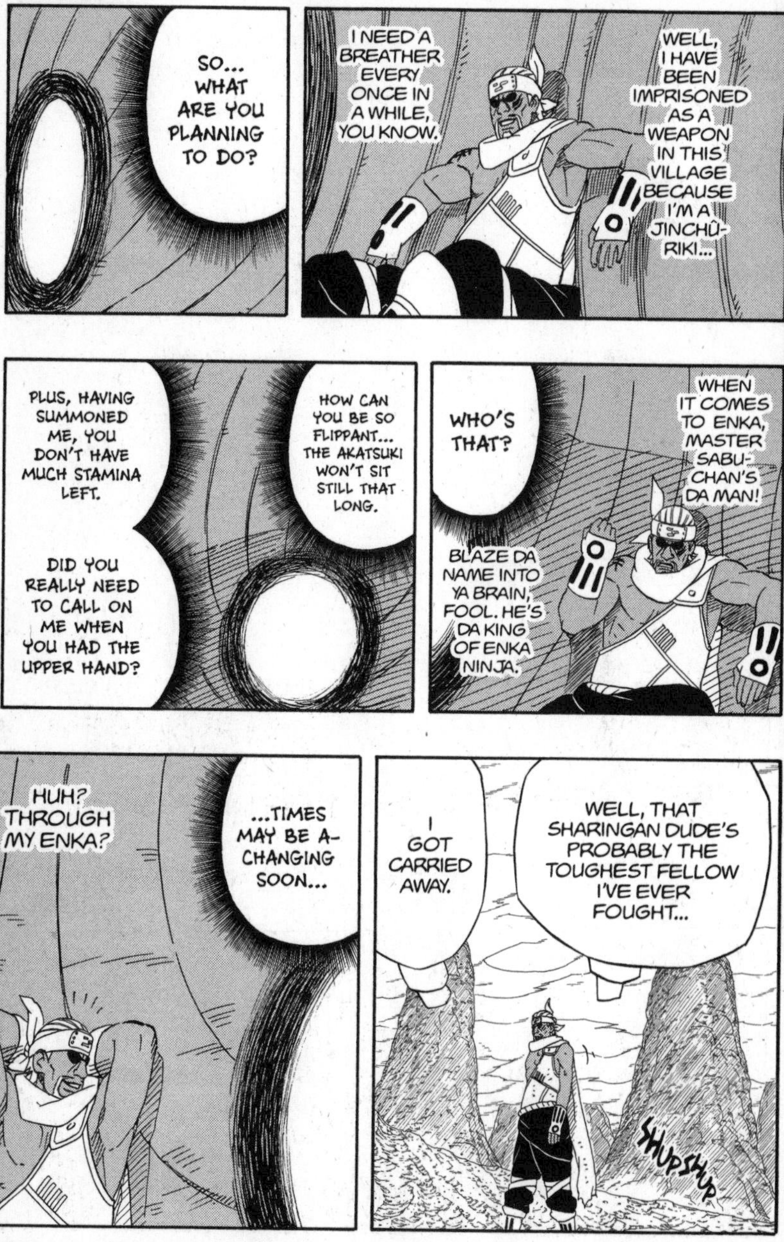
WELL, I HAVE BEEN IMPRISONED AS A WEAPON IN THIS VILLAGE BECAUSE I'M A JINCHŪ-RIKI...
I NEED A BREATHER EVERY ONCE IN A WHILE, YOU KNOW.
SO... WHAT ARE YOU PLANNING TO DO?
WHEN IT COMES TO ENKA, MASTER SABU-CHAN'S DA MAN!
WHO'S THAT?
BLAZE DA NAME INTO YA BRAIN, FOOL. HE'S DA KING OF ENKA NINJA.
HOW CAN YOU BE SO FLIPPANT... THE AKATSUKI WON'T SIT STILL THAT LONG.
PLUS, HAVING SUMMONED ME, YOU DON'T HAVE MUCH STAMINA LEFT.
DID YOU REALLY NEED TO CALL ON ME WHEN YOU HAD THE UPPER HAND?
WELL, THAT SHARINGAN DUDE'S PROBABLY THE TOUGHEST FELLOW I'VE EVER FOUGHT...
I GOT CARRIED AWAY.
SHUPSHUP
...TIMES MAY BE A-CHANGING SOON...
HUH? THROUGH MY ENKA?

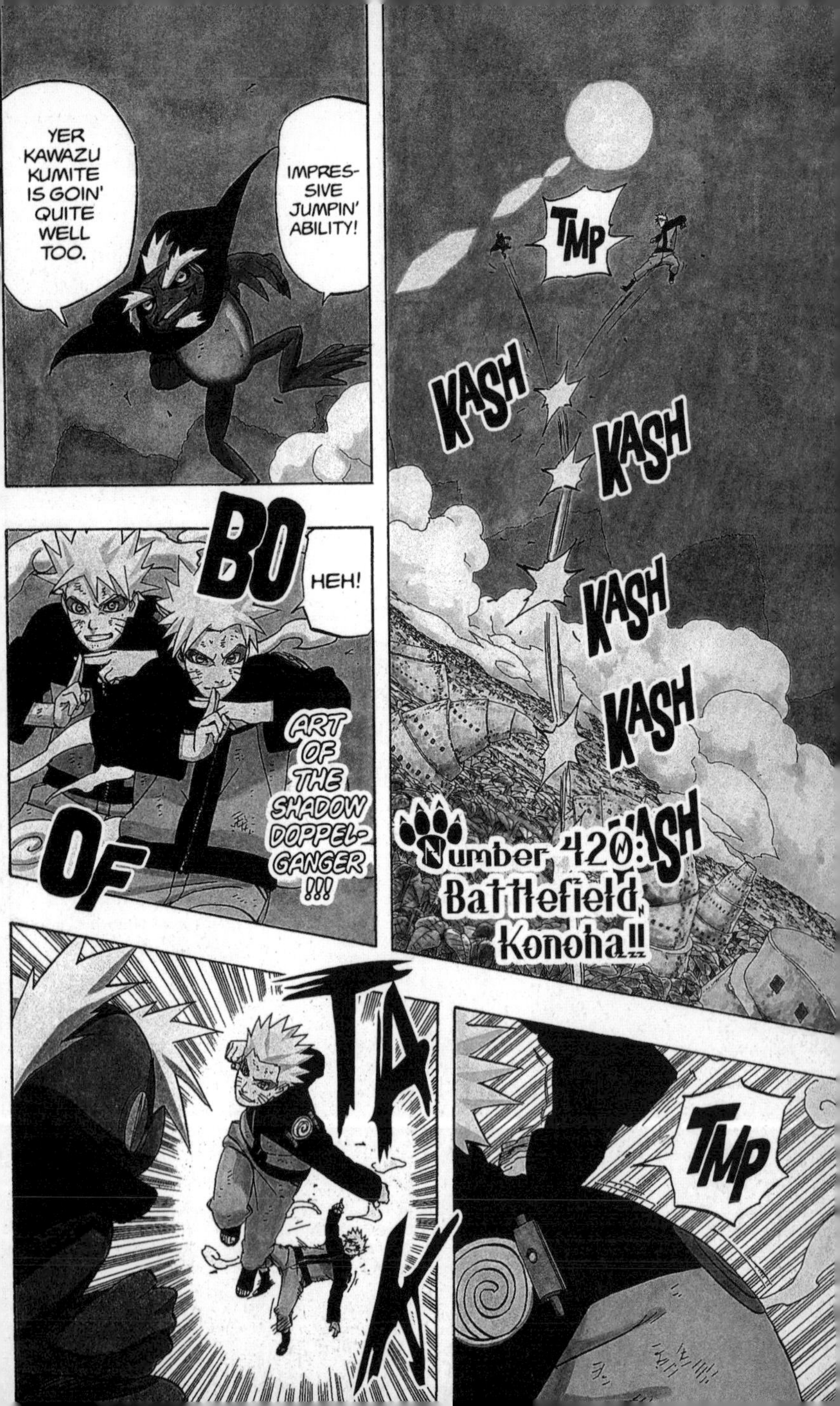

TMP
KASH
KASH
KASH
KASH
KASH
Number 420: Battlefield, Konoha!!
IMPRES-SIVE JUMPIN' ABILITY!
YER KAWAZU KUMITE IS GOIN' QUITE WELL TOO.
HEH!
BO
OF
ART OF THE SHADOW DOPPEL-GANGER!!!
TMP
TA
K

READ THIS WAY

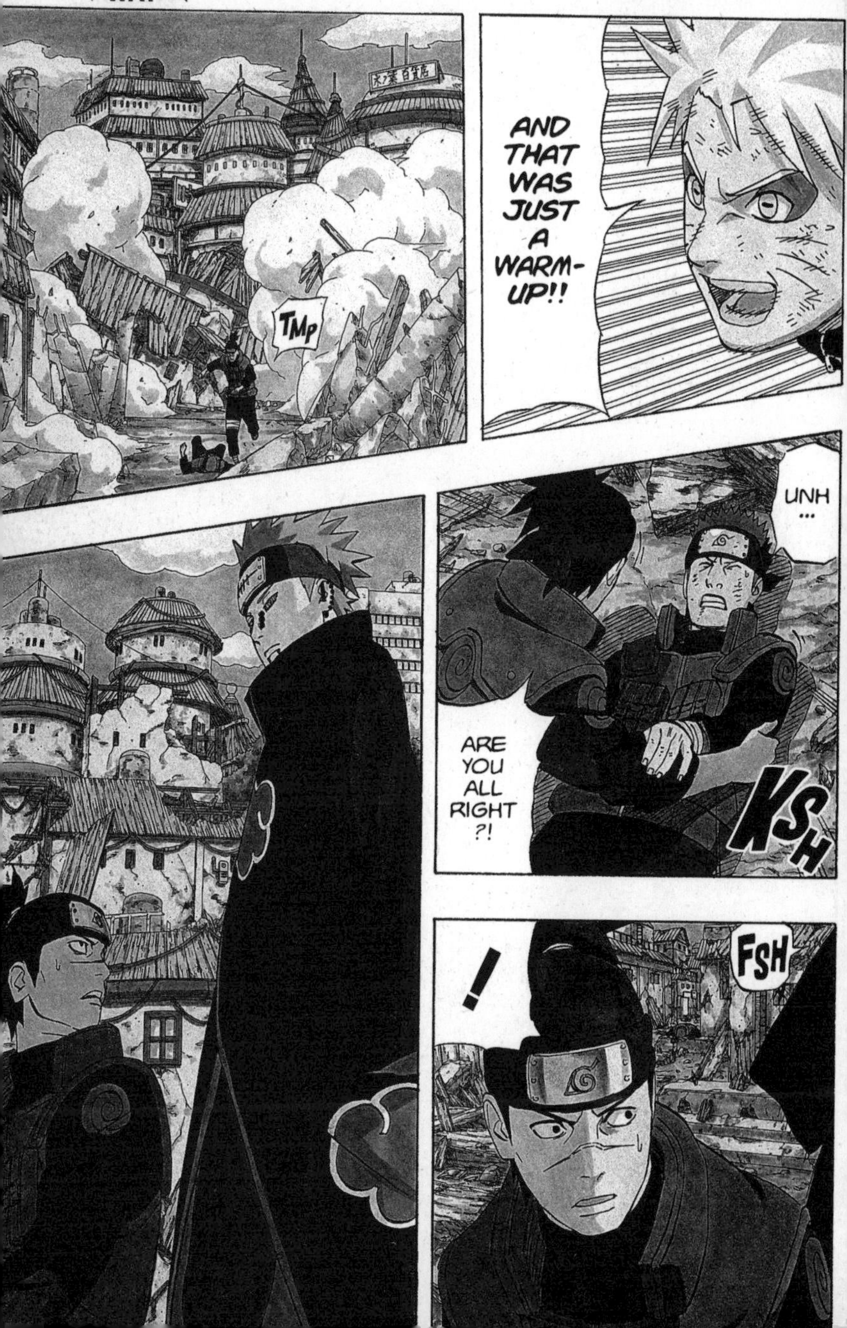
AND THAT WAS JUST A WARM-UP!!
TMP
UNH...
ARE YOU ALL RIGHT?!
KSH
!
FSH

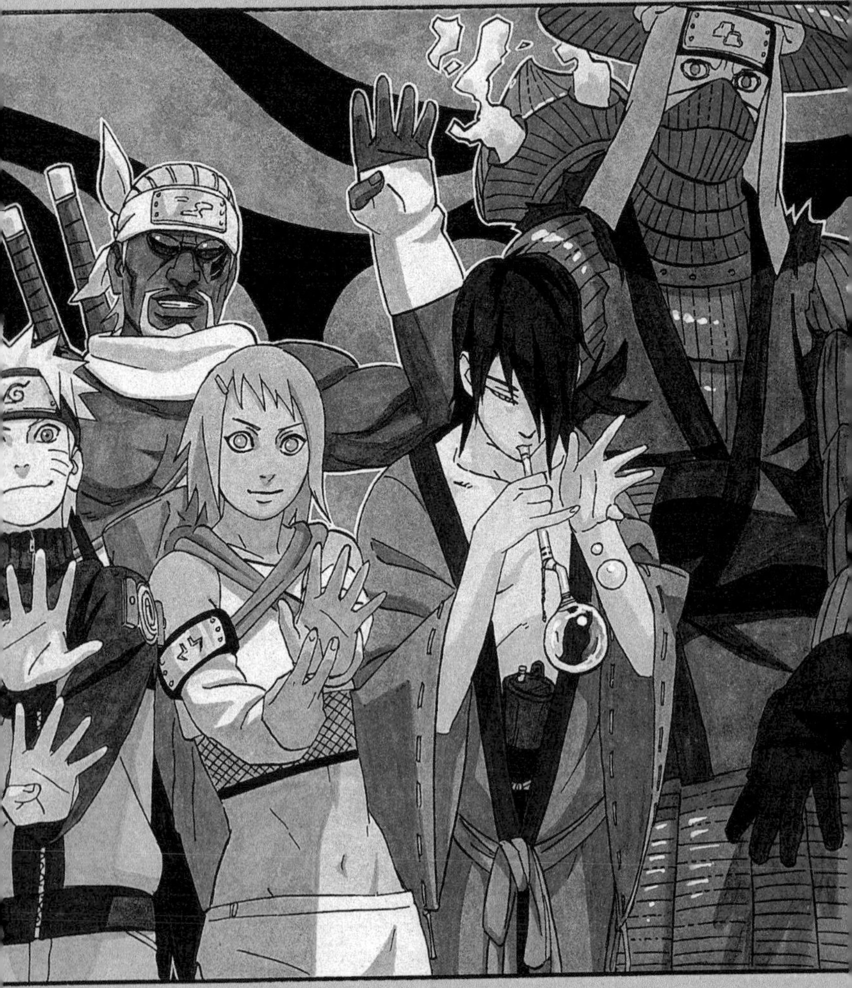

Number 420: Battlefield, Konoha!!

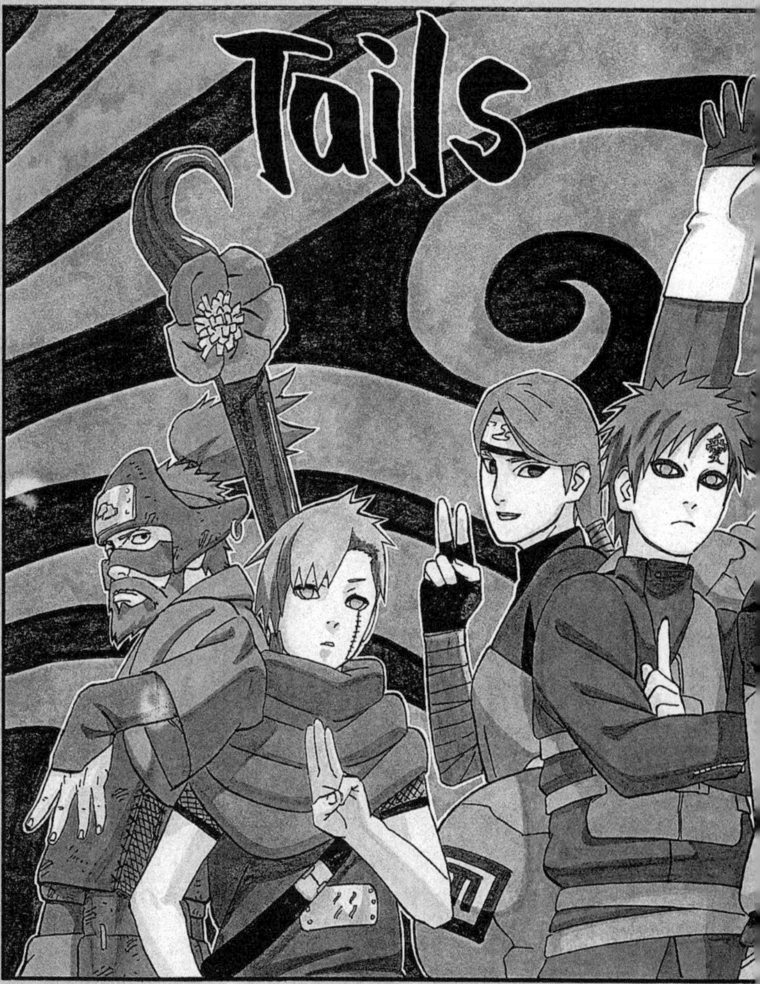
Tails

NARUTO

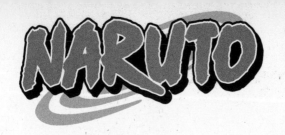

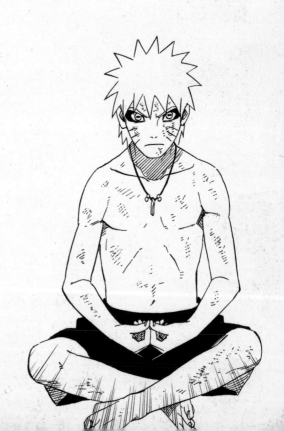

READ THIS WAY

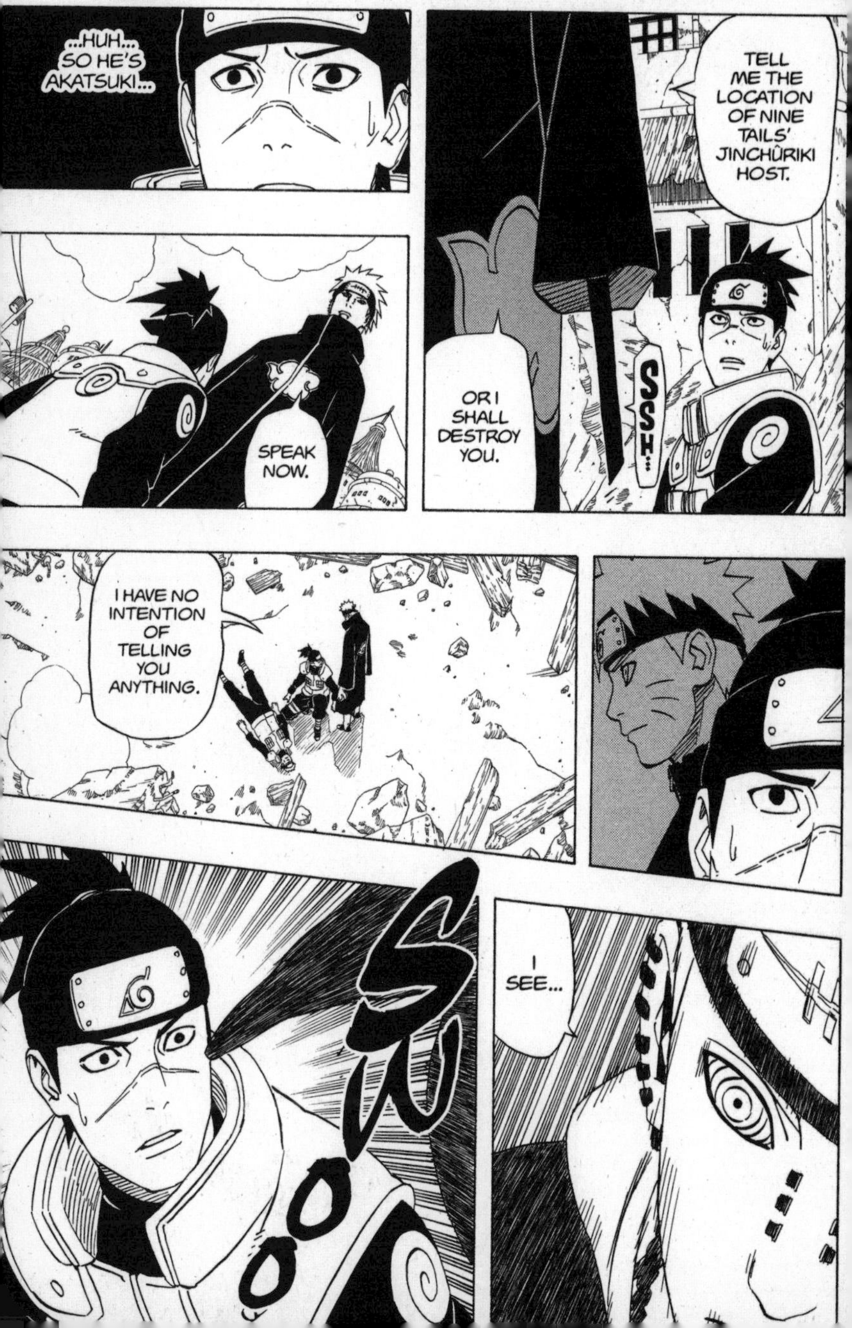
TELL ME THE LOCATION OF NINE TAILS' JINCHÛRIKI HOST.
SSH...
OR I SHALL DESTROY YOU.
...HUH... SO HE'S AKATSUKI...
SPEAK NOW.
I HAVE NO INTENTION OF TELLING YOU ANYTHING.
I SEE...

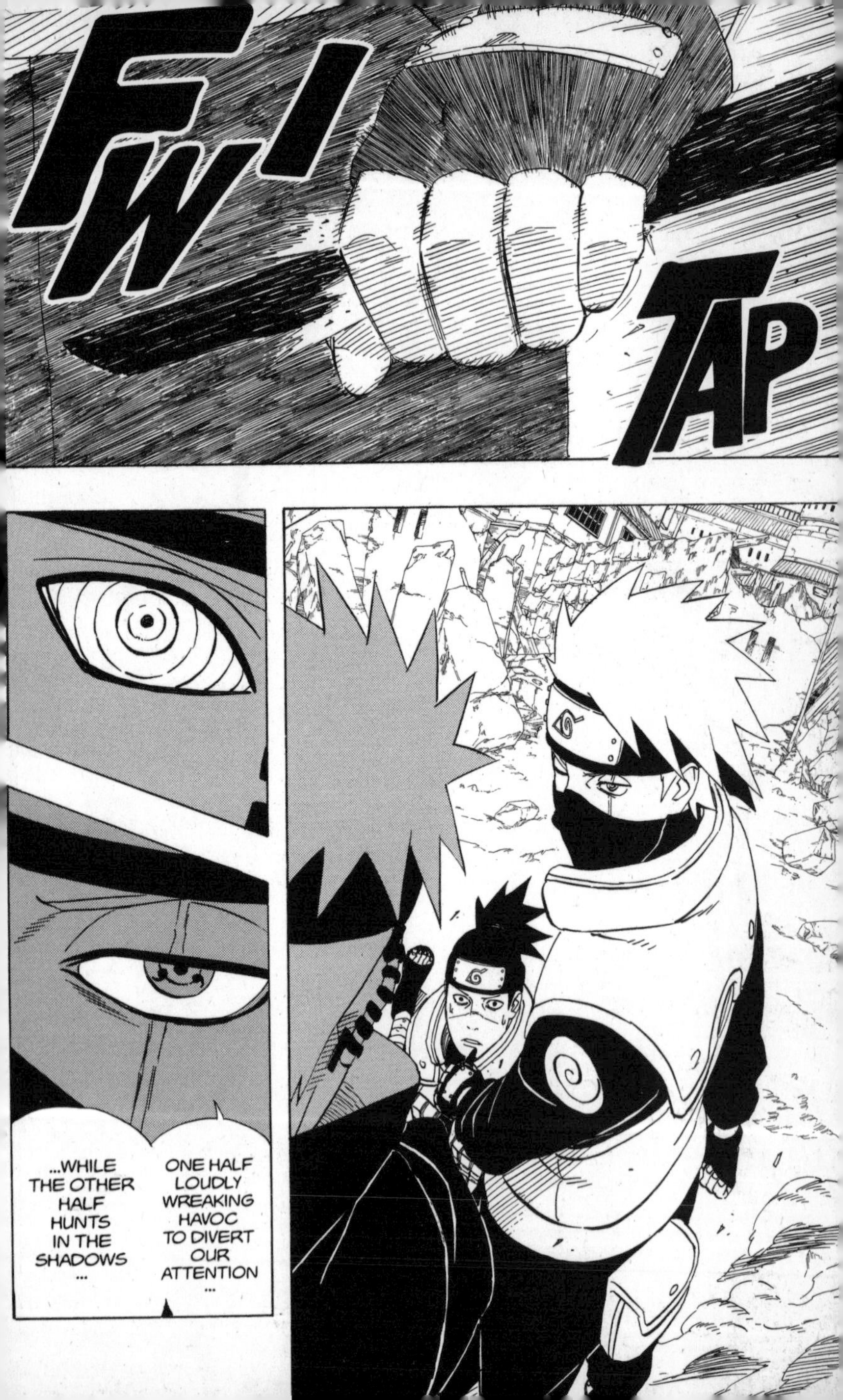
FWI
TAP
ONE HALF LOUDLY WREAKING HAVOC TO DIVERT OUR ATTENTION...
...WHILE THE OTHER HALF HUNTS IN THE SHADOWS...

READ THIS WAY

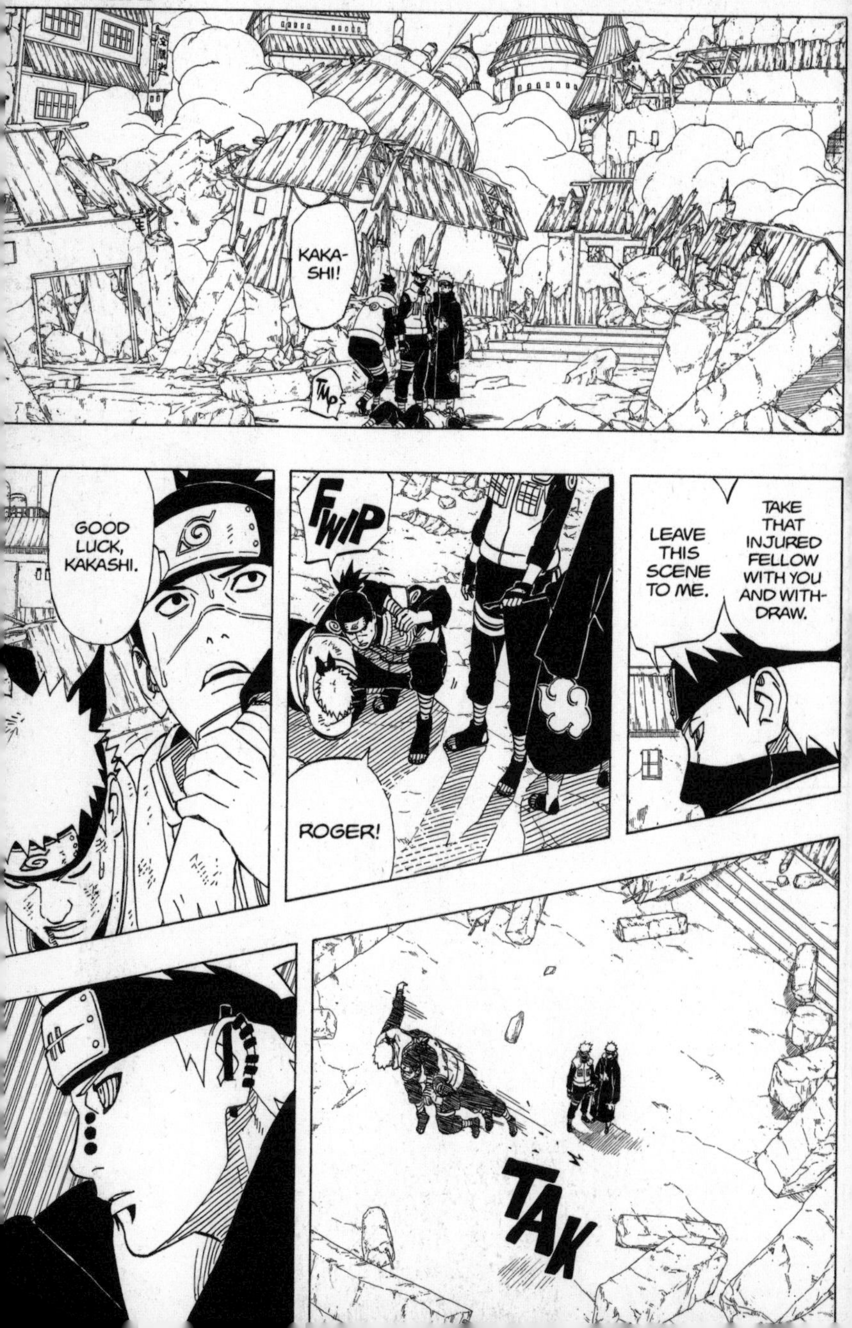

KAKA-SHI!
TMP
TAKE THAT INJURED FELLOW WITH YOU AND WITH-DRAW.
LEAVE THIS SCENE TO ME.
FWIP
ROGER!
GOOD LUCK, KAKASHI.
TAK

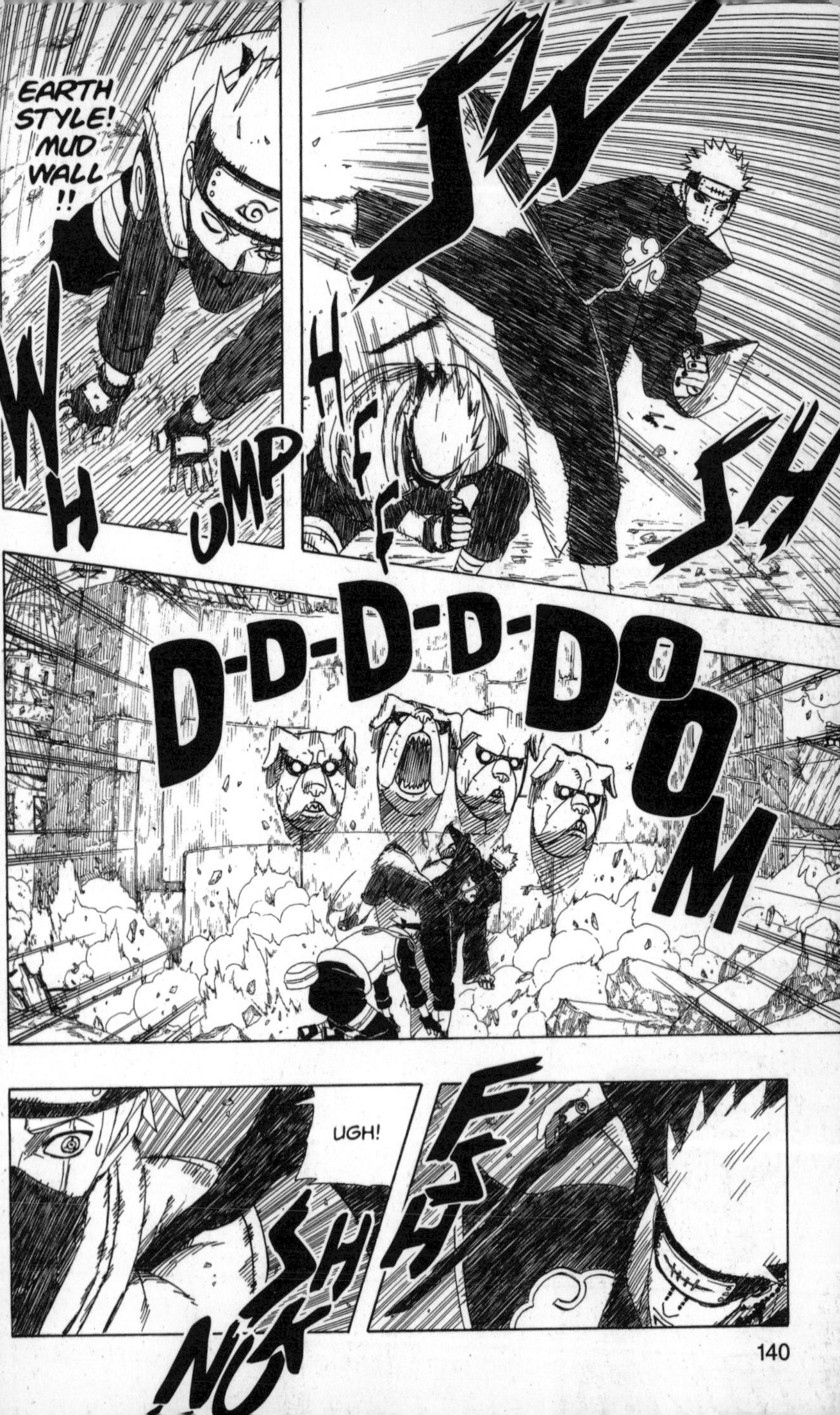

SW
SH
HFF
EARTH STYLE! MUD WALL!!
WHUMP
D-D-D-D-DOOM
FSSH
UGH!
NSHH

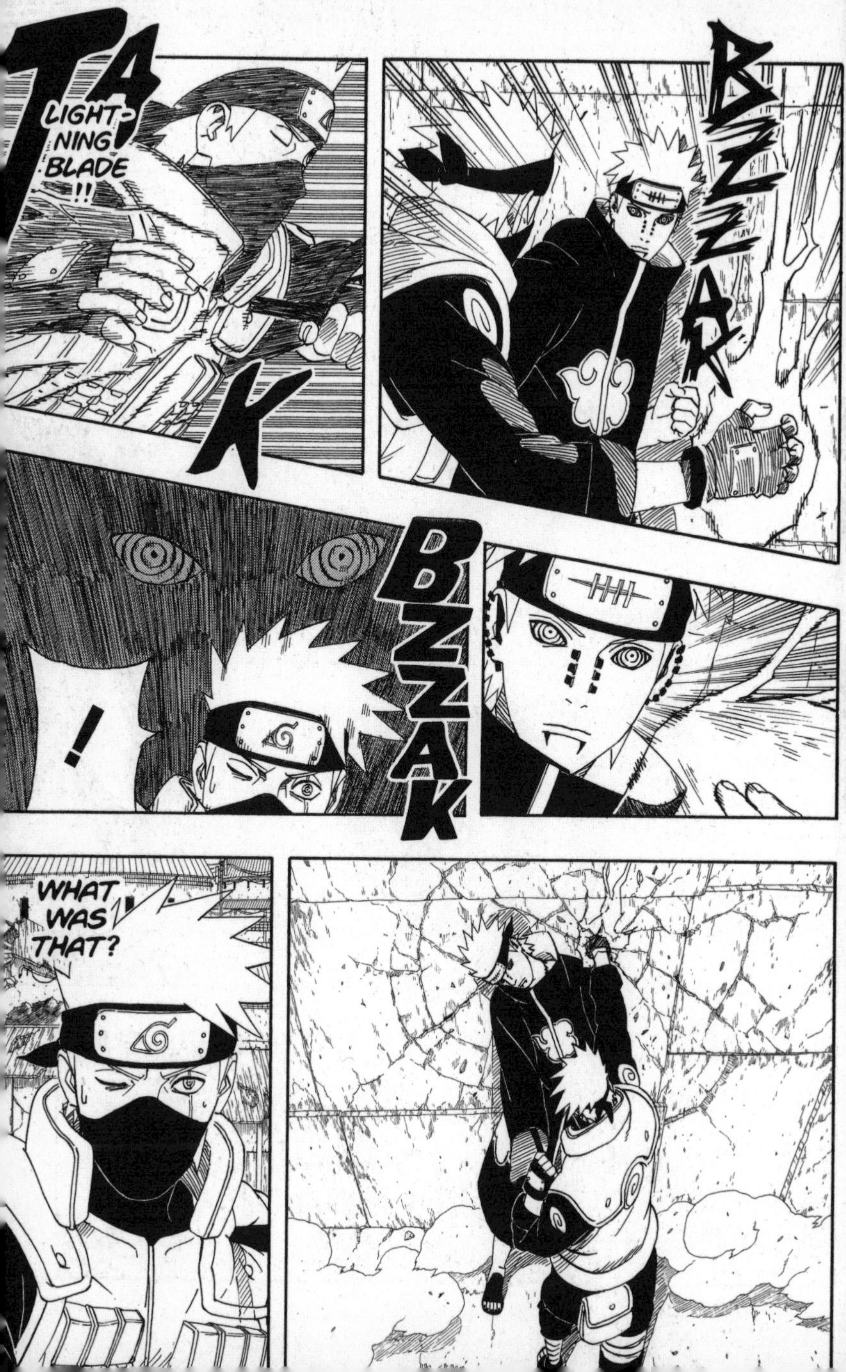
BZZZAK
TAK
LIGHTNING BLADE!!
BZZAK
!
WHAT WAS THAT?

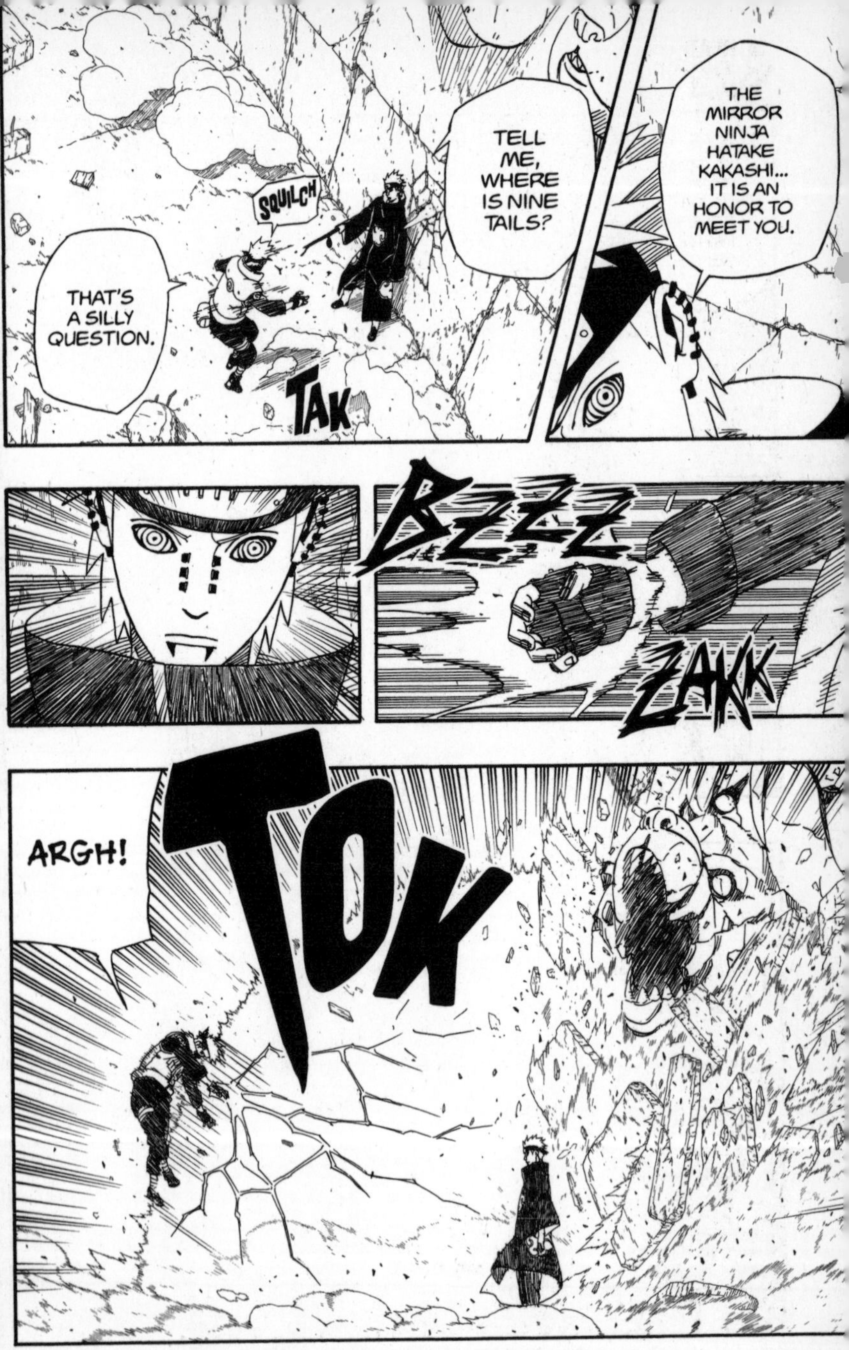
THE MIRROR NINJA HATAKE KAKASHI... IT IS AN HONOR TO MEET YOU.
TELL ME, WHERE IS NINE TAILS?
SQUILCH
THAT'S A SILLY QUESTION.
TAK
BZZZ
ZAKK
TOK
ARGH!

ALL RIGHT, I'M GONNA PROCURE US SOME FRESH INGREDIENTS.

ZZURP

MA, GET SOME STAMINA-BUILDIN' STUFF, EH!

NOT GROSS STUFF AGAIN... UGH...

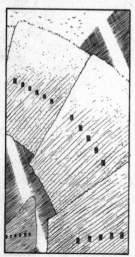

143

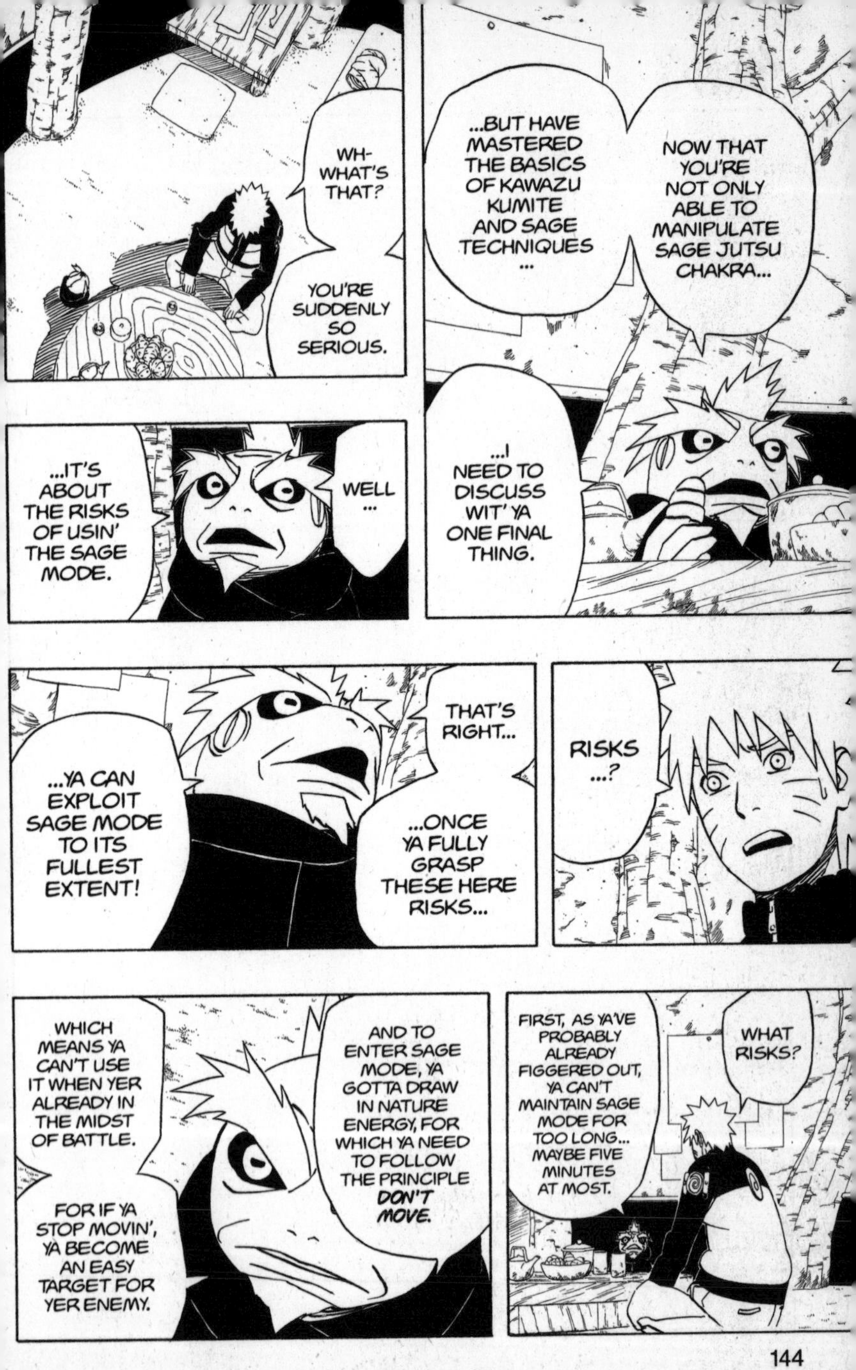
NOW THAT YOU'RE NOT ONLY ABLE TO MANIPULATE SAGE JUTSU CHAKRA...
...BUT HAVE MASTERED THE BASICS OF KAWAZU KUMITE AND SAGE TECHNIQUES ...
...I NEED TO DISCUSS WIT' YA ONE FINAL THING.
WH- WHAT'S THAT?
YOU'RE SUDDENLY SO SERIOUS.
WELL ...
...IT'S ABOUT THE RISKS OF USIN' THE SAGE MODE.
RISKS ...?
THAT'S RIGHT...
...ONCE YA FULLY GRASP THESE HERE RISKS...
...YA CAN EXPLOIT SAGE MODE TO ITS FULLEST EXTENT!
WHAT RISKS?
FIRST, AS YA'VE PROBABLY ALREADY FIGGERED OUT, YA CAN'T MAINTAIN SAGE MODE FOR TOO LONG... MAYBE FIVE MINUTES AT MOST.
AND TO ENTER SAGE MODE, YA GOTTA DRAW IN NATURE ENERGY, FOR WHICH YA NEED TO FOLLOW THE PRINCIPLE ***DON'T MOVE.***
WHICH MEANS YA CAN'T USE IT WHEN YER ALREADY IN THE MIDST OF BATTLE.
FOR IF YA STOP MOVIN', YA BECOME AN EASY TARGET FOR YER ENEMY.

READ THIS WAY

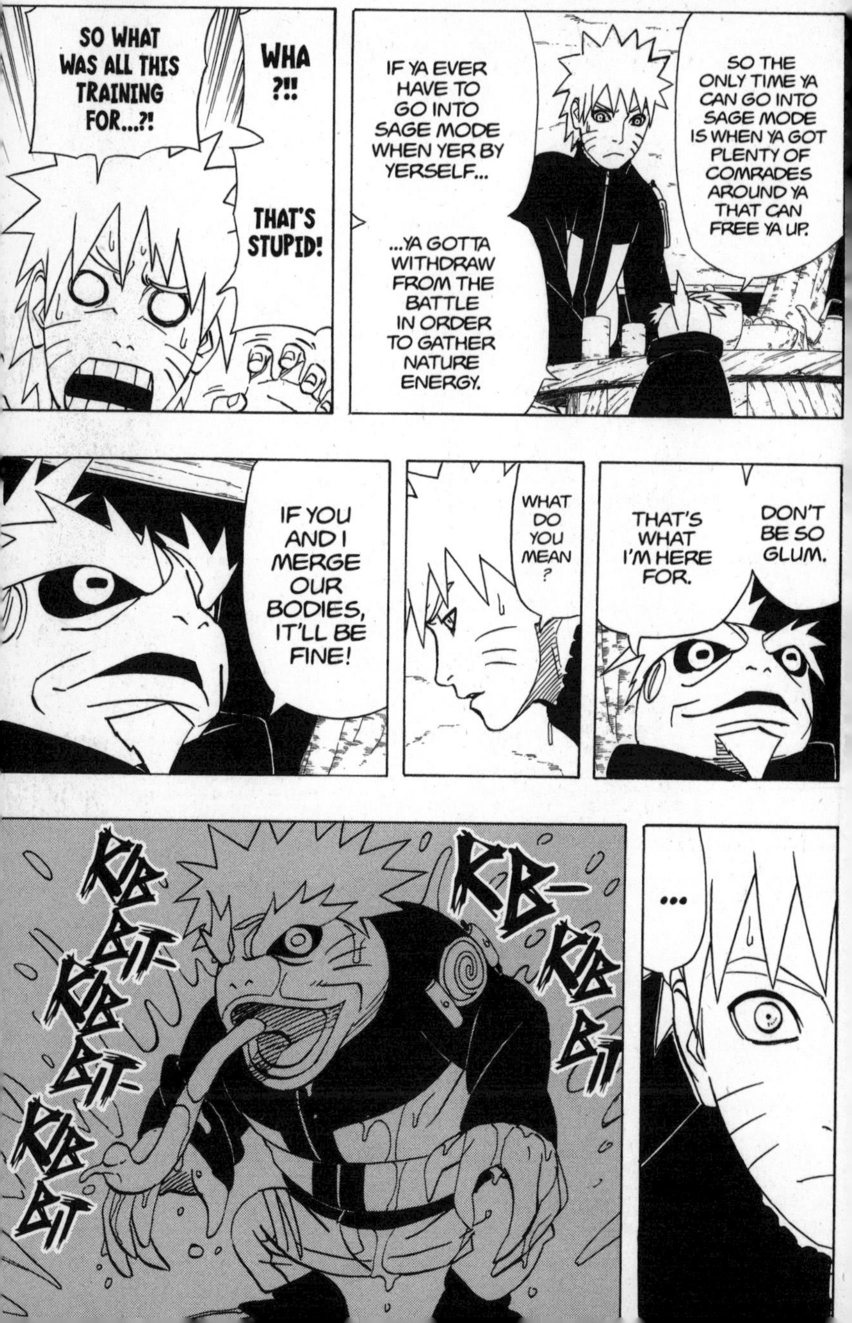
SO THE ONLY TIME YA CAN GO INTO SAGE MODE IS WHEN YA GOT PLENTY OF COMRADES AROUND YA THAT CAN FREE YA UP.
IF YA EVER HAVE TO GO INTO SAGE MODE WHEN YER BY YERSELF...
...YA GOTTA WITHDRAW FROM THE BATTLE IN ORDER TO GATHER NATURE ENERGY.
WHA ?!!
THAT'S STUPID!
SO WHAT WAS ALL THIS TRAINING FOR...?!
DON'T BE SO GLUM.
THAT'S WHAT I'M HERE FOR.
WHAT DO YOU MEAN?
IF YOU AND I MERGE OUR BODIES, IT'LL BE FINE!
...
KB-KB BIT
KB BIT-KB BIT-KB BIT-KB BIT

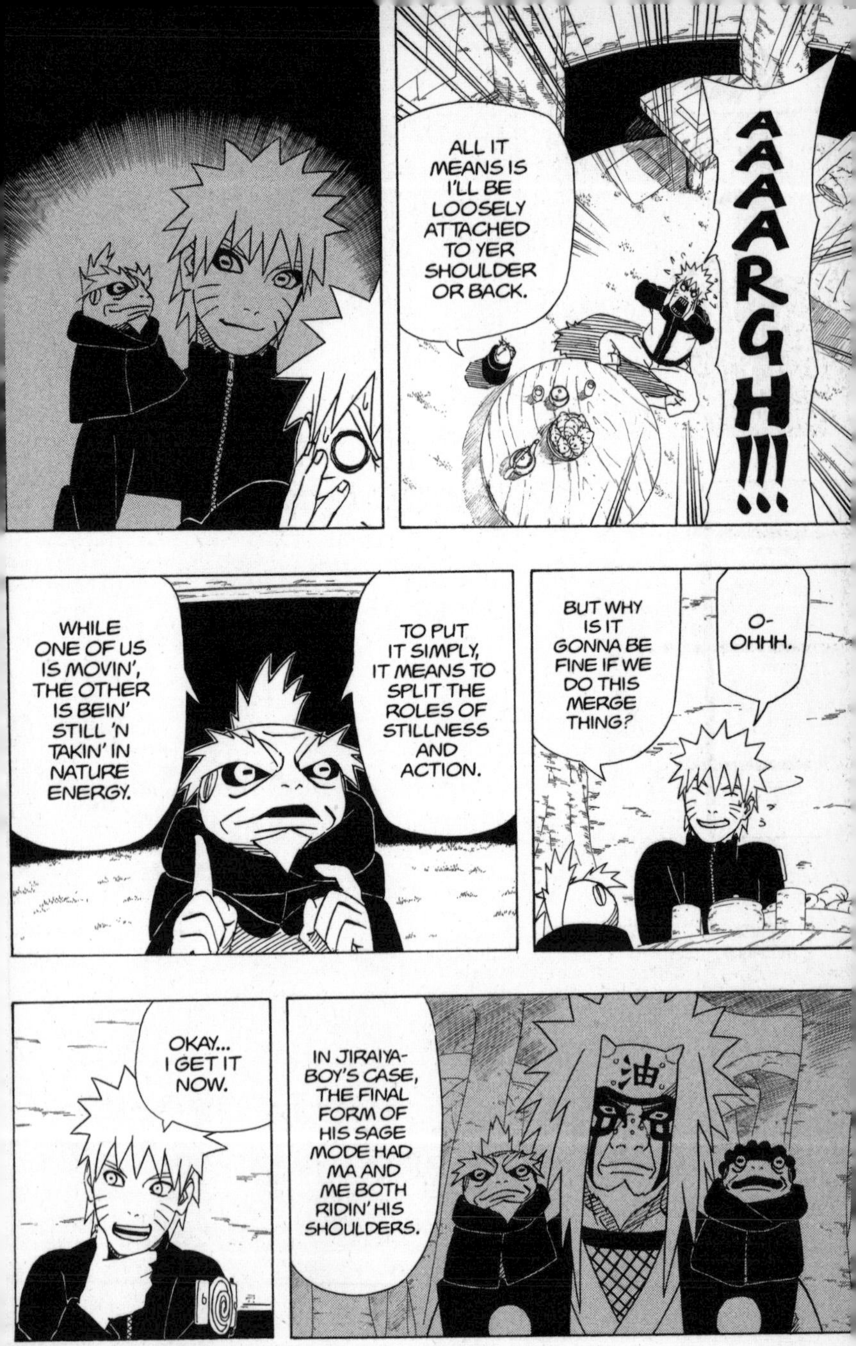
AAAARGH!!!
ALL IT MEANS IS I'LL BE LOOSELY ATTACHED TO YER SHOULDER OR BACK.
O-OHHH.
BUT WHY IS IT GONNA BE FINE IF WE DO THIS MERGE THING?
TO PUT IT SIMPLY, IT MEANS TO SPLIT THE ROLES OF STILLNESS AND ACTION.
WHILE ONE OF US IS MOVIN', THE OTHER IS BEIN' STILL 'N TAKIN' IN NATURE ENERGY.
IN JIRAIYA-BOY'S CASE, THE FINAL FORM OF HIS SAGE MODE HAD MA AND ME BOTH RIDIN' HIS SHOULDERS.
油
OKAY... I GET IT NOW.

READ THIS WAY

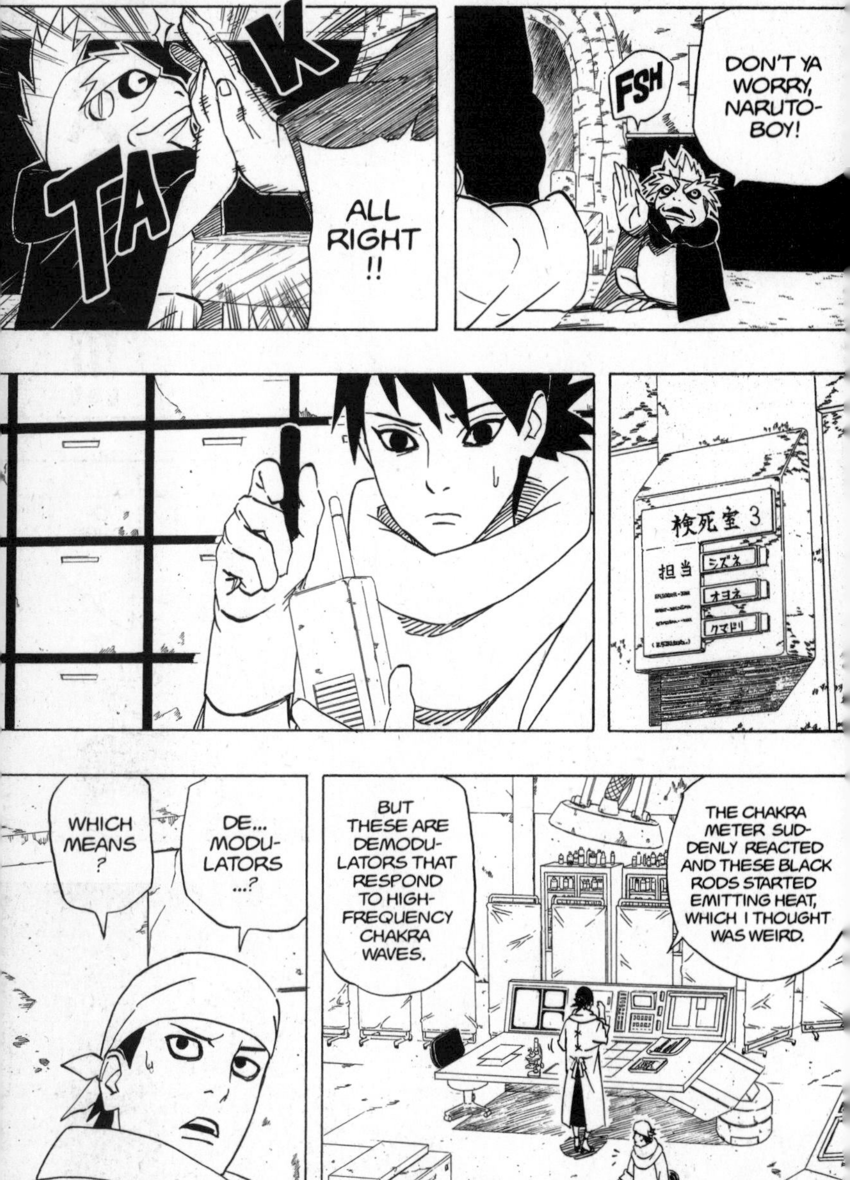
FSH
DON'T YA WORRY, NARUTO-BOY!
TAK
ALL RIGHT !!
検死室3
担当
シズネ
オヨネ
クマドリ
THE CHAKRA METER SUDDENLY REACTED AND THESE BLACK RODS STARTED EMITTING HEAT, WHICH I THOUGHT WAS WEIRD.
BUT THESE ARE DEMODULATORS THAT RESPOND TO HIGH-FREQUENCY CHAKRA WAVES.
DE... MODULATORS ...?
WHICH MEANS ?

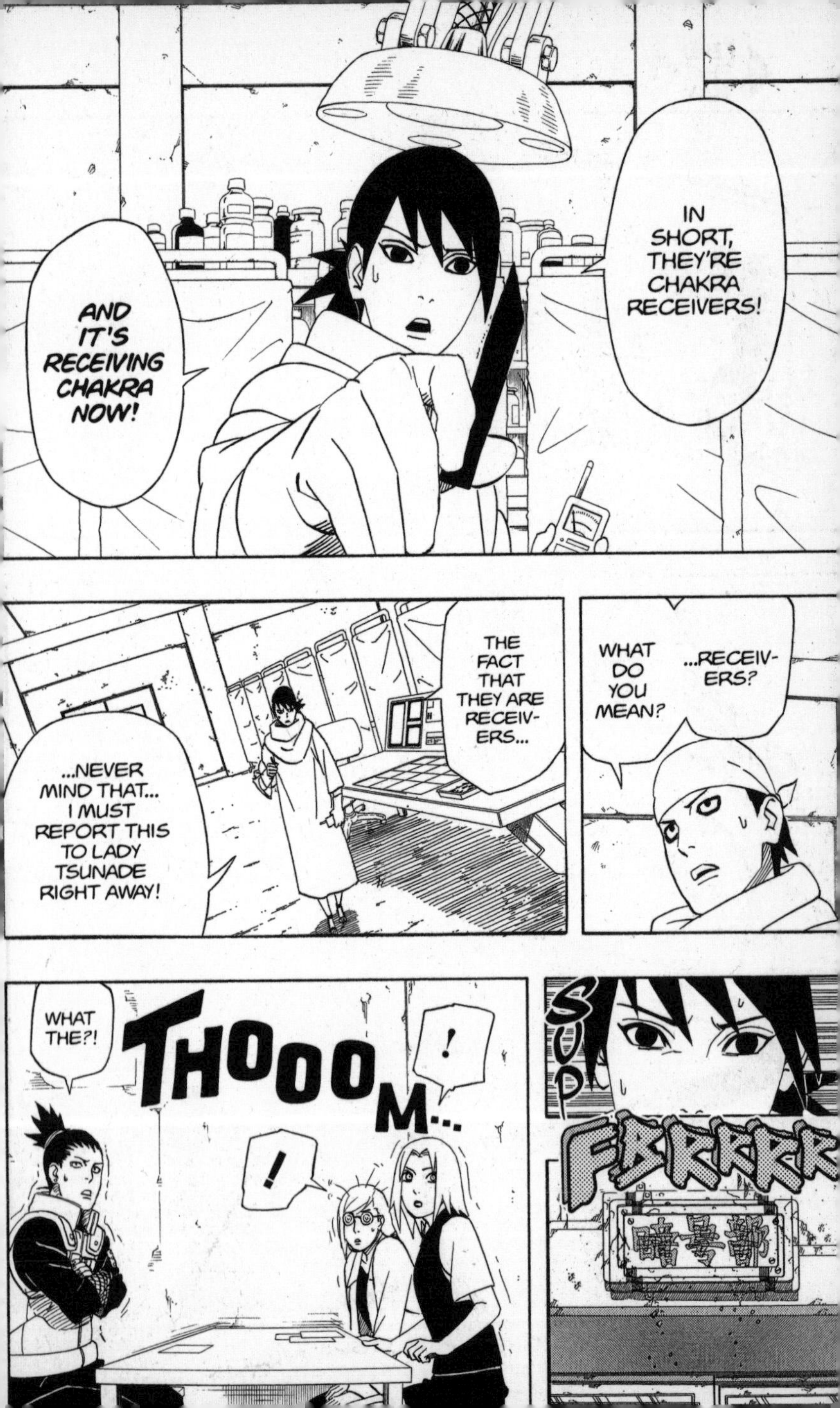
IN SHORT, THEY'RE CHAKRA RECEIVERS!
AND IT'S RECEIVING CHAKRA NOW!
...RECEIVERS?
WHAT DO YOU MEAN?
THE FACT THAT THEY ARE RECEIVERS...
...NEVER MIND THAT... I MUST REPORT THIS TO LADY TSUNADE RIGHT AWAY!
SUP
FBRRRR
THOOOM...
!
!
WHAT THE?!

READ THIS WAY

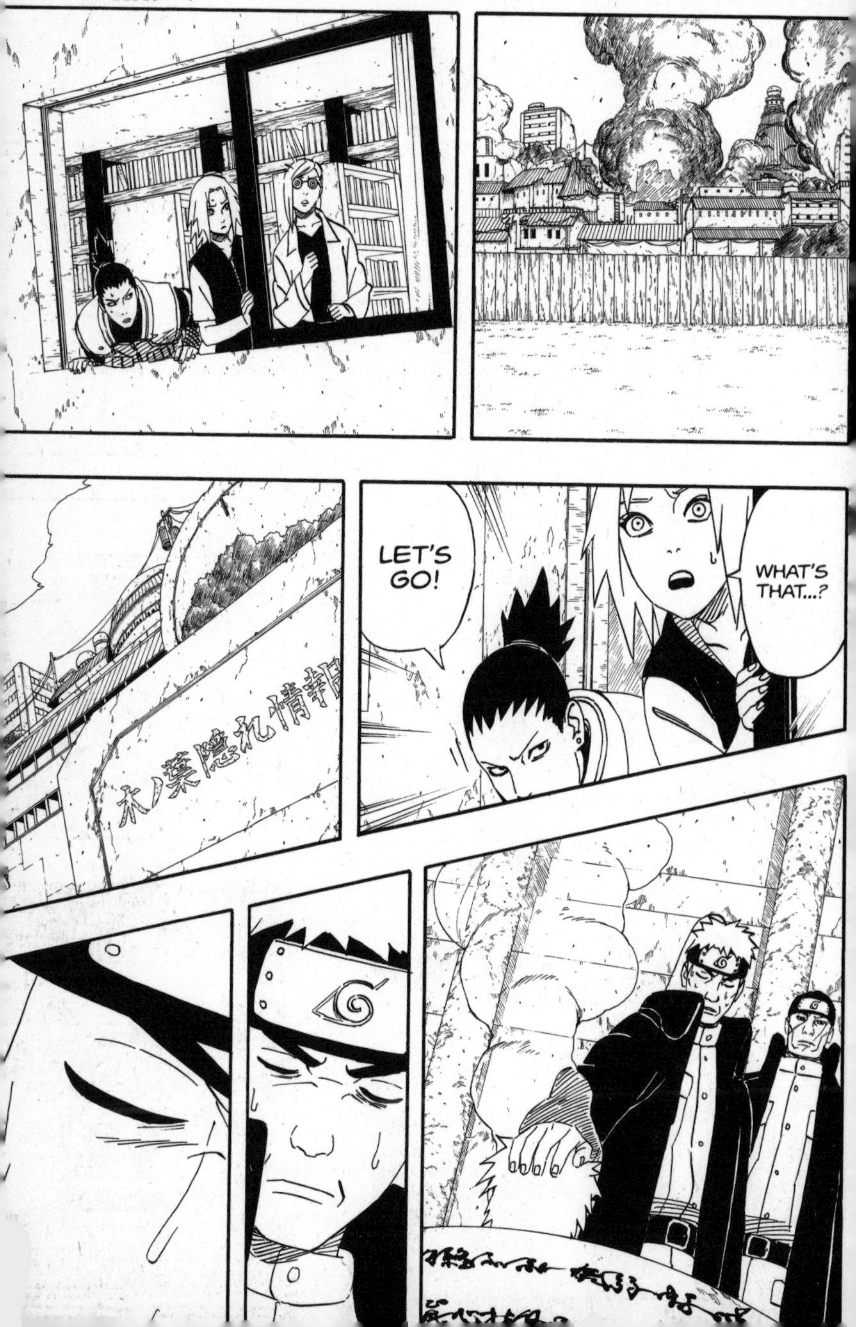
WHAT'S THAT...?
LET'S GO!

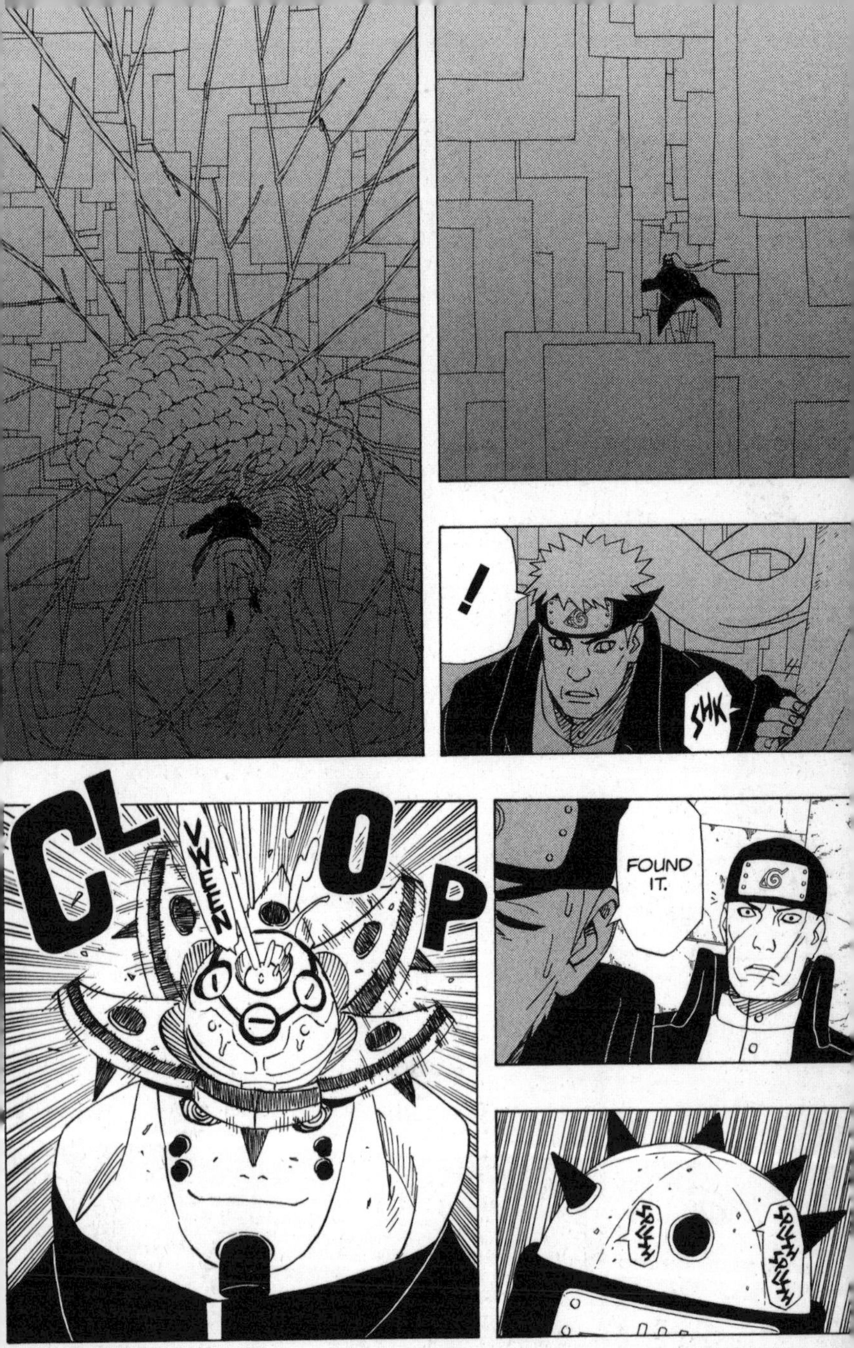
!
SHK
FOUND IT.
CLOP
VWEEN

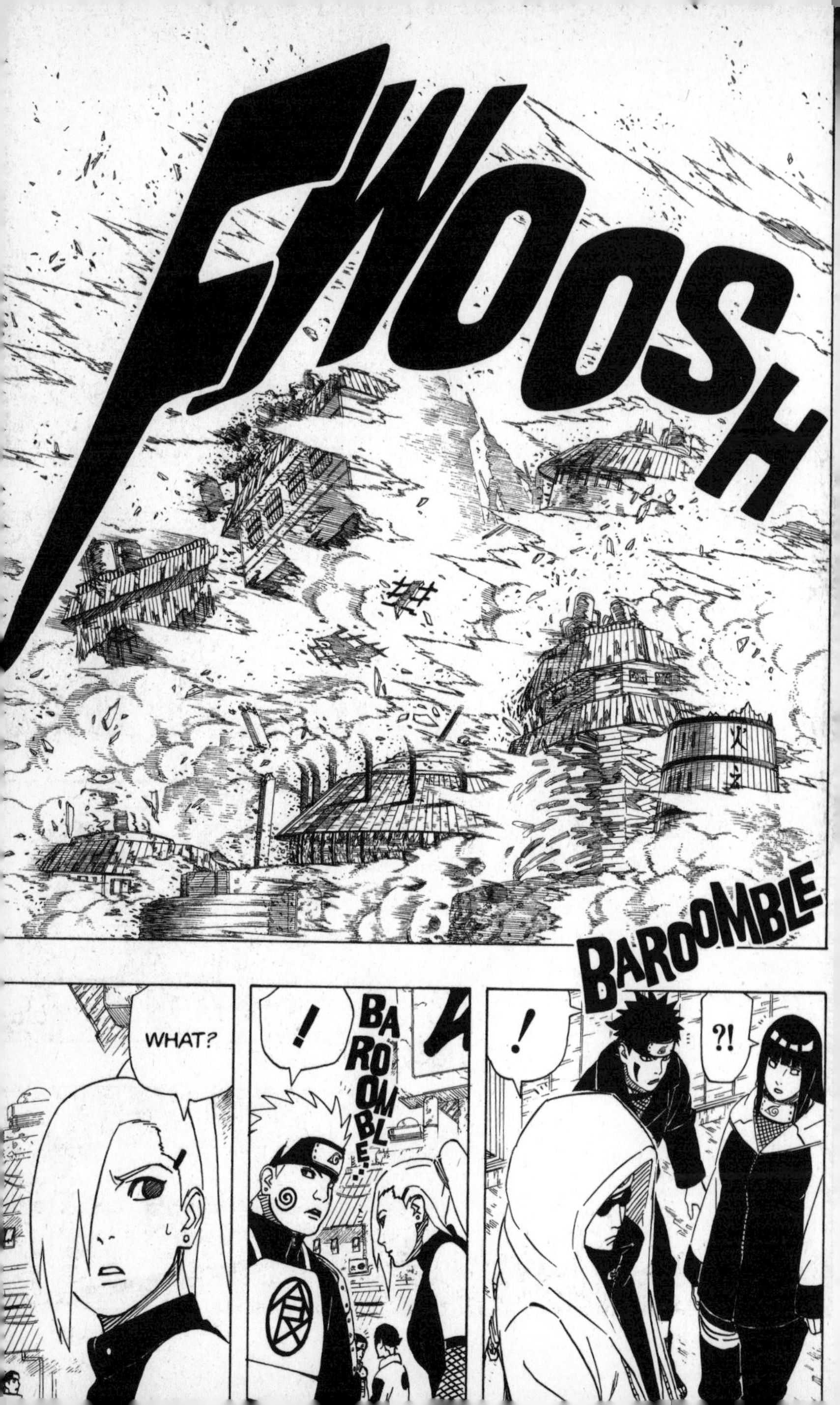
WHOOSH
BAROOMBLE
?!
!
BAROOMBLE...
!
WHAT?

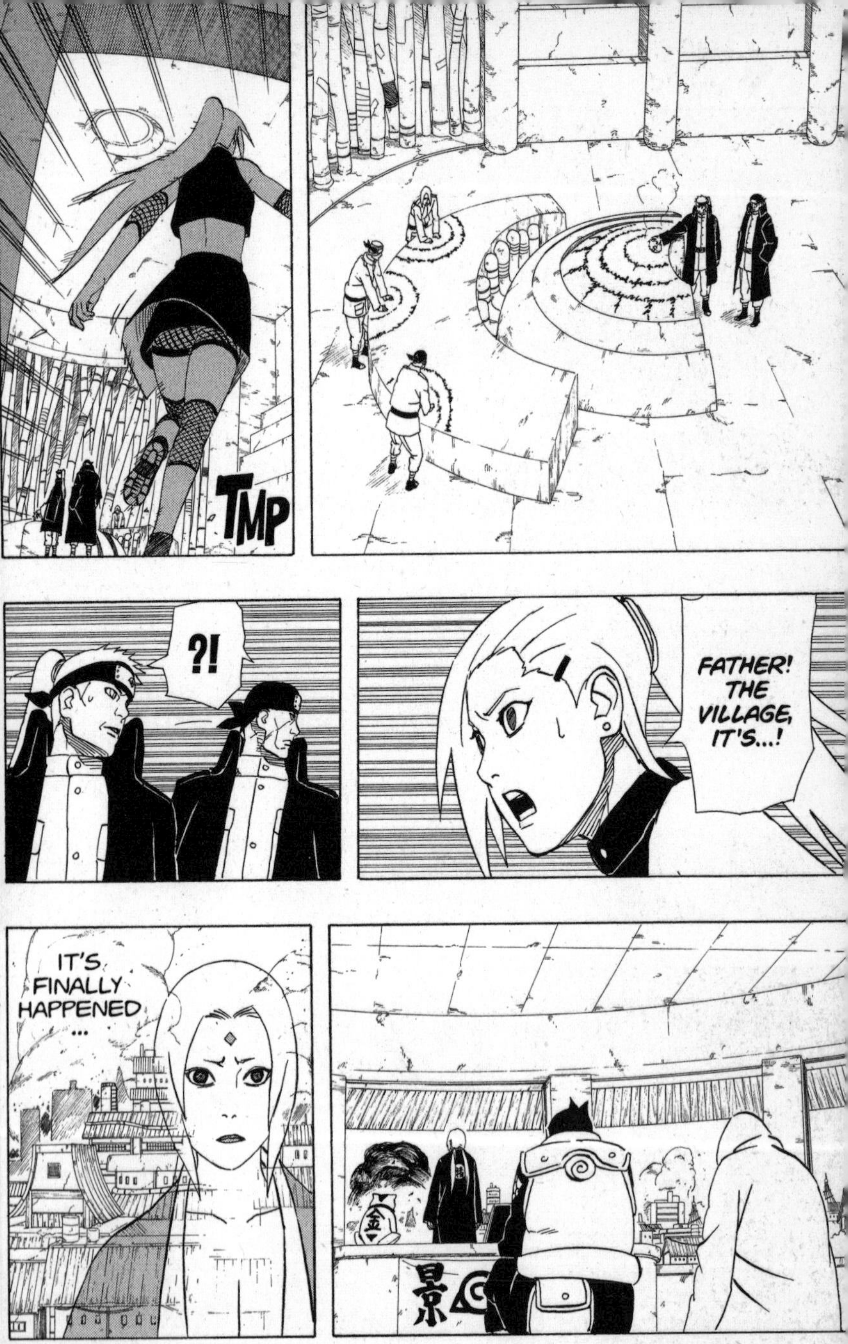
TMP
FATHER! THE VILLAGE, IT'S...!
?!
IT'S FINALLY HAPPENED...

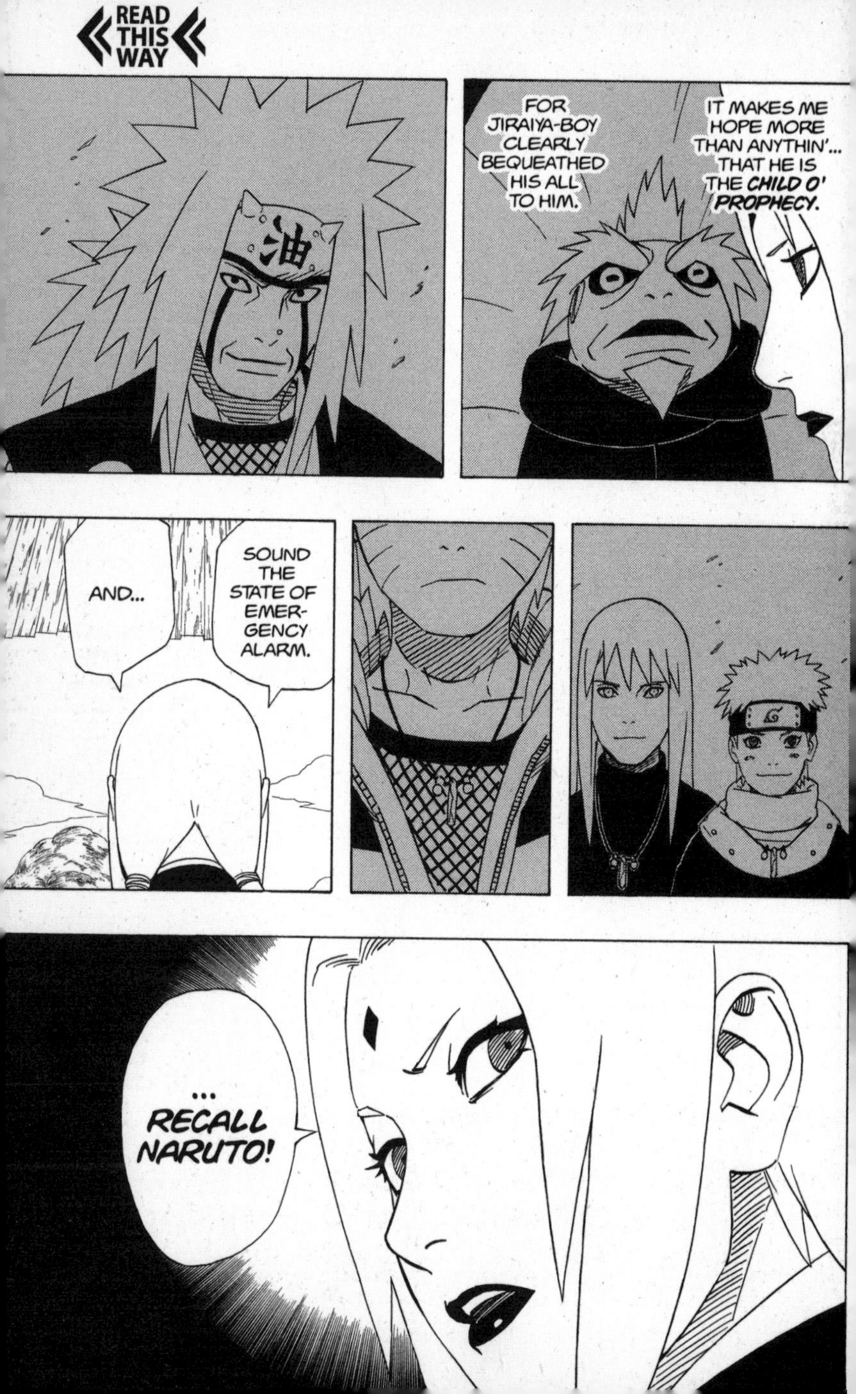
READ THIS WAY
IT MAKES ME HOPE MORE THAN ANYTHIN'... THAT HE IS THE CHILD O' PROPHECY.
FOR JIRAIYA-BOY CLEARLY BEQUEATHED HIS ALL TO HIM.
SOUND THE STATE OF EMER-GENCY ALARM.
AND...
... RECALL NARUTO!

NARUTO

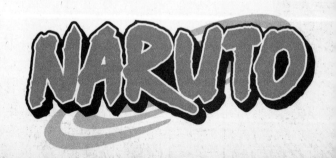

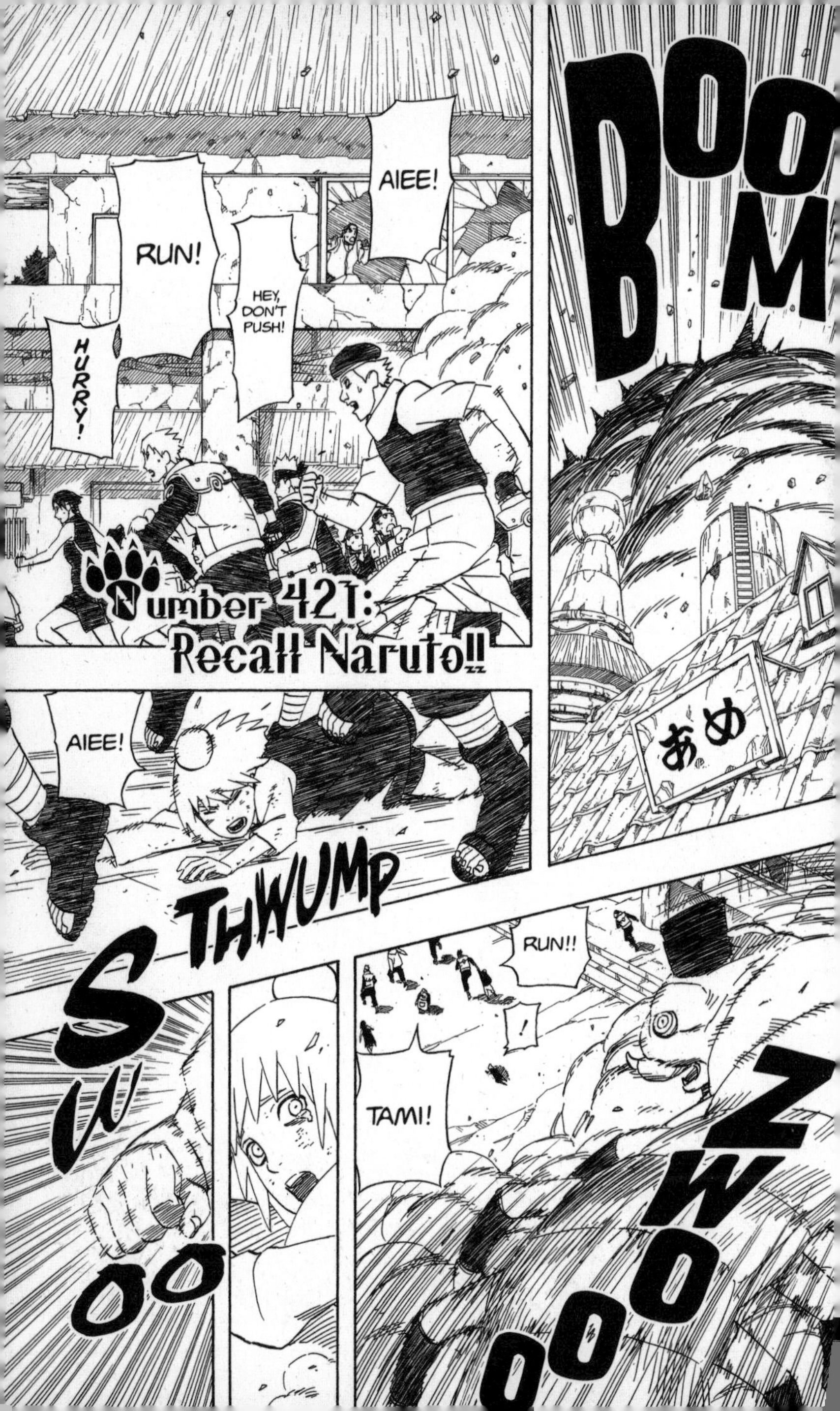

DOO
BM
あめ
AIEE!
HEY, DON'T PUSH!
RUN!
HURRY!
Number 421: Recall Naruto!!
AIEE!
THWUMP
RUN!!
!
TAMI!
ZWOOOO
SWOO

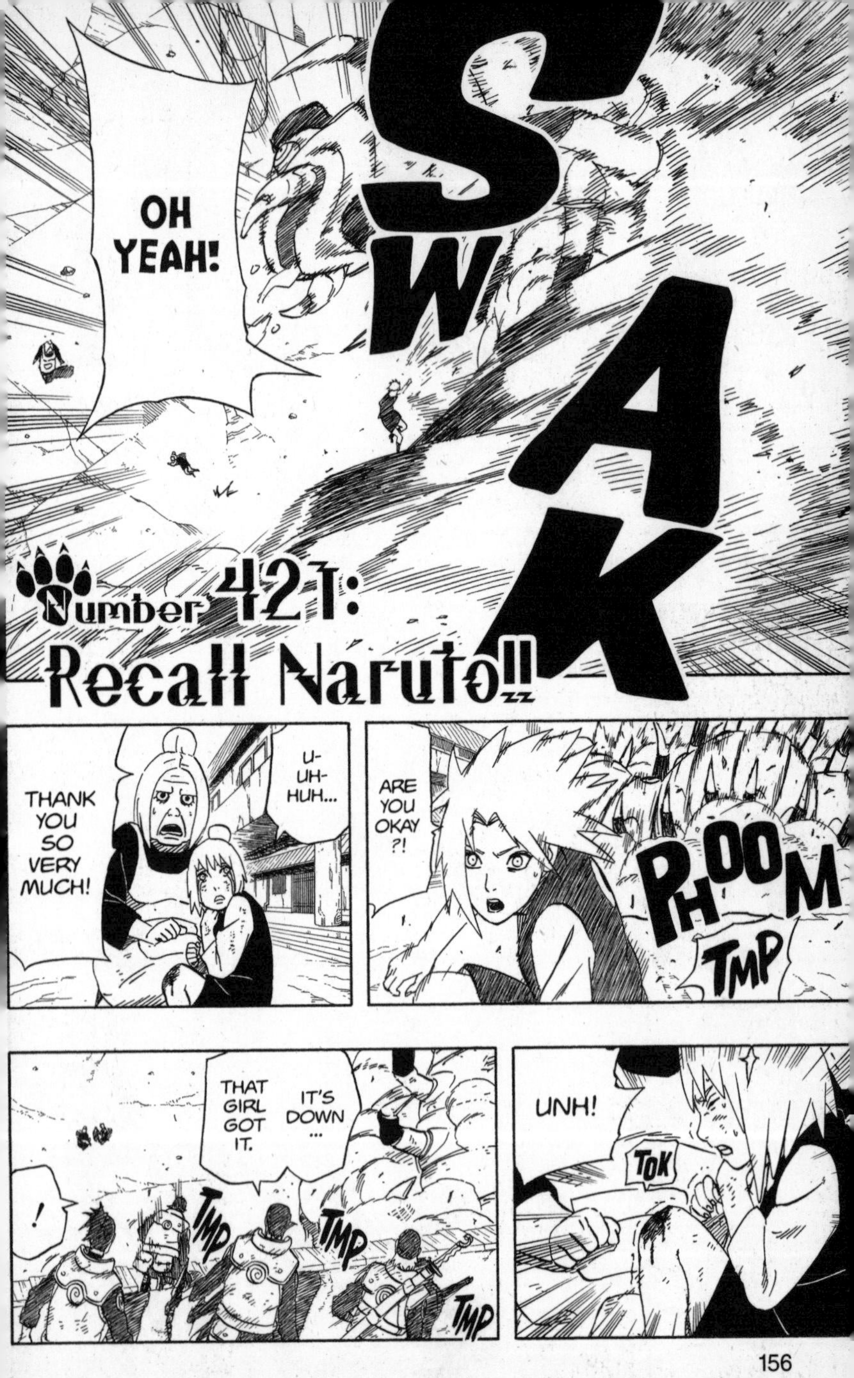
OH YEAH!
SWAK
Number 421: Recall Naruto!!
ARE YOU OKAY?!
PHOOM
TMP
U-UH-HUH...
THANK YOU SO VERY MUCH!
UNH!
TOK
IT'S DOWN...
THAT GIRL GOT IT.
!
TMP
TMP
TMP

READ THIS WAY

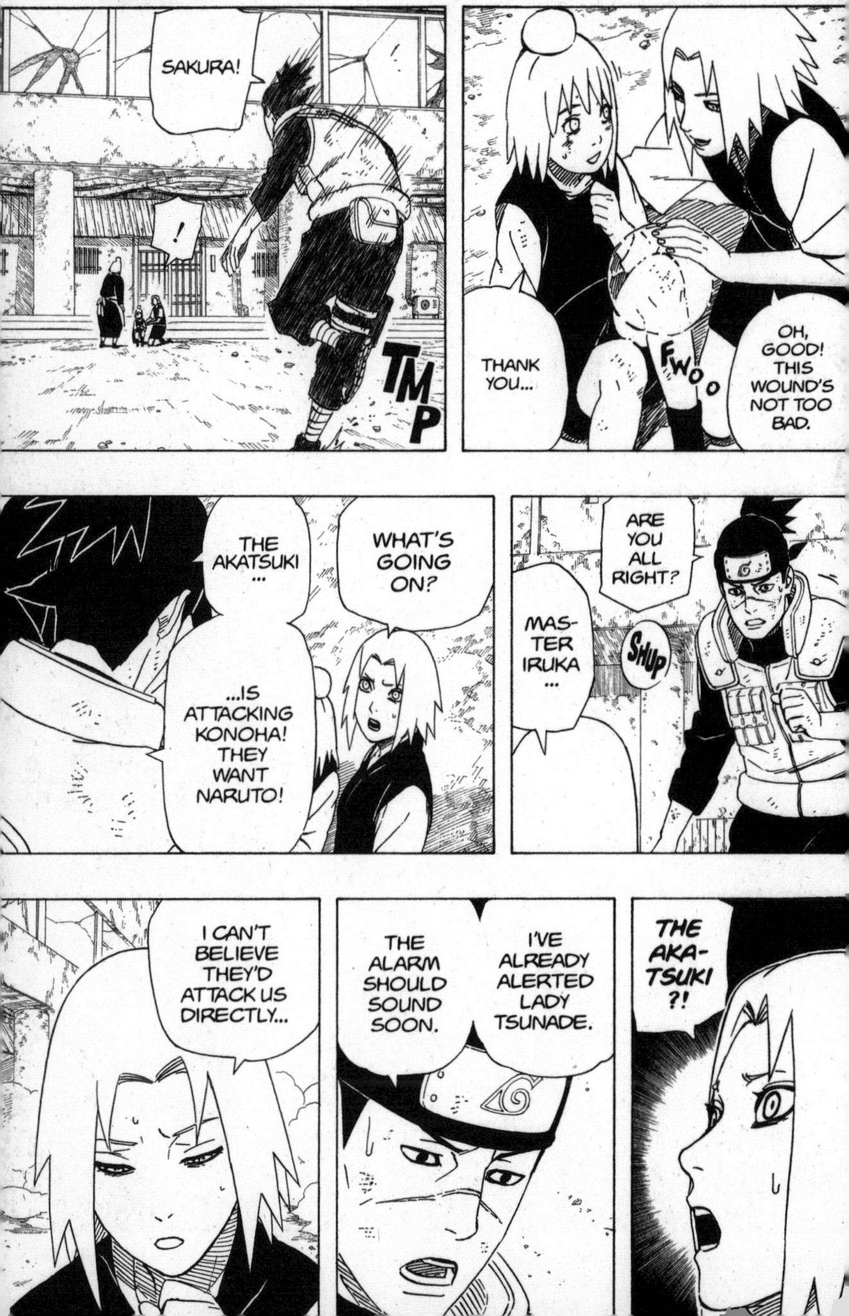
OH, GOOD! THIS WOUND'S NOT TOO BAD.
FWOO
THANK YOU...
SAKURA!
!
TMP
ARE YOU ALL RIGHT?
SHUP
MASTER IRUKA...
WHAT'S GOING ON?
THE AKATSUKI...
...IS ATTACKING KONOHA! THEY WANT NARUTO!
THE AKATSUKI?!
I'VE ALREADY ALERTED LADY TSUNADE.
THE ALARM SHOULD SOUND SOON.
I CAN'T BELIEVE THEY'D ACTTACK US DIRECTLY...

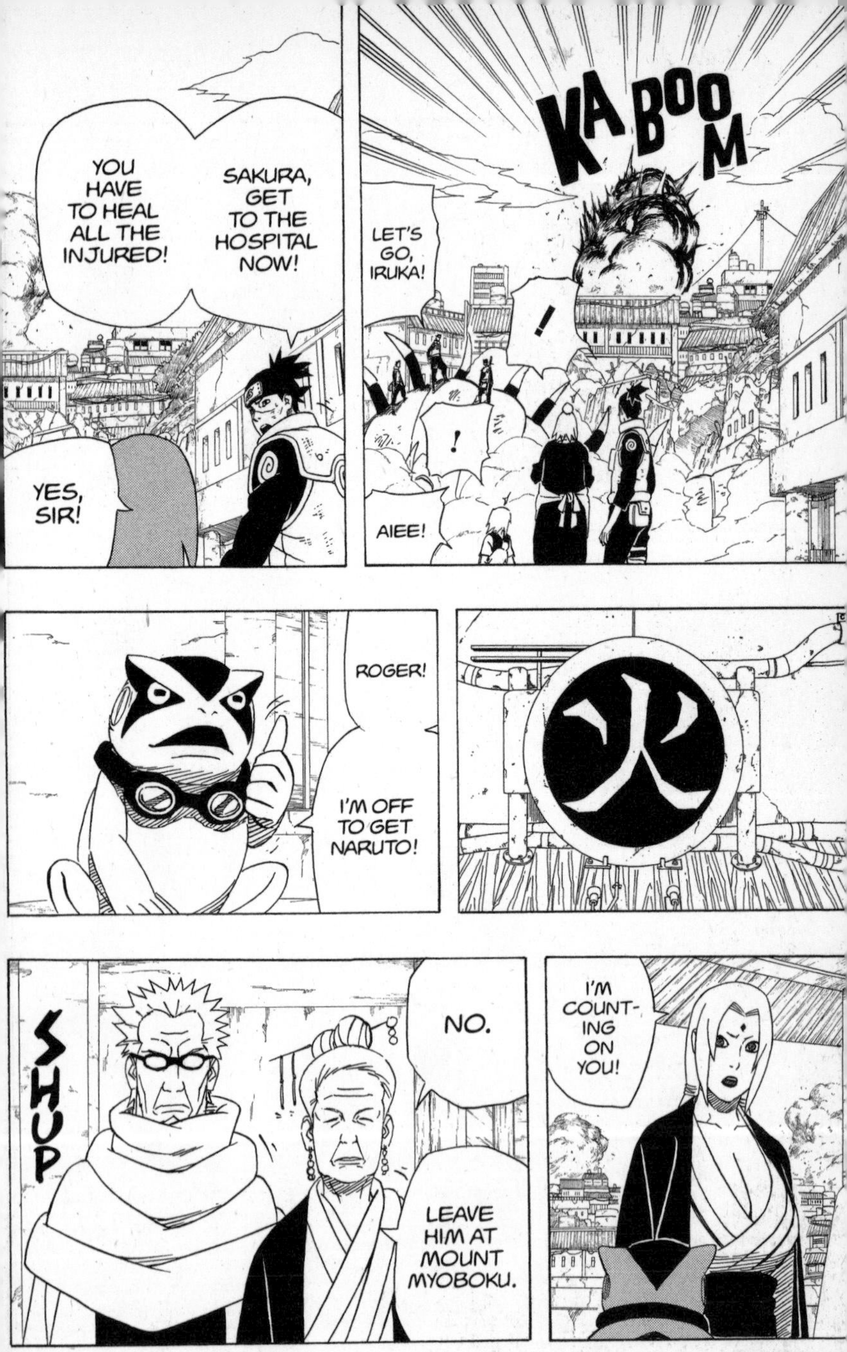
KABOOM
LET'S GO, IRUKA!
!
!
AIEE!
SAKURA, GET TO THE HOSPITAL NOW!
YOU HAVE TO HEAL ALL THE INJURED!
YES, SIR!
ROGER!
I'M OFF TO GET NARUTO!
I'M COUNTING ON YOU!
NO.
LEAVE HIM AT MOUNT MYOBOKU.
SHUP

READ THIS WAY

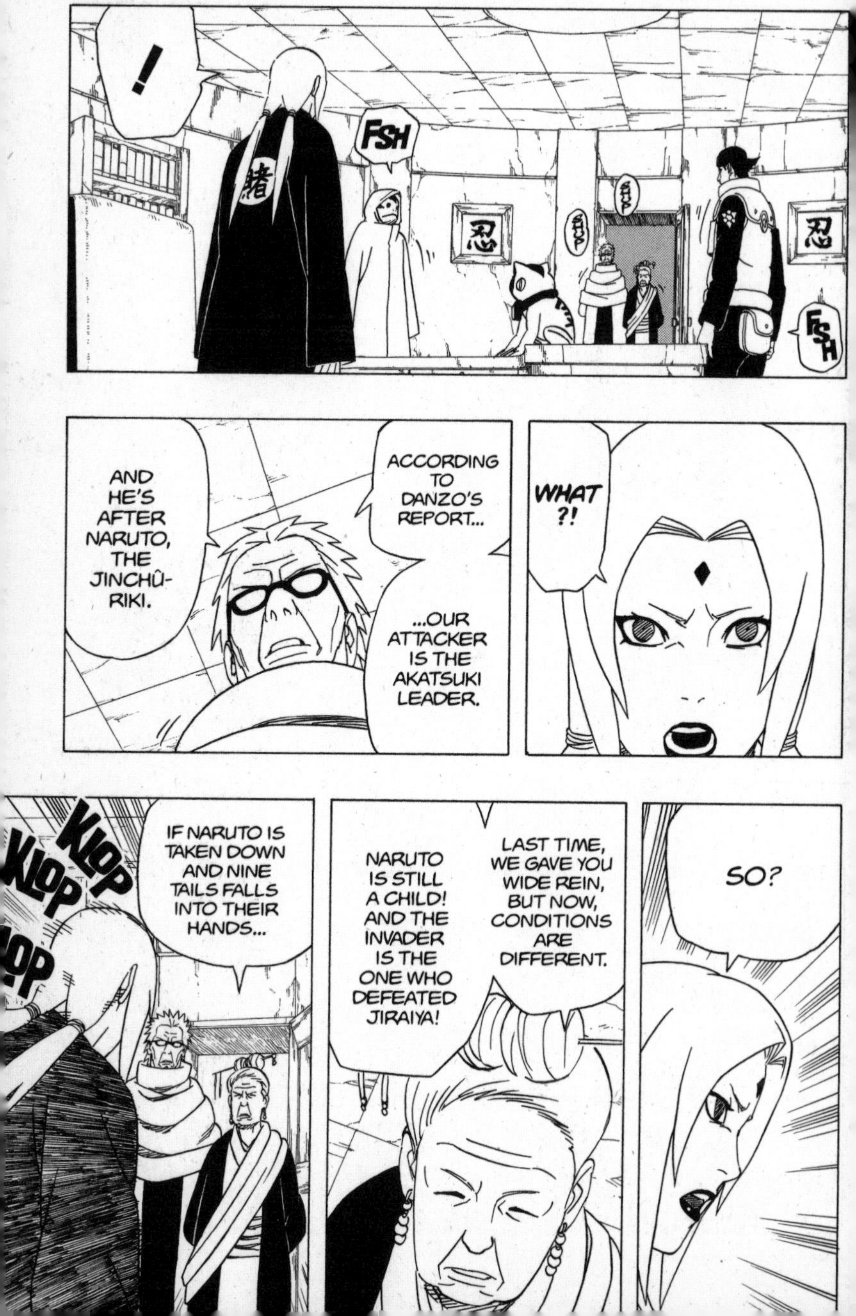
FSH
SHP
SHP
FSH
!
WHAT ?!
ACCORDING TO DANZO'S REPORT...
...OUR ATTACKER IS THE AKATSUKI LEADER.
AND HE'S AFTER NARUTO, THE JINCHÛ-RIKI.
SO?
LAST TIME, WE GAVE YOU WIDE REIN, BUT NOW, CONDITIONS ARE DIFFERENT.
NARUTO IS STILL A CHILD! AND THE INVADER IS THE ONE WHO DEFEATED JIRAIYA!
IF NARUTO IS TAKEN DOWN AND NINE TAILS FALLS INTO THEIR HANDS...
KLOP
KLOP
KLOP

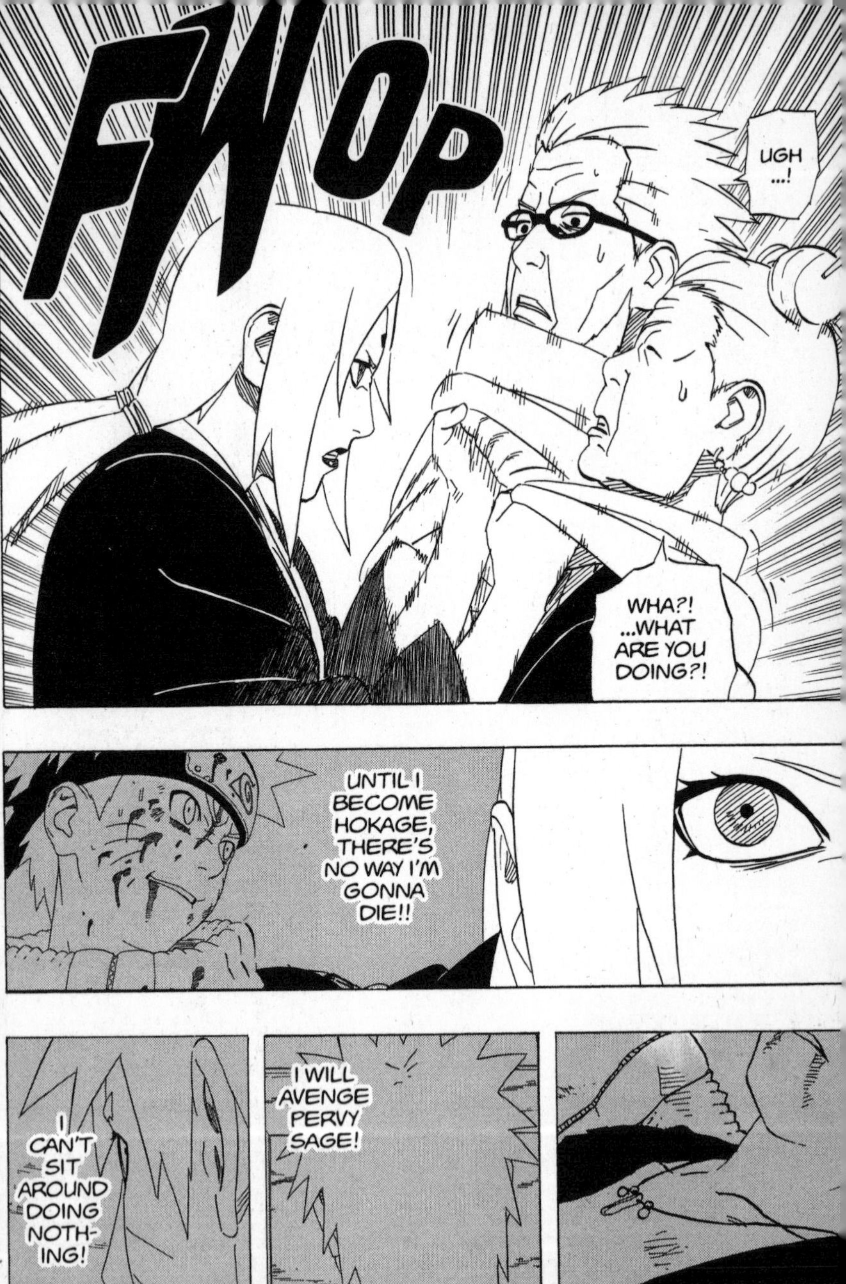
UGH ...!
FWOP
WHA?! ...WHAT ARE YOU DOING?!
UNTIL I BECOME HOKAGE, THERE'S NO WAY I'M GONNA DIE!!
I WILL AVENGE PERVY SAGE!
I CAN'T SIT AROUND DOING NOTH-ING!

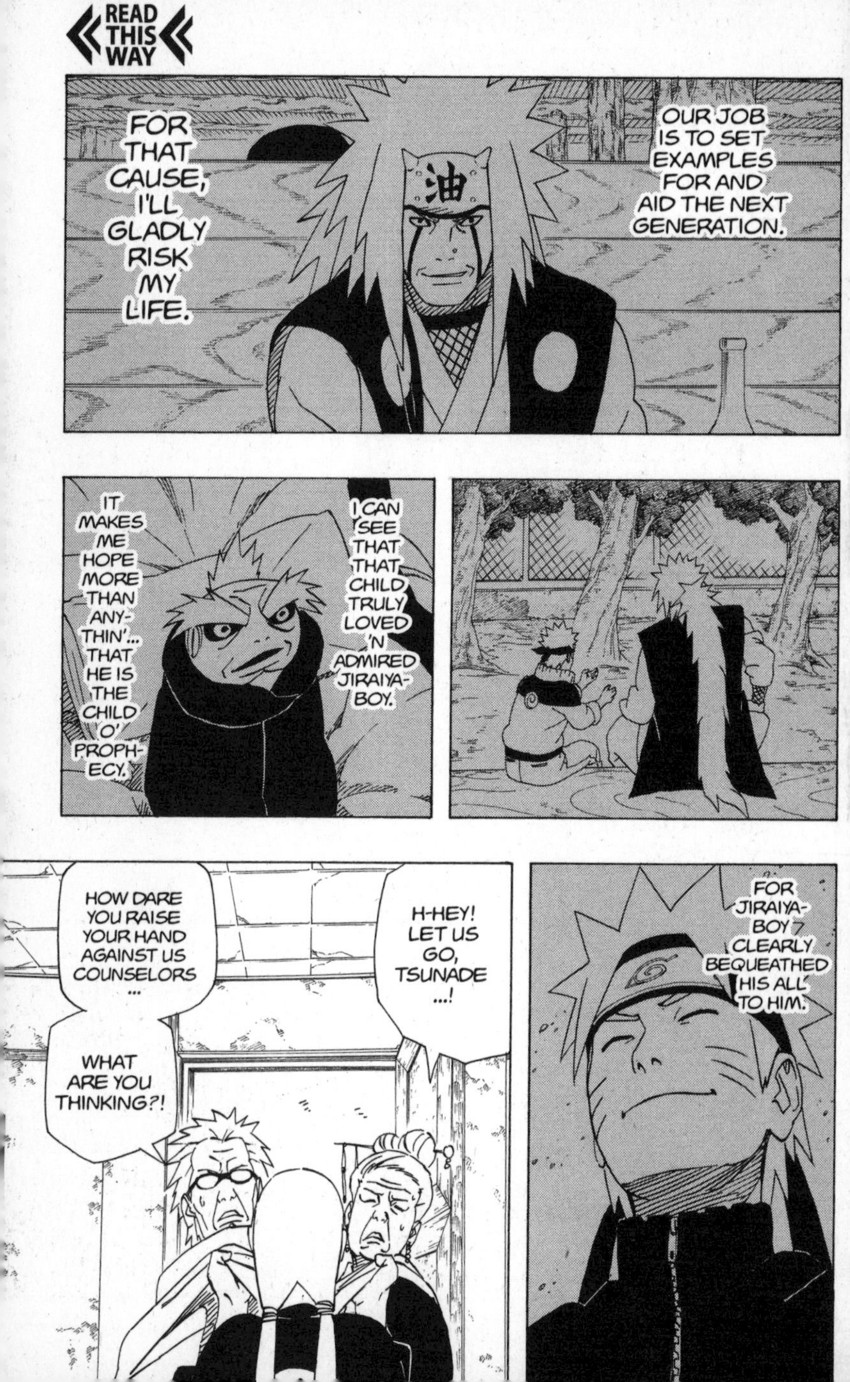
READ THIS WAY
OUR JOB IS TO SET EXAMPLES FOR AND AID THE NEXT GENERATION.
FOR THAT CAUSE, I'LL GLADLY RISK MY LIFE.
I CAN SEE THAT THAT CHILD TRULY LOVED 'N ADMIRED JIRAIYA-BOY.
IT MAKES ME HOPE MORE THAN ANY-THIN'... THAT HE IS THE CHILD O' PROPH-ECY.
FOR JIRAIYA-BOY CLEARLY BEQUEATHED HIS ALL TO HIM.
H-HEY! LET US GO, TSUNADE ...!
HOW DARE YOU RAISE YOUR HAND AGAINST US COUNSELORS ...
WHAT ARE YOU THINKING?!

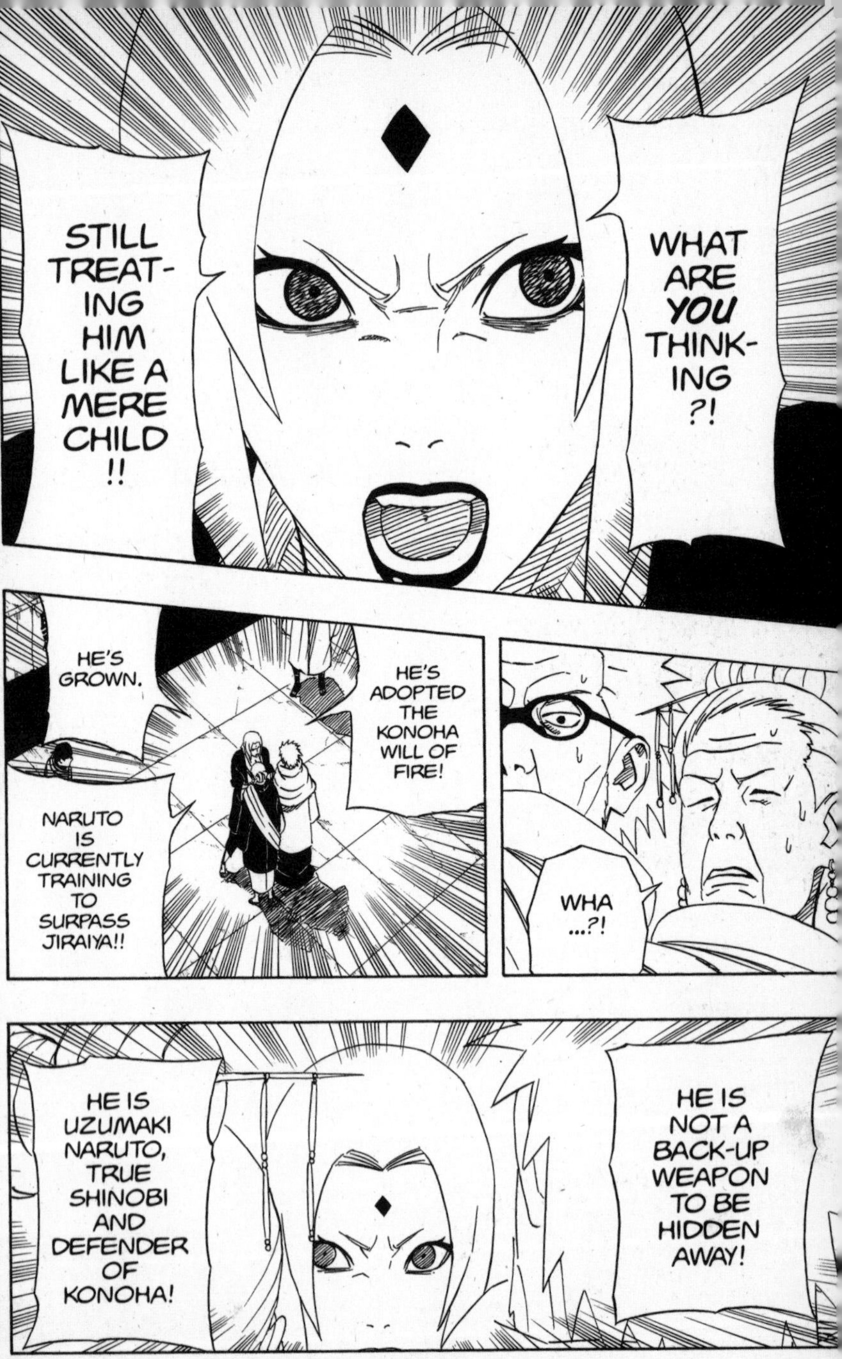

WHAT ARE *YOU* THINKING?!
STILL TREATING HIM LIKE A MERE CHILD!!
WHA...?!
HE'S ADOPTED THE KONOHA WILL OF FIRE!
HE'S GROWN.
NARUTO IS CURRENTLY TRAINING TO SURPASS JIRAIYA!!
HE IS NOT A BACK-UP WEAPON TO BE HIDDEN AWAY!
HE IS UZUMAKI NARUTO, TRUE SHINOBI AND DEFENDER OF KONOHA!

UGH...

WHA!

TH UMP

FFT

FFT

TH UMP

...THAT YOU LACK?!

...DO YOU KNOW WHAT JIRAIYA, MASTER SARUTOBI, AND EVEN GRANNY CHIYO OF THE SAND HAD...

...

...

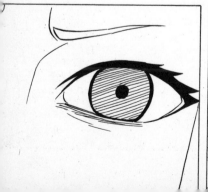

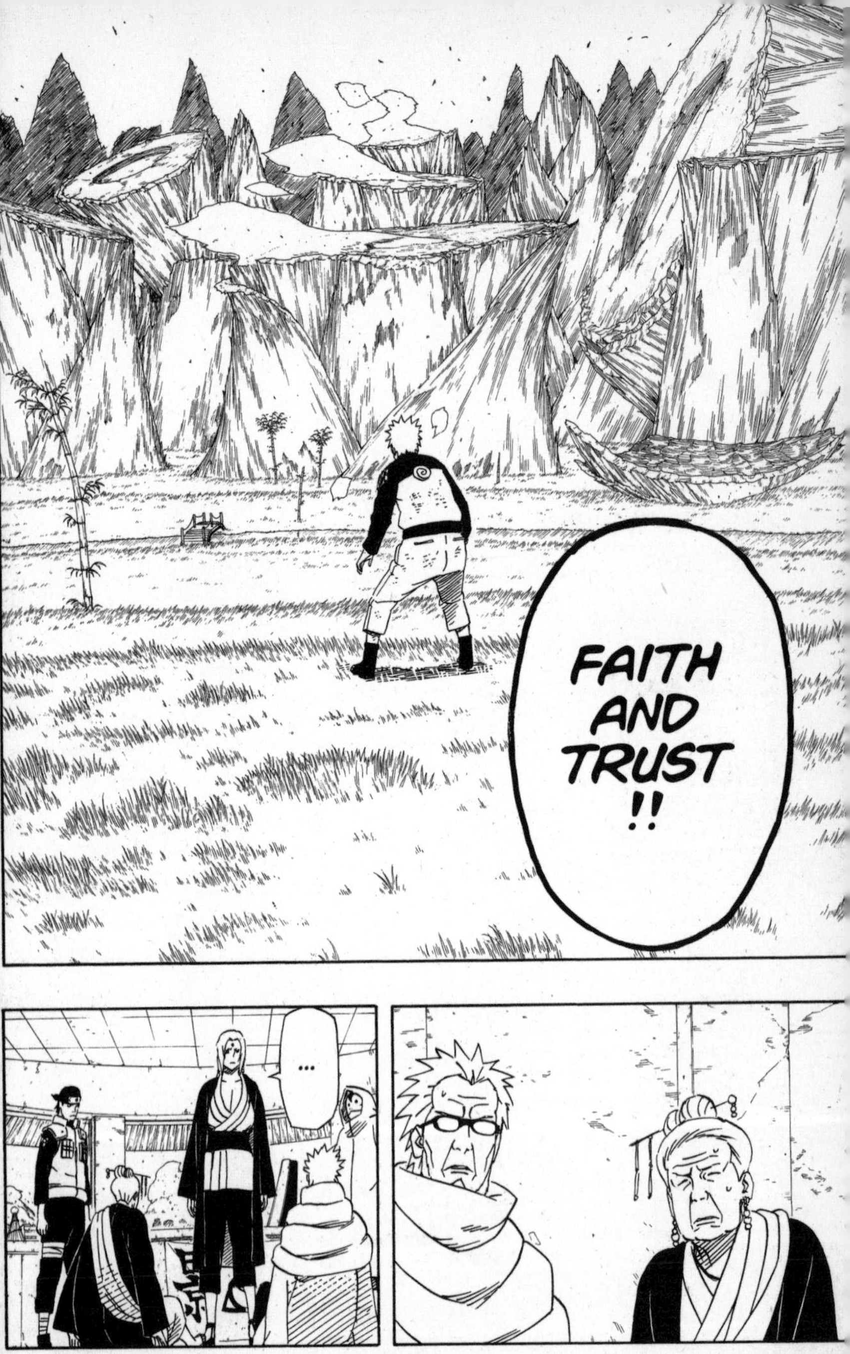
FAITH AND TRUST!!
...

READ THIS WAY

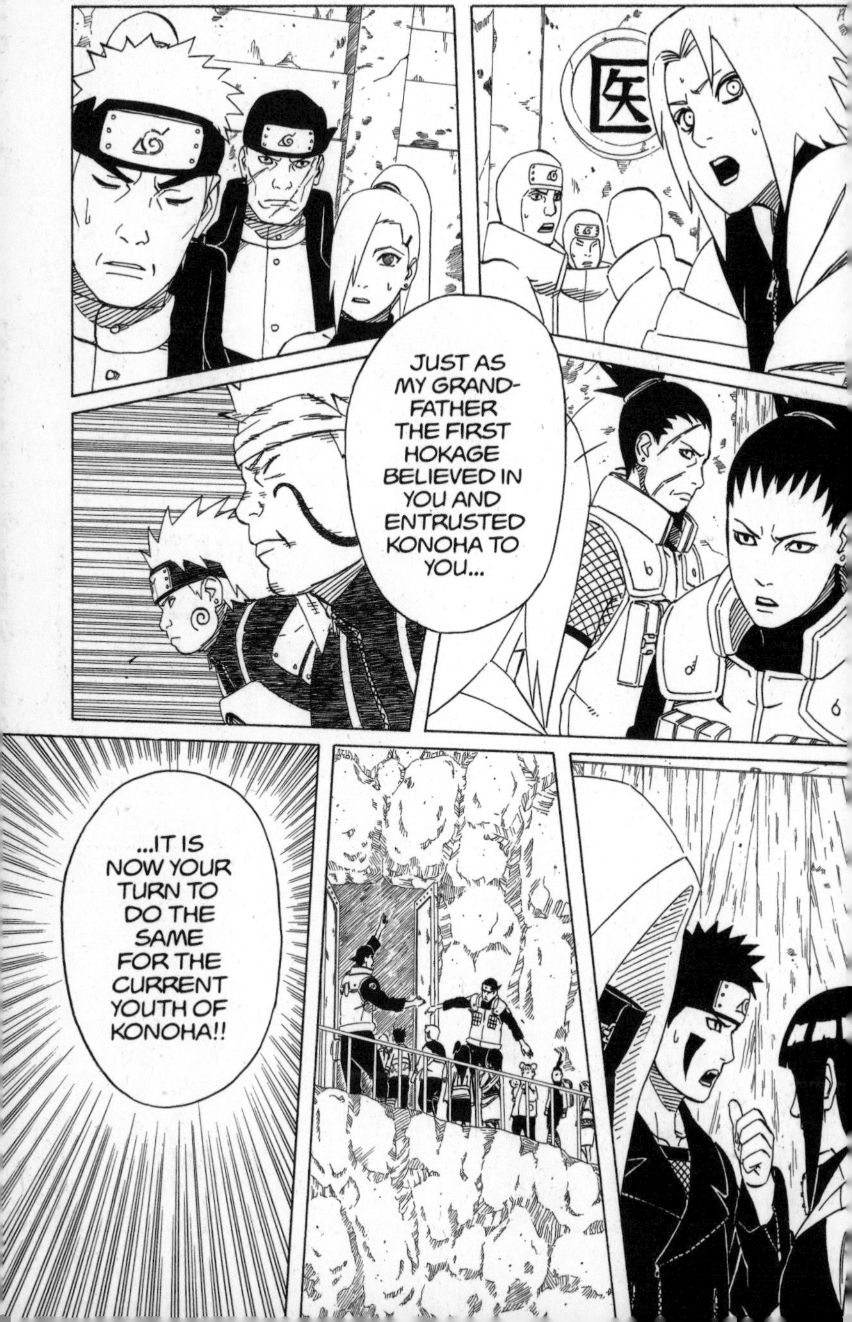

JUST AS MY GRAND-FATHER THE FIRST HOKAGE BELIEVED IN YOU AND ENTRUSTED KONOHA TO YOU...
...IT IS NOW YOUR TURN TO DO THE SAME FOR THE CURRENT YOUTH OF KONOHA!!

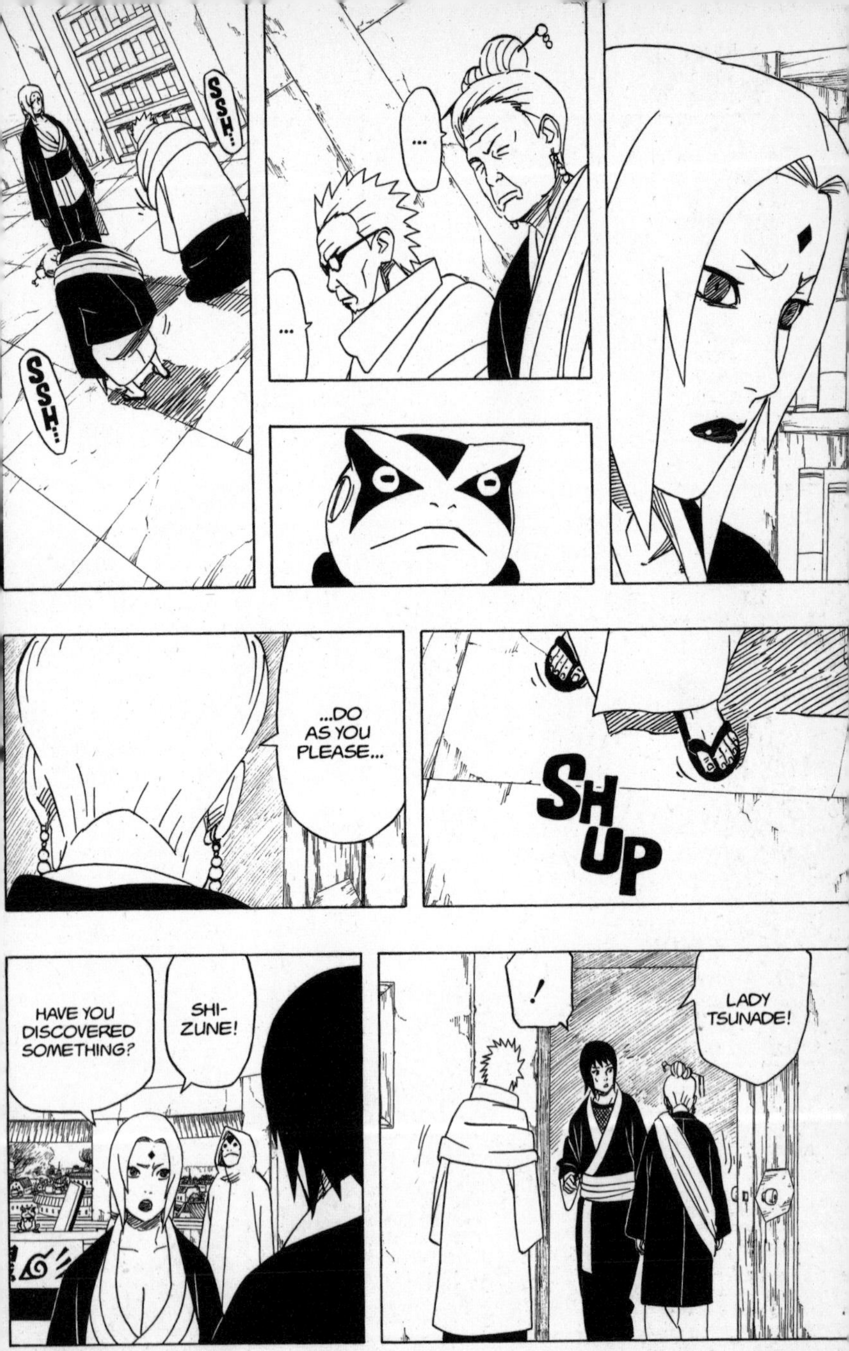
...
...
SSH...
SSH...
...DO AS YOU PLEASE...
SHUP
LADY TSUNADE!
!
SHI-ZUNE!
HAVE YOU DISCOVERED SOMETHING?

READ THIS WAY

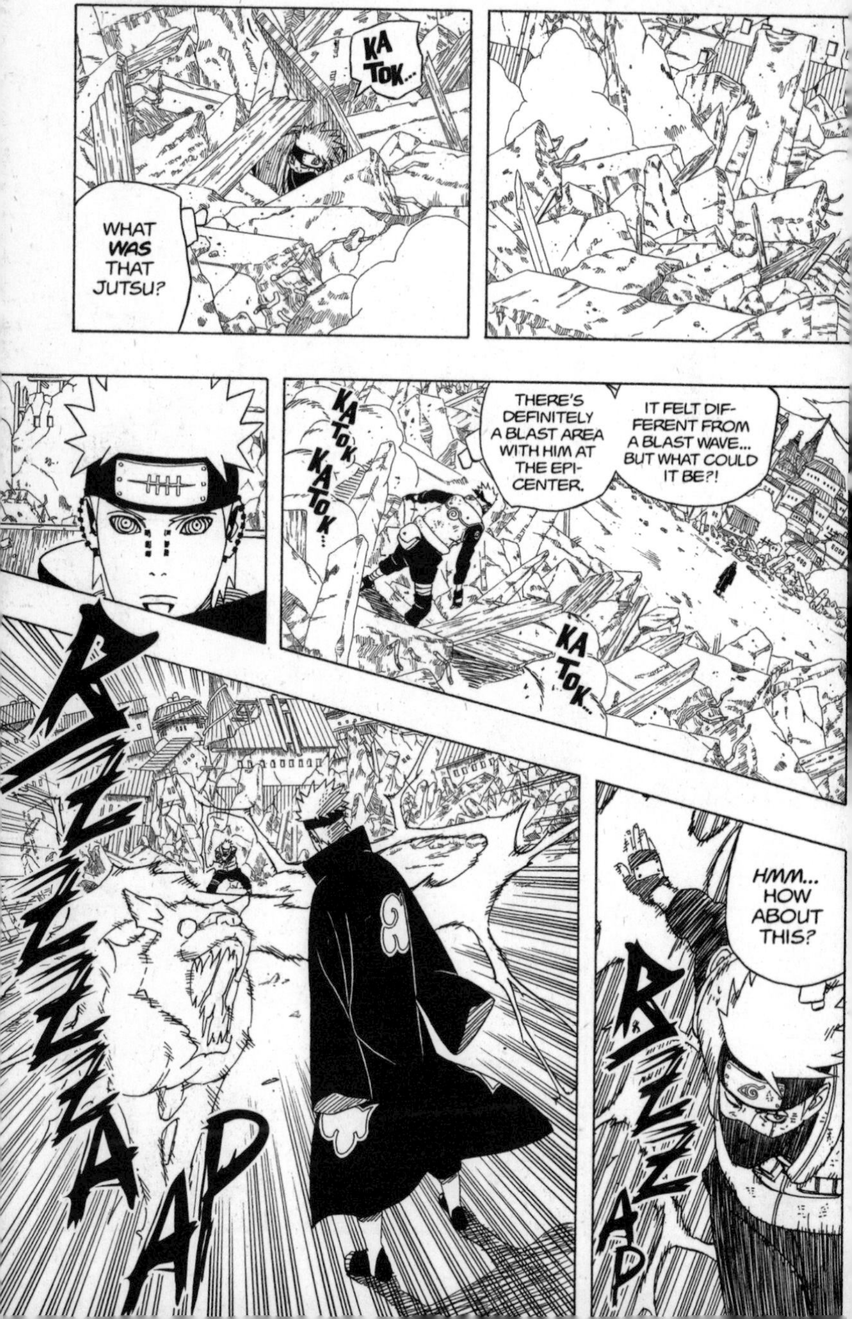

KA TOK...
WHAT WAS THAT JUTSU?
IT FELT DIFFERENT FROM A BLAST WAVE... BUT WHAT COULD IT BE?!
THERE'S DEFINITELY A BLAST AREA WITH HIM AT THE EPICENTER.
KA TOK KA TOK...
KA TOK...
HMM... HOW ABOUT THIS?
BZZZAP
BZZZZAAP

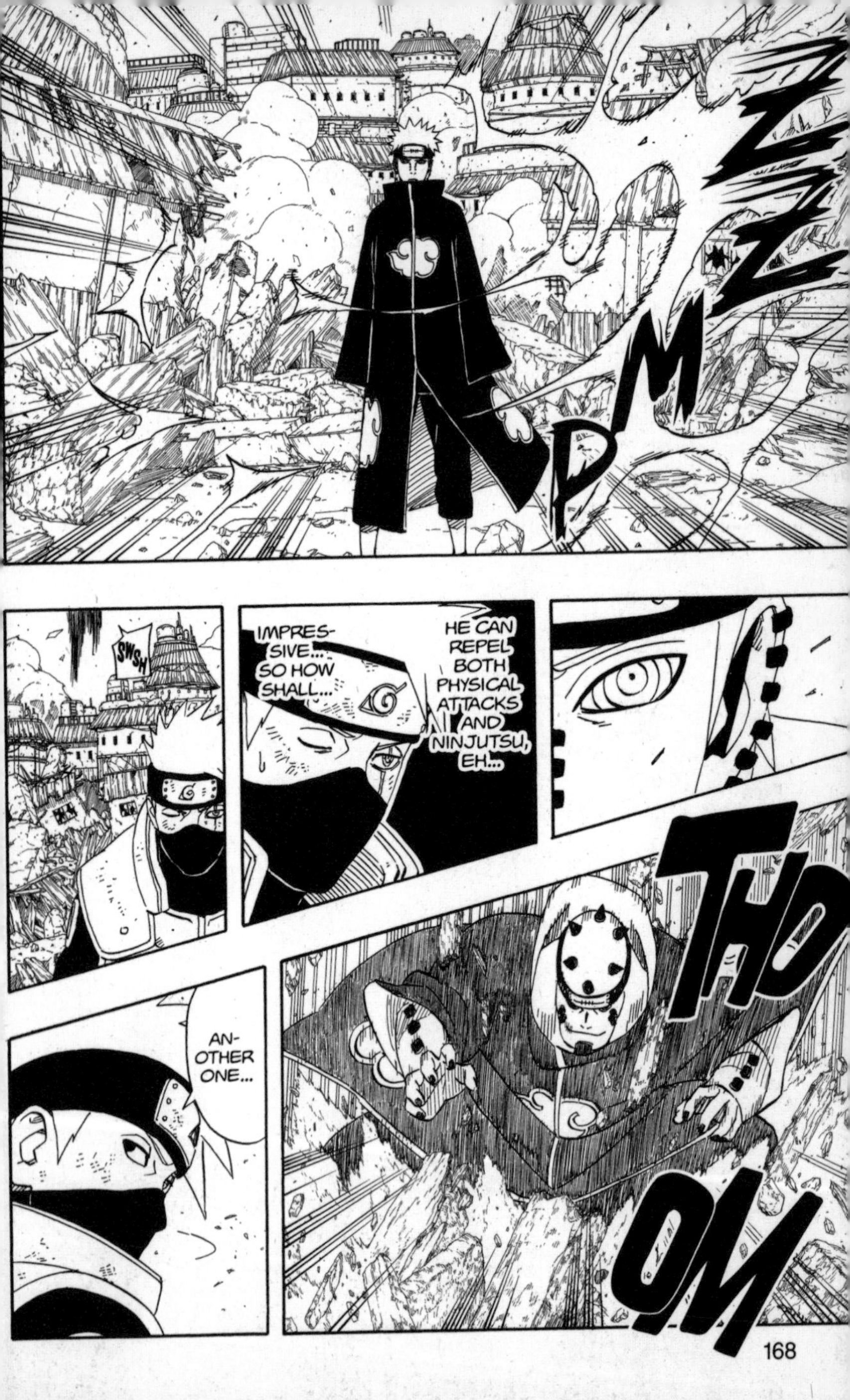
HE CAN REPEL BOTH PHYSICAL ATTACKS AND NINJUTSU, EH...
IMPRESSIVE... SO HOW SHALL...
SWSH
THOOM
ANOTHER ONE...

READ THIS WAY

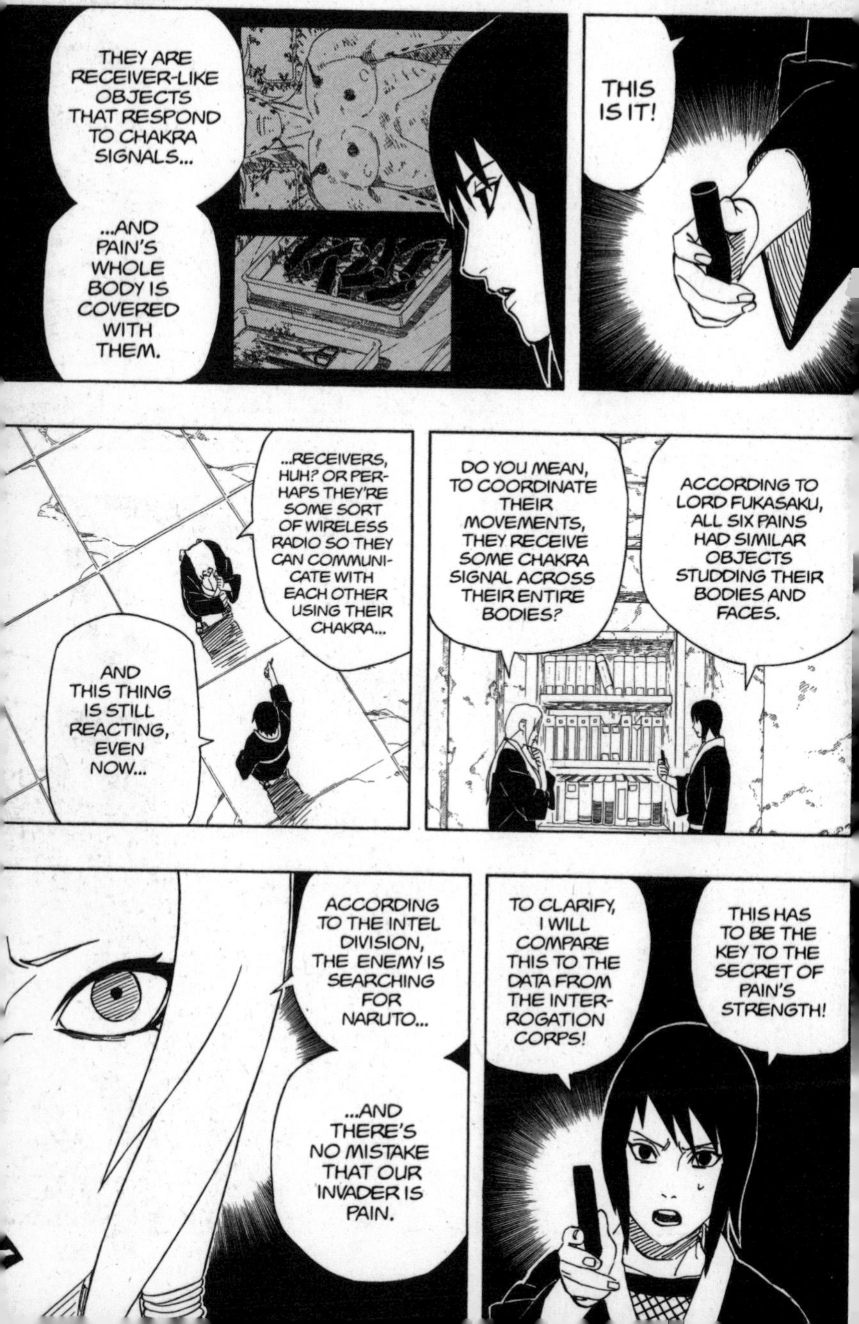
THIS IS IT!
THEY ARE RECEIVER-LIKE OBJECTS THAT RESPOND TO CHAKRA SIGNALS...
...AND PAIN'S WHOLE BODY IS COVERED WITH THEM.
ACCORDING TO LORD FUKASAKU, ALL SIX PAINS HAD SIMILAR OBJECTS STUDDING THEIR BODIES AND FACES.
DO YOU MEAN, TO COORDINATE THEIR MOVEMENTS, THEY RECEIVE SOME CHAKRA SIGNAL ACROSS THEIR ENTIRE BODIES?
...RECEIVERS, HUH? OR PERHAPS THEY'RE SOME SORT OF WIRELESS RADIO SO THEY CAN COMMUNICATE WITH EACH OTHER USING THEIR CHAKRA...
AND THIS THING IS STILL REACTING, EVEN NOW...
THIS HAS TO BE THE KEY TO THE SECRET OF PAIN'S STRENGTH!
TO CLARIFY, I WILL COMPARE THIS TO THE DATA FROM THE INTERROGATION CORPS!
ACCORDING TO THE INTEL DIVISION, THE ENEMY IS SEARCHING FOR NARUTO...
...AND THERE'S NO MISTAKE THAT OUR INVADER IS PAIN.

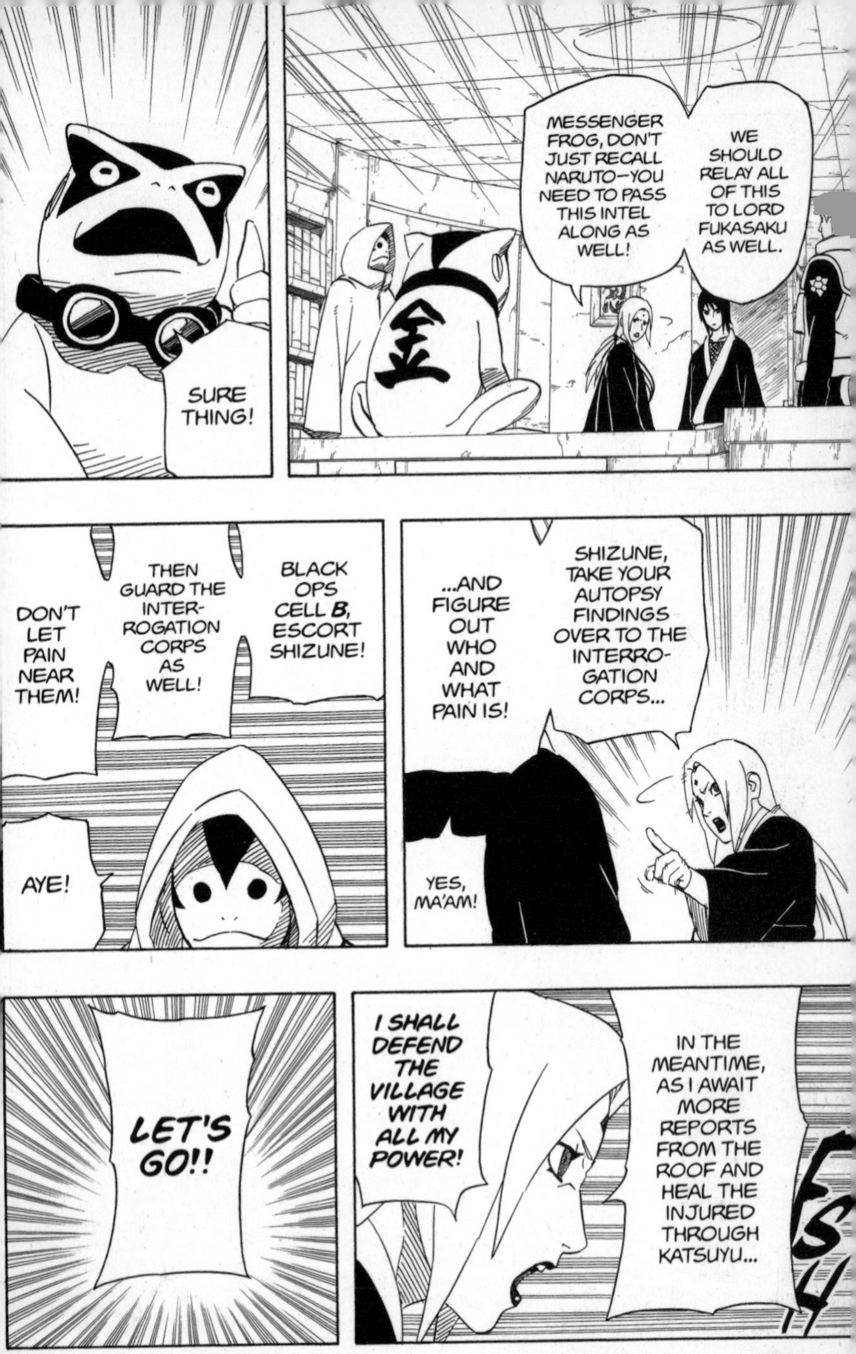
WE SHOULD RELAY ALL OF THIS TO LORD FUKASAKU AS WELL.
MESSENGER FROG, DON'T JUST RECALL NARUTO—YOU NEED TO PASS THIS INTEL ALONG AS WELL!
SURE THING!
SHIZUNE, TAKE YOUR AUTOPSY FINDINGS OVER TO THE INTERRO-GATION CORPS...
...AND FIGURE OUT WHO AND WHAT PAIN IS!
YES, MA'AM!
BLACK OPS CELL B, ESCORT SHIZUNE!
THEN GUARD THE INTER-ROGATION CORPS AS WELL!
DON'T LET PAIN NEAR THEM!
AYE!
IN THE MEANTIME, AS I AWAIT MORE REPORTS FROM THE ROOF AND HEAL THE INJURED THROUGH KATSUYU...
I SHALL DEFEND THE VILLAGE WITH ALL MY POWER!
LET'S GO!!

READ THIS WAY

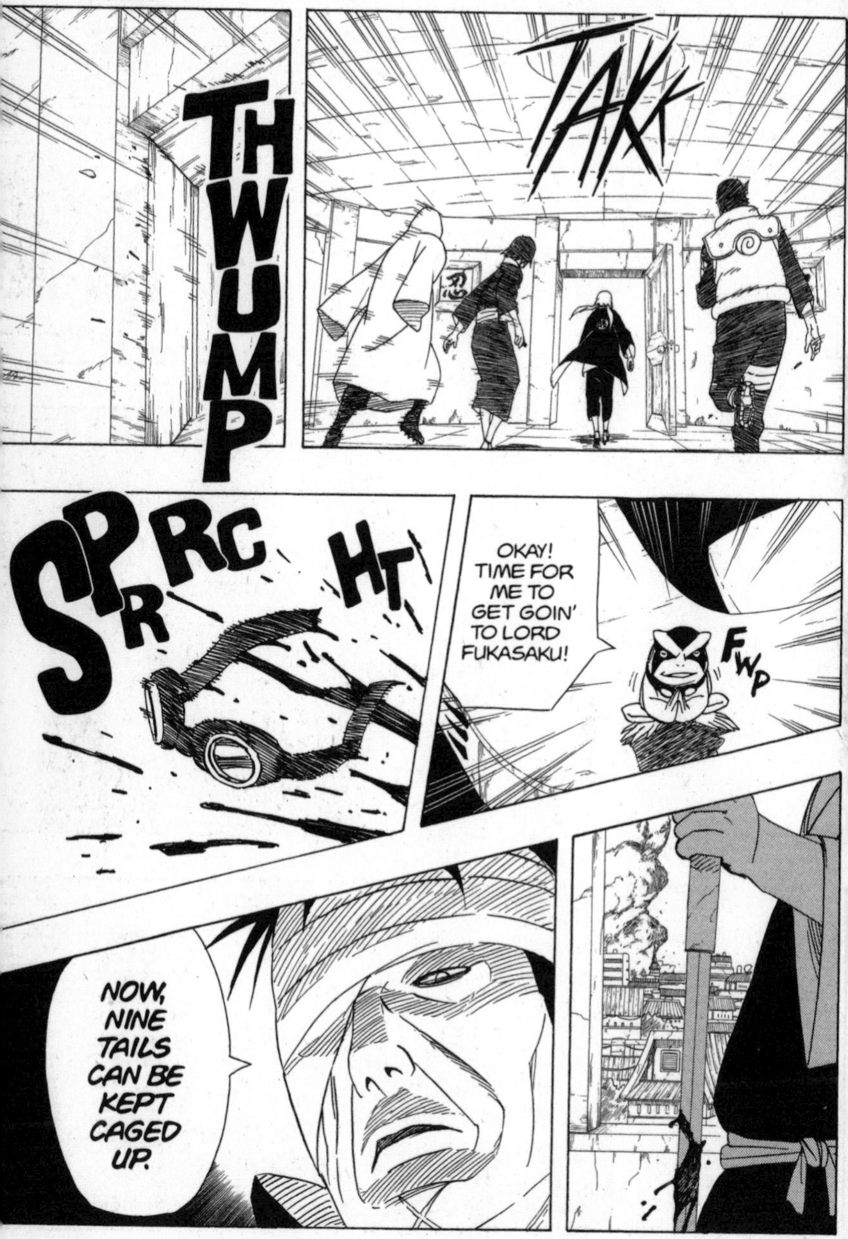
TAKK
THWUMP
OKAY! TIME FOR ME TO GET GOIN' TO LORD FUKASAKU!
FWP
SPRRCHT
NOW, NINE TAILS CAN BE KEPT CAGED UP.

NARUTO

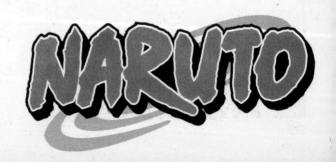

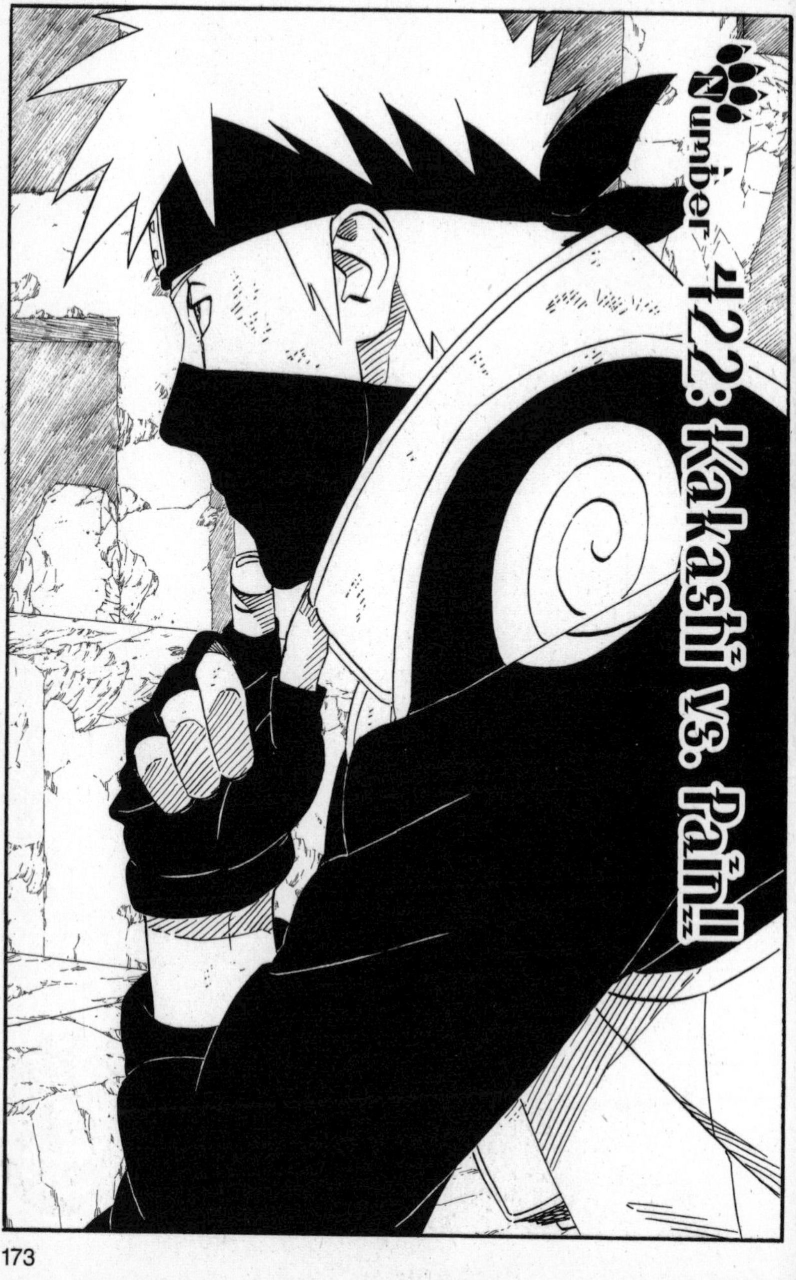
Number 422: Kakashi vs. Pain!!

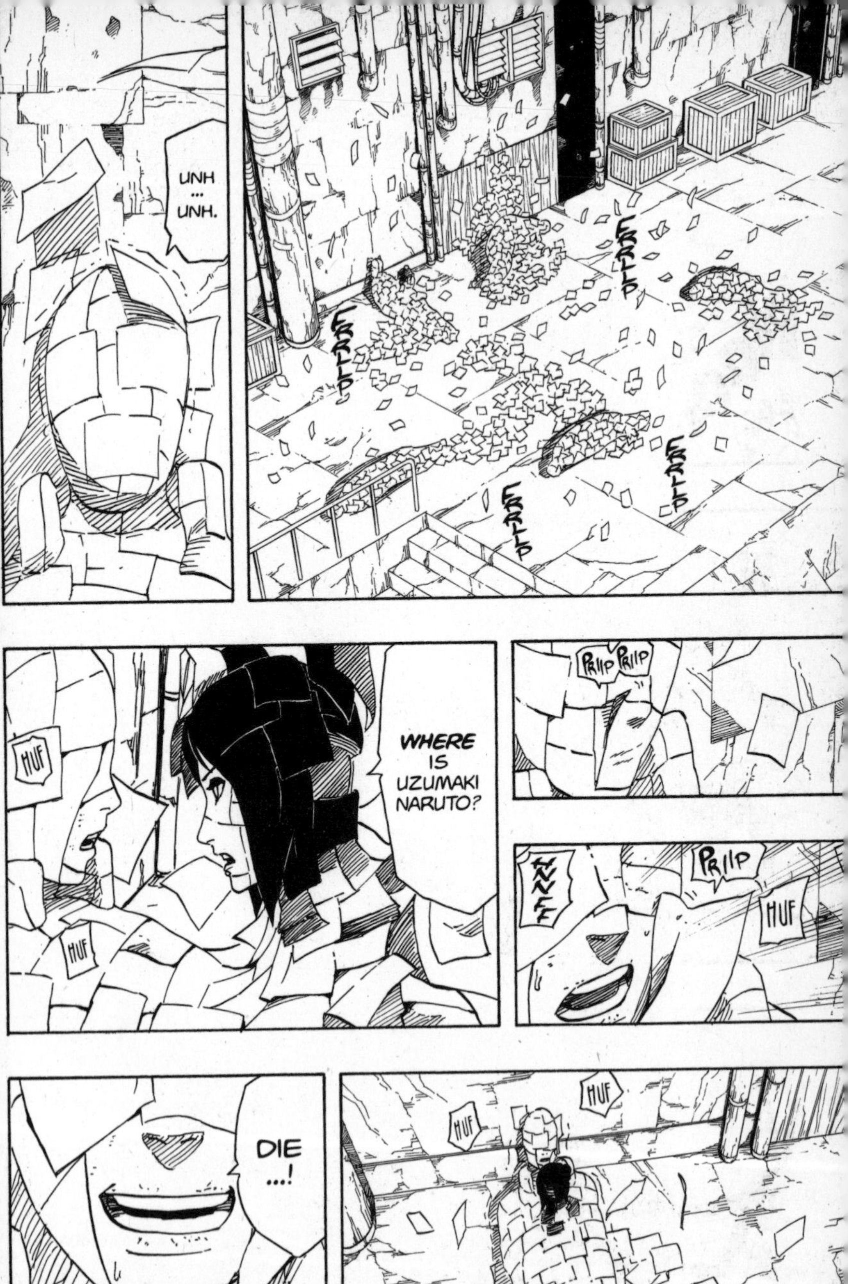
ERRLLP
ERRLLP
ERRLLP
ERRLLP
UNH ... UNH.
PRIIP PRIIP
PRIIP
HNNFF
HUF
HUF
WHERE IS UZUMAKI NARUTO?
HUF
HUF
HUF
DIE ...!

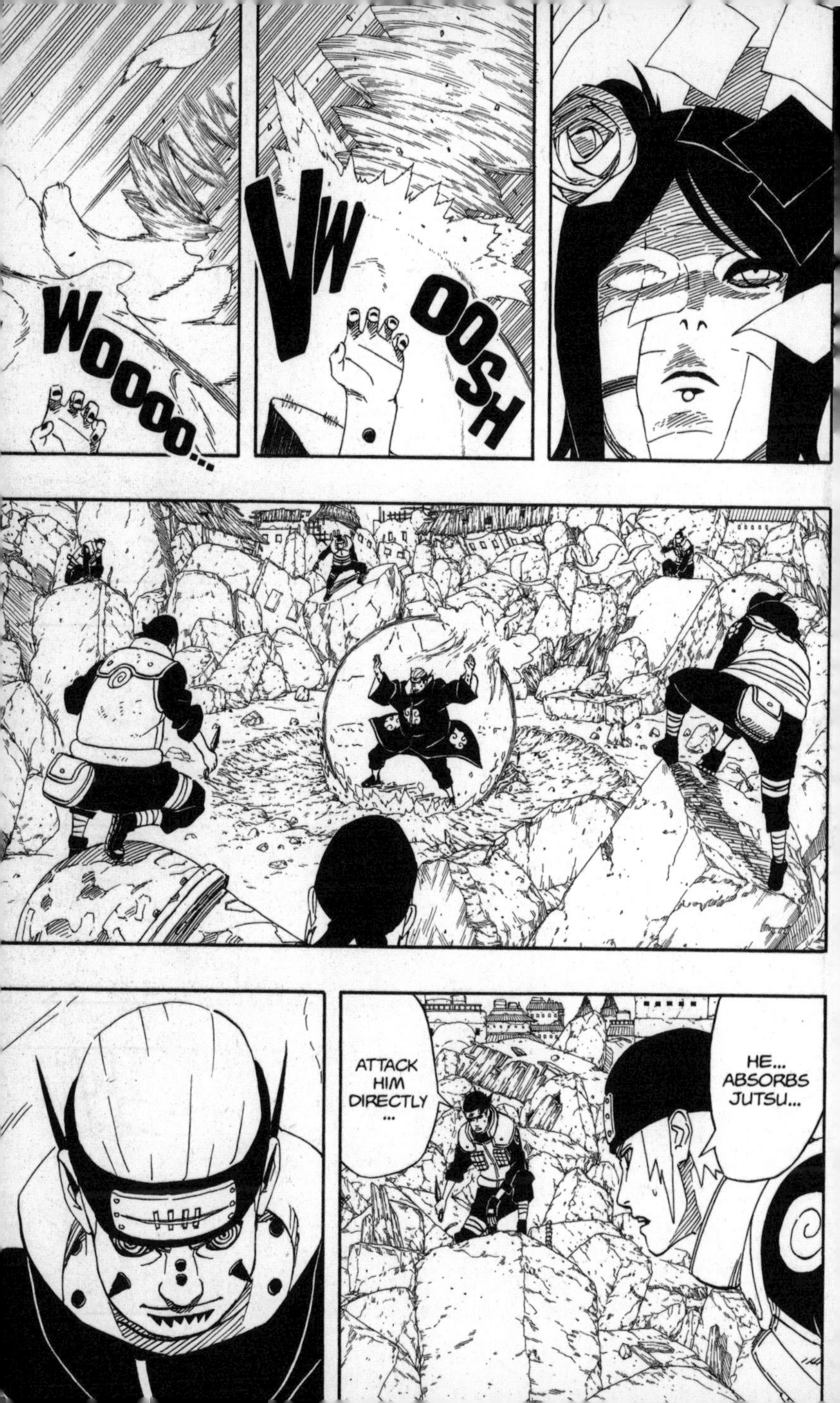
VWOOSH
WOOOOO...
HE... ABSORBS JUTSU...
ATTACK HIM DIRECTLY ...

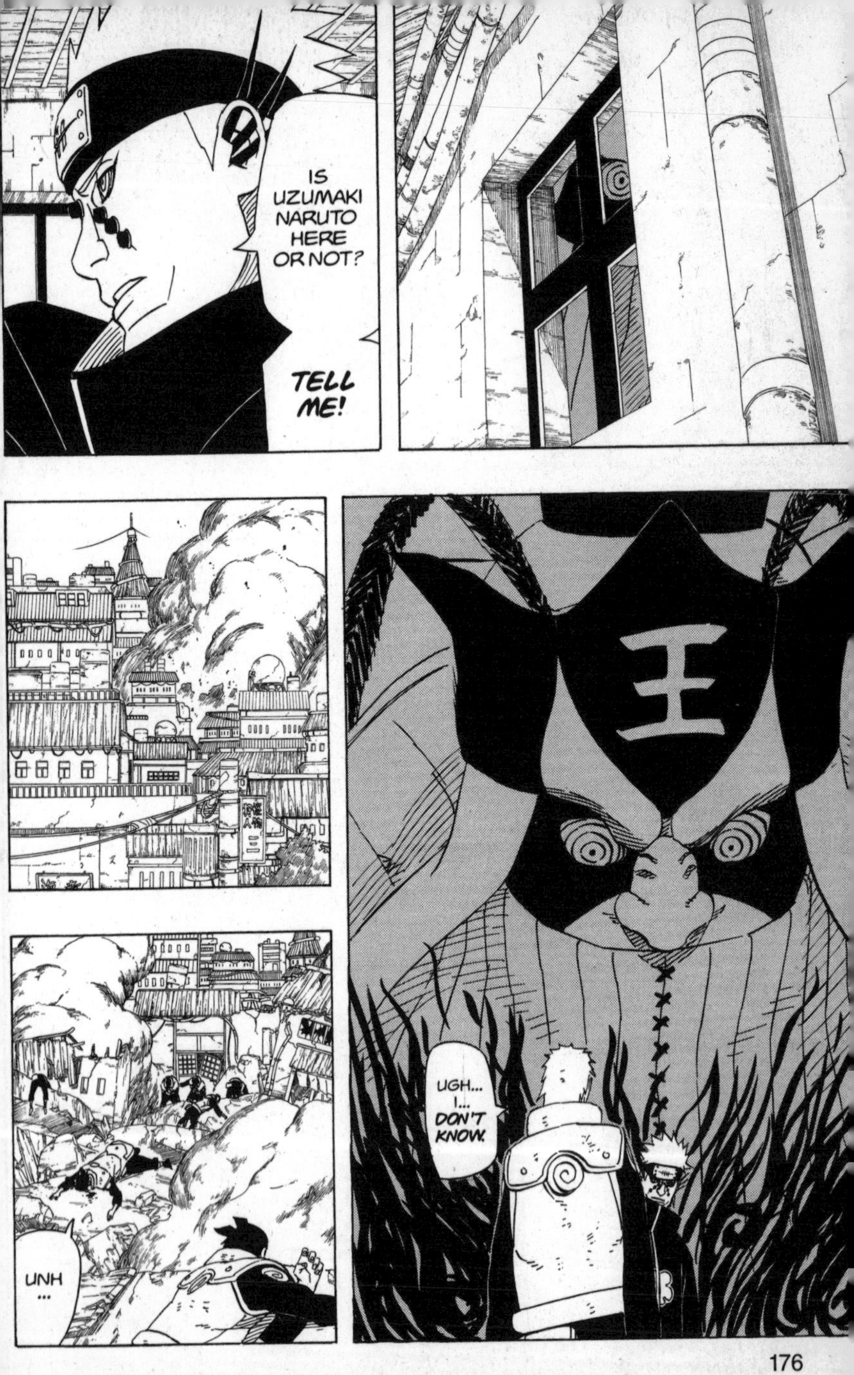
IS UZUMAKI NARUTO HERE OR NOT?
TELL ME!
UGH... I... DON'T KNOW.
UNH ...

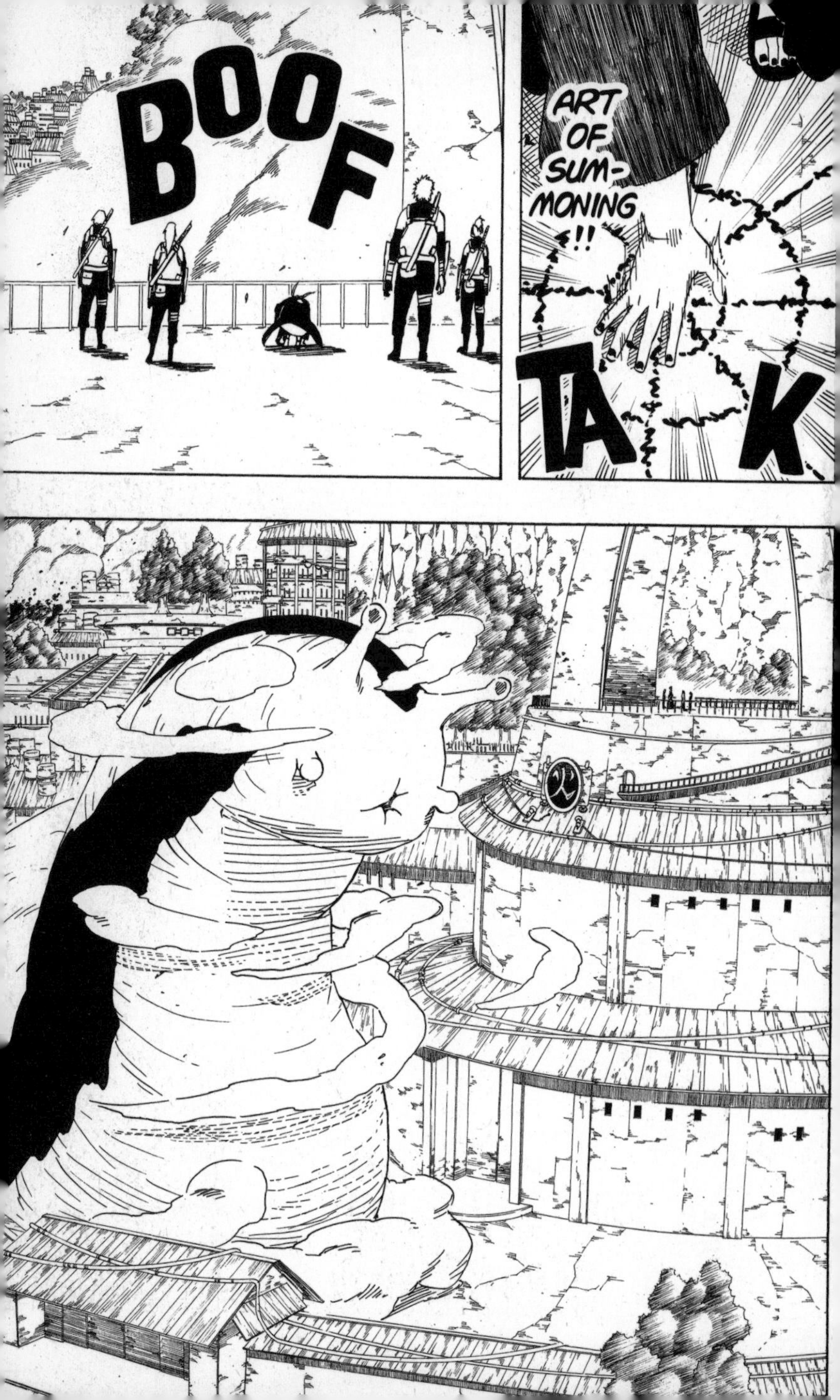
ART OF SUM-MONING!!
TAK
BOOF

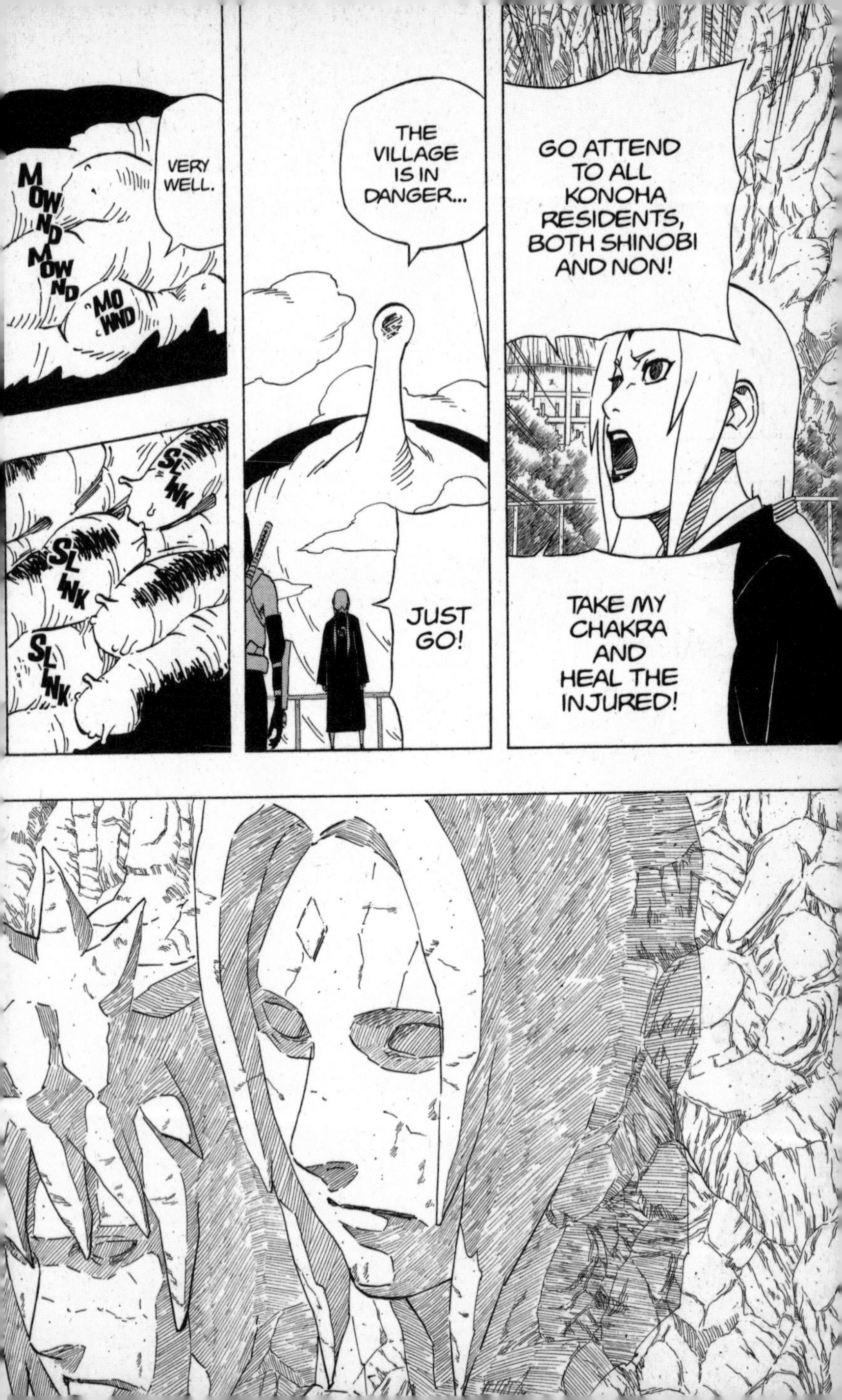
GO ATTEND TO ALL KONOHA RESIDENTS, BOTH SHINOBI AND NON!
TAKE MY CHAKRA AND HEAL THE INJURED!
THE VILLAGE IS IN DANGER...
JUST GO!
VERY WELL.
MOWND
MOWND
MOWND
SLINK
SLINK
SLINK

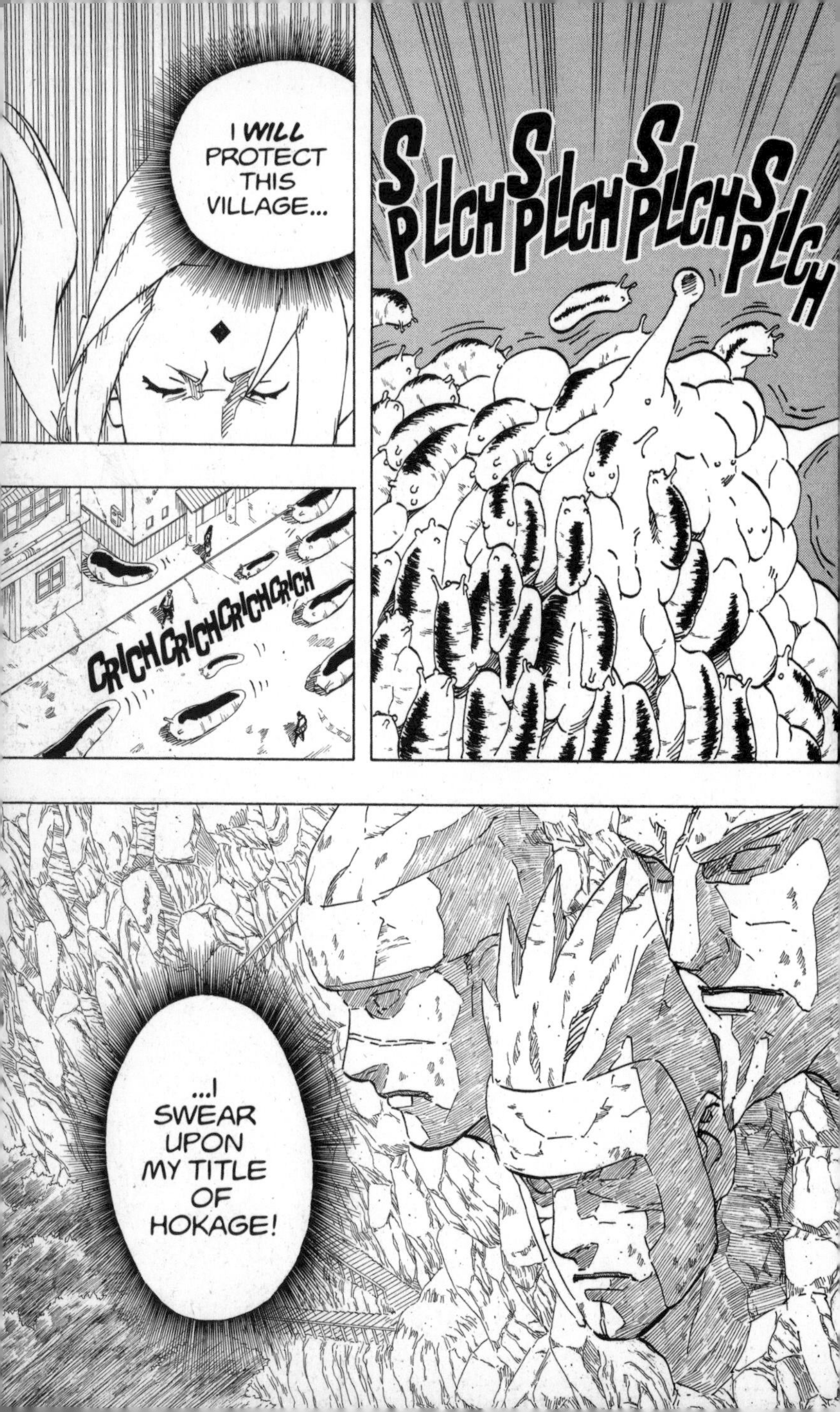
SPLICH SPLICH SPLICH SPLICH
I WILL PROTECT THIS VILLAGE...
CRICHCRICHCRICHCRICH
...I SWEAR UPON MY TITLE OF HOKAGE!

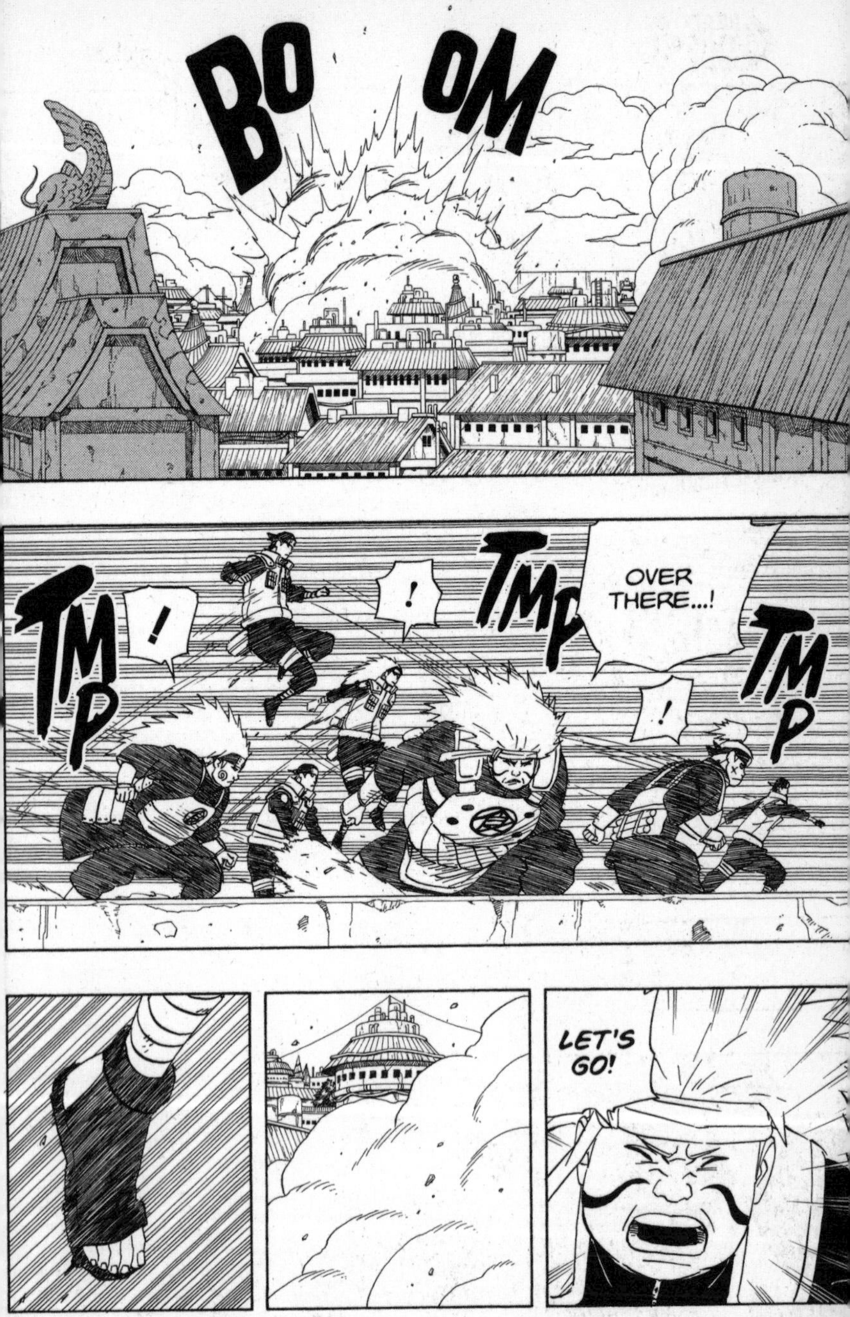
BOOM
TMP
!
OVER THERE...!
TMP
!
!
TMP
LET'S GO!

READ THIS WAY

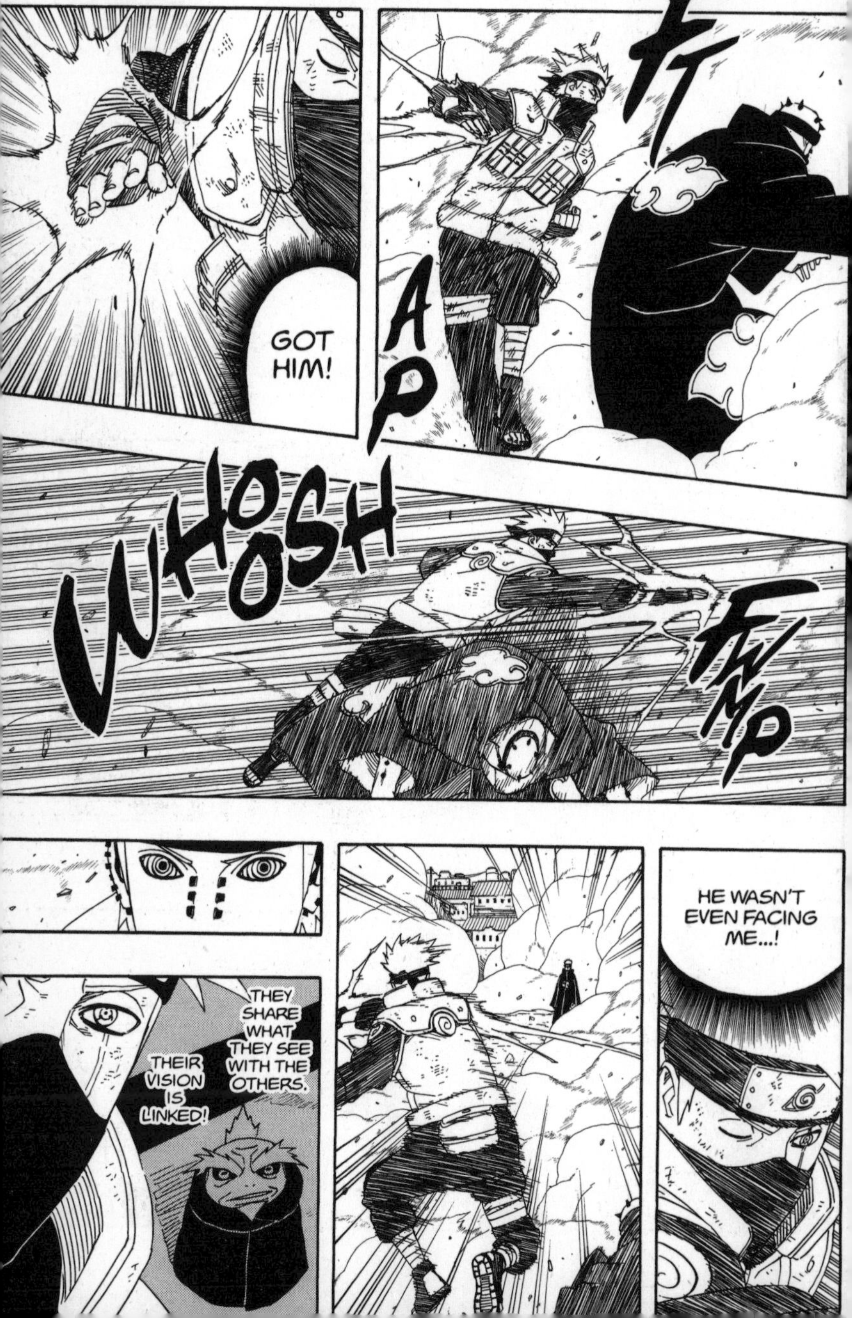
FT
AP
GOT HIM!
FWMP
WHOOSH
HE WASN'T EVEN FACING ME...!
THEY SHARE WHAT THEY SEE WITH THE OTHERS.
THEIR VISION IS LINKED!

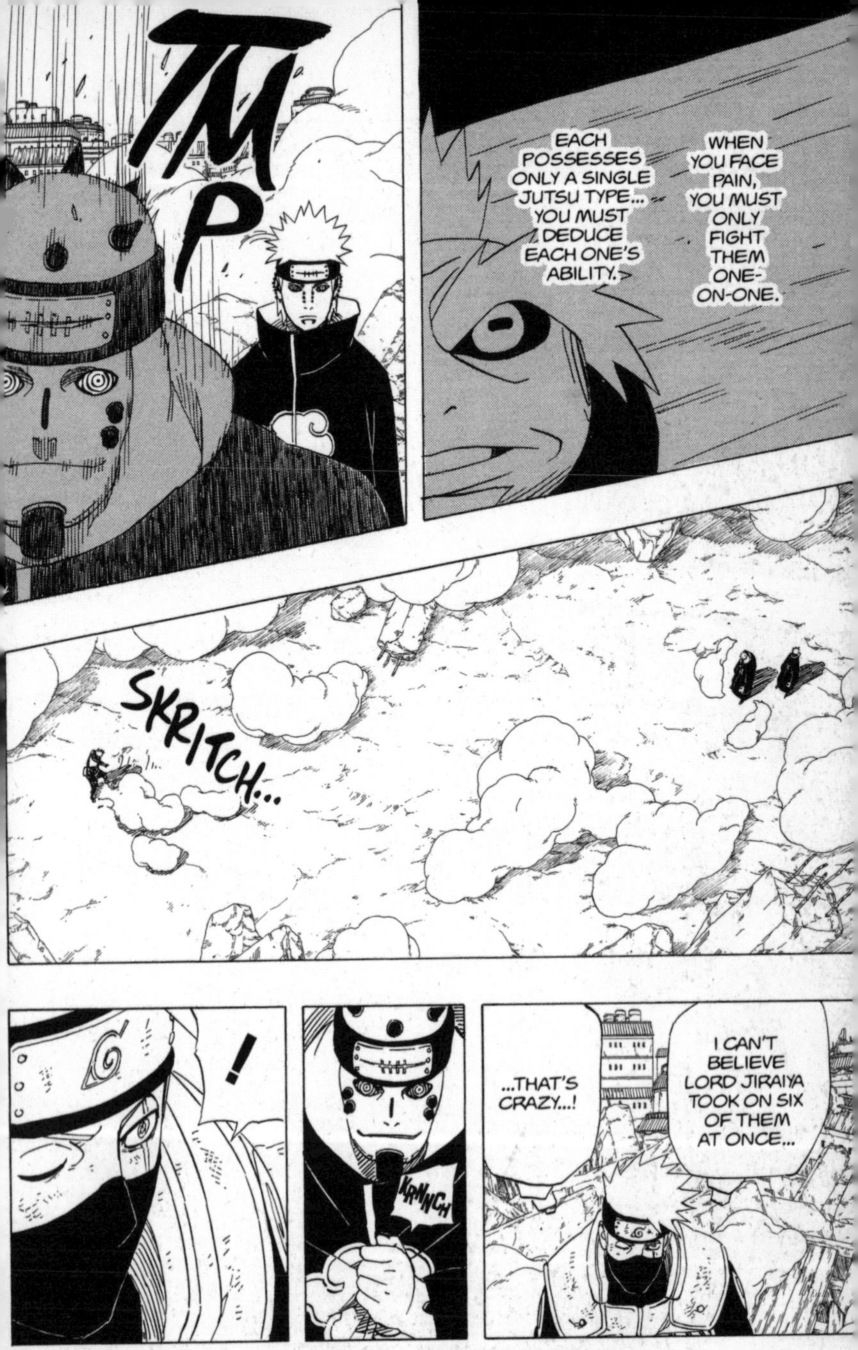
WHEN YOU FACE PAIN, YOU MUST ONLY FIGHT THEM ONE-ON-ONE.
EACH POSSESSES ONLY A SINGLE JUTSU TYPE... YOU MUST DEDUCE EACH ONE'S ABILITY.
TMP
SKRITCH...
I CAN'T BELIEVE LORD JIRAIYA TOOK ON SIX OF THEM AT ONCE...
...THAT'S CRAZY...!
KRNNCH
!

READ THIS WAY

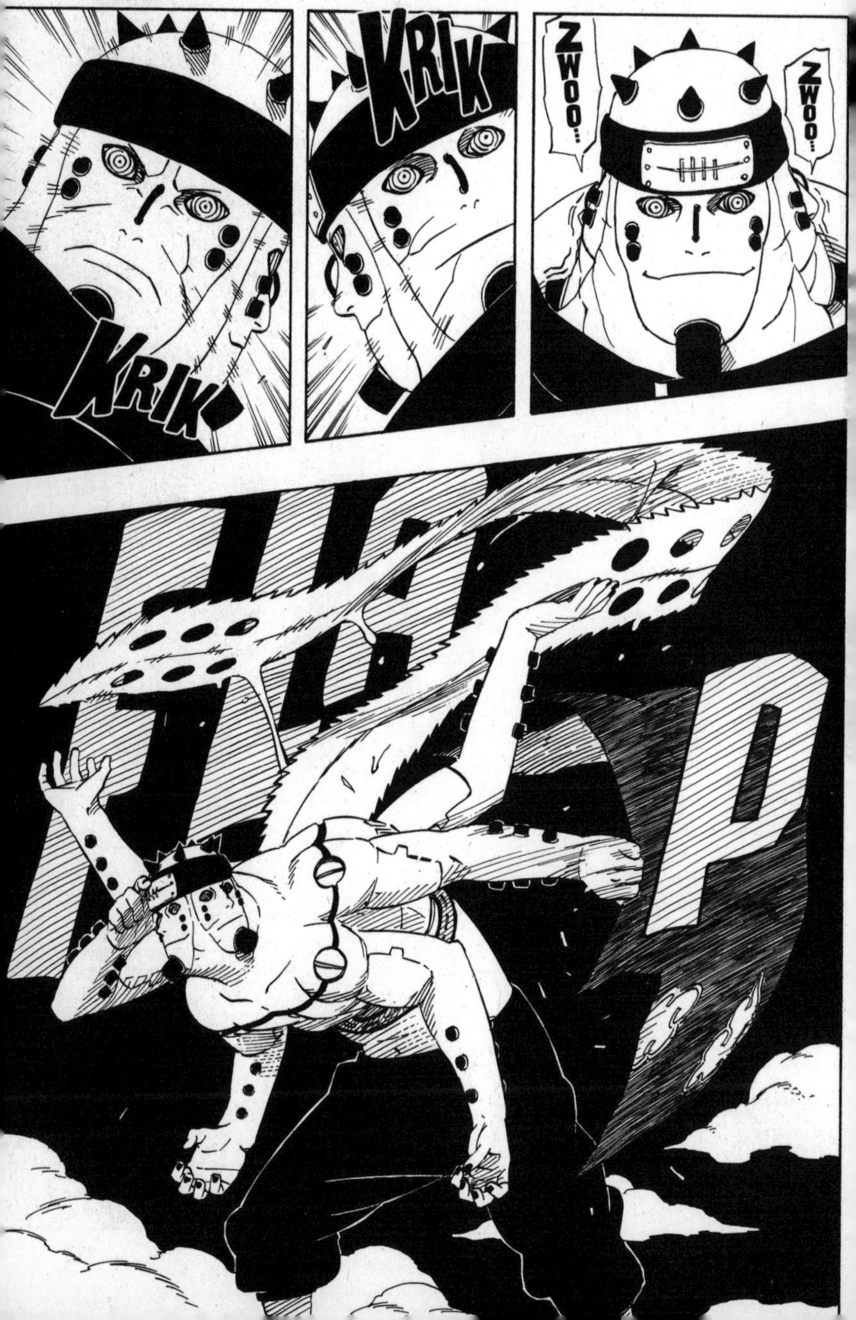
ZWOO...
ZWOO...
KRIK
KRIK

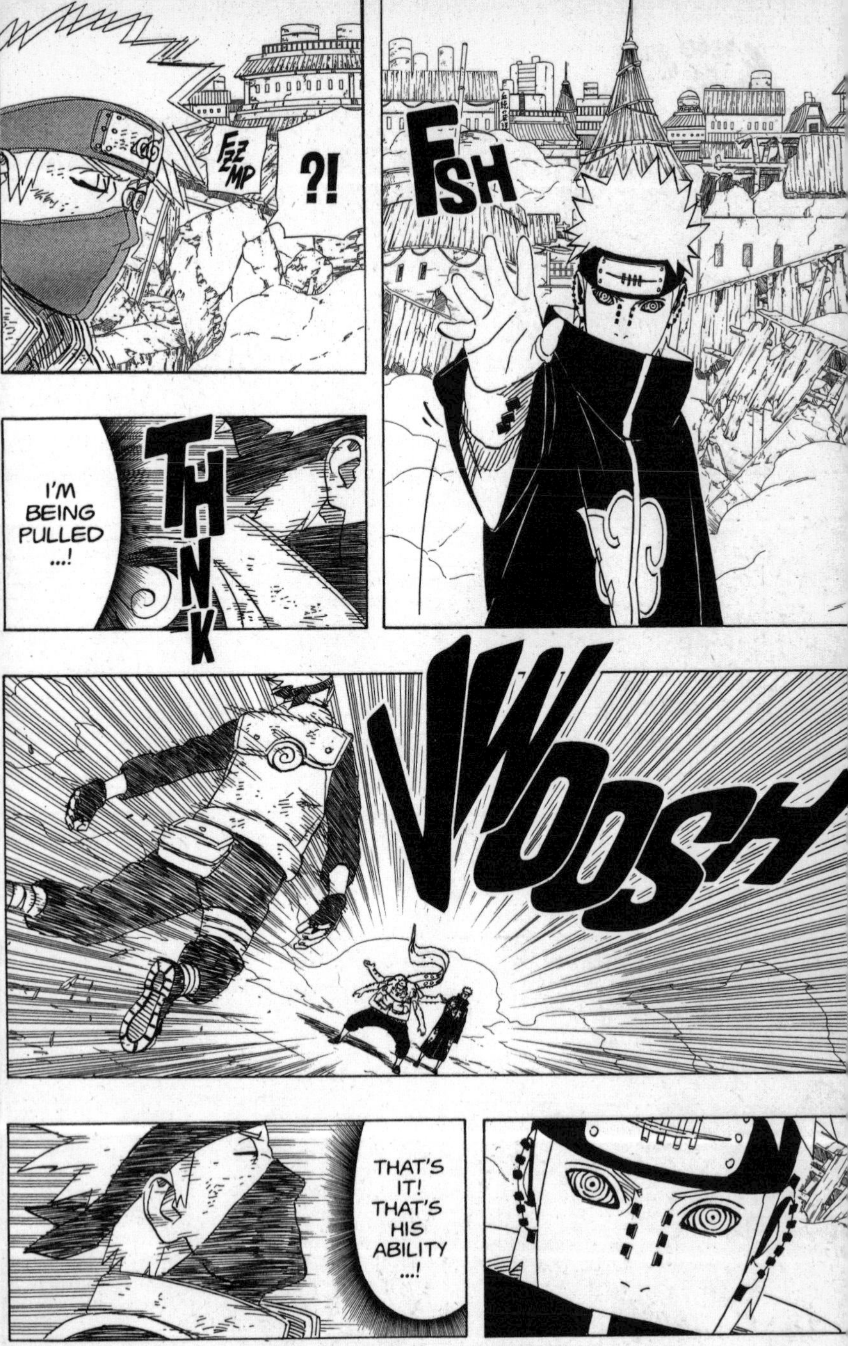
FSH
FZZZMP
?!
THNK
I'M BEING PULLED ...!
WOOSH
THAT'S IT! THAT'S HIS ABILITY ...!

READ THIS WAY

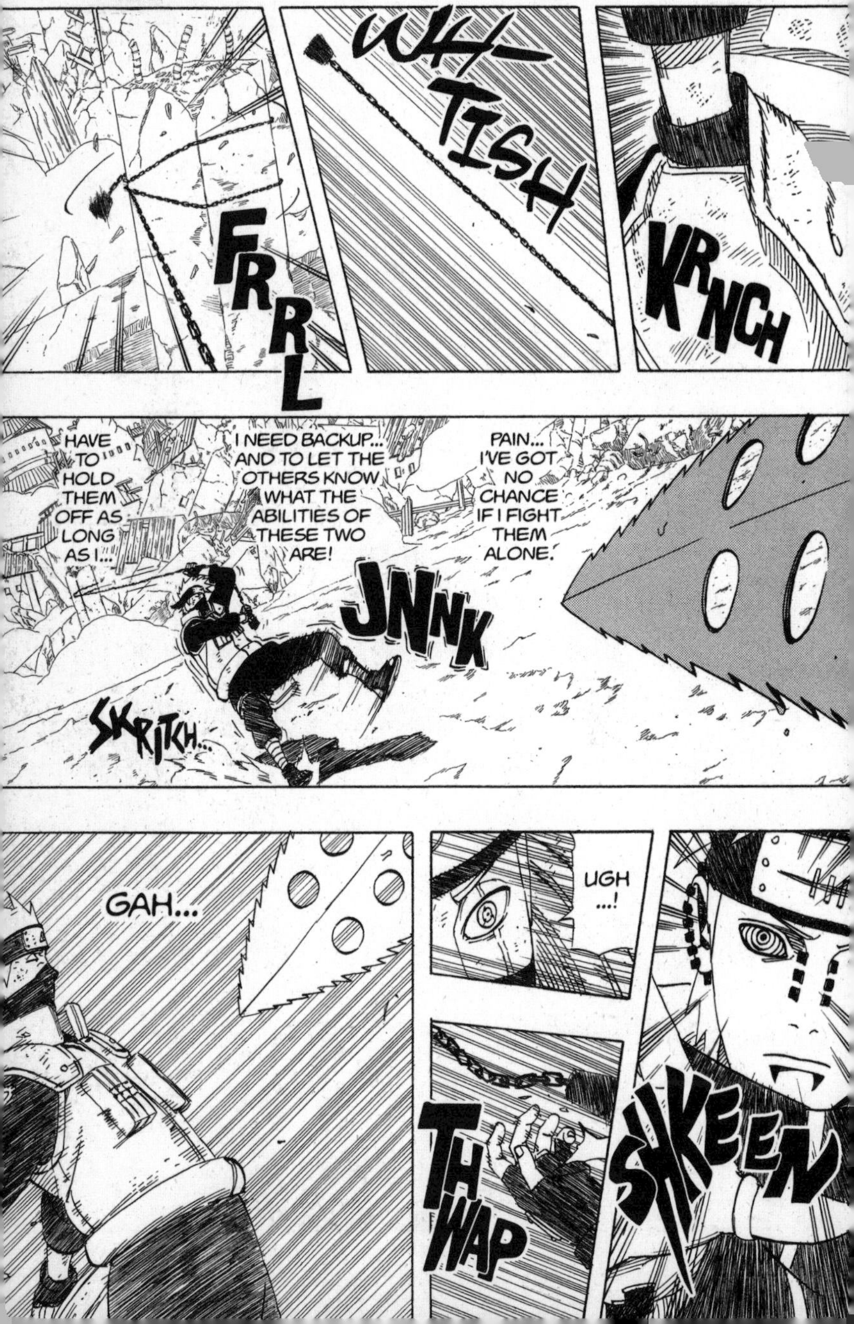
KRNCH
WHTISH
FRRRL
PAIN... I'VE GOT NO CHANCE IF I FIGHT THEM ALONE.
I NEED BACKUP... AND TO LET THE OTHERS KNOW WHAT THE ABILITIES OF THESE TWO ARE!
HAVE TO HOLD THEM OFF AS LONG AS I...
JNNK
SKRITCH...
SKEEN
UGH ...!
THWAP
GAH...

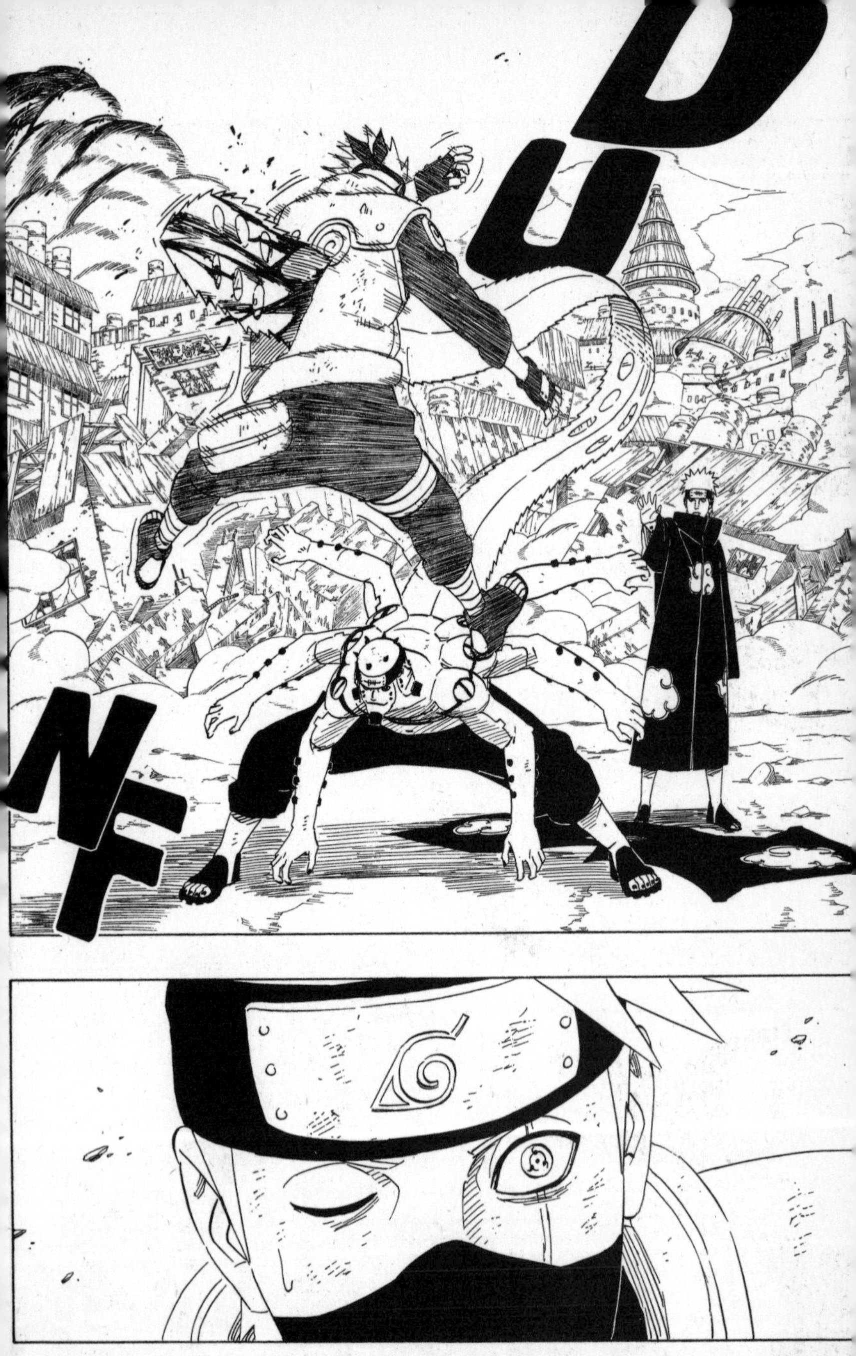
DUNF

READ THIS WAY

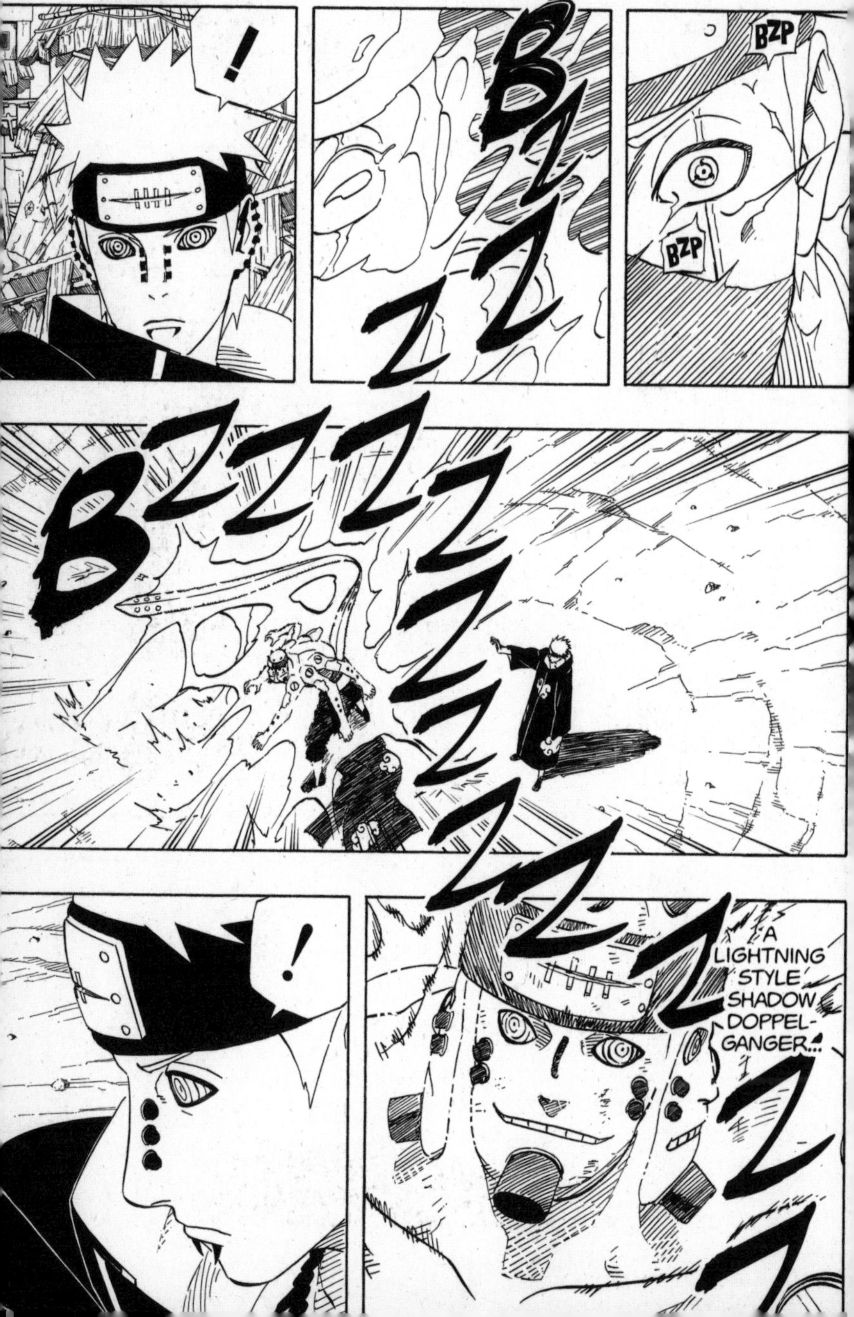
BZP
BZP
BZZZZ
!
BZZZZZZZZZZZZ
A LIGHTNING STYLE SHADOW DOPPELGANGER...!
!

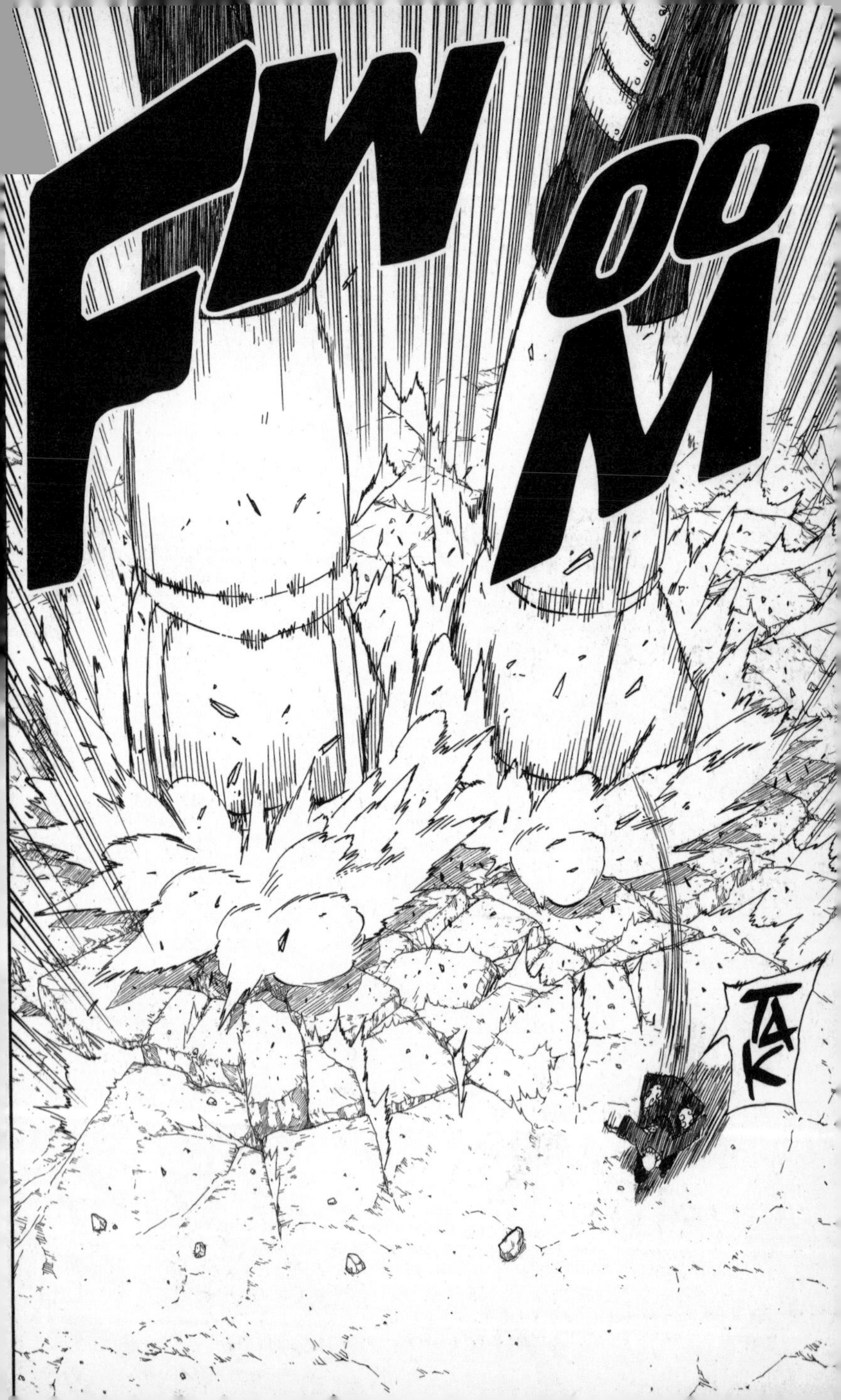
FWOOM
TAK

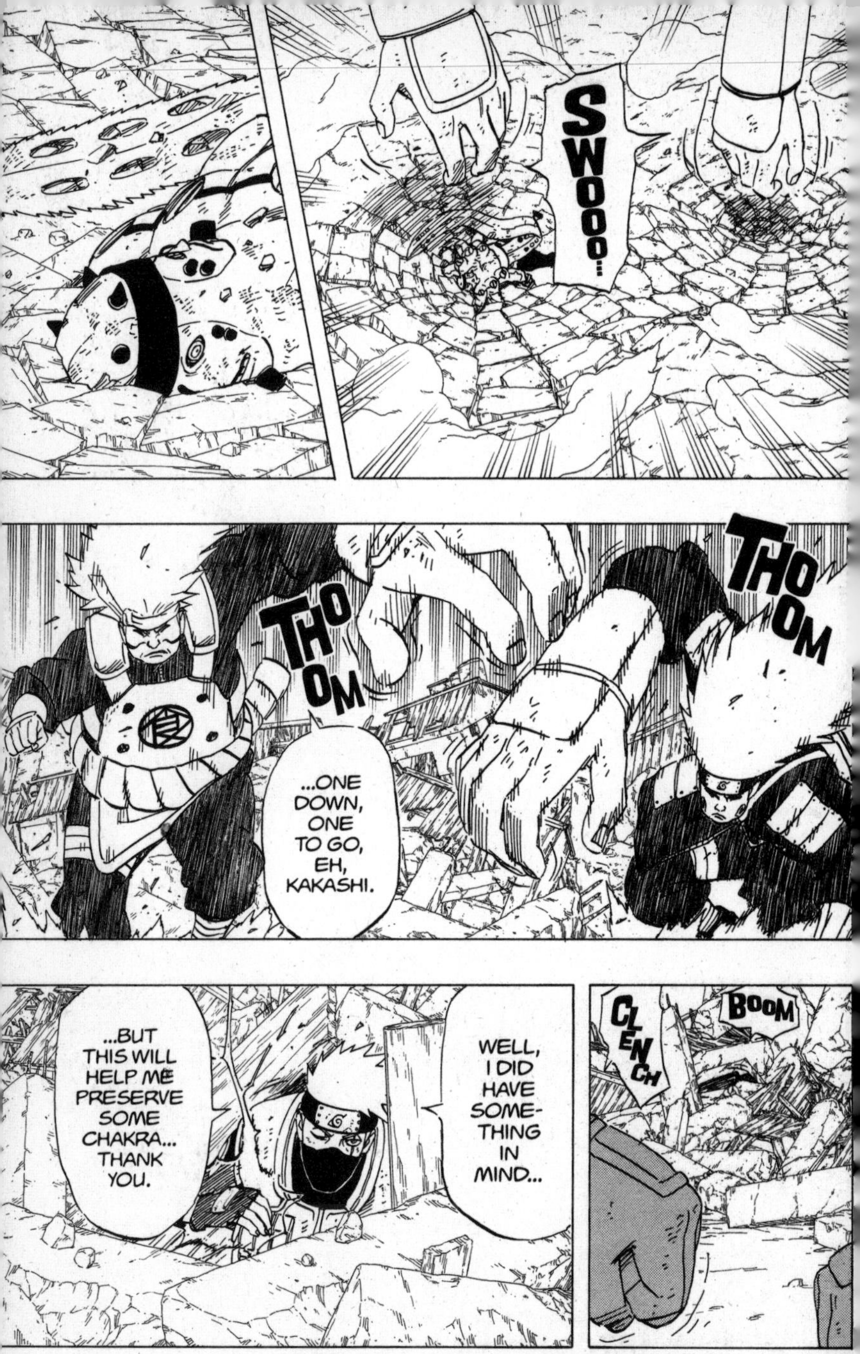
SWOOO...
THOOM
THOOM
...ONE DOWN, ONE TO GO, EH, KAKASHI.
BOOM
CLENCH
WELL, I DID HAVE SOME-THING IN MIND...
...BUT THIS WILL HELP ME PRESERVE SOME CHAKRA... THANK YOU.

TO BE CONTINUED IN *NARUTO* VOLUME 46!

IN THE NEXT VOLUME...

KNOW THY PAIN

The determination of Naruto and his comrades is tested beyond measure when Kakashi is injured and an attempt to overthrow Tsunade begins. Naruto's friends must fight or fall as Pain commences the final destruction of Konoha. Is the fate of Naruto's beloved village—and that of everyone he loves—finally truly sealed?

AVAILABLE OCTOBER 2009!
READ IT FIRST IN SHONEN JUMP MAGAZINE!